The first time I ever dipped my pen in ink and drew manga I was in my second year of junior high. That was around 26 years ago now, but my methods haven't changed. Lately, a lot of people create their work digitally, but I still go the analog route. Depending on the design and style, I'm sure there are some manga that are better suited for the digital medium, but I just don't think I could get used to it. Though I guess I could say that I'm still not very good at drawing in general (sniffle). So I'll probably still be challenged enough using the analog medium. (My current weight...70 kg!!)

—Mitsutoshi Shimabukuro, 2015

Mitsutoshi Shimabukuro made his debut in **Weekly Shonen Jump** in 1996. He is best known for **Seikimatsu Leader Den Takeshi!**, for which he won the 46th Shogakukan Manga Award for children's manga in 2001. His current series, **Toriko**, began serialization in Japan in 2008

TORIKO VOL. 36
SHONEN JUMP Manga Edition

STORY AND ART BY MITSUTOSHI SHIMABUKURO

Translation/Christine Dashiell
Weekly Shonen Jump Lettering/Erika Terriquez
Graphic Novel Touch-Up Art & Lettering/Elena Diaz
Design/Veronica Casson
Editor/Marlene First

Printed in the U.S.A.

Published by VIZ Media, LLC
P.O. Box 77010
San Francisco, CA 94107

10 9 8 7 6 5 4 3 2 1
First printing, November 2016

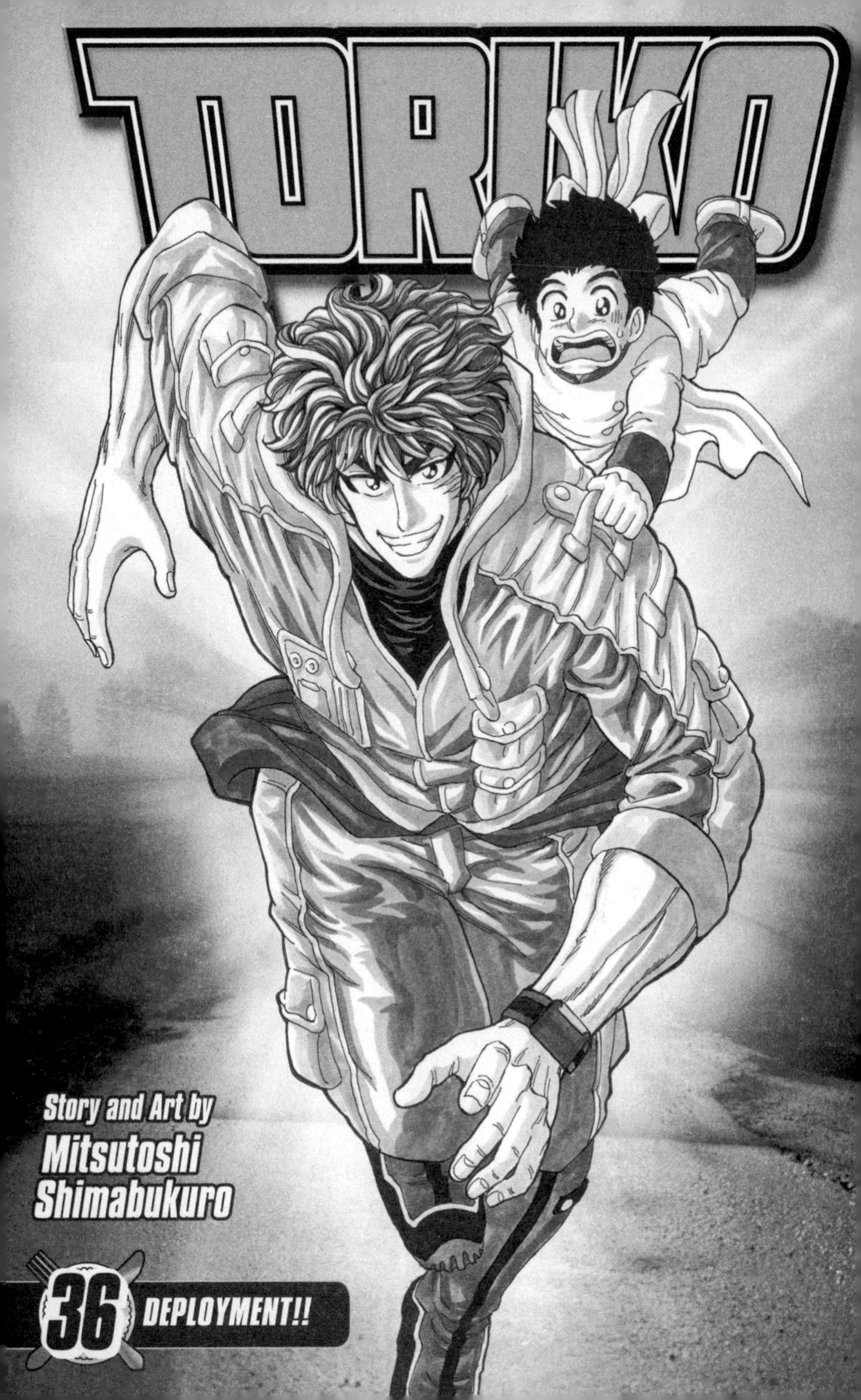
TORIKO
Story and Art by
Mitsutoshi
Shimabukuro
36
DEPLOYMENT!!

TORIKO

THE ULTIMATE GOURMET HUNTER WHO'S ON A NEVER-ENDING QUEST TO FIND AND SCARF UP THE RAREST FOODS ON EARTH! HE FIGHTS WITH A KNIFE (HIS FIST), A FORK (HIS FIST), AND SPIKED PUNCH (ALSO HIS FISTS).

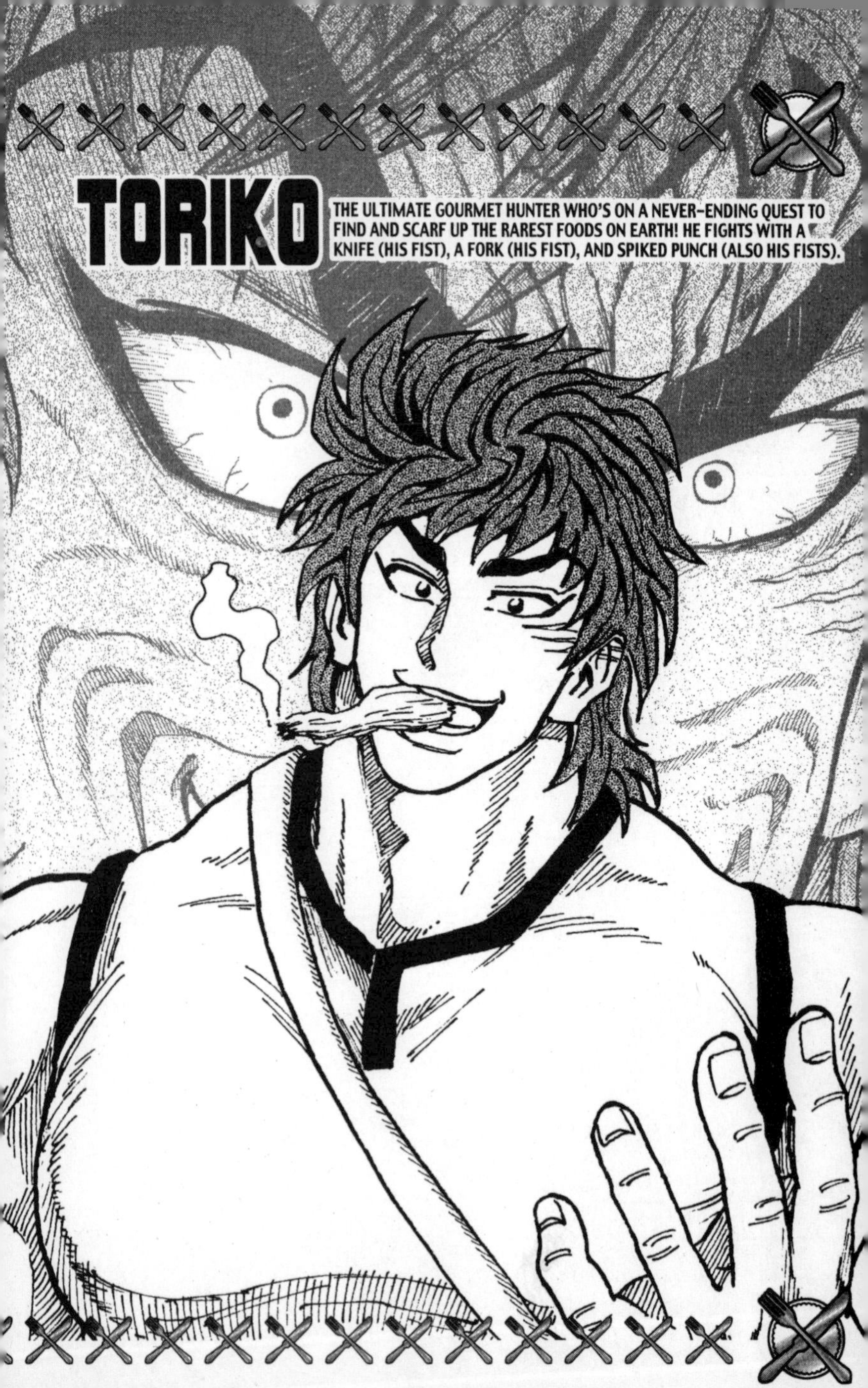

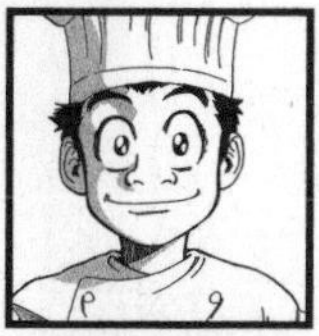

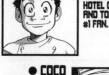

●KOMATSU

TALENTED IGO HOTEL CHEF AND TORIKO'S #1 FAN.

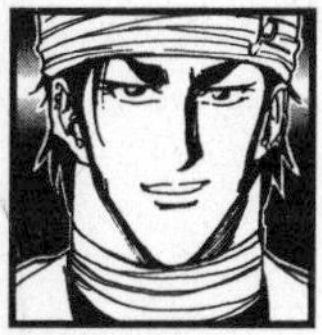

● COCO

ONE OF THE FOUR KINGS, THOUGH HE IS ALSO A FORTUNETELLER. SPECIAL ABILITY: POISON FLOWS IN HIS VEINS.

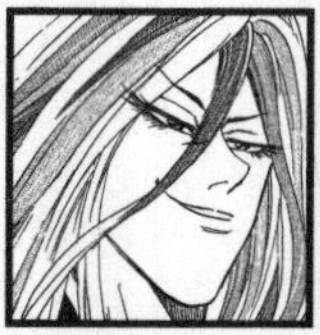

●SUNNY

ONE OF THE FOUR KINGS. SENSORS IN HIS LONG HAIR ENABLE HIM TO "TASTE" THE WORLD. OBSESSED WITH ALL THAT IS BEAUTIFUL.

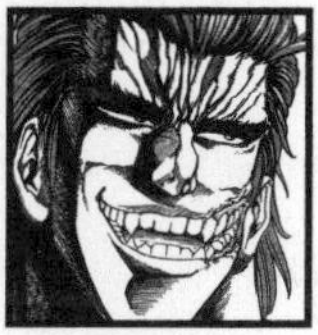

● ZEBRA

ONE OF THE FOUR KINGS. A DANGEROUS INDIVIDUAL WITH SUPERHUMAN HEARING AND VOCAL POWERS.

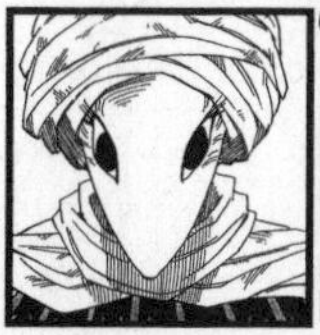

●KAKA

A TASTE HERMIT NITRO WHO AWOKE FROM DROUGHT DORMANCY. SHE MET TORIKO AND THE GANG IN AREA 7 AND BECAME THEIR GUIDE.

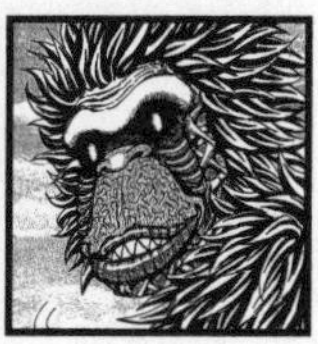

●MONKEY KING BAMBINA

ONE OF THE EIGHT KINGS AND THE RULER OF AREA 7. HE'S THE GREATEST PRACTITIONER OF MONKEY MARTIAL ARTS.

WHAT'S FOR DINNER

THE AGE OF GOURMET IS DECLARED OVER. IN ORDER TO REVIVE IT, TORIKO AND THE GANG TAKE AN ENORMOUS ORDER. THEY MUST TRAVEL TO THE GOURMET WORLD AND FIND ACACIA'S FULL-COURSE MEAL. ARMED WITH THE INFORMATION AND THE OCTOMELON CAMPER MONSTER GIVEN TO THEM BY ICHIRYU'S MYSTERIOUS FRIEND CHICHI, THE FIVE MEN SET THEIR SIGHTS ON THE GOURMET WORLD.

THEIR FIRST STOP IS AREA 8, WHERE TORIKO MUST FACE OFF AGAINST THE RULER OF THE CONTINENT, NIGHTMARE HERACLES, IN ORDER TO OBTAIN ACACIA'S SALAD, "AIR." BUT THE OVERWHELMING DIFFERENCE IN STRENGTH LEAVES TORIKO ON THE BRINK OF DEATH.

MEANWHILE, KOMATSU REACHES "AIR" AND USES HIS MASTERFUL CULINARY SKILLS TO PREPARE IT. THIS MAGNIFICENT FEAT SAVES THE NIGHTMARES AND ALL OF AREA 8! AT LAST, TORIKO AND HIS FRIENDS SAMPLE "AIR", WHICH GIVES TORIKO AND HIS FRIENDS THE POWER TO CONTROL THEIR GOURMET CELLS, AND HE EVEN ADDS IT TO HIS OWN FULL-COURSE MEAL. THAT'S WHEN THE REVIVER, TEPPEI, WHO HAD DEFECTED TO NEO, ATTACKS KOMATSU.

TORIKO AND THE GANG HEAD TO AREA 7 TO CAPTURE ACACIA'S SOUP, "PAIR", WHICH IS THE ONLY THING THAT CAN SAVE KOMATSU. THERE IS ONLY ONE, VERY BIG PROBLEM THAT STANDS IN THEIR WAY... ONE OF THE EIGHT KINGS--THE MISCHIEVOUS MONKEY KING BAMBINA. AND TO MAKE MATTERS WORSE, THEY LEARN FROM THEIR GUIDE KAKA THAT THE FOOD TREASURE PAIR IS ACTUALLY A PART OF BAMBINA'S BODY!

IN ORDER TO OBTAIN "PAIR", TORIKO AND THE GANG MUST UNDERGO MONKEY MARTIAL ARTS TRAINING TO BE ABLE TO GO TOE-TO-TOE AGAINST THE MONKEY KING. TORIKO AND THE GANG FINALLY TRIUMPH, CAPTURING PAIR AND SAVING KOMATSU'S LIFE. TORIKO, KOMATSU, THE GANG AND THE MONKEYS SIT DOWN TO ENJOY PAIR AND PARTAKE IN A FLAVOR THAT UNIFIES EVERYTHING. THE DEAD JOIN THE LIVING, THE MEN BECOME WOMEN...AND THEN THE REAL KAKA APPROACHES TORIKO...

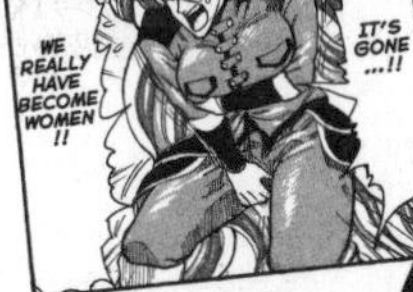
IT'S GONE ...!!
WE REALLY HAVE BECOME WOMEN !!

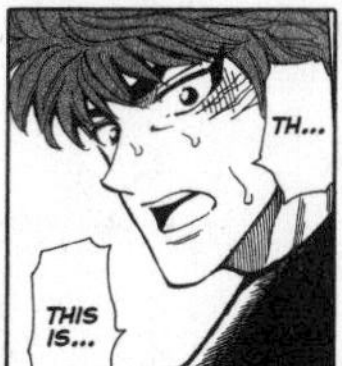
TH...
THIS IS...

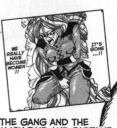

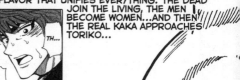

Contents

TORIKO

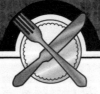

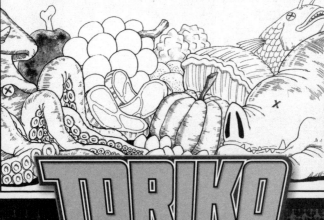

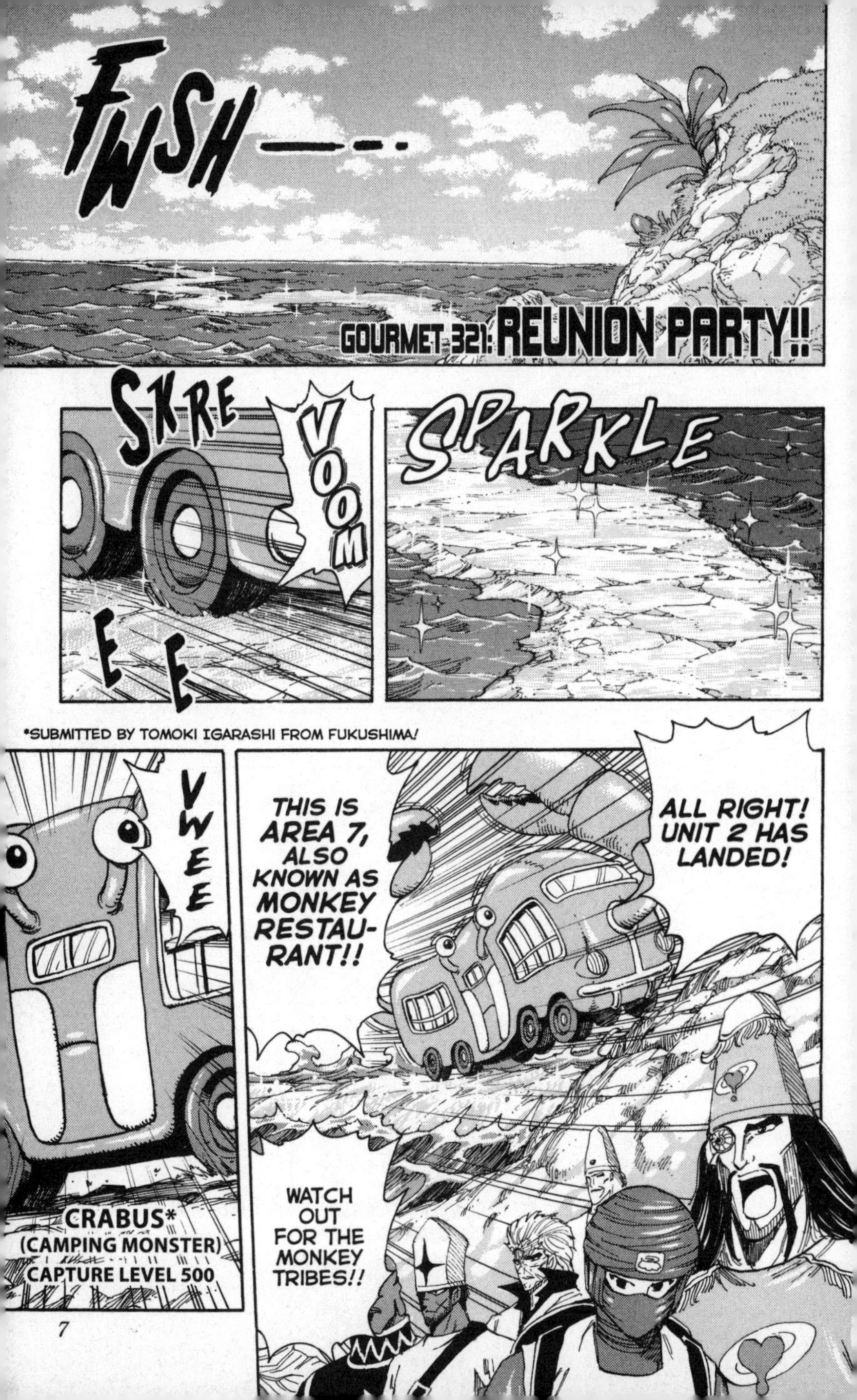

FWSH
GOURMET 321: REUNION PARTY!!
SPARKLE
VOOM
SKREEE
ALL RIGHT! UNIT 2 HAS LANDED!
THIS IS AREA 7, ALSO KNOWN AS MONKEY RESTAURANT!!
WATCH OUT FOR THE MONKEY TRIBES!!
VWEE
CRABUS* (CAMPING MONSTER) CAPTURE LEVEL 500
*SUBMITTED BY TOMOKI IGARASHI FROM FUKUSHIMA!

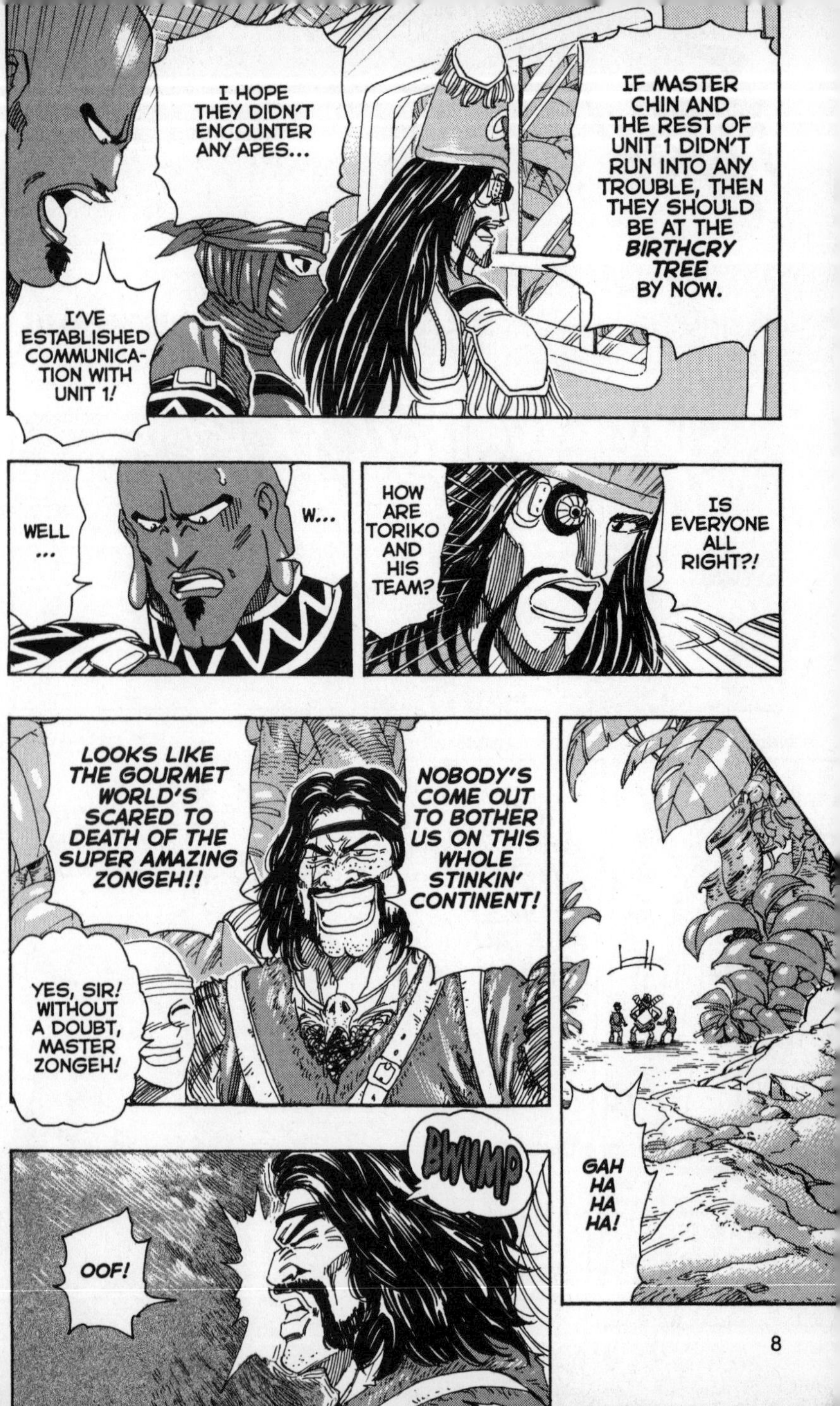
IF MASTER CHIN AND THE REST OF UNIT 1 DIDN'T RUN INTO ANY TROUBLE, THEN THEY SHOULD BE AT THE *BIRTHCRY TREE* BY NOW.
I HOPE THEY DIDN'T ENCOUNTER ANY APES...
I'VE ESTABLISHED COMMUNICATION WITH UNIT 1!
IS EVERYONE ALL RIGHT?!
HOW ARE TORIKO AND HIS TEAM?
W...
WELL ...
GAH HA HA HA!
NOBODY'S COME OUT TO BOTHER US ON THIS WHOLE STINKIN' CONTINENT!
LOOKS LIKE THE GOURMET WORLD'S SCARED TO DEATH OF THE SUPER AMAZING ZONGEH!!
YES, SIR! WITHOUT A DOUBT, MASTER ZONGEH!
BWUMP
OOF!

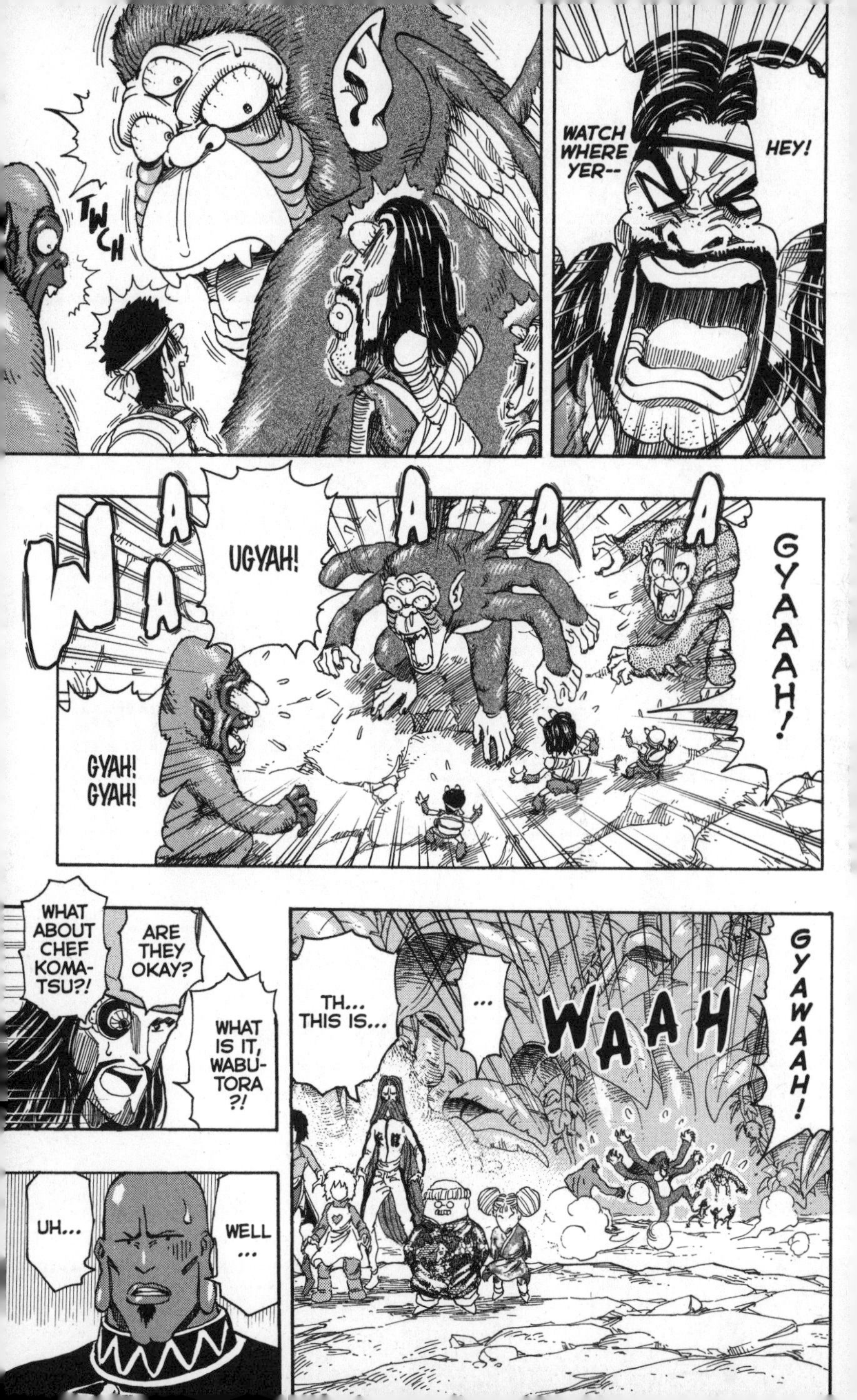
HEY!
WATCH WHERE YER--
TWCH
GYAAAAH!
A A A
UGYAH!
WA A
GYAH! GYAH!
GYAWAAAH!
WAAH
...
TH... THIS IS...
ARE THEY OKAY?
WHAT ABOUT CHEF KOMATSU?!
WHAT IS IT, WABUTORA?!
WELL...
UH...

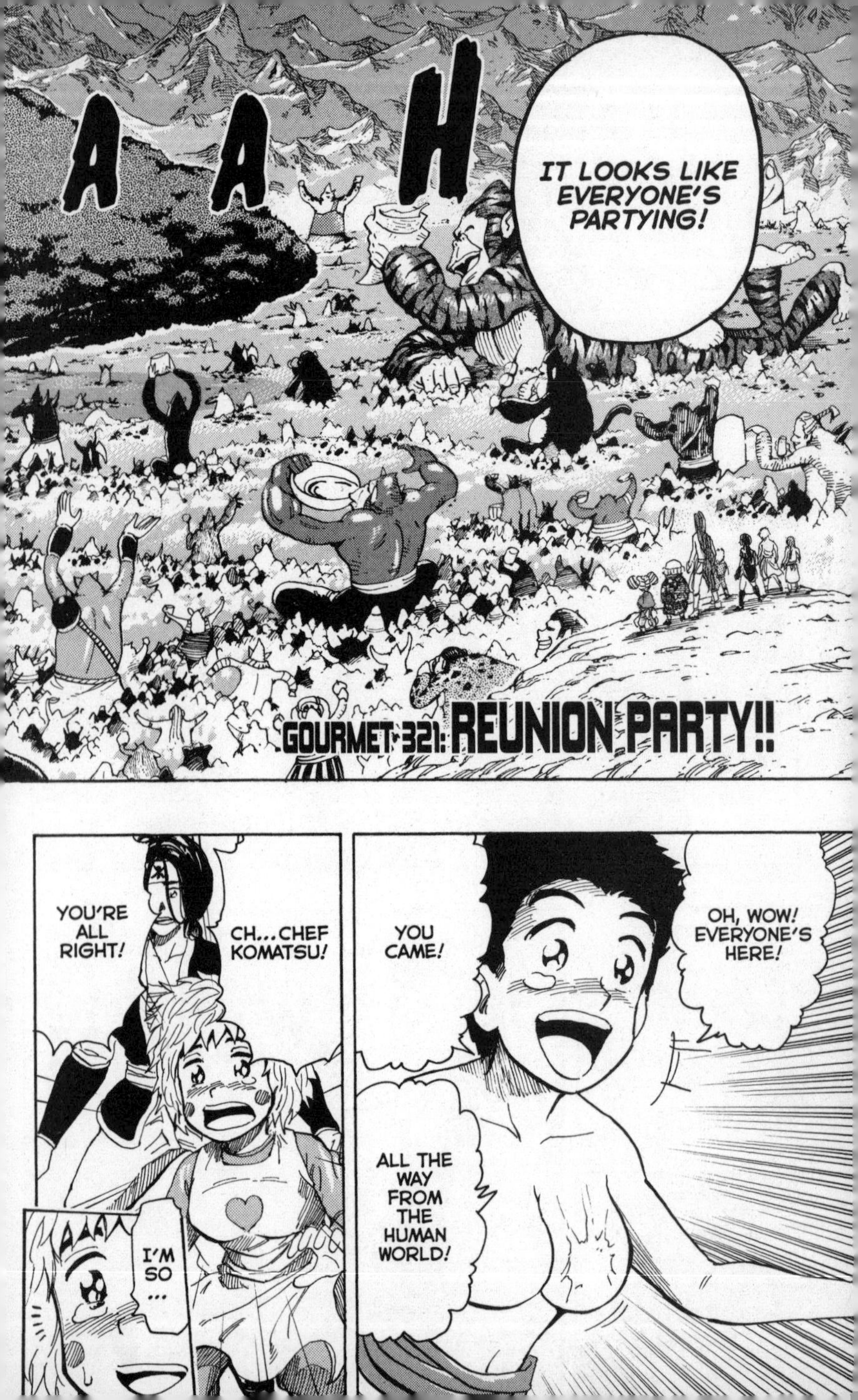
AAH
IT LOOKS LIKE EVERYONE'S PARTYING!
GOURMET 321: REUNION PARTY!!
OH, WOW! EVERYONE'S HERE!
YOU CAME!
ALL THE WAY FROM THE HUMAN WORLD!
CH...CHEF KOMATSU!
YOU'RE ALL RIGHT!
I'M SO ...

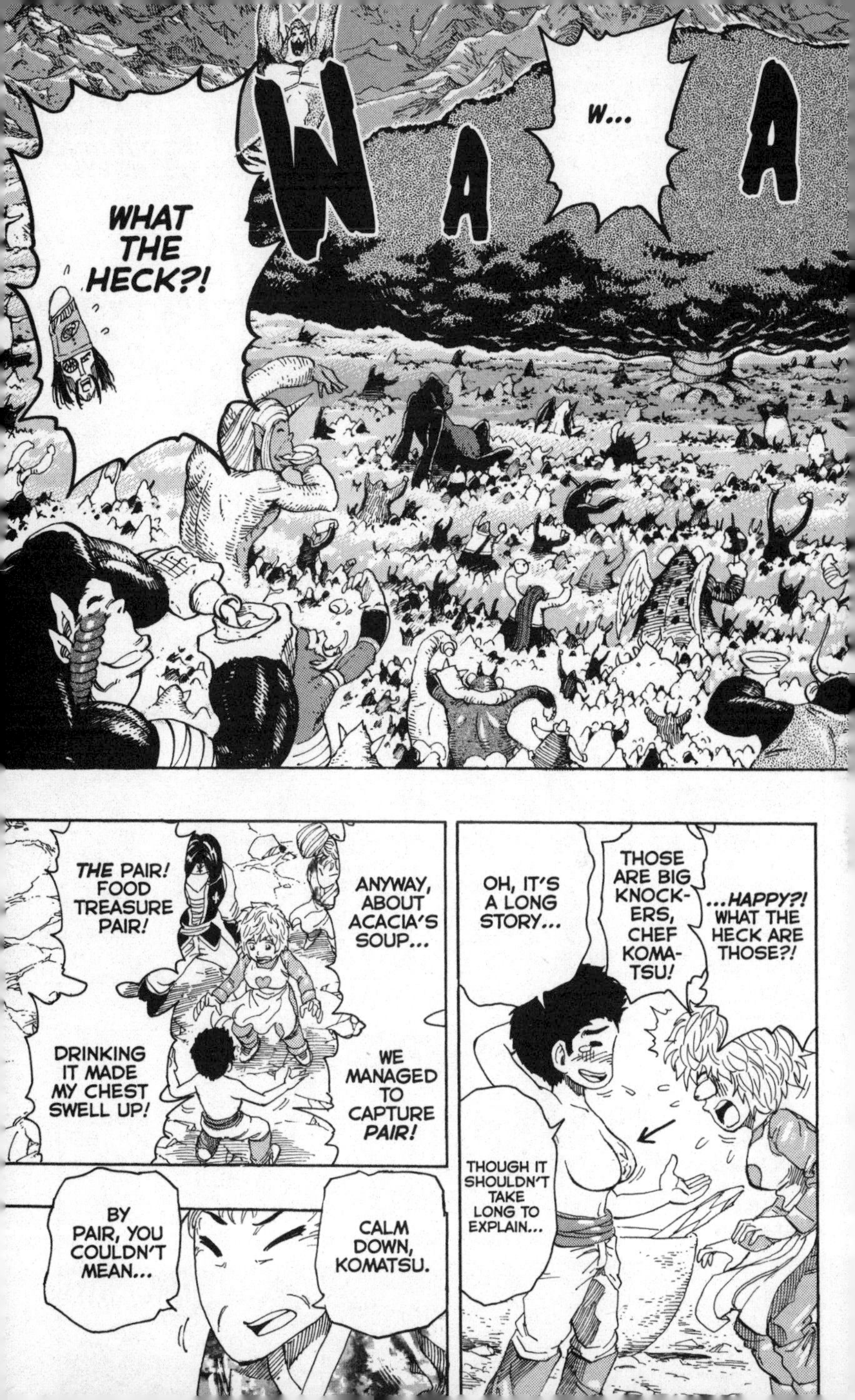
W...
WAA
WHAT THE HECK?!
...HAPPY?! WHAT THE HECK ARE THOSE?!
THOSE ARE BIG KNOCK-ERS, CHEF KOMA-TSU!
OH, IT'S A LONG STORY...
THOUGH IT SHOULDN'T TAKE LONG TO EXPLAIN...
ANYWAY, ABOUT ACACIA'S SOUP...
WE MANAGED TO CAPTURE PAIR!
THE PAIR! FOOD TREASURE PAIR!
DRINKING IT MADE MY CHEST SWELL UP!
CALM DOWN, KOMATSU.
BY PAIR, YOU COULDN'T MEAN...

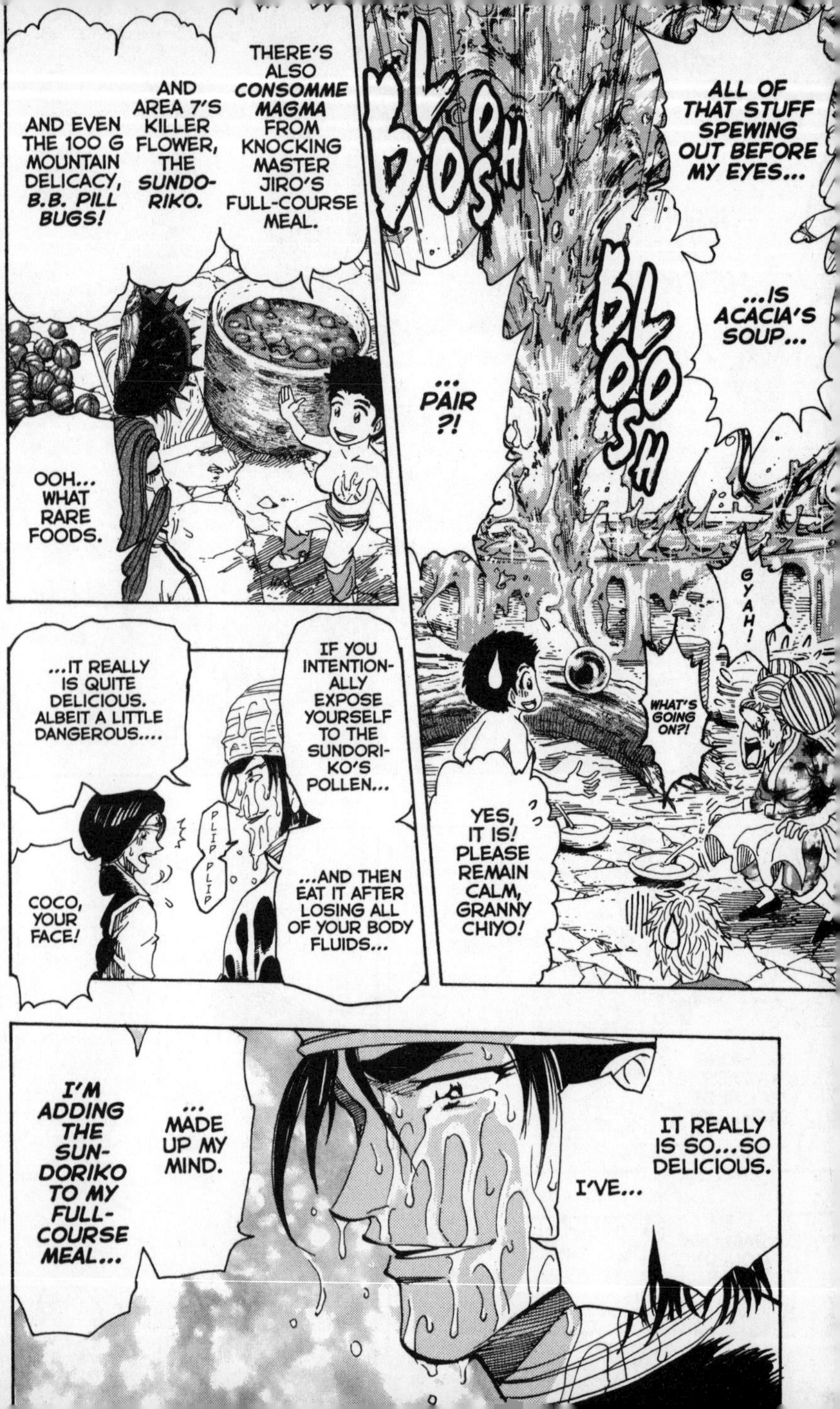

ALL OF THAT STUFF SPEWING OUT BEFORE MY EYES...
BLOOSH
...IS ACACIA'S SOUP...
BLOOSH
...PAIR?!
GYAH!
WHAT'S GOING ON?!
YES, IT IS! PLEASE REMAIN CALM, GRANNY CHIYO!
THERE'S ALSO CONSOMME MAGMA FROM KNOCKING MASTER JIRO'S FULL-COURSE MEAL.
AND AREA 7'S KILLER FLOWER, THE SUNDO-RIKO.
AND EVEN THE 100 G MOUNTAIN DELICACY, B.B. PILL BUGS!
OOH... WHAT RARE FOODS.
IF YOU INTENTION-ALLY EXPOSE YOURSELF TO THE SUNDORI-KO'S POLLEN...
...AND THEN EAT IT AFTER LOSING ALL OF YOUR BODY FLUIDS...
PLIP PLIP
...IT REALLY IS QUITE DELICIOUS. ALBEIT A LITTLE DANGEROUS....
COCO, YOUR FACE!
IT REALLY IS SO...SO DELICIOUS.
I'VE...
...MADE UP MY MIND.
I'M ADDING THE SUN-DORIKO TO MY FULL-COURSE MEAL...

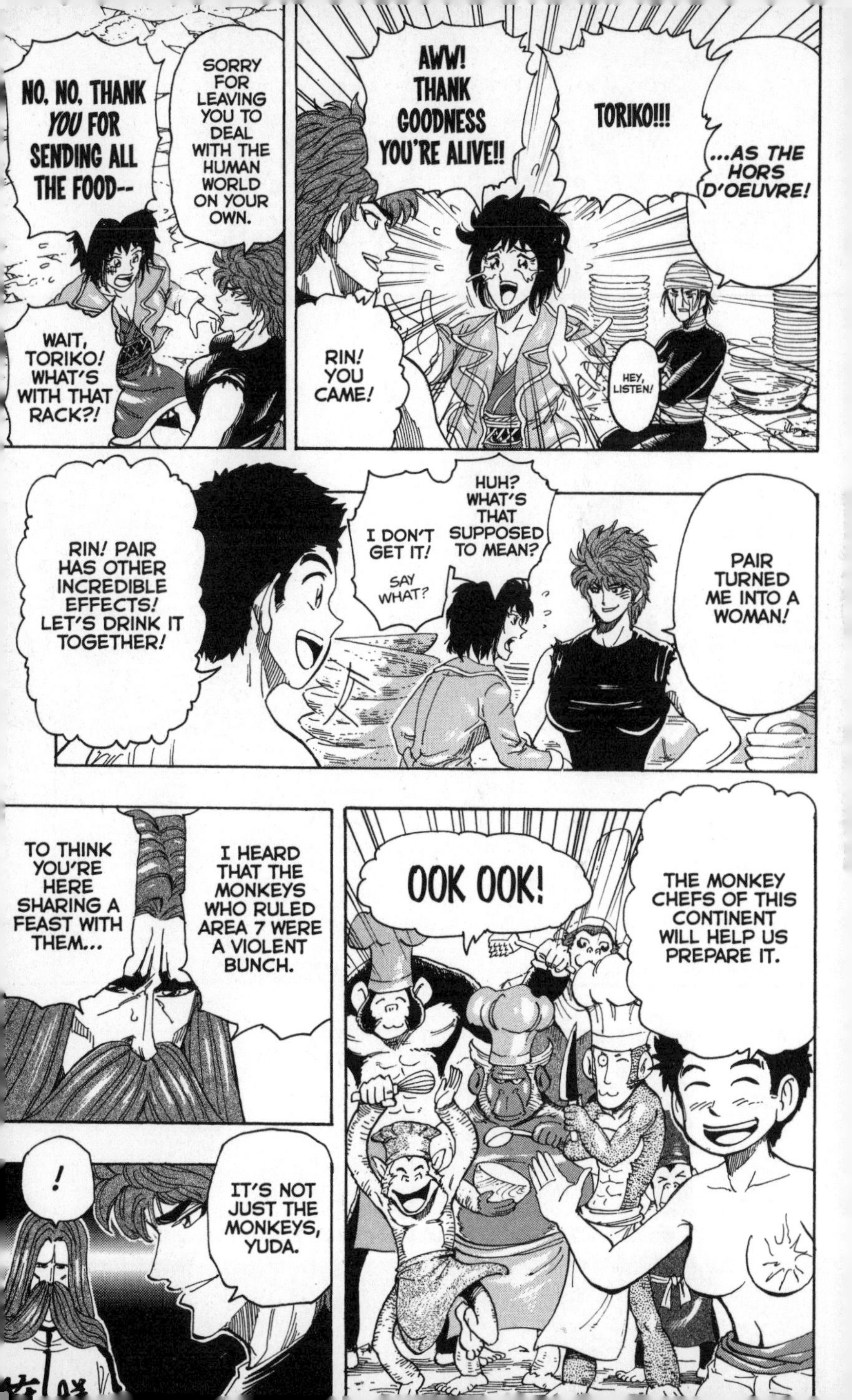
...AS THE HORS D'OEUVRE!
TORIKO!!!
AWW! THANK GOODNESS YOU'RE ALIVE!!
HEY, LISTEN!
RIN! YOU CAME!
SORRY FOR LEAVING YOU TO DEAL WITH THE HUMAN WORLD ON YOUR OWN.
NO, NO, THANK *YOU* FOR SENDING ALL THE FOOD--
WAIT, TORIKO! WHAT'S WITH THAT RACK?!
PAIR TURNED ME INTO A WOMAN!
HUH? WHAT'S THAT SUPPOSED TO MEAN?
I DON'T GET IT!
SAY WHAT?
RIN! PAIR HAS OTHER INCREDIBLE EFFECTS! LET'S DRINK IT TOGETHER!
THE MONKEY CHEFS OF THIS CONTINENT WILL HELP US PREPARE IT.
OOK OOK!
I HEARD THAT THE MONKEYS WHO RULED AREA 7 WERE A VIOLENT BUNCH.
TO THINK YOU'RE HERE SHARING A FEAST WITH THEM...
IT'S NOT JUST THE MONKEYS, YUDA.
!

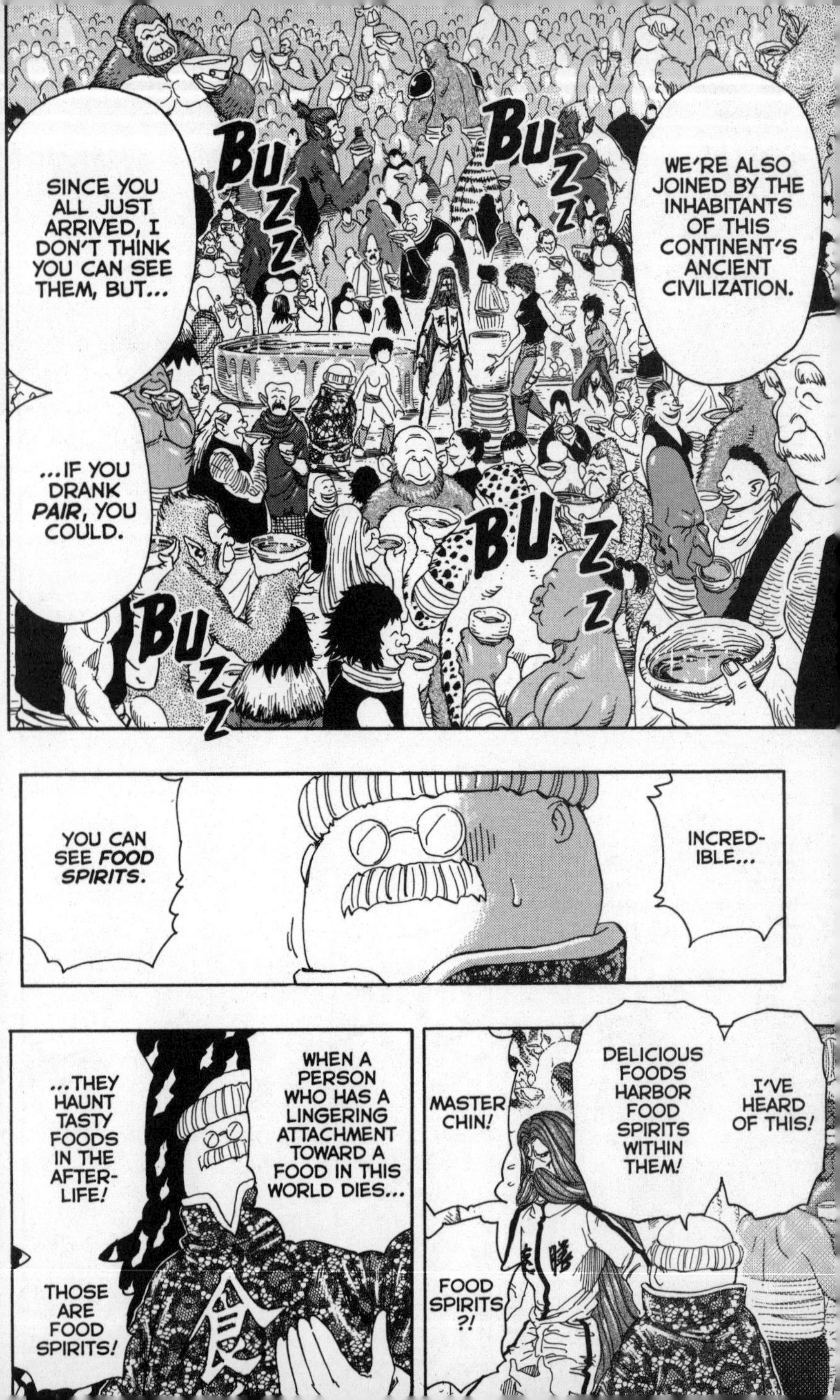
WE'RE ALSO JOINED BY THE INHABITANTS OF THIS CONTINENT'S ANCIENT CIVILIZATION.
BUZZ
BUZZ
SINCE YOU ALL JUST ARRIVED, I DON'T THINK YOU CAN SEE THEM, BUT...
...IF YOU DRANK *PAIR*, YOU COULD.
BUZZ
BUZZ
INCRED-IBLE...
YOU CAN SEE *FOOD SPIRITS*.
I'VE HEARD OF THIS!
DELICIOUS FOODS HARBOR FOOD SPIRITS WITHIN THEM!
MASTER CHIN!
FOOD SPIRITS?!
WHEN A PERSON WHO HAS A LINGERING ATTACHMENT TOWARD A FOOD IN THIS WORLD DIES...
...THEY HAUNT TASTY FOODS IN THE AFTER-LIFE!
THOSE ARE FOOD SPIRITS!

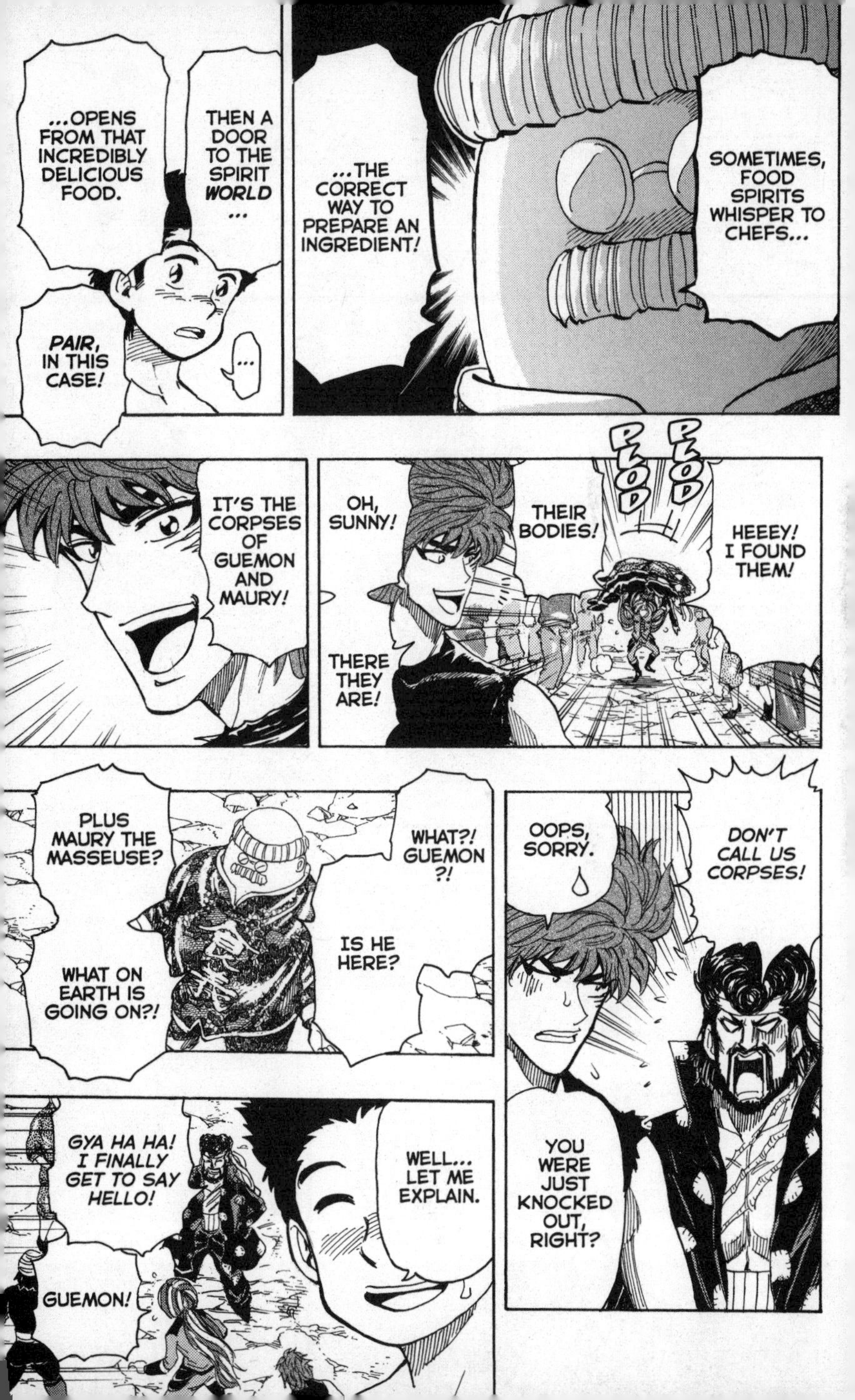
SOMETIMES, FOOD SPIRITS WHISPER TO CHEFS...
...THE CORRECT WAY TO PREPARE AN INGREDIENT!
THEN A DOOR TO THE SPIRIT *WORLD*...
...OPENS FROM THAT INCREDIBLY DELICIOUS FOOD.
...
PAIR, IN THIS CASE!
PLOD PLOD
HEEEY! I FOUND THEM!
THEIR BODIES!
OH, SUNNY!
THERE THEY ARE!
IT'S THE CORPSES OF GUEMON AND MAURY!
DON'T CALL US CORPSES!
OOPS, SORRY.
YOU WERE JUST KNOCKED OUT, RIGHT?
WHAT?! GUEMON?!
IS HE HERE?
PLUS MAURY THE MASSEUSE?
WHAT ON EARTH IS GOING ON?!
WELL... LET ME EXPLAIN.
GYA HA HA! I FINALLY GET TO SAY HELLO!
GUEMON!

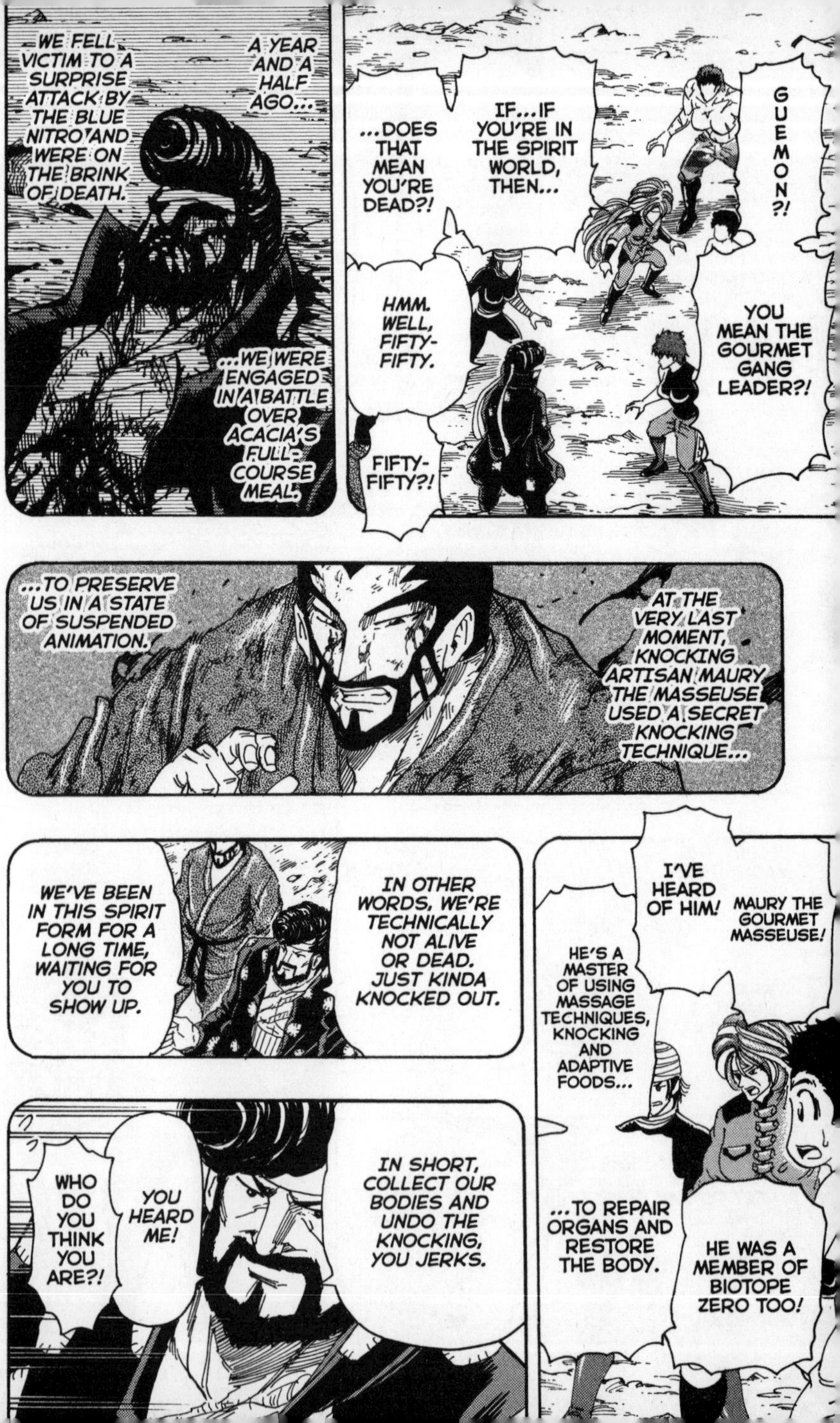
GUEMON?!
YOU MEAN THE GOURMET GANG LEADER?!
IF...IF YOU'RE IN THE SPIRIT WORLD, THEN...
...DOES THAT MEAN YOU'RE DEAD?!
HMM. WELL, FIFTY-FIFTY.
FIFTY-FIFTY?!
A YEAR AND A HALF AGO...
...WE WERE ENGAGED IN A BATTLE OVER ACACIA'S FULL-COURSE MEAL.
WE FELL VICTIM TO A SURPRISE ATTACK BY THE BLUE NITRO AND WERE ON THE BRINK OF DEATH.
AT THE VERY LAST MOMENT, KNOCKING ARTISAN MAURY THE MASSEUSE USED A SECRET KNOCKING TECHNIQUE...
...TO PRESERVE US IN A STATE OF SUSPENDED ANIMATION.
MAURY THE GOURMET MASSEUSE!
I'VE HEARD OF HIM!
HE'S A MASTER OF USING MASSAGE TECHNIQUES, KNOCKING AND ADAPTIVE FOODS...
...TO REPAIR ORGANS AND RESTORE THE BODY.
HE WAS A MEMBER OF BIOTOPE ZERO TOO!
IN OTHER WORDS, WE'RE TECHNICALLY NOT ALIVE OR DEAD. JUST KINDA KNOCKED OUT.
WE'VE BEEN IN THIS SPIRIT FORM FOR A LONG TIME, WAITING FOR YOU TO SHOW UP.
IN SHORT, COLLECT OUR BODIES AND UNDO THE KNOCKING, YOU JERKS.
WHO DO YOU THINK YOU ARE?!
YOU HEARD ME!

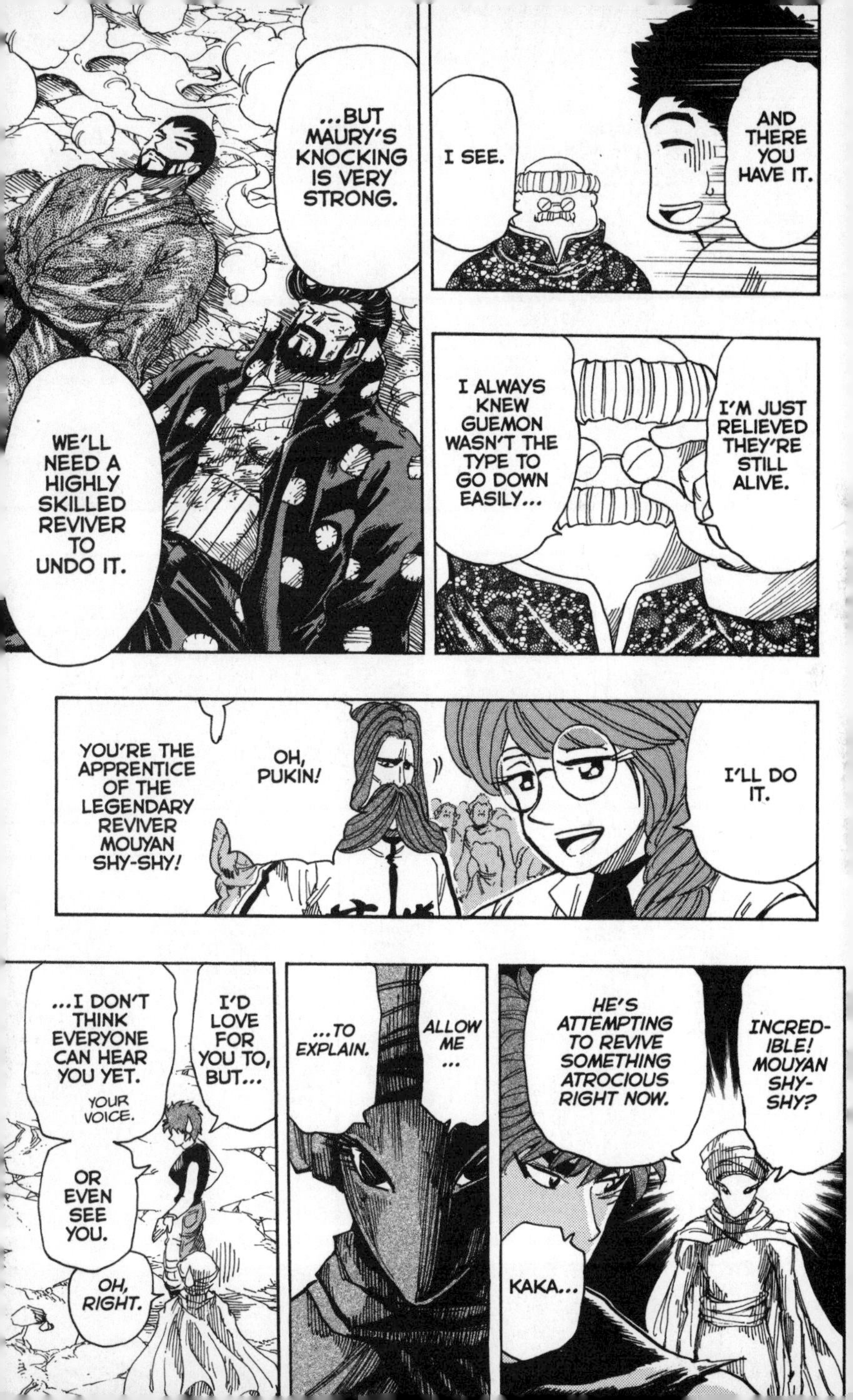
AND THERE YOU HAVE IT.
I SEE.
I'M JUST RELIEVED THEY'RE STILL ALIVE.
I ALWAYS KNEW GUEMON WASN'T THE TYPE TO GO DOWN EASILY...
...BUT MAURY'S KNOCKING IS VERY STRONG.
WE'LL NEED A HIGHLY SKILLED REVIVER TO UNDO IT.
I'LL DO IT.
OH, PUKIN!
YOU'RE THE APPRENTICE OF THE LEGENDARY REVIVER MOUYAN SHY-SHY!
INCRED-IBLE! MOUYAN SHY-SHY?
HE'S ATTEMPTING TO REVIVE SOMETHING ATROCIOUS RIGHT NOW.
KAKA...
ALLOW ME...
...TO EXPLAIN.
I'D LOVE FOR YOU TO, BUT...
...I DON'T THINK EVERYONE CAN HEAR YOU YET.
YOUR VOICE.
OR EVEN SEE YOU.
OH, RIGHT.

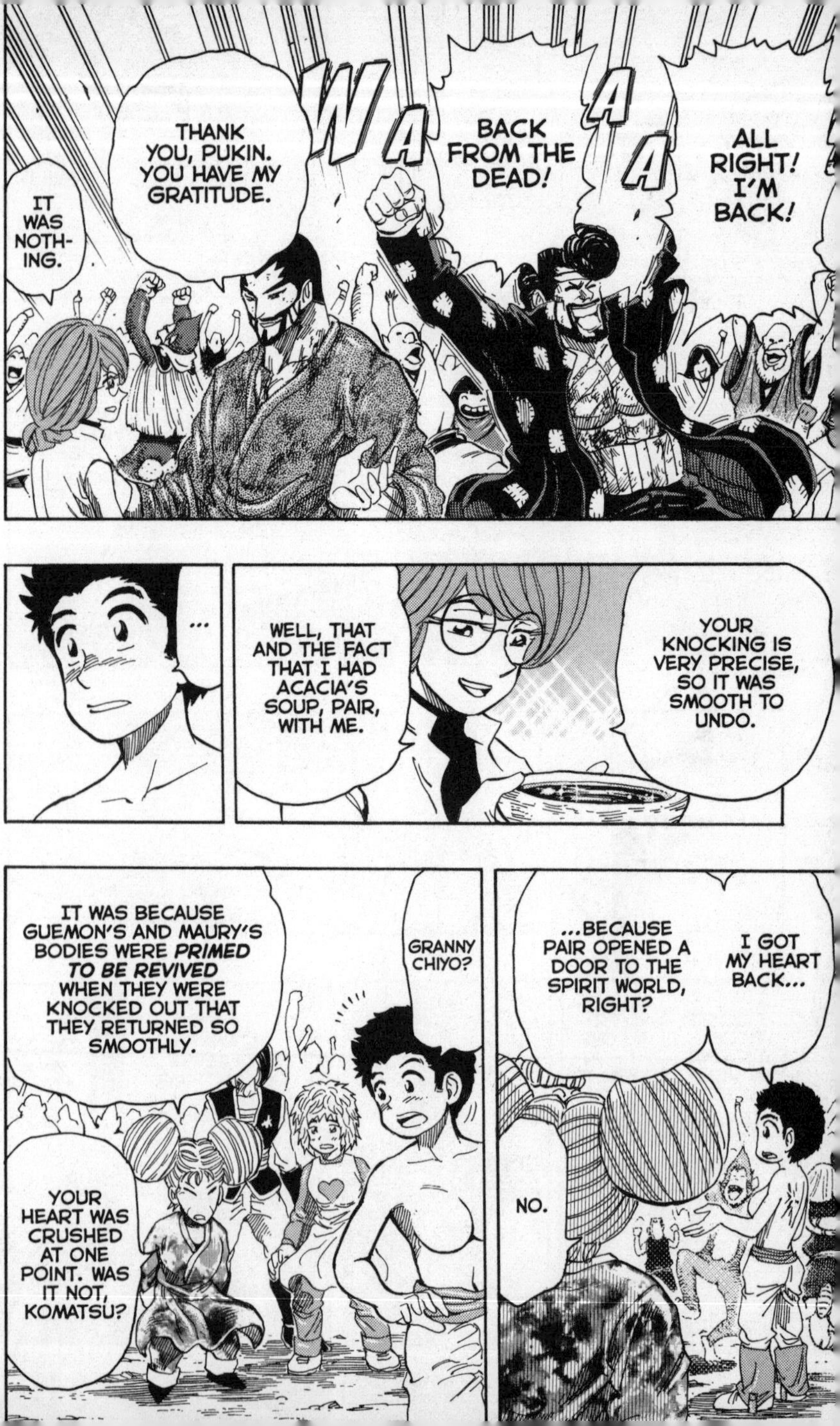
ALL RIGHT! I'M BACK!
WAAA
BACK FROM THE DEAD!
THANK YOU, PUKIN. YOU HAVE MY GRATITUDE.
IT WAS NOTHING.
YOUR KNOCKING IS VERY PRECISE, SO IT WAS SMOOTH TO UNDO.
WELL, THAT AND THE FACT THAT I HAD ACACIA'S SOUP, PAIR, WITH ME.
...
I GOT MY HEART BACK...
...BECAUSE PAIR OPENED A DOOR TO THE SPIRIT WORLD, RIGHT?
NO.
GRANNY CHIYO?
IT WAS BECAUSE GUEMON'S AND MAURY'S BODIES WERE *PRIMED TO BE REVIVED* WHEN THEY WERE KNOCKED OUT THAT THEY RETURNED SO SMOOTHLY.
YOUR HEART WAS CRUSHED AT ONE POINT. WAS IT NOT, KOMATSU?

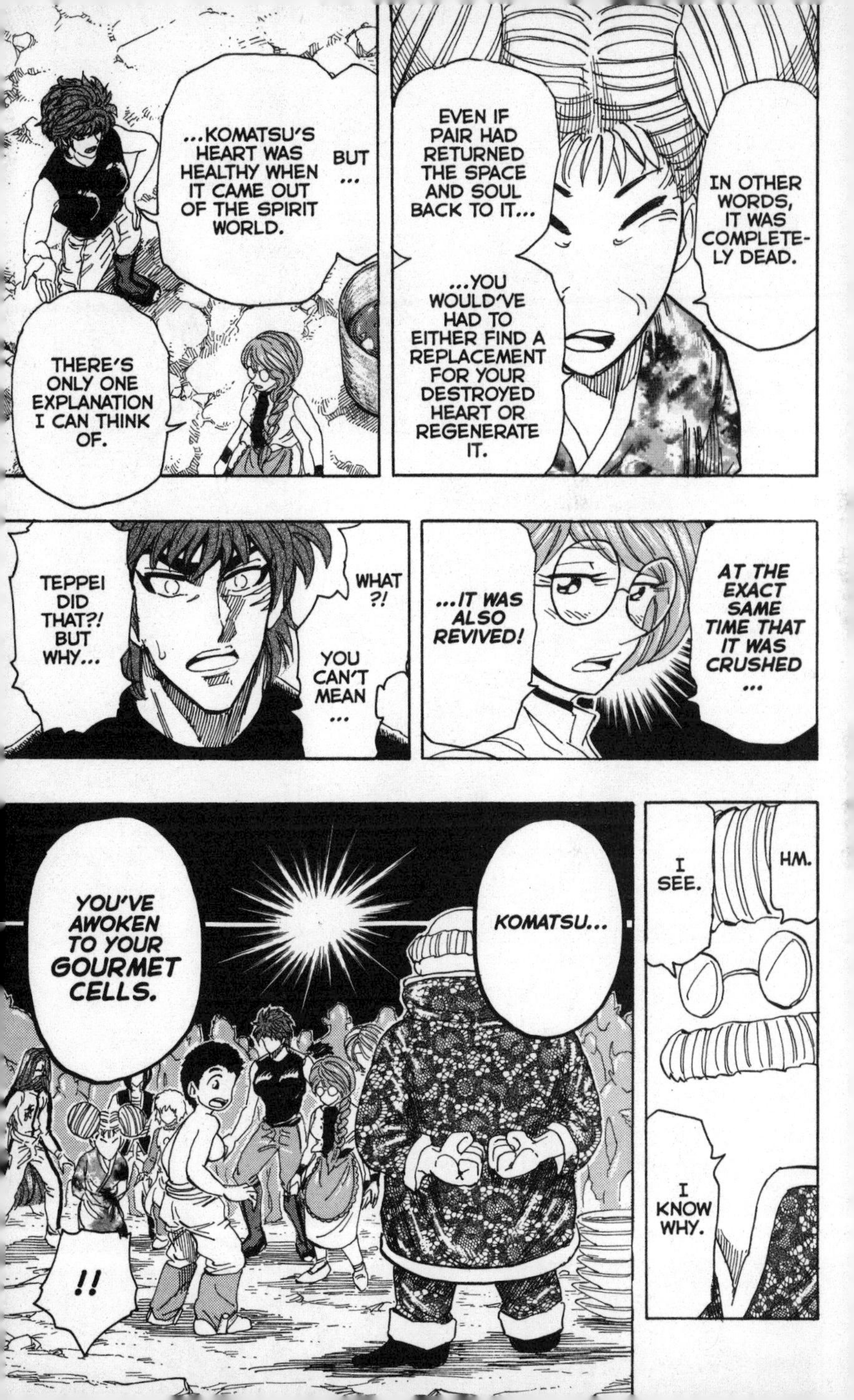
IN OTHER WORDS, IT WAS COMPLETE-LY DEAD.
EVEN IF PAIR HAD RETURNED THE SPACE AND SOUL BACK TO IT...
...YOU WOULD'VE HAD TO EITHER FIND A REPLACEMENT FOR YOUR DESTROYED HEART OR REGENERATE IT.
BUT...
...KOMATSU'S HEART WAS HEALTHY WHEN IT CAME OUT OF THE SPIRIT WORLD.
THERE'S ONLY ONE EXPLANATION I CAN THINK OF.
AT THE EXACT SAME TIME THAT IT WAS CRUSHED...
...IT WAS ALSO REVIVED!
WHAT?!
YOU CAN'T MEAN...
TEPPEI DID THAT?! BUT WHY...
HM.
I SEE.
I KNOW WHY.
KOMATSU...
YOU'VE AWOKEN TO YOUR GOURMET CELLS.
!!

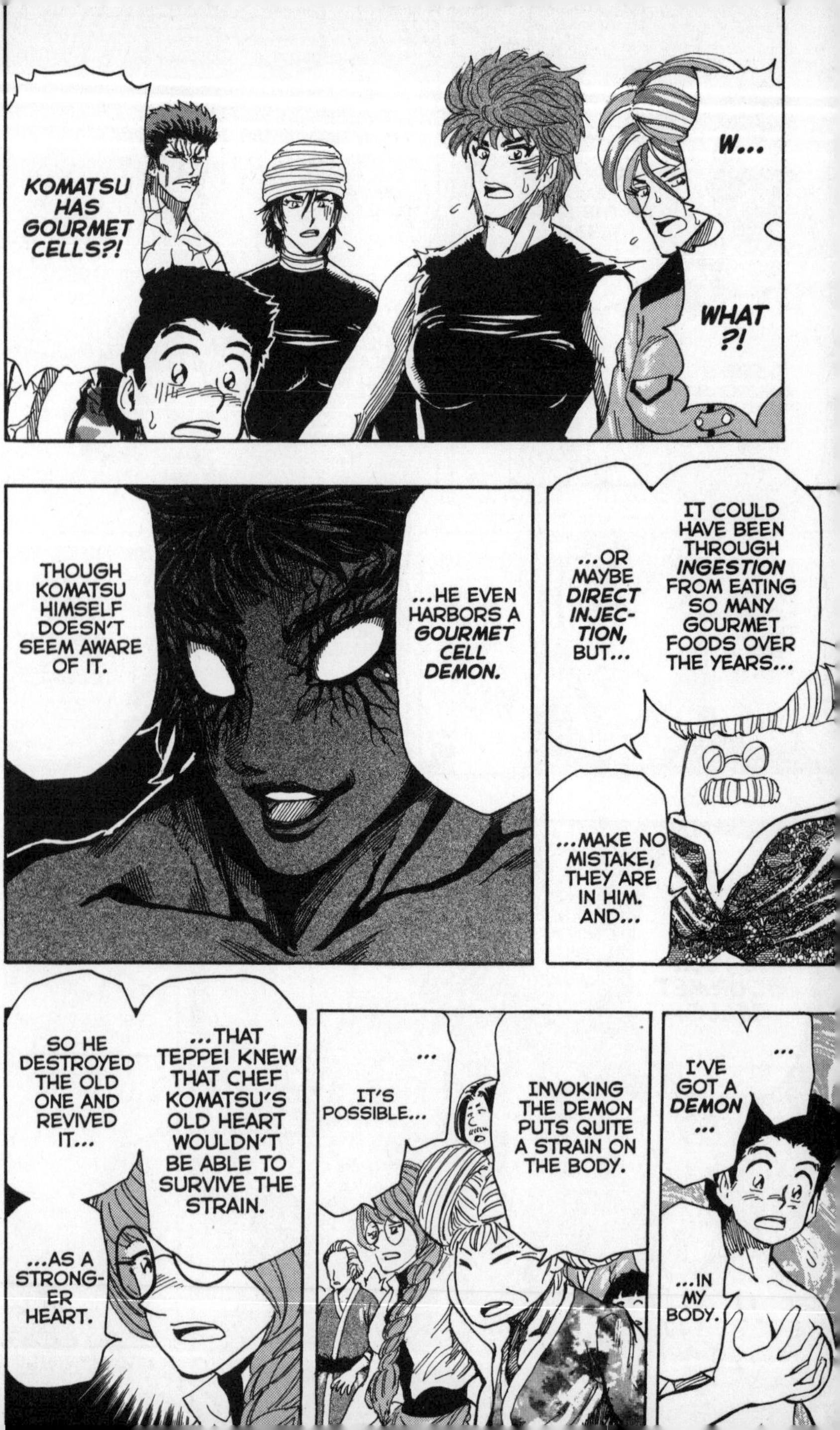
W...
WHAT ?!
KOMATSU HAS GOURMET CELLS?!
IT COULD HAVE BEEN THROUGH *INGESTION* FROM EATING SO MANY GOURMET FOODS OVER THE YEARS...
...OR MAYBE *DIRECT INJECTION,* BUT...
...MAKE NO MISTAKE, THEY ARE IN HIM. AND...
...HE EVEN HARBORS A *GOURMET CELL DEMON.*
THOUGH KOMATSU HIMSELF DOESN'T SEEM AWARE OF IT.
...
I'VE GOT A *DEMON* ...
...IN MY BODY.
INVOKING THE DEMON PUTS QUITE A STRAIN ON THE BODY.
...
IT'S POSSIBLE...
...THAT TEPPEI KNEW THAT CHEF KOMATSU'S OLD HEART WOULDN'T BE ABLE TO SURVIVE THE STRAIN.
SO HE DESTROYED THE OLD ONE AND REVIVED IT...
...AS A STRONG-ER HEART.

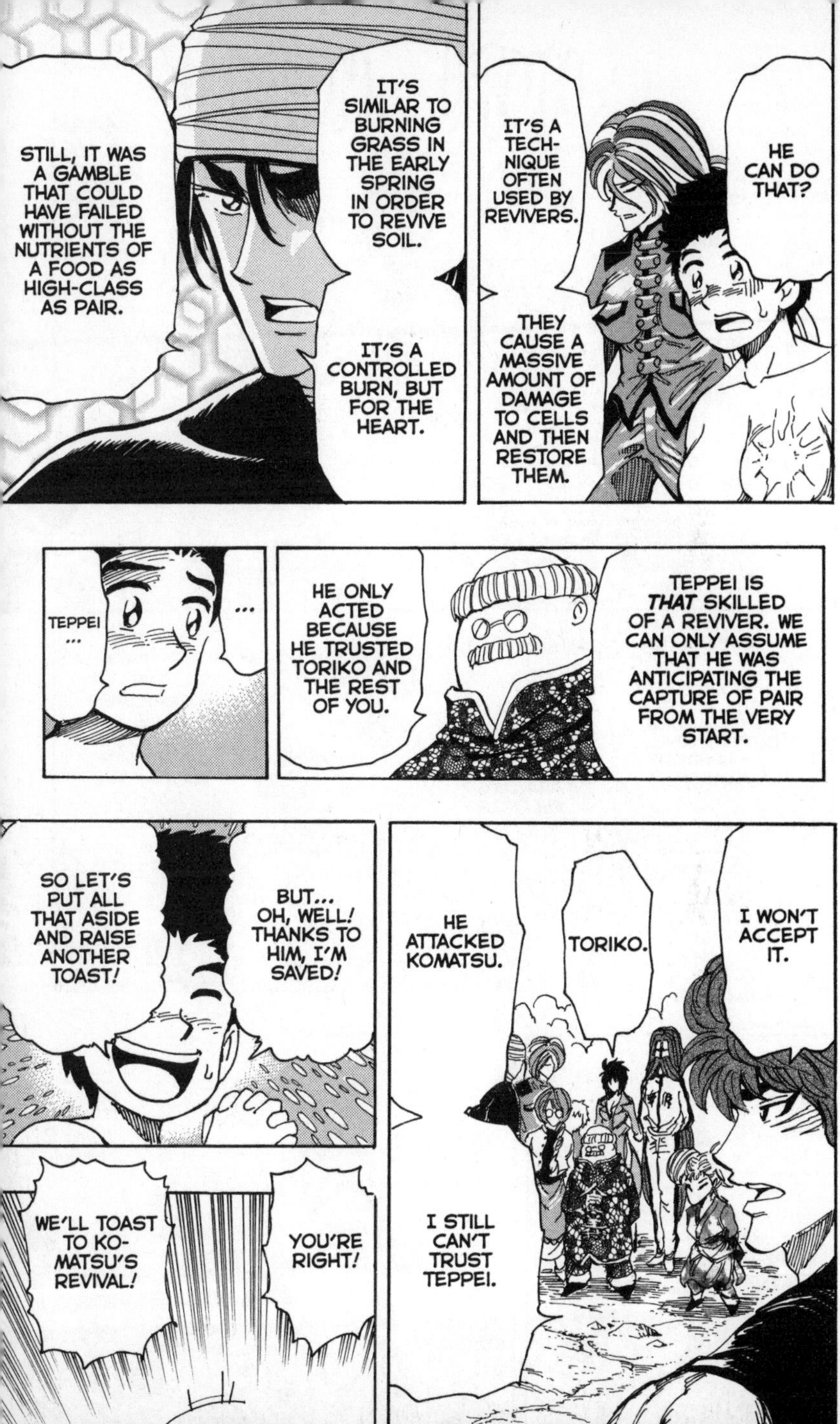
HE CAN DO THAT?
IT'S A TECHNIQUE OFTEN USED BY REVIVERS.
THEY CAUSE A MASSIVE AMOUNT OF DAMAGE TO CELLS AND THEN RESTORE THEM.
IT'S SIMILAR TO BURNING GRASS IN THE EARLY SPRING IN ORDER TO REVIVE SOIL.
IT'S A CONTROLLED BURN, BUT FOR THE HEART.
STILL, IT WAS A GAMBLE THAT COULD HAVE FAILED WITHOUT THE NUTRIENTS OF A FOOD AS HIGH-CLASS AS PAIR.
TEPPEI IS THAT SKILLED OF A REVIVER. WE CAN ONLY ASSUME THAT HE WAS ANTICIPATING THE CAPTURE OF PAIR FROM THE VERY START.
HE ONLY ACTED BECAUSE HE TRUSTED TORIKO AND THE REST OF YOU.
...
TEPPEI ...
I WON'T ACCEPT IT.
TORIKO.
HE ATTACKED KOMATSU.
I STILL CAN'T TRUST TEPPEI.
BUT... OH, WELL! THANKS TO HIM, I'M SAVED!
SO LET'S PUT ALL THAT ASIDE AND RAISE ANOTHER TOAST!
YOU'RE RIGHT!
WE'LL TOAST TO KOMATSU'S REVIVAL!

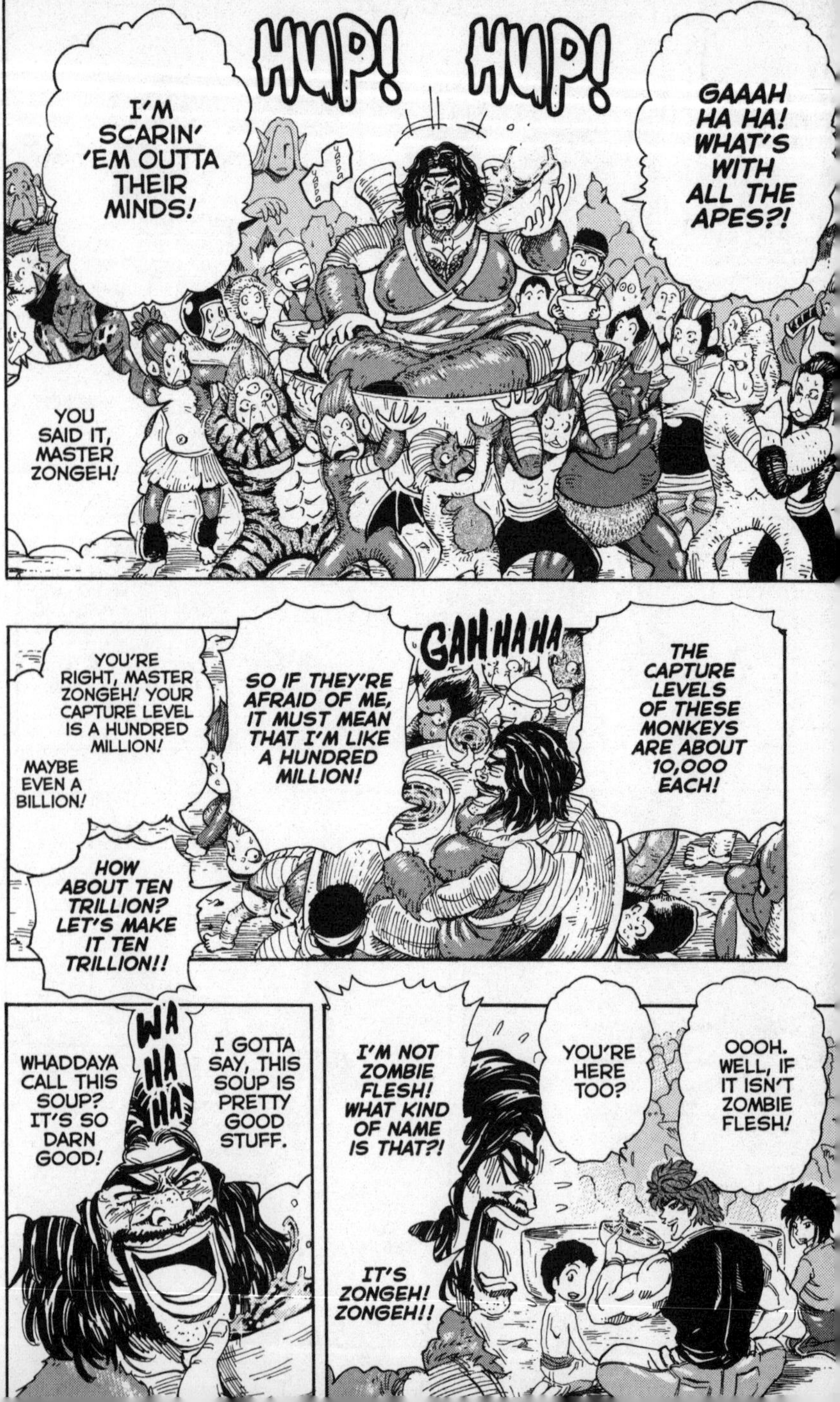
HUP! HUP!
GAAAH HA HA! WHAT'S WITH ALL THE APES?!
I'M SCARIN' 'EM OUTTA THEIR MINDS!
YOU SAID IT, MASTER ZONGEH!
THE CAPTURE LEVELS OF THESE MONKEYS ARE ABOUT 10,000 EACH!
GAH HA HA
SO IF THEY'RE AFRAID OF ME, IT MUST MEAN THAT I'M LIKE A HUNDRED MILLION!
YOU'RE RIGHT, MASTER ZONGEH! YOUR CAPTURE LEVEL IS A HUNDRED MILLION!
MAYBE EVEN A BILLION!
HOW ABOUT TEN TRILLION? LET'S MAKE IT TEN TRILLION!!
OOOH. WELL, IF IT ISN'T ZOMBIE FLESH!
YOU'RE HERE TOO?
I'M NOT ZOMBIE FLESH! WHAT KIND OF NAME IS THAT?!
IT'S ZONGEH! ZONGEH!!
I GOTTA SAY, THIS SOUP IS PRETTY GOOD STUFF.
WA HA HA HA
WHADDAYA CALL THIS SOUP? IT'S SO DARN GOOD!

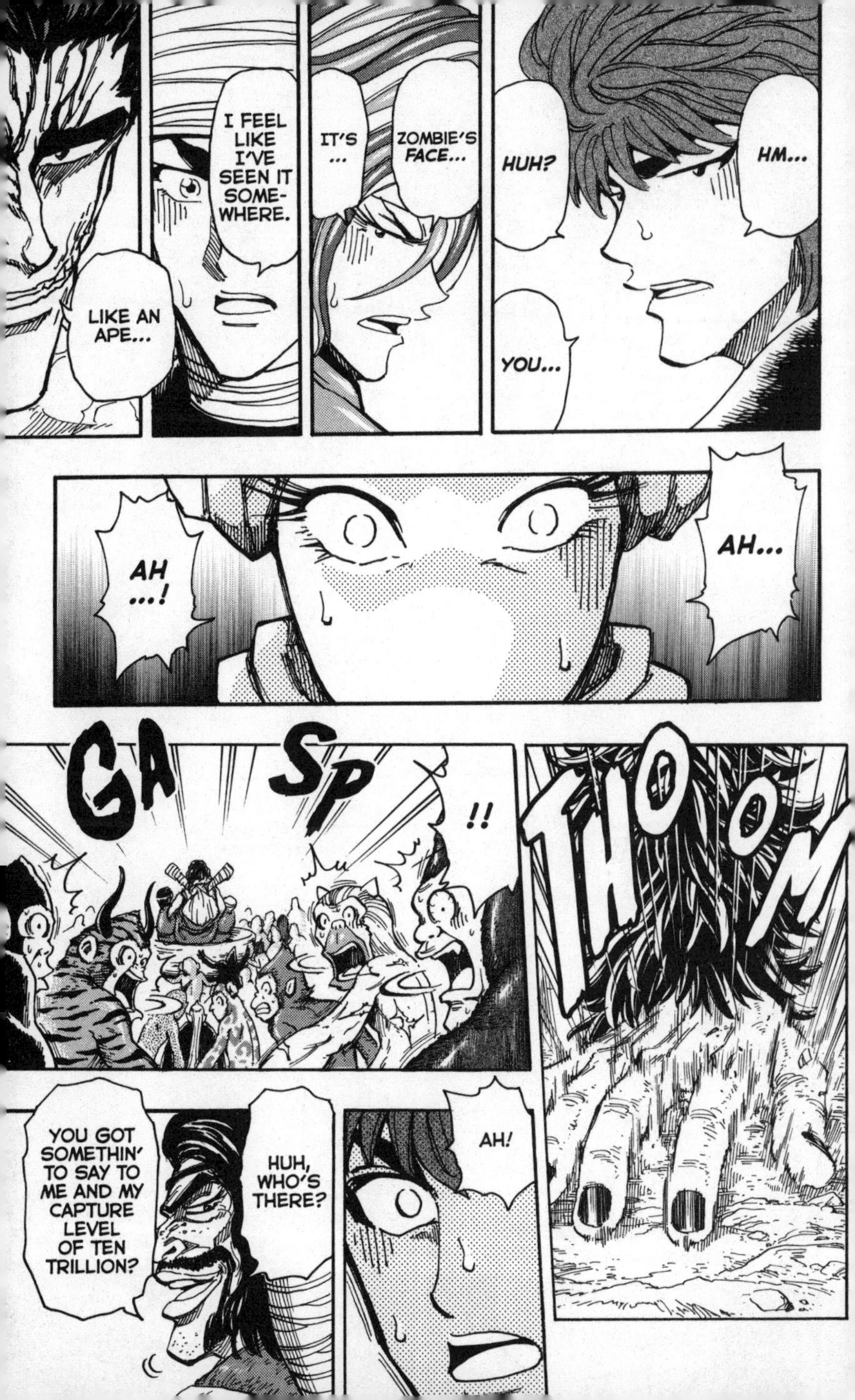
HM...
HUH?
YOU...
ZOMBIE'S FACE...
IT'S ...
I FEEL LIKE I'VE SEEN IT SOME-WHERE.
LIKE AN APE...
AH...
AH ...!
THOOM
GASP!!
AH!
HUH, WHO'S THERE?
YOU GOT SOMETHIN' TO SAY TO ME AND MY CAPTURE LEVEL OF TEN TRILLION?

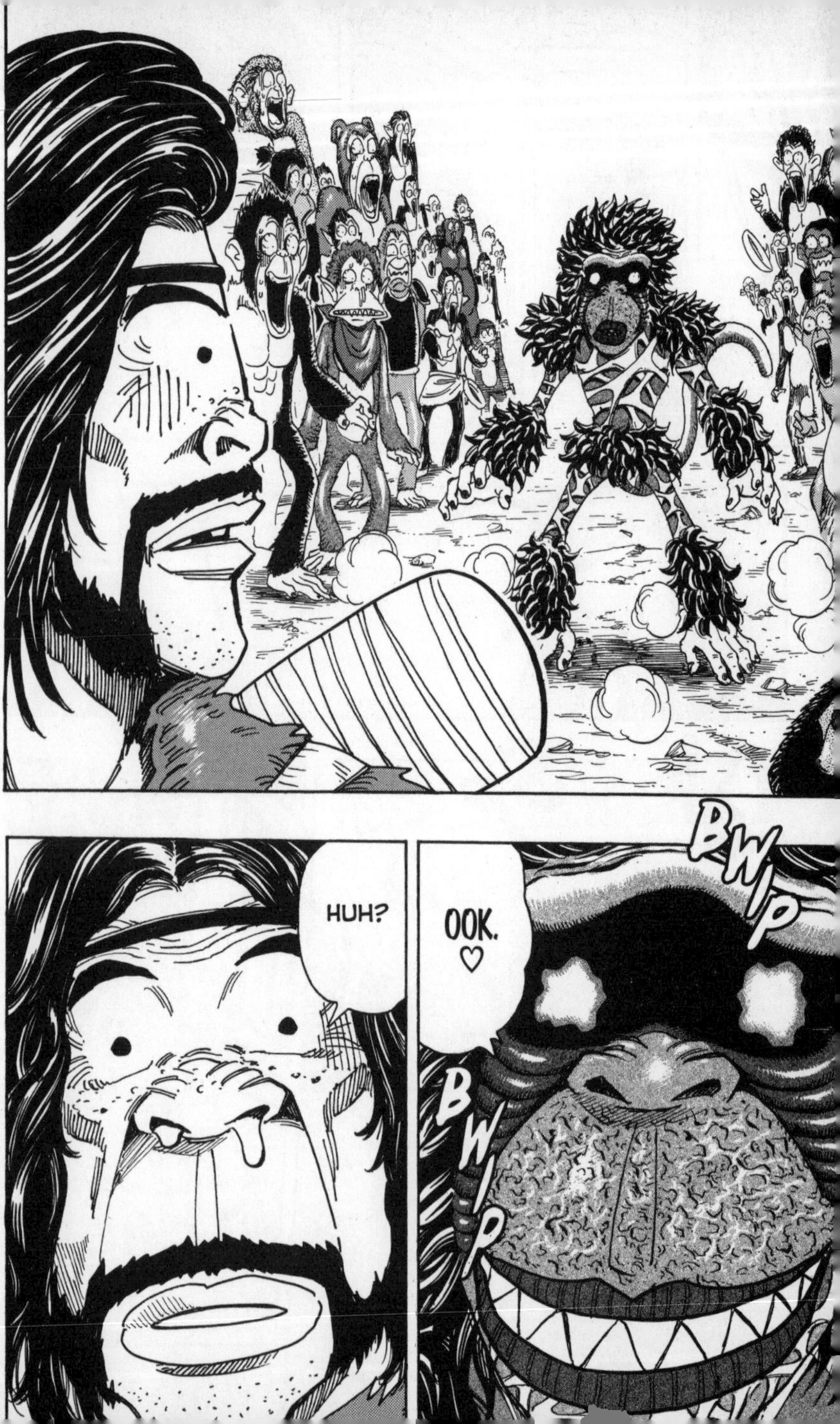
BWIP
OOK. ♡
BWIP
HUH?

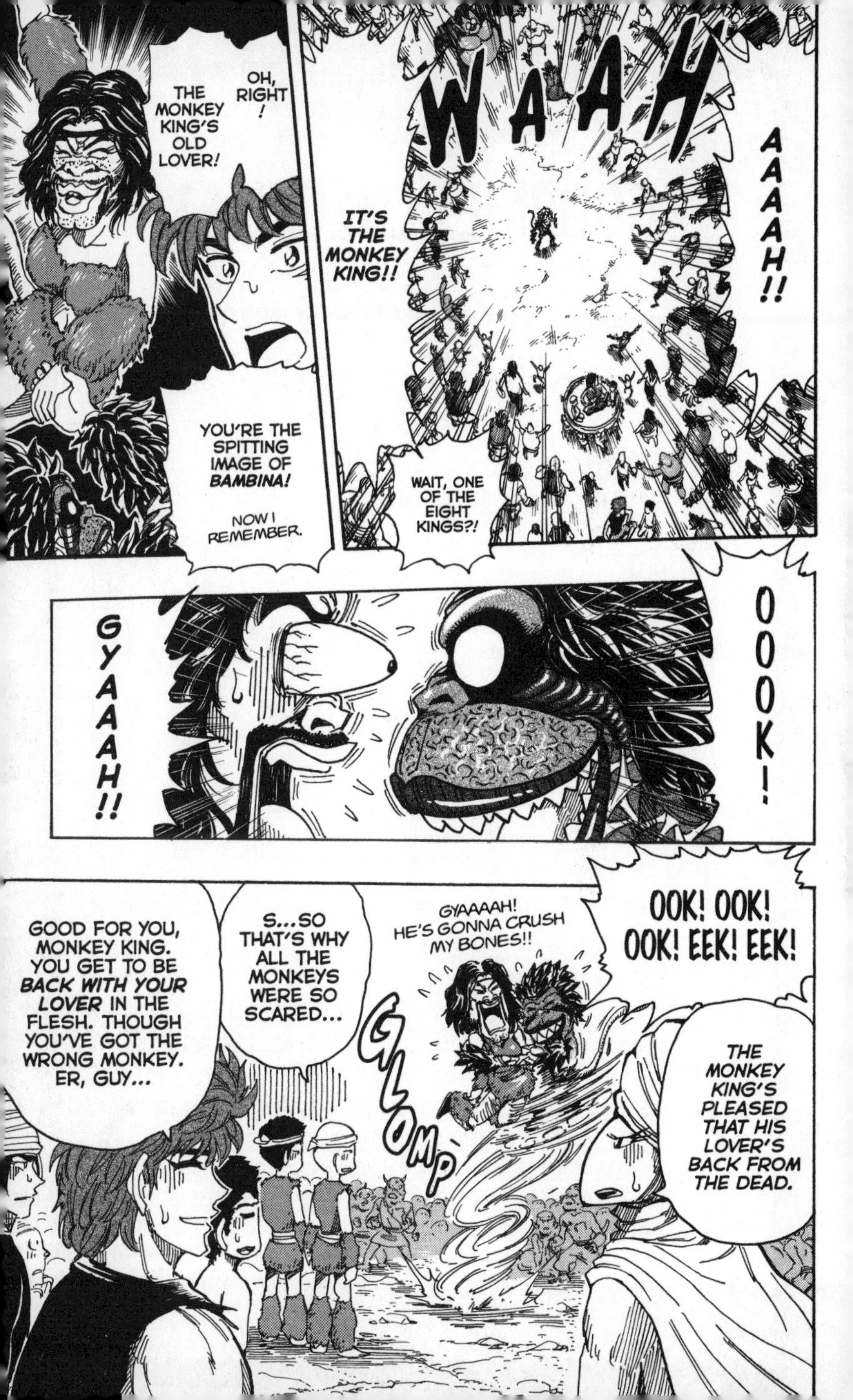
WAAH
AAAAAH!!
IT'S THE MONKEY KING!!
WAIT, ONE OF THE EIGHT KINGS?!
OH, RIGHT!
THE MONKEY KING'S OLD LOVER!
YOU'RE THE SPITTING IMAGE OF BAMBINA!
NOW I REMEMBER.
OOOOK!
GYAAAAH!!
OOK! OOK! OOK! EEK! EEK!
THE MONKEY KING'S PLEASED THAT HIS LOVER'S BACK FROM THE DEAD.
GYAAAAH! HE'S GONNA CRUSH MY BONES!!
GLOMP
S...SO THAT'S WHY ALL THE MONKEYS WERE SO SCARED...
GOOD FOR YOU, MONKEY KING. YOU GET TO BE BACK WITH YOUR LOVER IN THE FLESH. THOUGH YOU'VE GOT THE WRONG MONKEY. ER, GUY...

TORIKO

GOURMET CHECKLIST

Vol. 351

BREATH DRAGON

(MAMMAL)

CAPTURE LEVEL: 219

HABITAT: ZIRBEL ISLAND IN THE GOURMET WORLD

SIZE: 300 M

HEIGHT: 260 M

WEIGHT: 1.2 MILLION TONS

PRICE: 6,000 YEN PER KILOGRAM

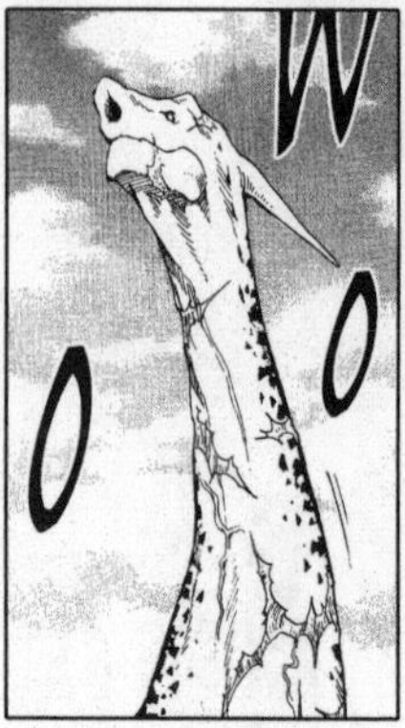
WOO

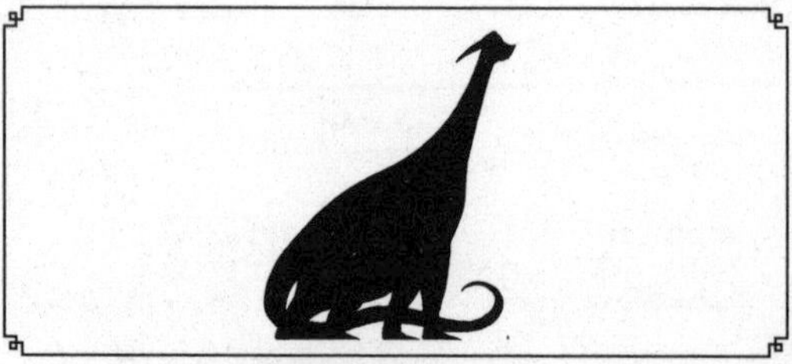

SCALE

THE FIRST TIME TORIKO WENT TO THE GOURMET WORLD, THIS MONSTER PUT HIM IN A WORLD OF HURT. THIS POWERFUL ENEMY BLASTS AIR OUT OF ITS NOSE. BUT SINCE TORIKO HAD ALREADY BEEN TRAINING AND STEADILY LEVELING UP, THIS MONSTER DIDN'T STAND A CHANCE. YOU CAN SEE THE VESTIGES OF TORIKO'S PROGRESS EMBEDDED INTO THIS MONSTER.

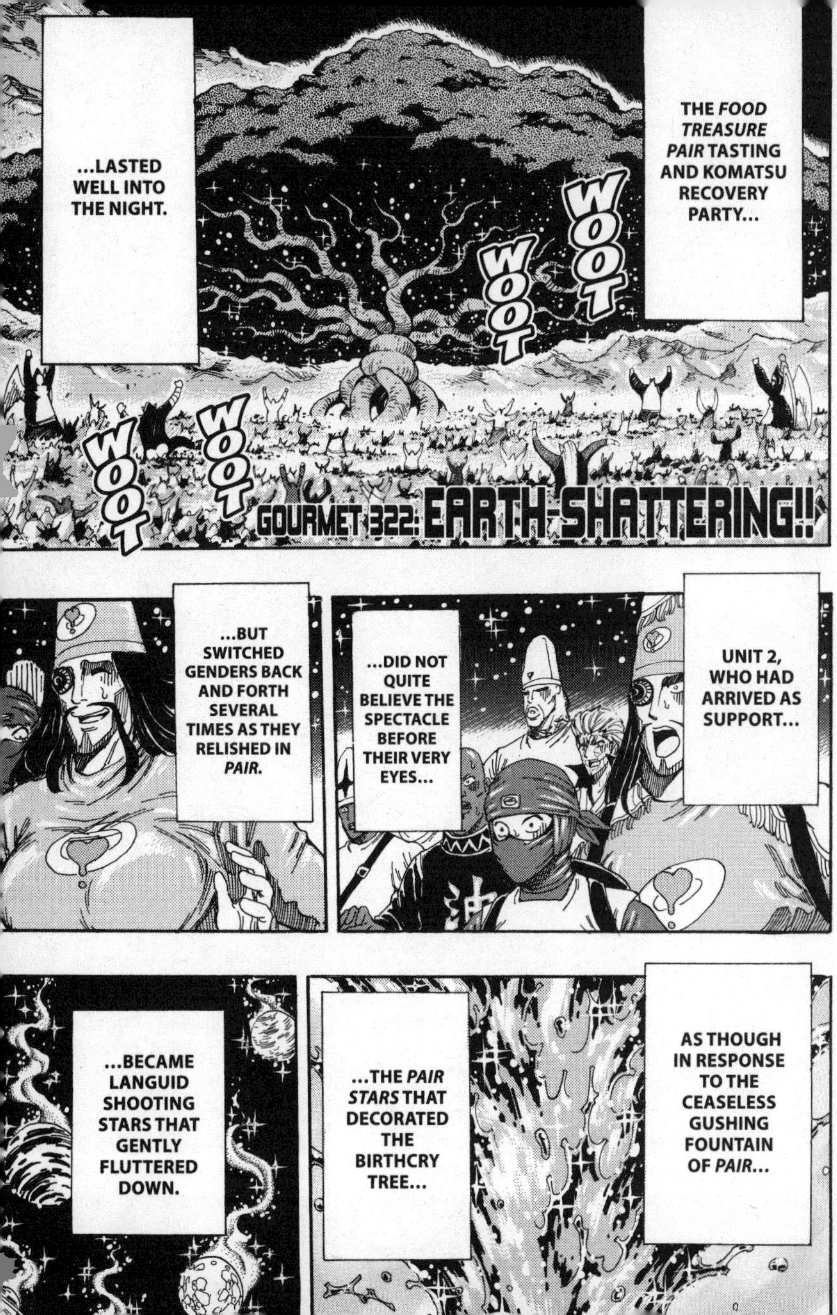
THE *FOOD TREASURE PAIR* TASTING AND KOMATSU RECOVERY PARTY...
WOOT
WOOT
...LASTED WELL INTO THE NIGHT.
WOOT
WOOT
GOURMET 322: EARTH-SHATTERING!!
UNIT 2, WHO HAD ARRIVED AS SUPPORT...
...DID NOT QUITE BELIEVE THE SPECTACLE BEFORE THEIR VERY EYES...
...BUT SWITCHED GENDERS BACK AND FORTH SEVERAL TIMES AS THEY RELISHED IN *PAIR*.
AS THOUGH IN RESPONSE TO THE CEASELESS GUSHING FOUNTAIN OF *PAIR*...
...THE *PAIR STARS* THAT DECORATED THE BIRTHCRY TREE...
...BECAME LANGUID SHOOTING STARS THAT GENTLY FLUTTERED DOWN.

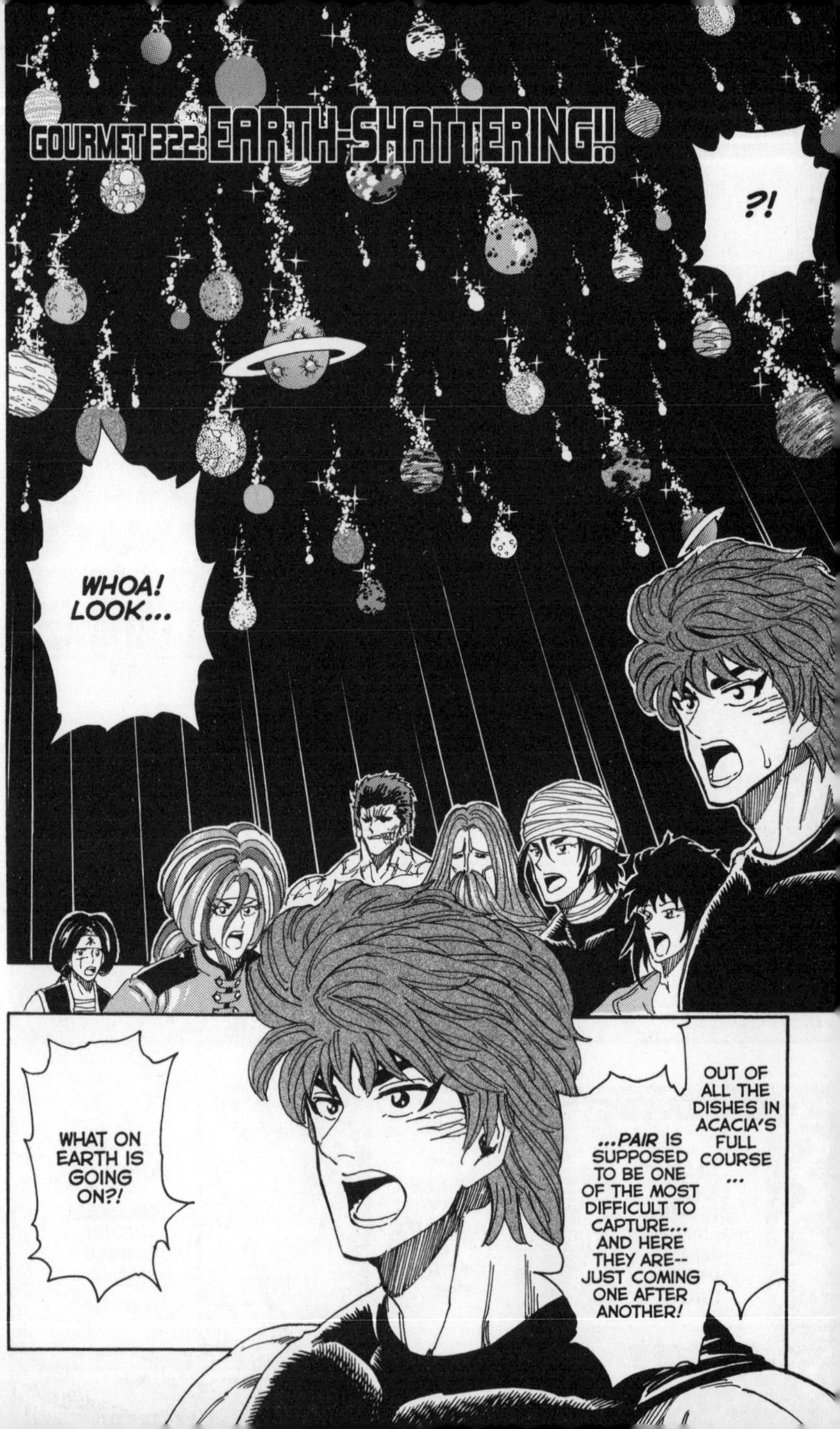
GOURMET 322: EARTH-SHATTERING!!
?!
WHOA! LOOK...
OUT OF ALL THE DISHES IN ACACIA'S FULL COURSE ...
...PAIR IS SUPPOSED TO BE ONE OF THE MOST DIFFICULT TO CAPTURE... AND HERE THEY ARE--JUST COMING ONE AFTER ANOTHER!
WHAT ON EARTH IS GOING ON?!

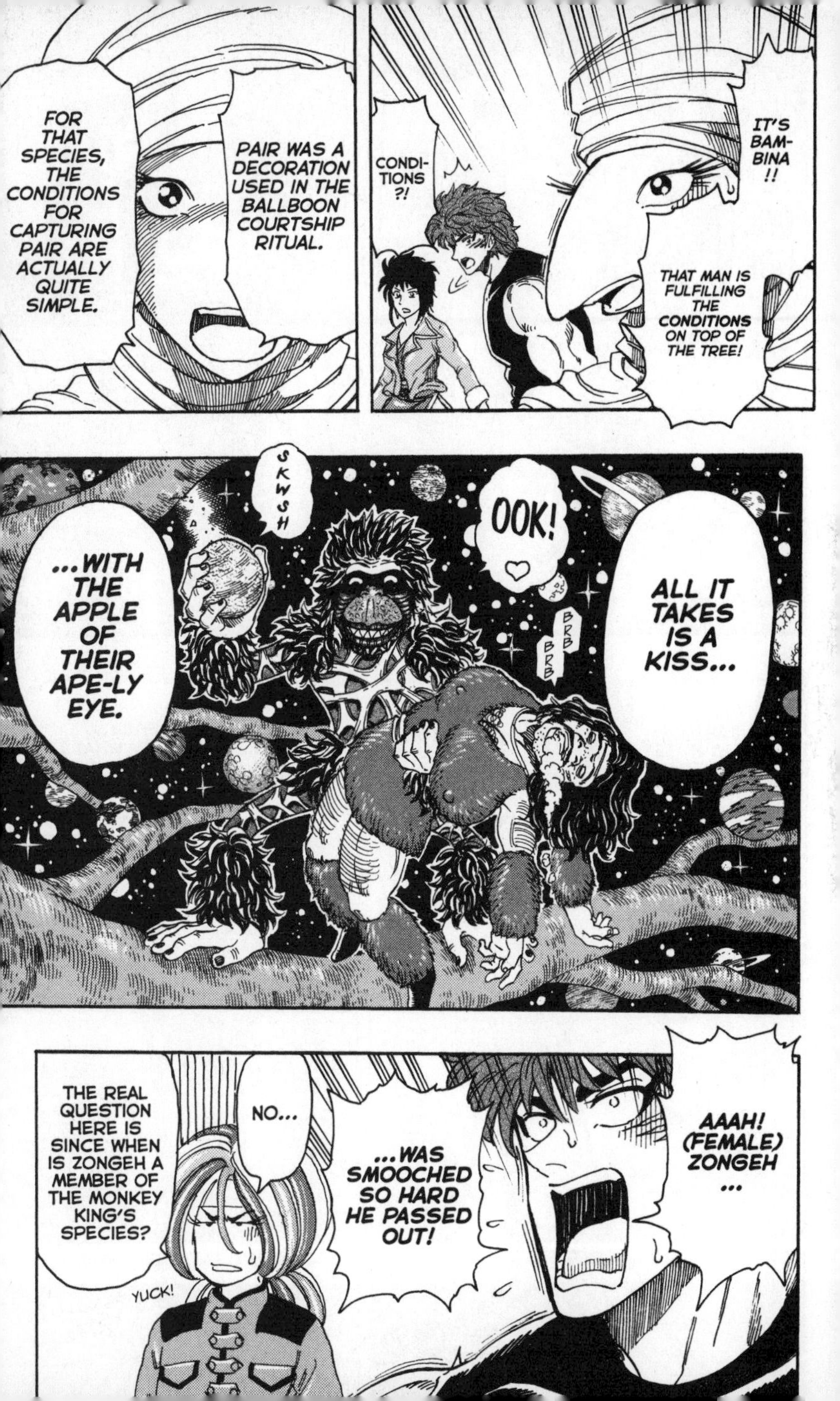
IT'S BAMBINA!!
THAT MAN IS FULFILLING THE CONDITIONS ON TOP OF THE TREE!
CONDITIONS?!
PAIR WAS A DECORATION USED IN THE BALLBOON COURTSHIP RITUAL.
FOR THAT SPECIES, THE CONDITIONS FOR CAPTURING PAIR ARE ACTUALLY QUITE SIMPLE.
ALL IT TAKES IS A KISS...
OOK!
BRB BRB
SKWSH
...WITH THE APPLE OF THEIR APE-LY EYE.
AAAH! (FEMALE) ZONGEH ...
...WAS SMOOCHED SO HARD HE PASSED OUT!
NO...
THE REAL QUESTION HERE IS SINCE WHEN IS ZONGEH A MEMBER OF THE MONKEY KING'S SPECIES?
YUCK!

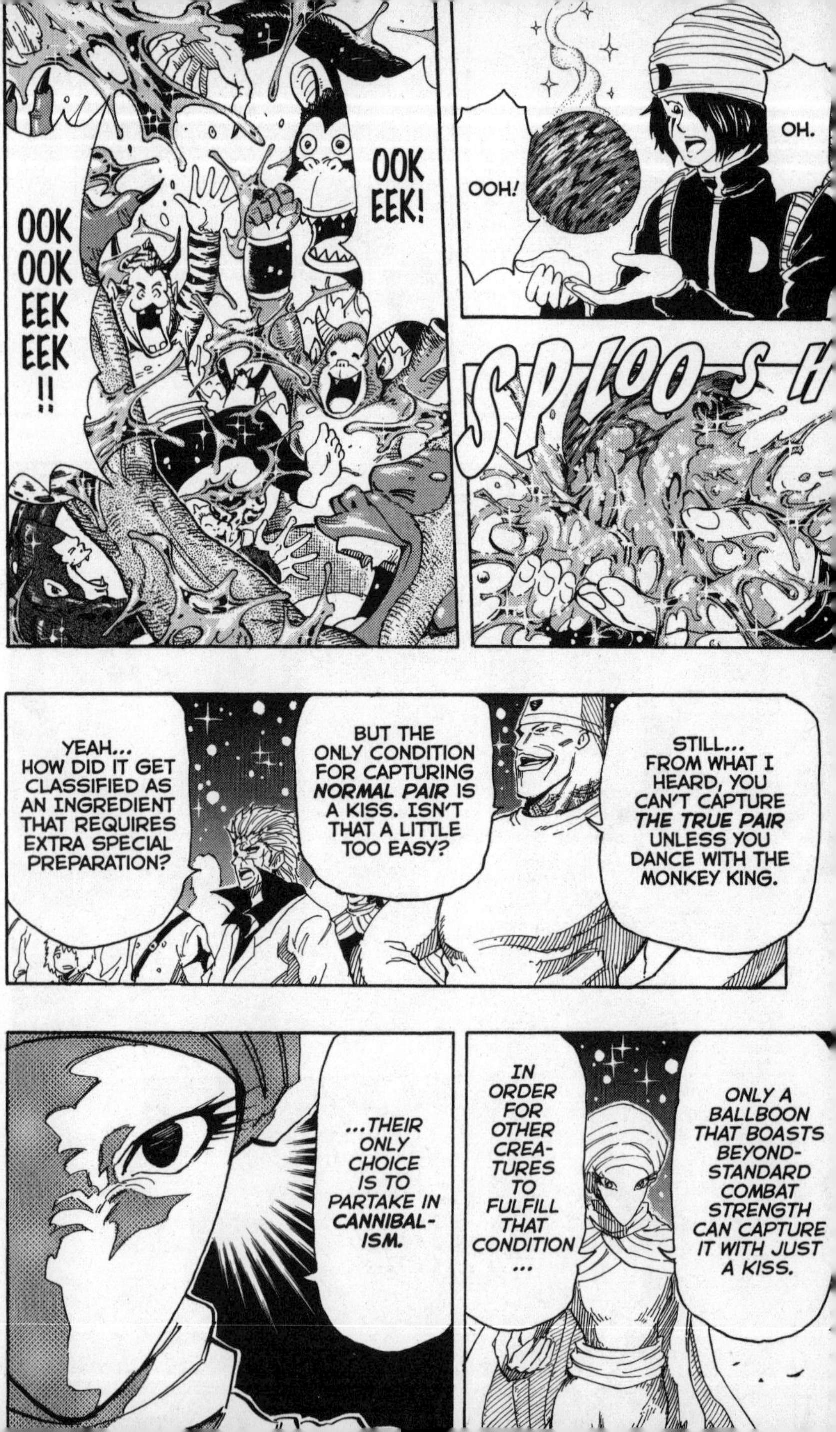
OH.
OOH!
SPLOOSH
OOK EEK!
OOK OOK EEK EEK !!
STILL... FROM WHAT I HEARD, YOU CAN'T CAPTURE *THE TRUE PAIR* UNLESS YOU DANCE WITH THE MONKEY KING.
BUT THE ONLY CONDITION FOR CAPTURING *NORMAL PAIR* IS A KISS. ISN'T THAT A LITTLE TOO EASY?
YEAH... HOW DID IT GET CLASSIFIED AS AN INGREDIENT THAT REQUIRES EXTRA SPECIAL PREPARATION?
ONLY A BALLBOON THAT BOASTS BEYOND-STANDARD COMBAT STRENGTH CAN CAPTURE IT WITH JUST A KISS.
IN ORDER FOR OTHER CREA-TURES TO FULFILL THAT CONDITION...
...THEIR ONLY CHOICE IS TO PARTAKE IN CANNIBAL-ISM.

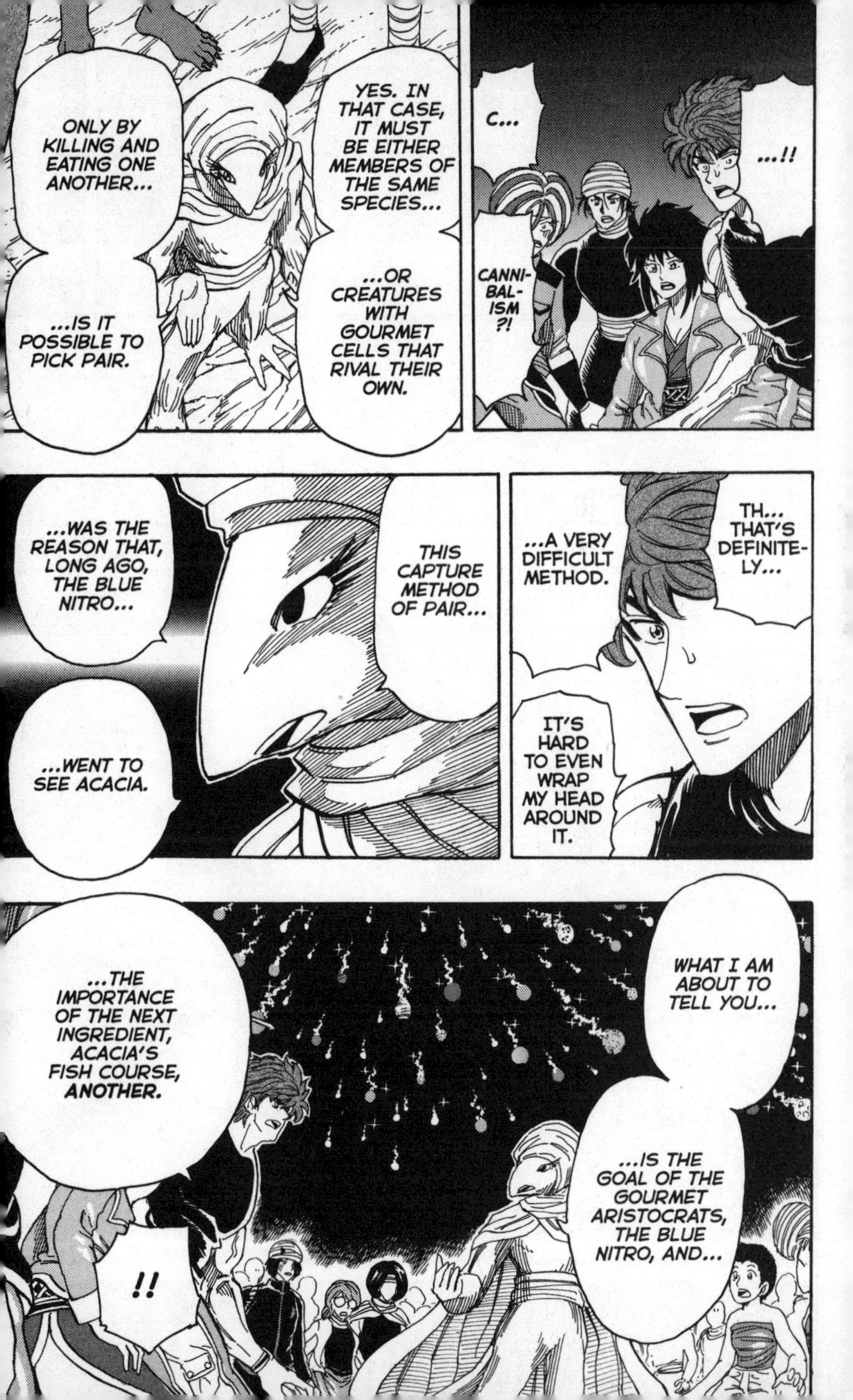
C...
...!!
CANNI-BAL-ISM?!
YES. IN THAT CASE, IT MUST BE EITHER MEMBERS OF THE SAME SPECIES...
...OR CREATURES WITH GOURMET CELLS THAT RIVAL THEIR OWN.
ONLY BY KILLING AND EATING ONE ANOTHER...
...IS IT POSSIBLE TO PICK PAIR.
TH... THAT'S DEFINITE-LY...
...A VERY DIFFICULT METHOD.
IT'S HARD TO EVEN WRAP MY HEAD AROUND IT.
THIS CAPTURE METHOD OF PAIR...
...WAS THE REASON THAT, LONG AGO, THE BLUE NITRO...
...WENT TO SEE ACACIA.
WHAT I AM ABOUT TO TELL YOU...
...IS THE GOAL OF THE GOURMET ARISTOCRATS, THE BLUE NITRO, AND...
...THE IMPORTANCE OF THE NEXT INGREDIENT, ACACIA'S FISH COURSE, **ANOTHER.**
!!

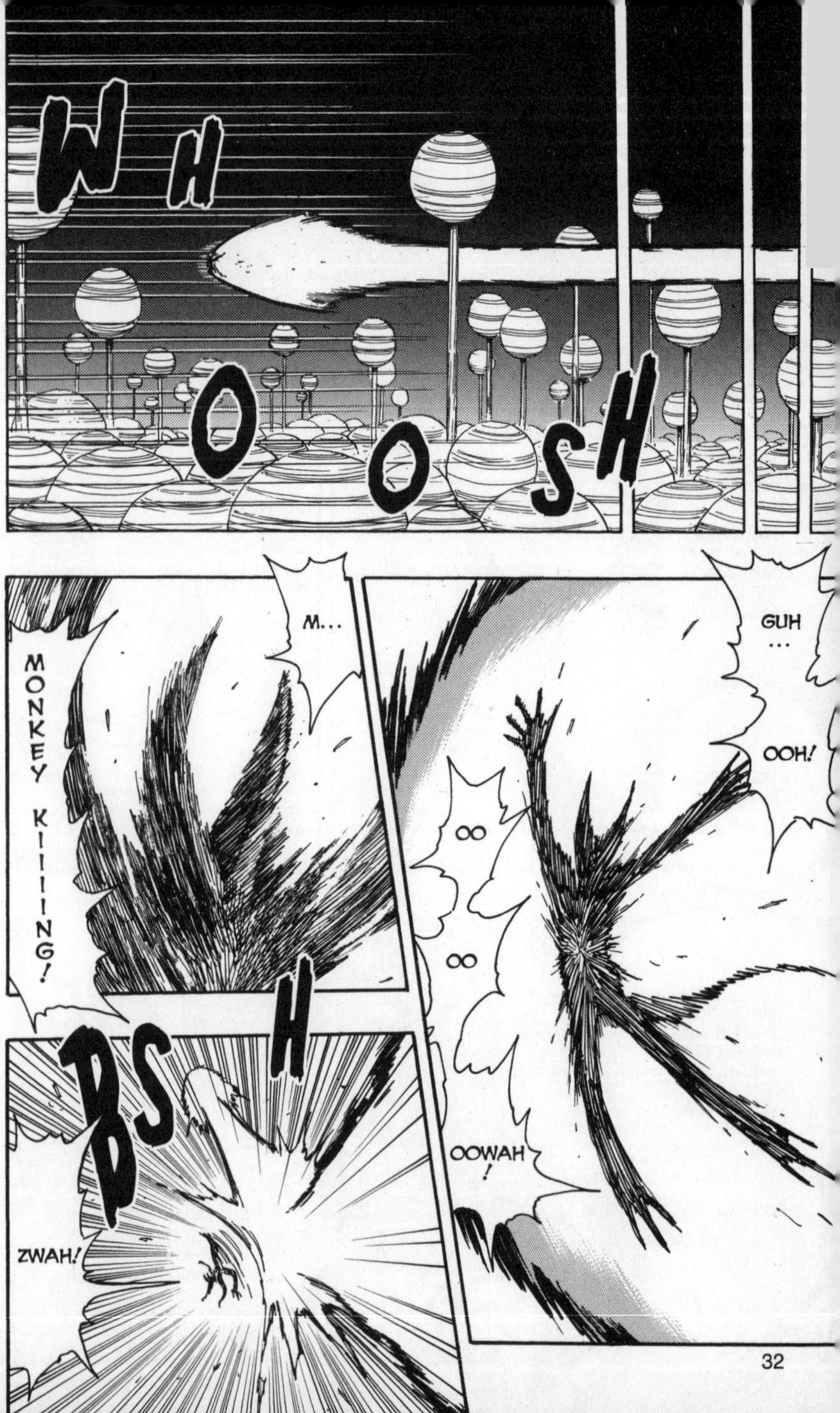
WHOOSH
GUH... OOH!
∞ ∞
OOWAH!
M...
MONKEY KIIIING!
BSH
ZWAH!

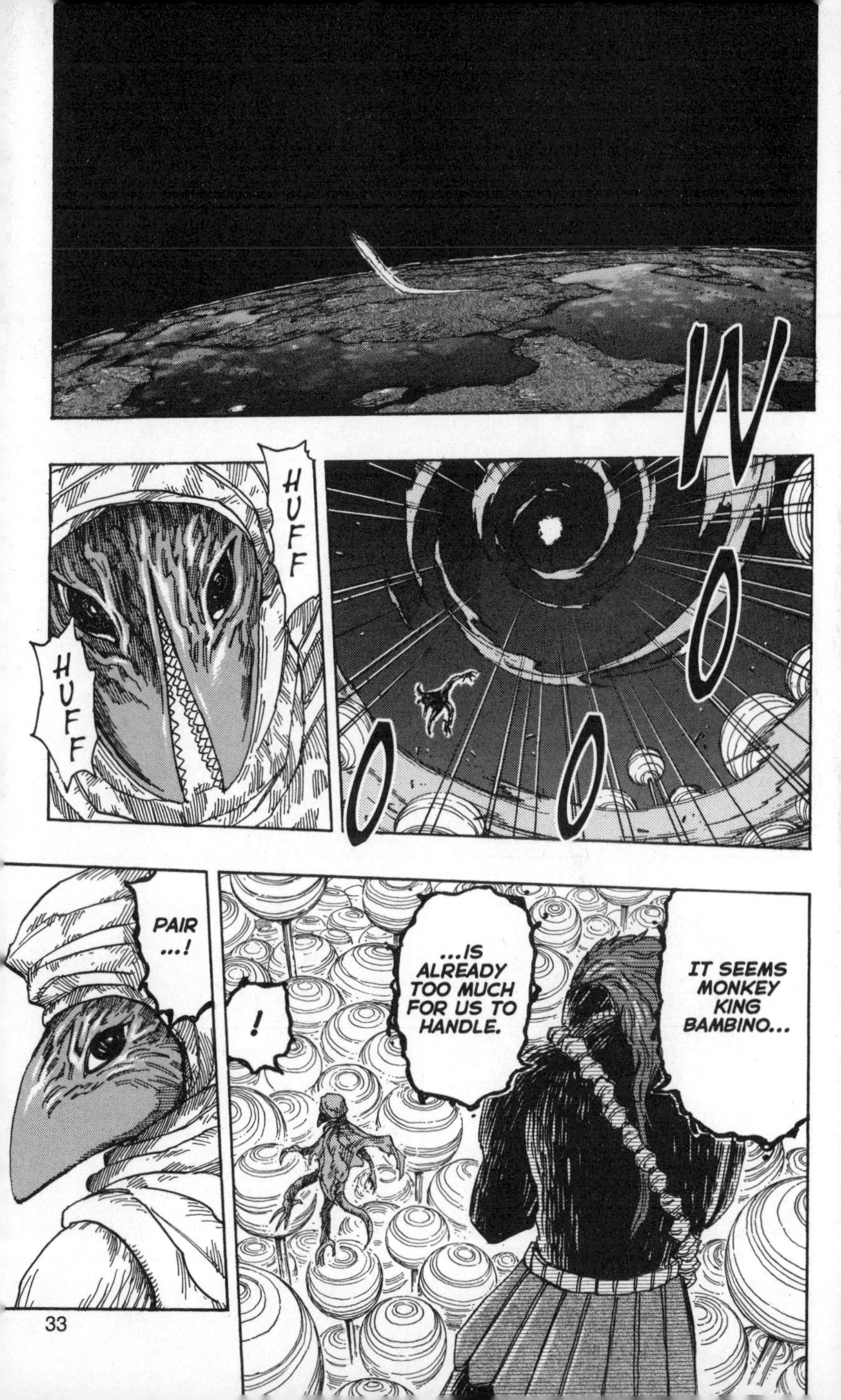
WOOO
HUFF
HUFF
IT SEEMS MONKEY KING BAMBINO...
...IS ALREADY TOO MUCH FOR US TO HANDLE.
!
PAIR ...!

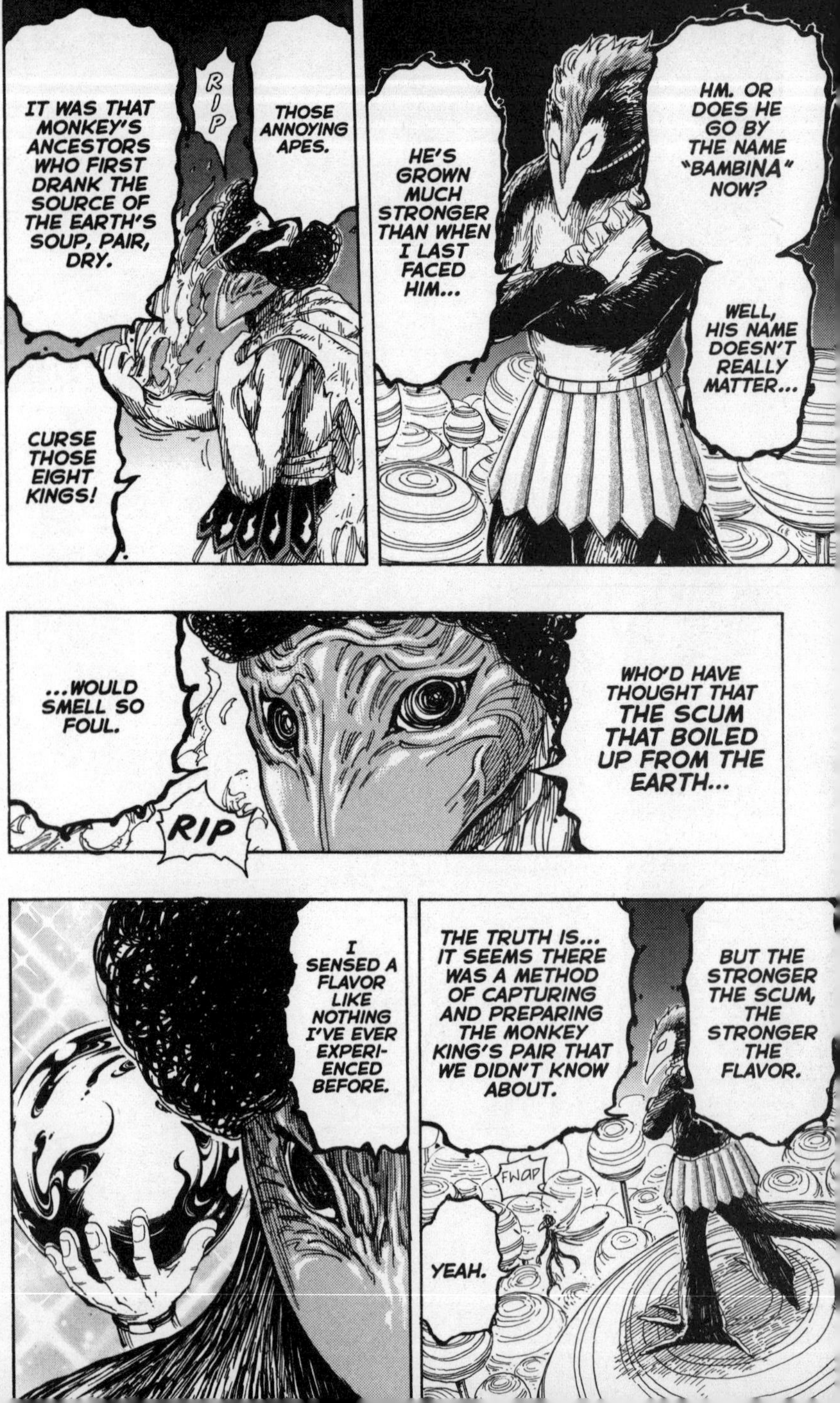
HM. OR DOES HE GO BY THE NAME "BAMBINA" NOW?
HE'S GROWN MUCH STRONGER THAN WHEN I LAST FACED HIM...
WELL, HIS NAME DOESN'T REALLY MATTER...
THOSE ANNOYING APES.
RIP
IT WAS THAT MONKEY'S ANCESTORS WHO FIRST DRANK THE SOURCE OF THE EARTH'S SOUP, PAIR, DRY.
CURSE THOSE EIGHT KINGS!
WHO'D HAVE THOUGHT THAT THE SCUM THAT BOILED UP FROM THE EARTH...
...WOULD SMELL SO FOUL.
RIP
BUT THE STRONGER THE SCUM, THE STRONGER THE FLAVOR.
THE TRUTH IS... IT SEEMS THERE WAS A METHOD OF CAPTURING AND PREPARING THE MONKEY KING'S PAIR THAT WE DIDN'T KNOW ABOUT.
FWAP
YEAH.
I SENSED A FLAVOR LIKE NOTHING I'VE EVER EXPERI-ENCED BEFORE.

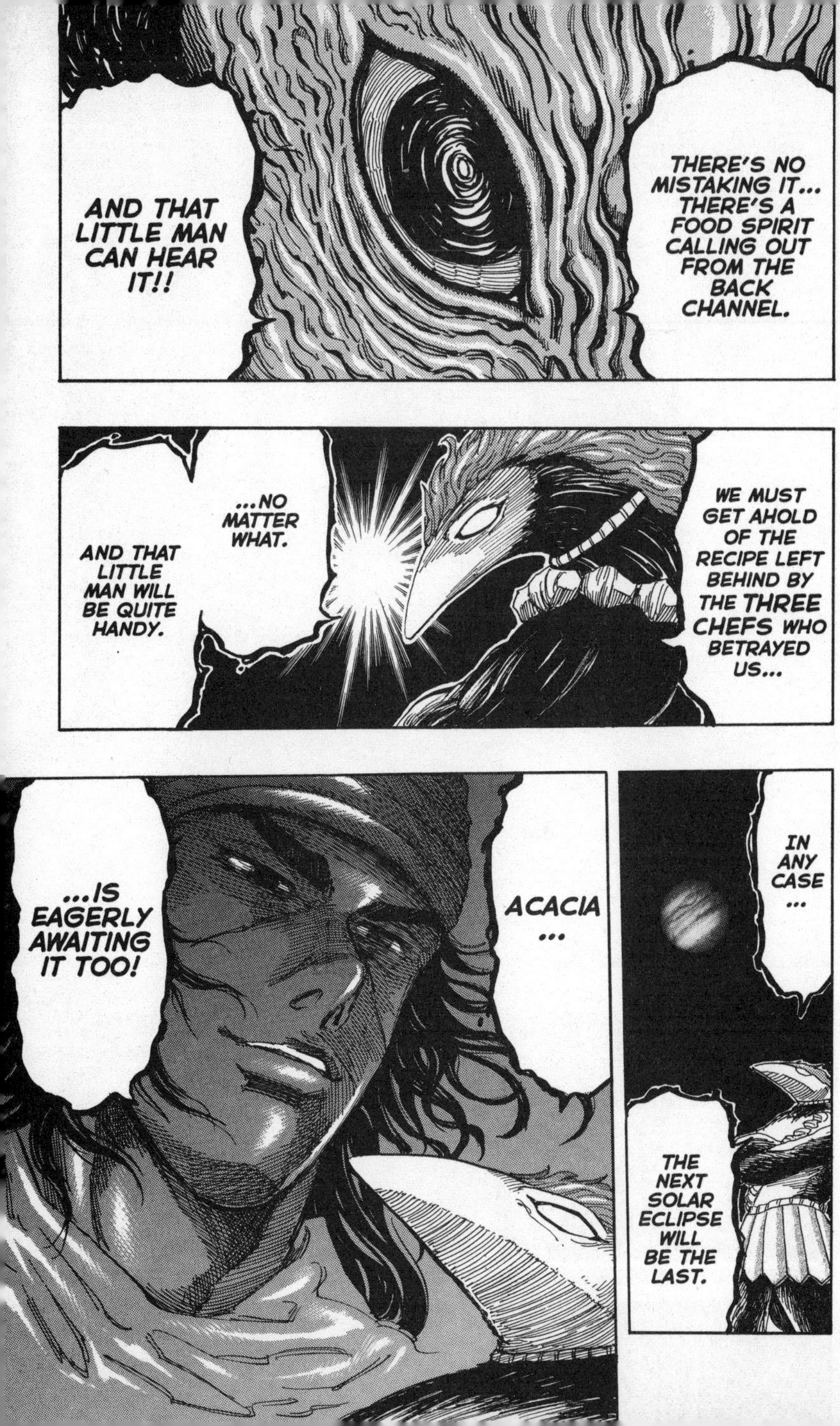
THERE'S NO MISTAKING IT... THERE'S A FOOD SPIRIT CALLING OUT FROM THE BACK CHANNEL.
AND THAT LITTLE MAN CAN HEAR IT!!
WE MUST GET AHOLD OF THE RECIPE LEFT BEHIND BY THE THREE CHEFS WHO BETRAYED US...
...NO MATTER WHAT.
AND THAT LITTLE MAN WILL BE QUITE HANDY.
IN ANY CASE...
THE NEXT SOLAR ECLIPSE WILL BE THE LAST.
ACACIA...
...IS EAGERLY AWAITING IT TOO!

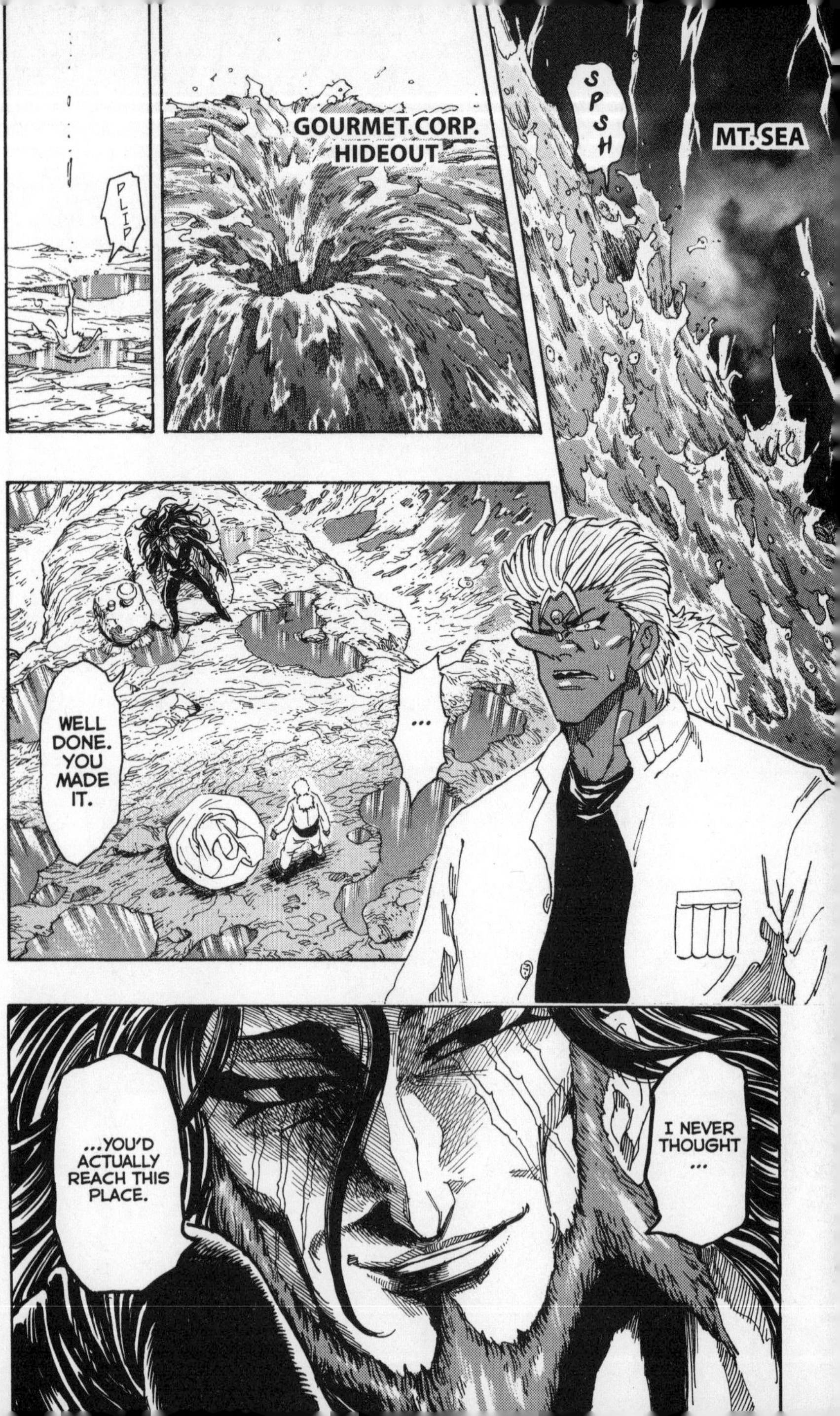
MT. SEA
SPSH
GOURMET CORP. HIDEOUT
PLIP
...
WELL DONE. YOU MADE IT.
I NEVER THOUGHT ...
...YOU'D ACTUALLY REACH THIS PLACE.

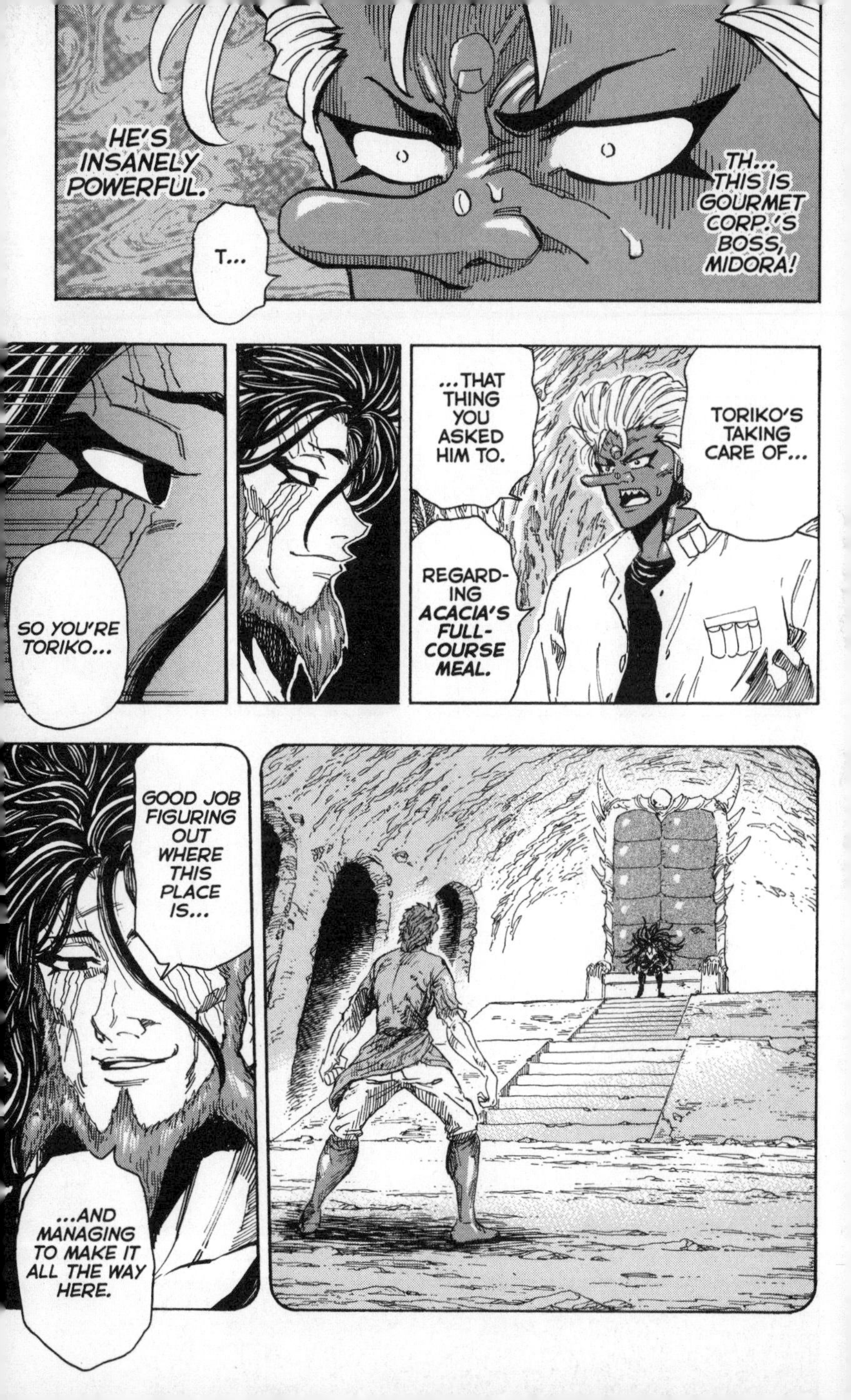
TH... THIS IS GOURMET CORP.'S BOSS, MIDORA!
HE'S INSANELY POWERFUL.
T...
TORIKO'S TAKING CARE OF...
...THAT THING YOU ASKED HIM TO.
REGARDING ACACIA'S FULL-COURSE MEAL.
SO YOU'RE TORIKO...
GOOD JOB FIGURING OUT WHERE THIS PLACE IS...
...AND MANAGING TO MAKE IT ALL THE WAY HERE.

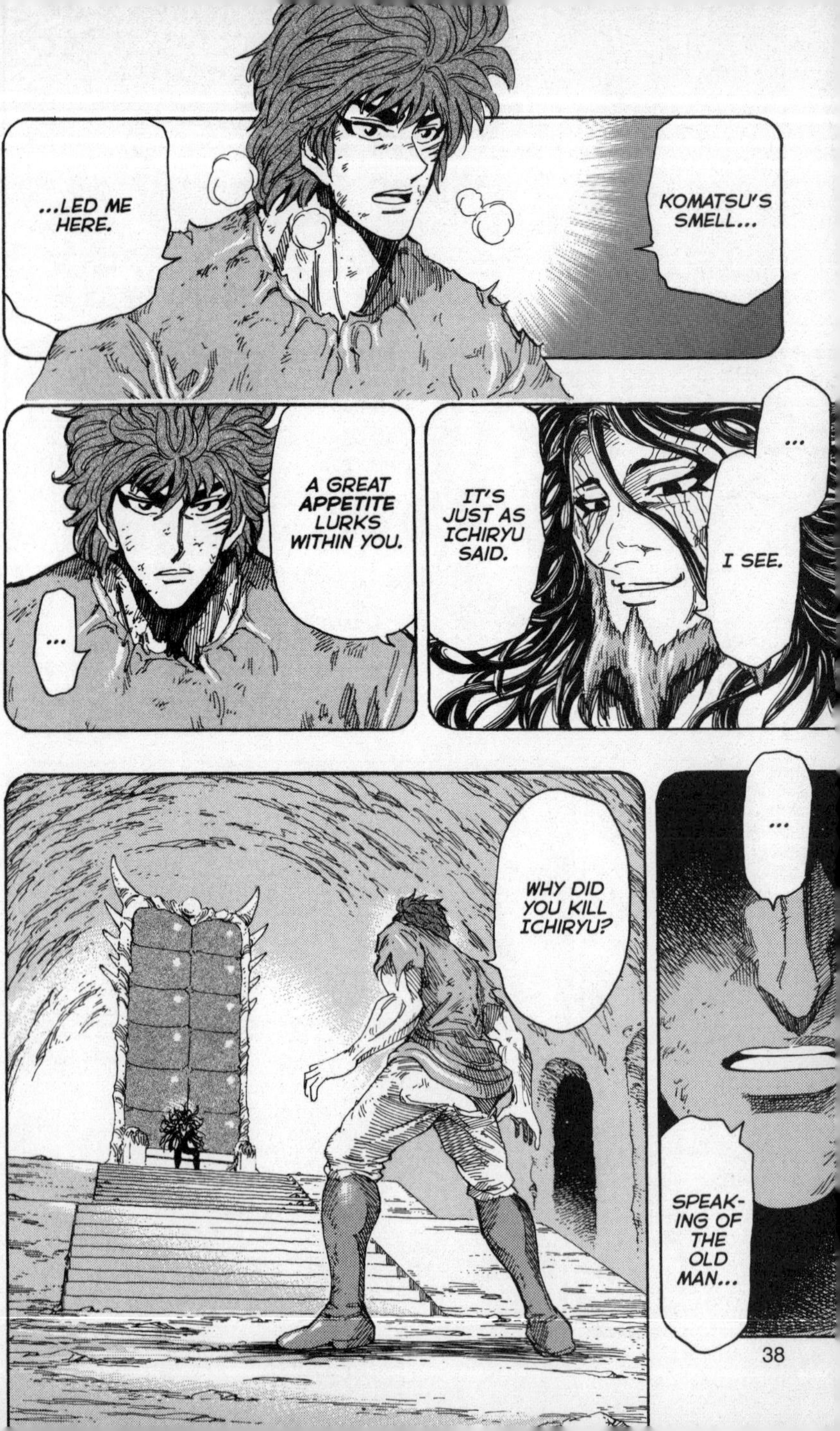
KOMATSU'S SMELL...
...LED ME HERE.
...
I SEE.
IT'S JUST AS ICHIRYU SAID.
A GREAT APPETITE LURKS WITHIN YOU.
...
...
SPEAK-ING OF THE OLD MAN...
WHY DID YOU KILL ICHIRYU?

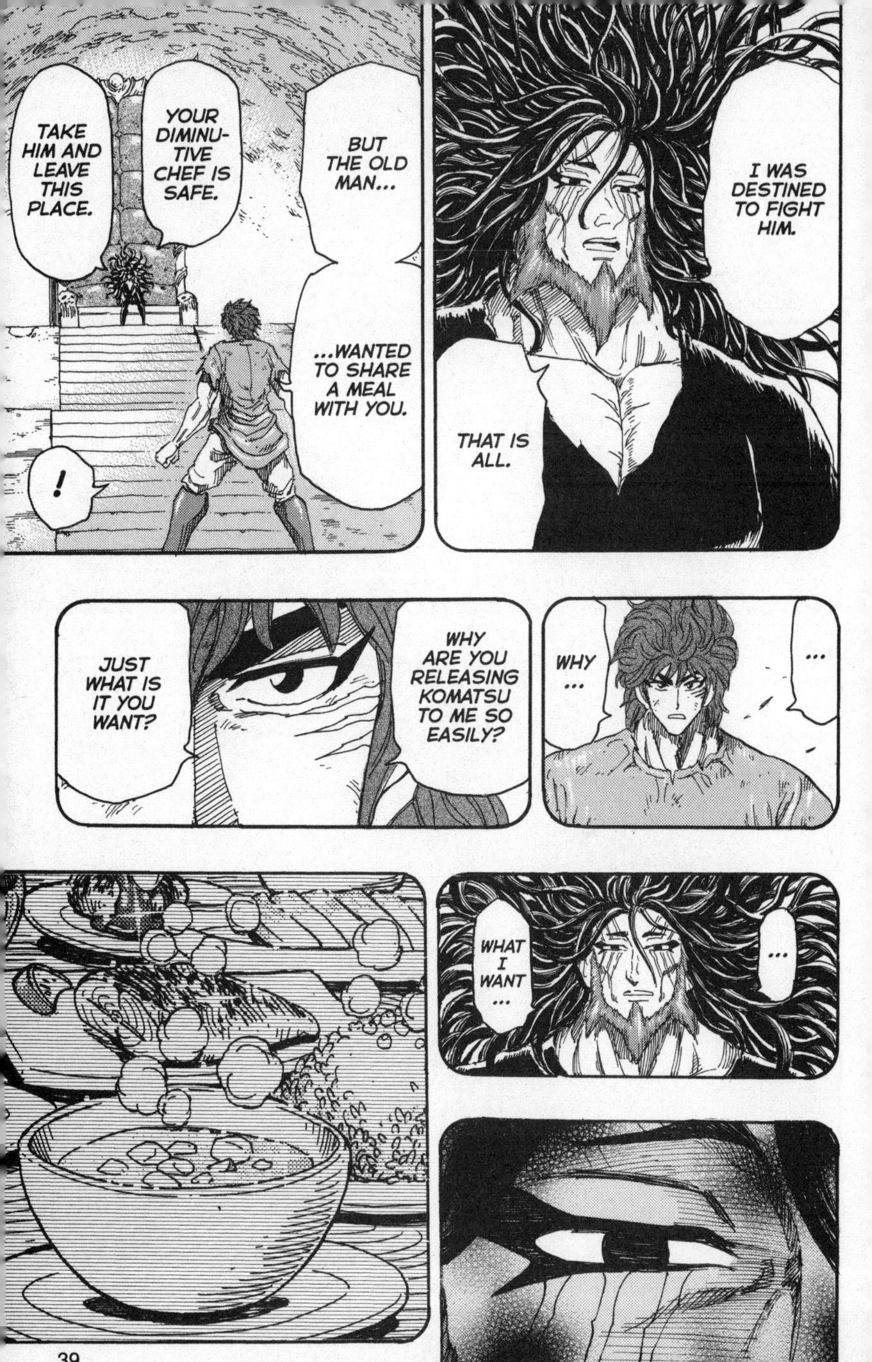
I WAS DESTINED TO FIGHT HIM.
THAT IS ALL.
BUT THE OLD MAN...
...WANTED TO SHARE A MEAL WITH YOU.
YOUR DIMINU-TIVE CHEF IS SAFE.
TAKE HIM AND LEAVE THIS PLACE.
!
...
WHY...
WHY ARE YOU RELEASING KOMATSU TO ME SO EASILY?
JUST WHAT IS IT YOU WANT?
...
WHAT I WANT...

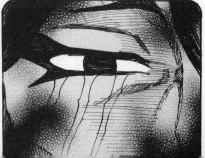

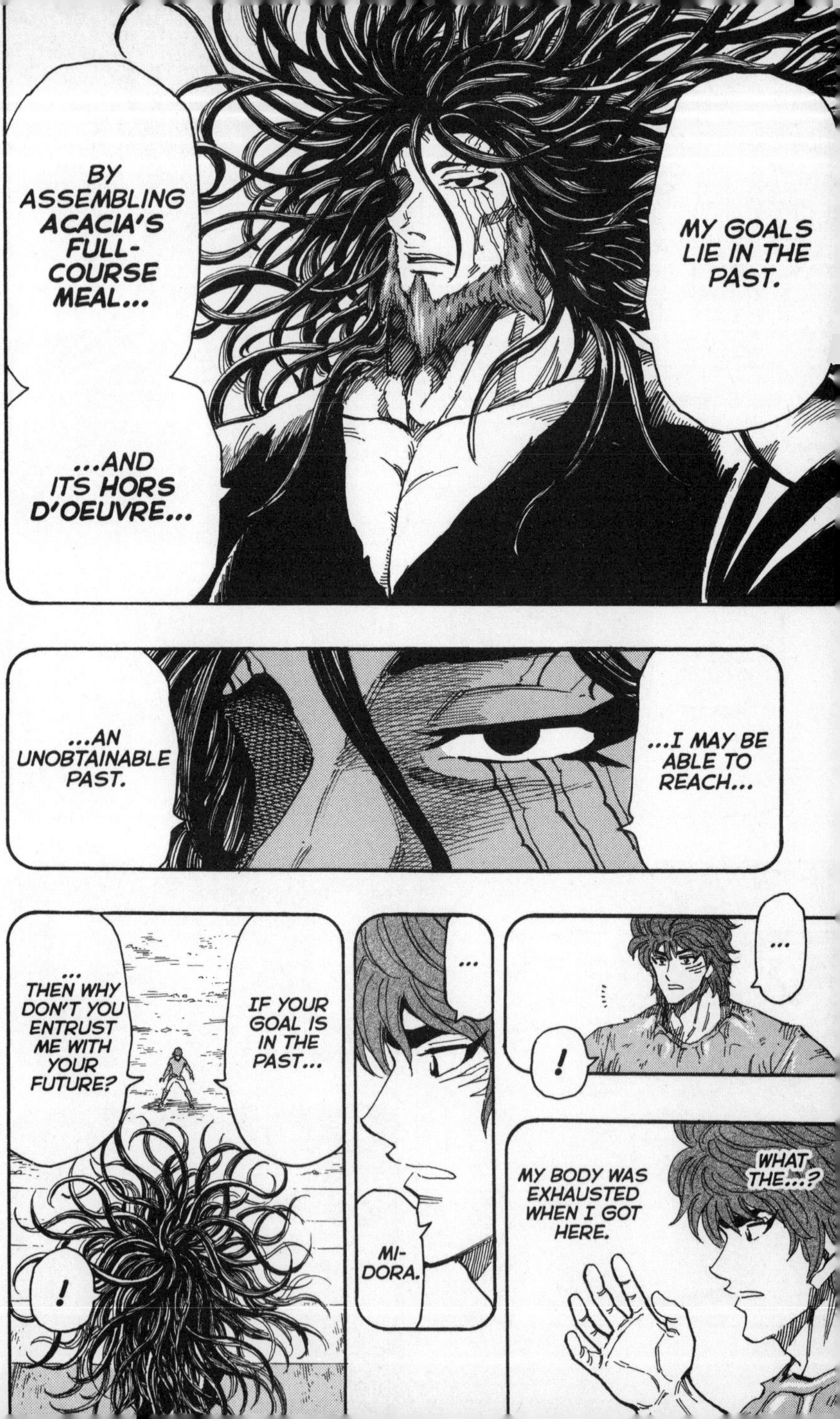
MY GOALS LIE IN THE PAST.
BY ASSEMBLING ACACIA'S FULL-COURSE MEAL...
...AND ITS HORS D'OEUVRE...
...I MAY BE ABLE TO REACH...
...AN UNOBTAINABLE PAST.
...
!
WHAT THE...?
MY BODY WAS EXHAUSTED WHEN I GOT HERE.
...
MI-DORA.
IF YOUR GOAL IS IN THE PAST...
... THEN WHY DON'T YOU ENTRUST ME WITH YOUR FUTURE?
!

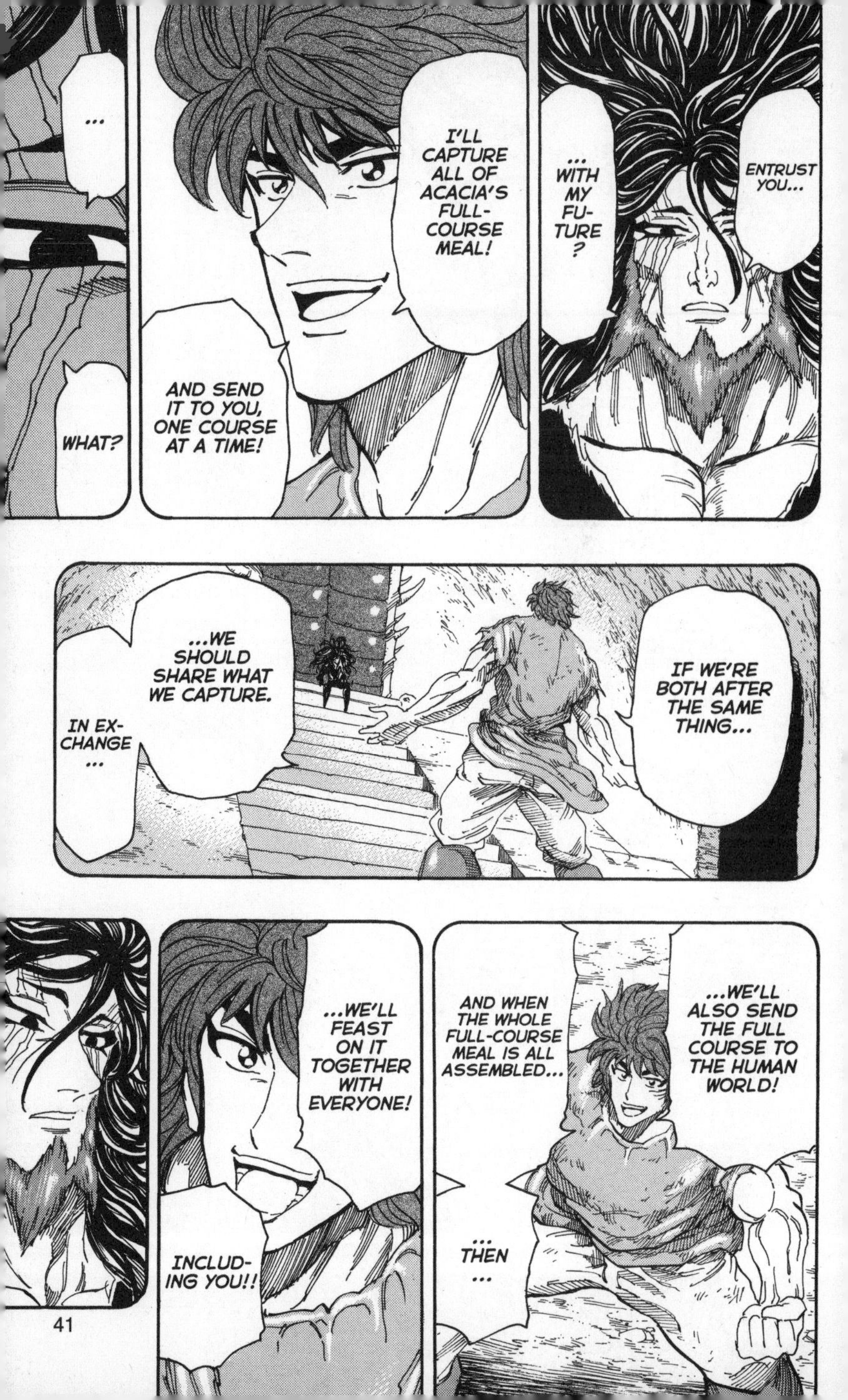
ENTRUST YOU...
...WITH MY FU-TURE?
I'LL CAPTURE ALL OF ACACIA'S FULL-COURSE MEAL!
AND SEND IT TO YOU, ONE COURSE AT A TIME!
...
WHAT?
IF WE'RE BOTH AFTER THE SAME THING...
...WE SHOULD SHARE WHAT WE CAPTURE.
IN EX-CHANGE...
...WE'LL ALSO SEND THE FULL COURSE TO THE HUMAN WORLD!
AND WHEN THE WHOLE FULL-COURSE MEAL IS ALL ASSEMBLED...
...THEN...
...WE'LL FEAST ON IT TOGETHER WITH EVERYONE!
INCLUD-ING YOU!!

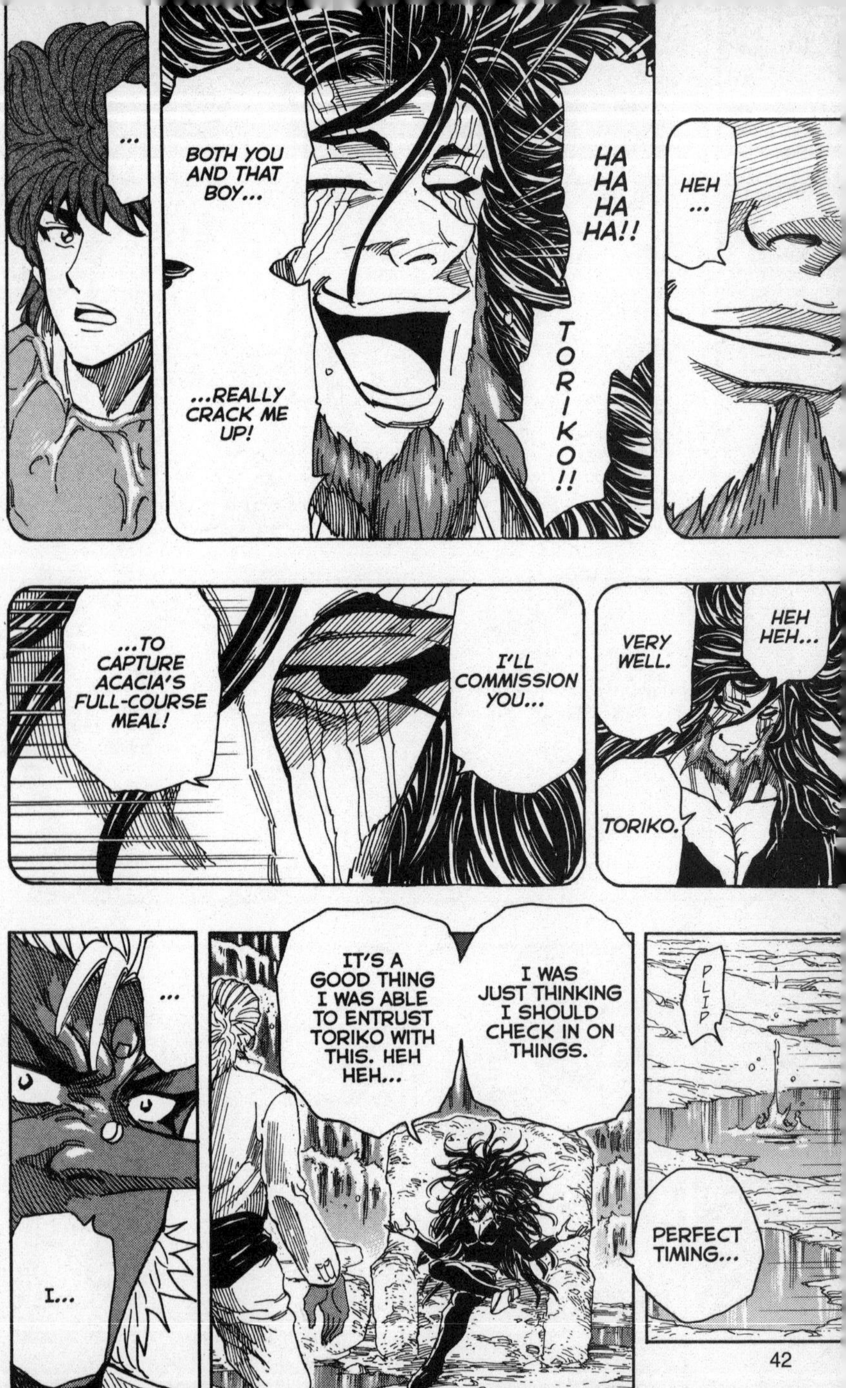
HEH ...
HA HA HA HA!!
TORIKO!!
BOTH YOU AND THAT BOY...
...REALLY CRACK ME UP!
...
HEH HEH...
VERY WELL.
TORIKO.
I'LL COMMISSION YOU...
...TO CAPTURE ACACIA'S FULL-COURSE MEAL!
PLIP
PERFECT TIMING...
I WAS JUST THINKING I SHOULD CHECK IN ON THINGS.
IT'S A GOOD THING I WAS ABLE TO ENTRUST TORIKO WITH THIS. HEH HEH...
...
I...

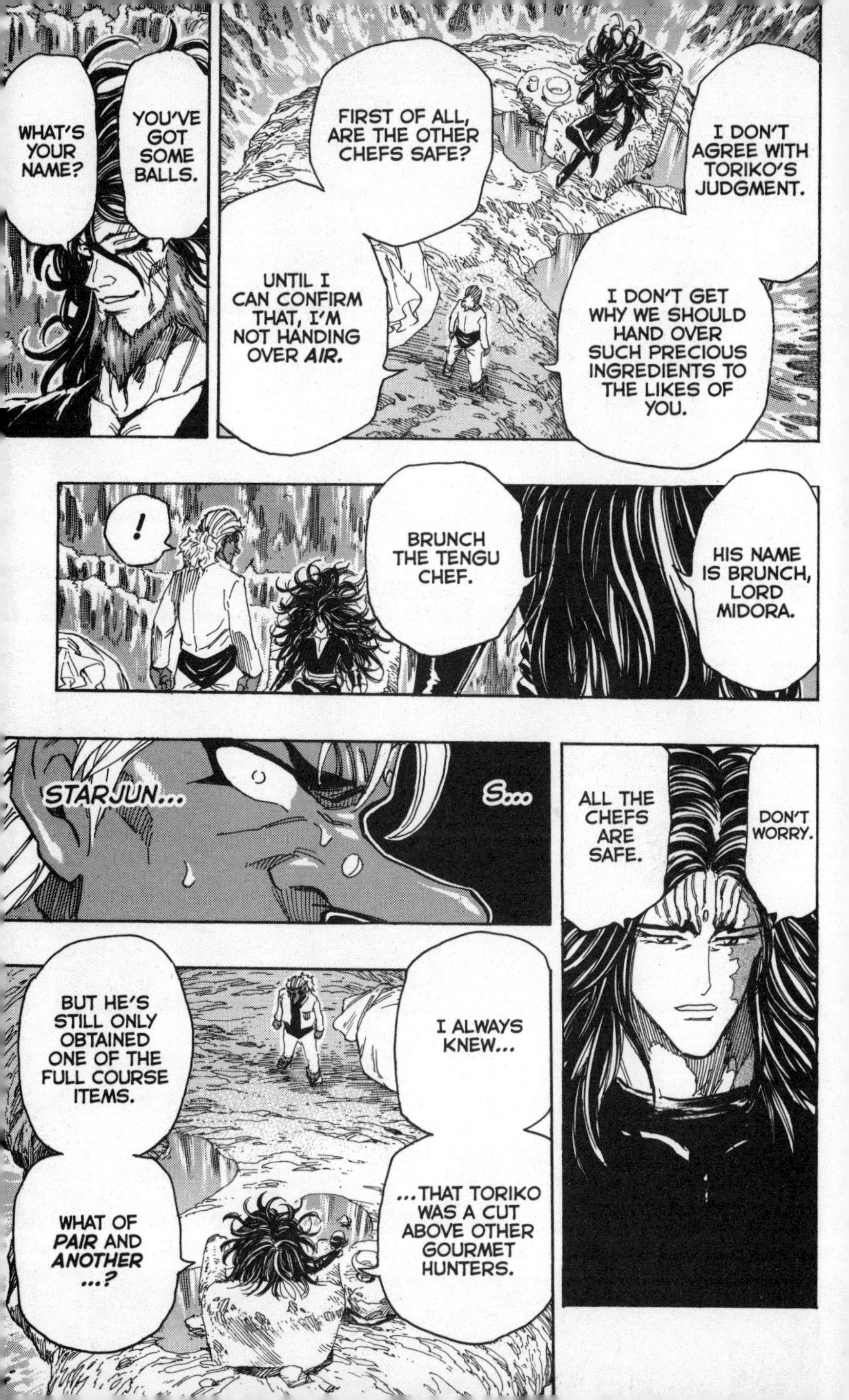
I DON'T AGREE WITH TORIKO'S JUDGMENT.
I DON'T GET WHY WE SHOULD HAND OVER SUCH PRECIOUS INGREDIENTS TO THE LIKES OF YOU.
FIRST OF ALL, ARE THE OTHER CHEFS SAFE?
UNTIL I CAN CONFIRM THAT, I'M NOT HANDING OVER *AIR.*
YOU'VE GOT SOME BALLS.
WHAT'S YOUR NAME?
HIS NAME IS BRUNCH, LORD MIDORA.
BRUNCH THE TENGU CHEF.
!
DON'T WORRY.
ALL THE CHEFS ARE SAFE.
S...
STARJUN...
I ALWAYS KNEW...
...THAT TORIKO WAS A CUT ABOVE OTHER GOURMET HUNTERS.
BUT HE'S STILL ONLY OBTAINED ONE OF THE FULL COURSE ITEMS.
WHAT OF *PAIR* AND *ANOTHER* ...?

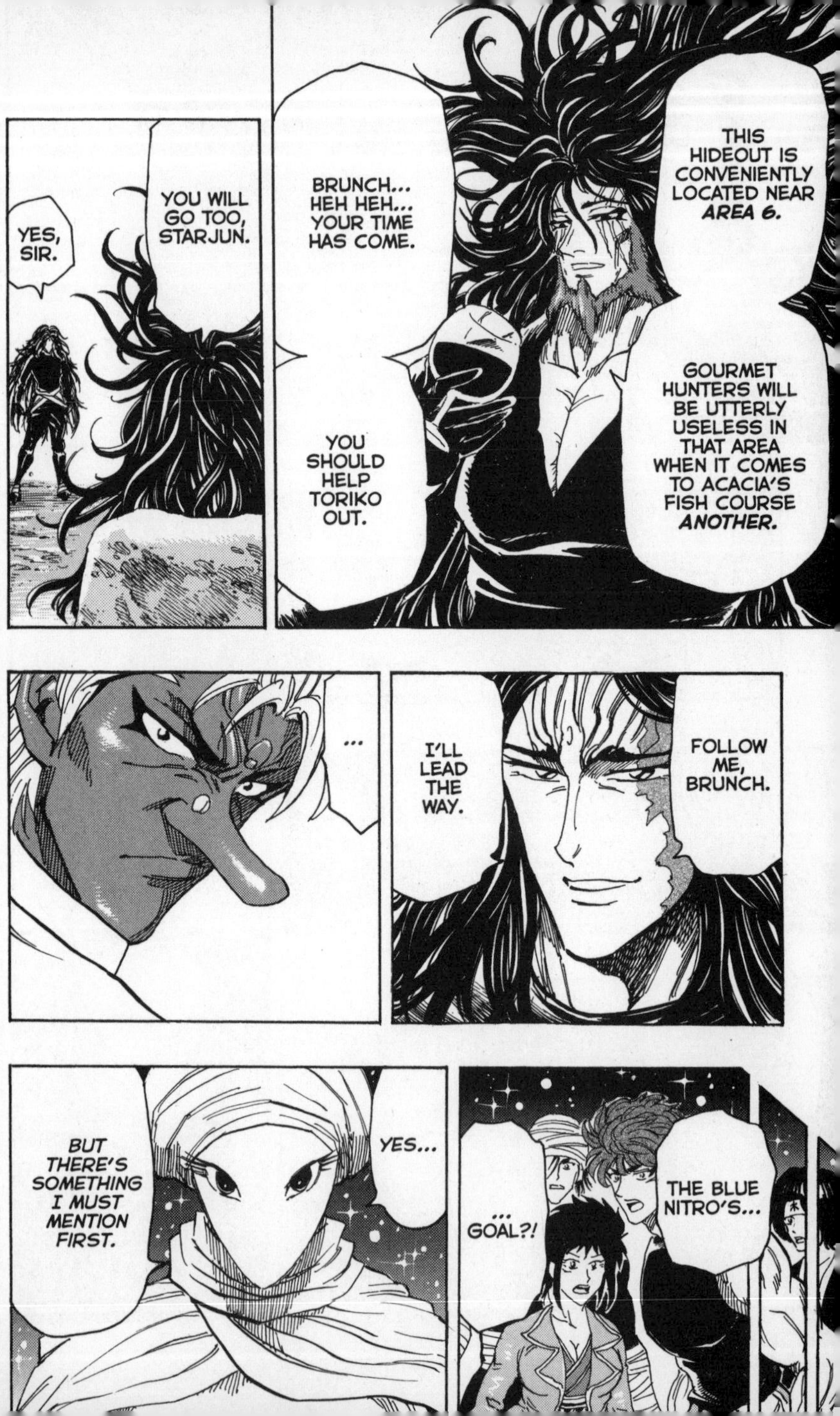
THIS HIDEOUT IS CONVENIENTLY LOCATED NEAR *AREA 6.*
GOURMET HUNTERS WILL BE UTTERLY USELESS IN THAT AREA WHEN IT COMES TO ACACIA'S FISH COURSE *ANOTHER.*
BRUNCH... HEH HEH... YOUR TIME HAS COME.
YOU SHOULD HELP TORIKO OUT.
YOU WILL GO TOO, STARJUN.
YES, SIR.
FOLLOW ME, BRUNCH.
I'LL LEAD THE WAY.
...
THE BLUE NITRO'S...
...GOAL?!
YES...
BUT THERE'S SOMETHING I MUST MENTION FIRST.

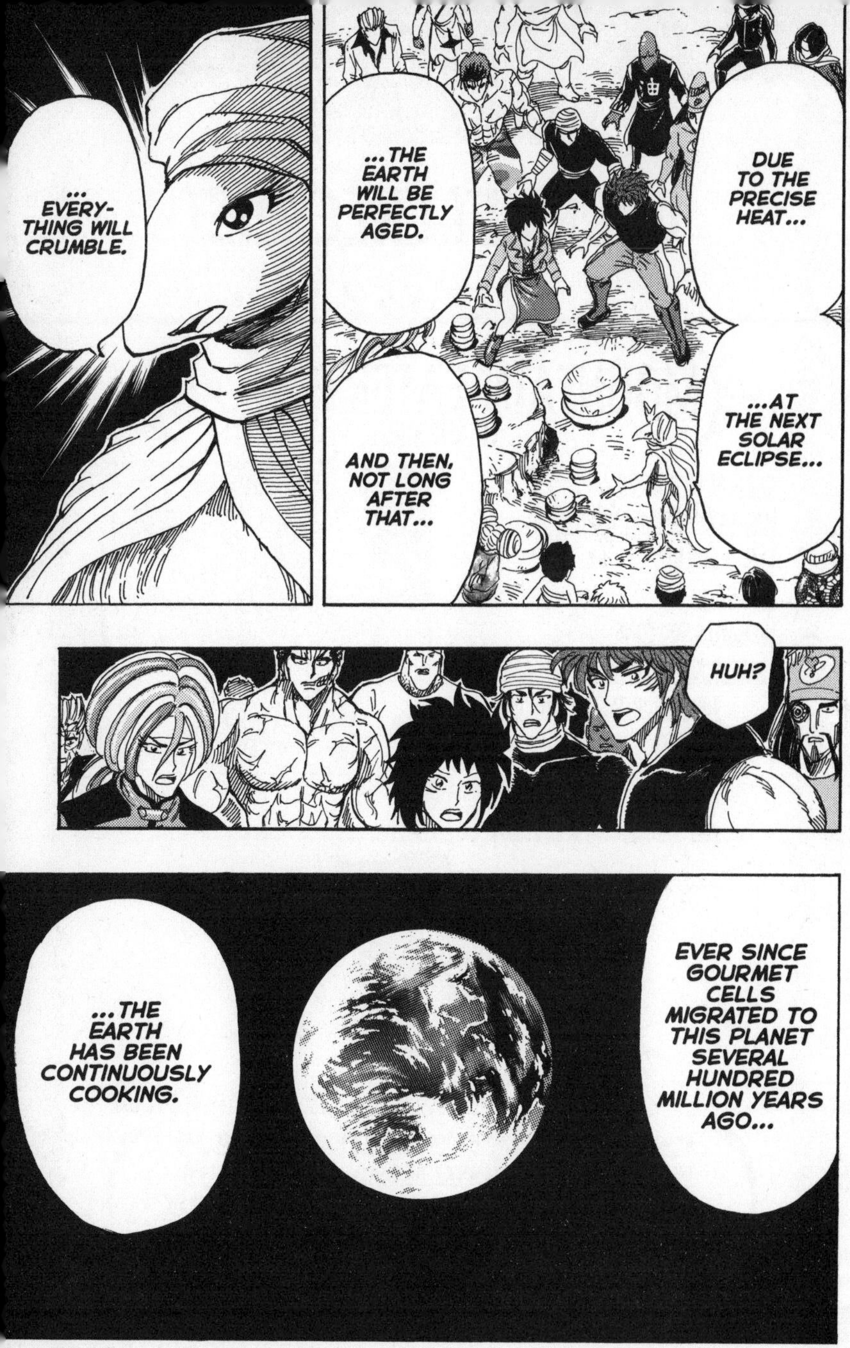
DUE TO THE PRECISE HEAT...
...AT THE NEXT SOLAR ECLIPSE...
...THE EARTH WILL BE PERFECTLY AGED.
AND THEN, NOT LONG AFTER THAT...
... EVERY-THING WILL CRUMBLE.
HUH?
EVER SINCE GOURMET CELLS MIGRATED TO THIS PLANET SEVERAL HUNDRED MILLION YEARS AGO...
...THE EARTH HAS BEEN CONTINUOUSLY COOKING.

TORIKO

GOURMET CHECKLIST

Vol. 352

❖ MOUNTAIN-EATER PELICAN ❖
(GIANT BIRD)

CAPTURE LEVEL: 770
HABITAT: GOURMET WORLD
SIZE: 1,500 M
HEIGHT: ---
WEIGHT: 9,500 TONS
PRICE: 700,000 YEN PER KILOGRAM
     100 HUNDRED MILLION YEN
     PER EGG

SCALE

A GIANT PELICAN THAT LIVES IN THE GOURMET WORLD. IT HAS A SUPER LARGE BILL THAT CAN SWALLOW MOUNTAINS WHOLE. THE BIRD IS EXTREMELY RARE AND ONLY LIVES IN CLIMATES WHERE IT RAINS MOUNTAINS. JUST TO GIVE AN IDEA OF HOW BIG THE ADULTS ARE, ONE OF ITS EGGS CAN MAKE 100,000 SERVINGS OF SCRAMBLED EGGS.

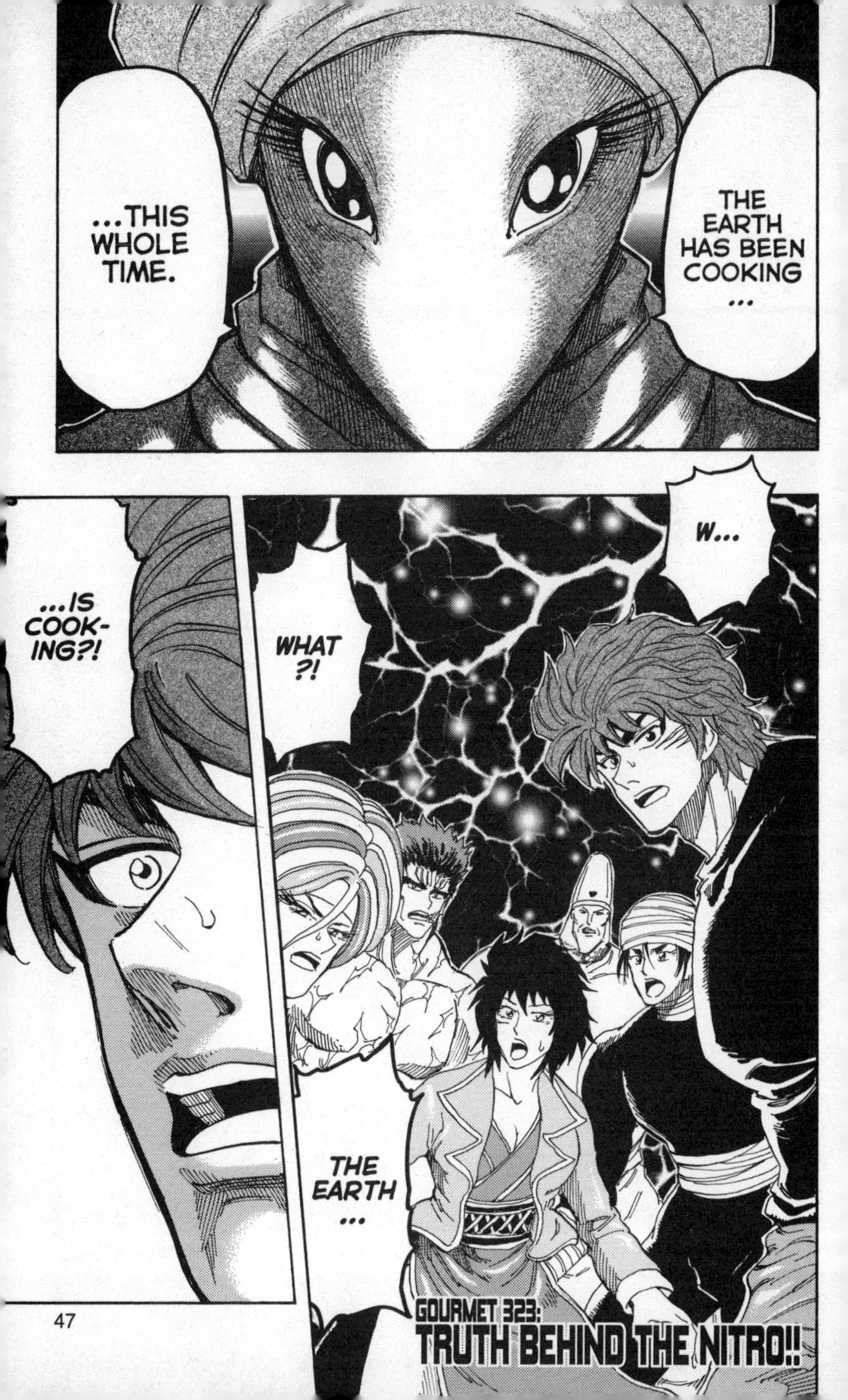
THE EARTH HAS BEEN COOKING ...
...THIS WHOLE TIME.
W...
WHAT ?!
THE EARTH ...
...IS COOKING?!
GOURMET 323:
TRUTH BEHIND THE NITRO!!

GOURMET 323: TRUTH BEHIND THE NITRO!!

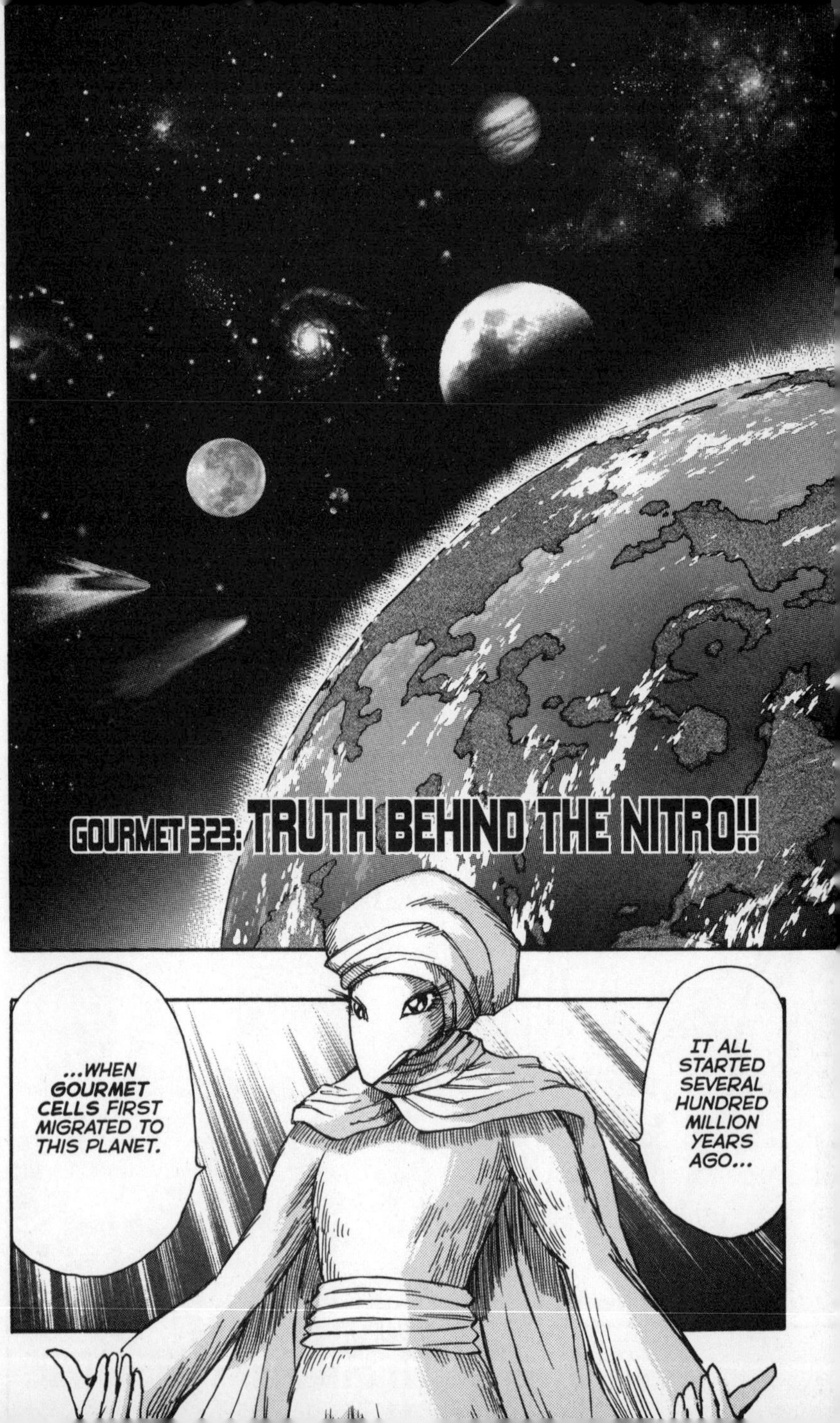
IT ALL STARTED SEVERAL HUNDRED MILLION YEARS AGO...
...WHEN GOURMET CELLS FIRST MIGRATED TO THIS PLANET.

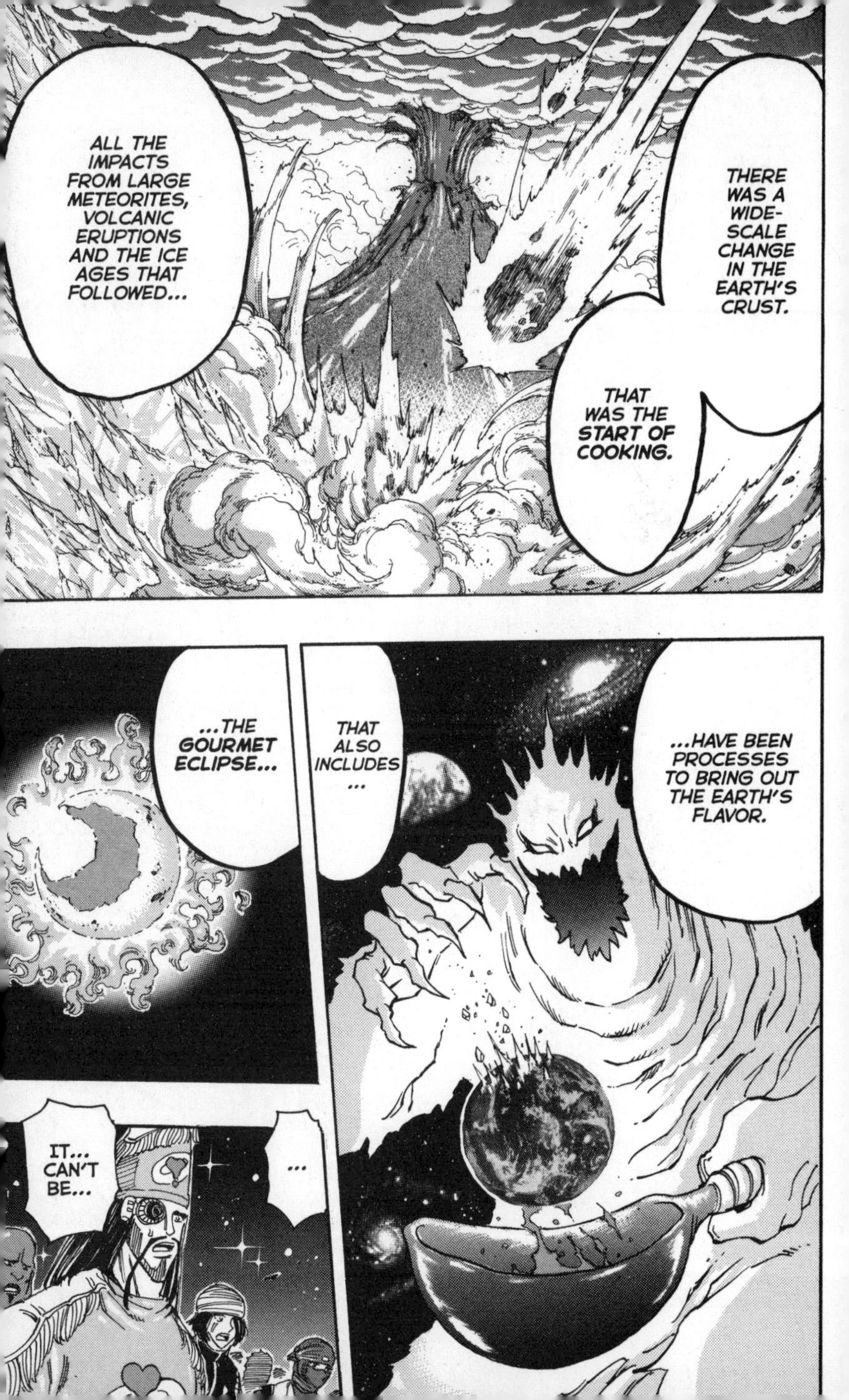

THERE WAS A WIDE-SCALE CHANGE IN THE EARTH'S CRUST.
THAT WAS THE START OF COOKING.
ALL THE IMPACTS FROM LARGE METEORITES, VOLCANIC ERUPTIONS AND THE ICE AGES THAT FOLLOWED...
...HAVE BEEN PROCESSES TO BRING OUT THE EARTH'S FLAVOR.
THAT ALSO INCLUDES...
...THE GOURMET ECLIPSE...
...
IT... CAN'T BE...

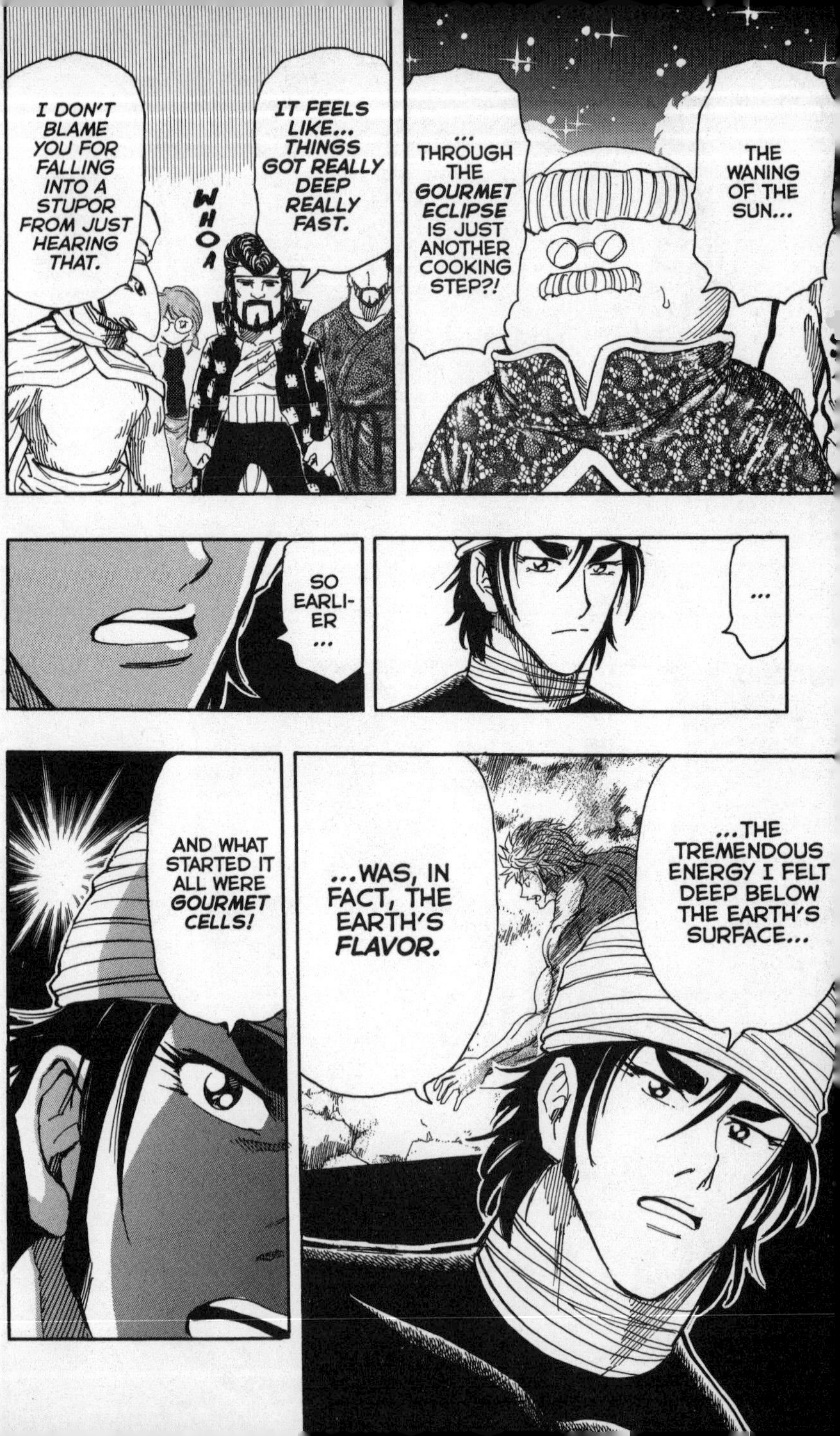
THE WANING OF THE SUN...
...THROUGH THE GOURMET ECLIPSE IS JUST ANOTHER COOKING STEP?!
IT FEELS LIKE... THINGS GOT REALLY DEEP REALLY FAST.
WHOA
I DON'T BLAME YOU FOR FALLING INTO A STUPOR FROM JUST HEARING THAT.
...
SO EARLIER...
...THE TREMENDOUS ENERGY I FELT DEEP BELOW THE EARTH'S SURFACE...
...WAS, IN FACT, THE EARTH'S FLAVOR.
AND WHAT STARTED IT ALL WERE GOURMET CELLS!

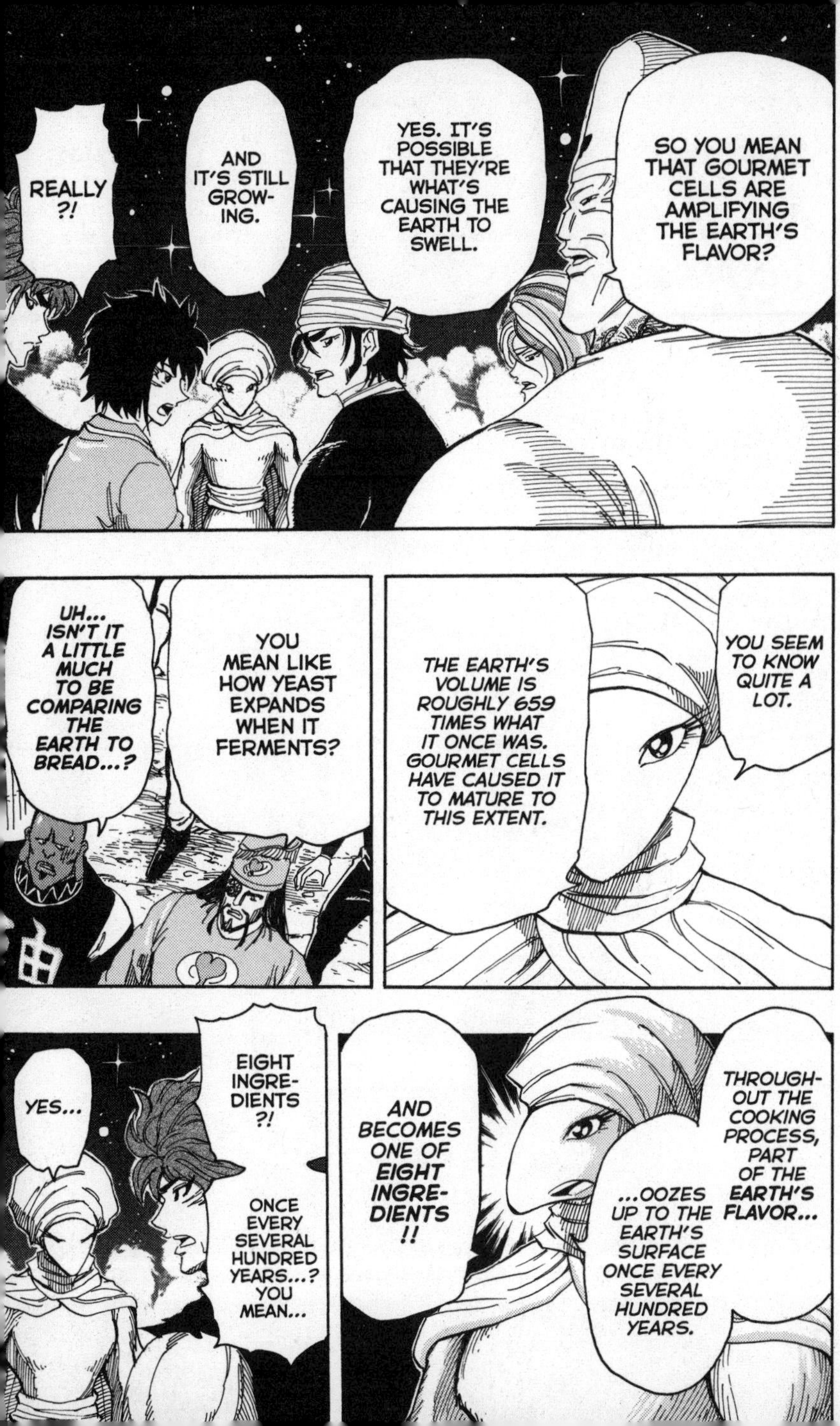
SO YOU MEAN THAT GOURMET CELLS ARE AMPLIFYING THE EARTH'S FLAVOR?
YES. IT'S POSSIBLE THAT THEY'RE WHAT'S CAUSING THE EARTH TO SWELL.
AND IT'S STILL GROW-ING.
REALLY?!
YOU SEEM TO KNOW QUITE A LOT.
THE EARTH'S VOLUME IS ROUGHLY 659 TIMES WHAT IT ONCE WAS. GOURMET CELLS HAVE CAUSED IT TO MATURE TO THIS EXTENT.
YOU MEAN LIKE HOW YEAST EXPANDS WHEN IT FERMENTS?
UH... ISN'T IT A LITTLE MUCH TO BE COMPARING THE EARTH TO BREAD...?
THROUGH-OUT THE COOKING PROCESS, PART OF THE EARTH'S FLAVOR...
...OOZES UP TO THE EARTH'S SURFACE ONCE EVERY SEVERAL HUNDRED YEARS.
AND BECOMES ONE OF EIGHT INGRE-DIENTS!!
EIGHT INGRE-DIENTS?!
ONCE EVERY SEVERAL HUNDRED YEARS...? YOU MEAN...
YES...

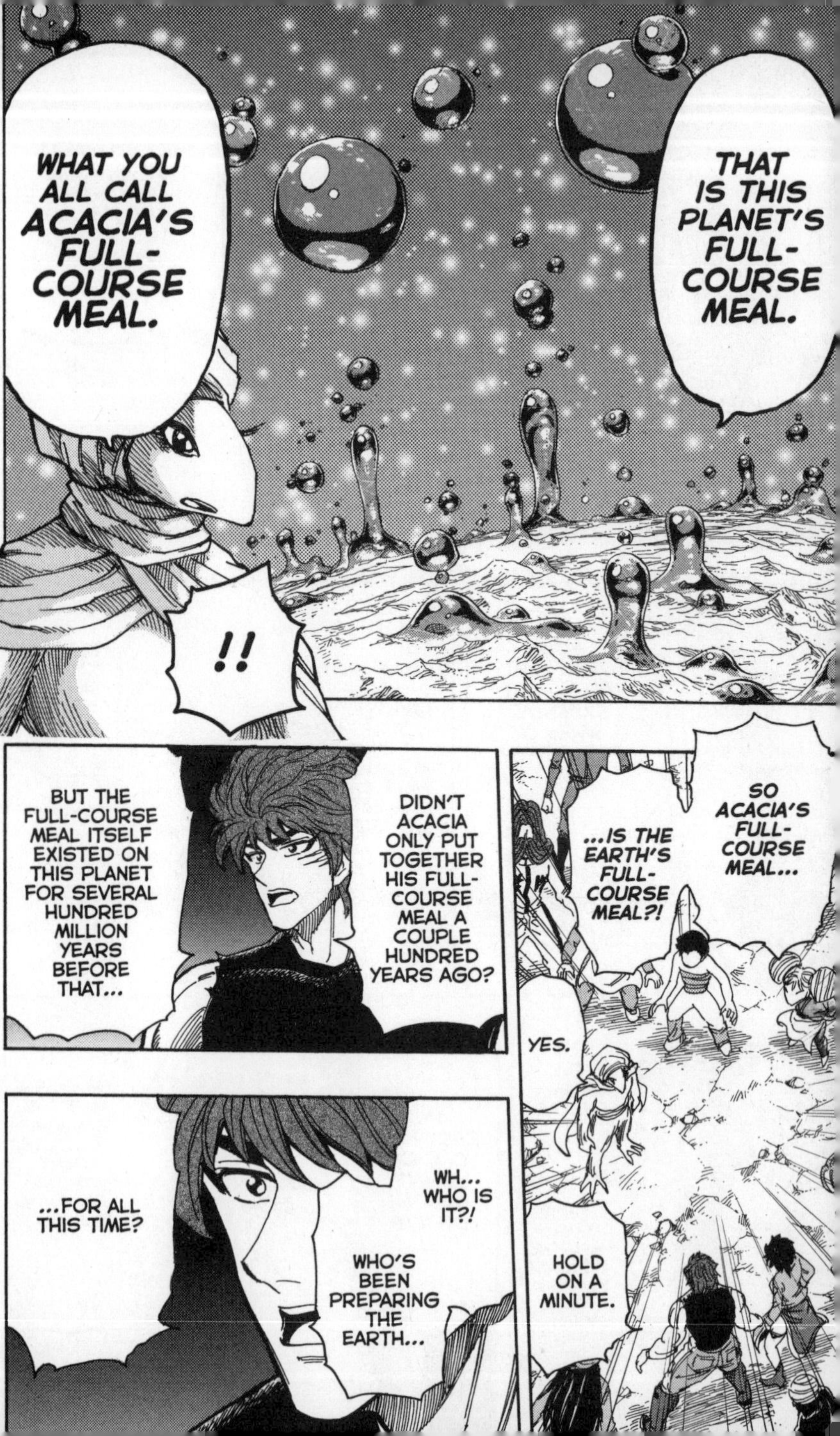
THAT IS THIS PLANET'S FULL-COURSE MEAL.
WHAT YOU ALL CALL ACACIA'S FULL-COURSE MEAL.
!!
SO ACACIA'S FULL-COURSE MEAL...
...IS THE EARTH'S FULL-COURSE MEAL?!
YES.
HOLD ON A MINUTE.
DIDN'T ACACIA ONLY PUT TOGETHER HIS FULL-COURSE MEAL A COUPLE HUNDRED YEARS AGO?
BUT THE FULL-COURSE MEAL ITSELF EXISTED ON THIS PLANET FOR SEVERAL HUNDRED MILLION YEARS BEFORE THAT...
WH... WHO IS IT?!
WHO'S BEEN PREPARING THE EARTH...
...FOR ALL THIS TIME?

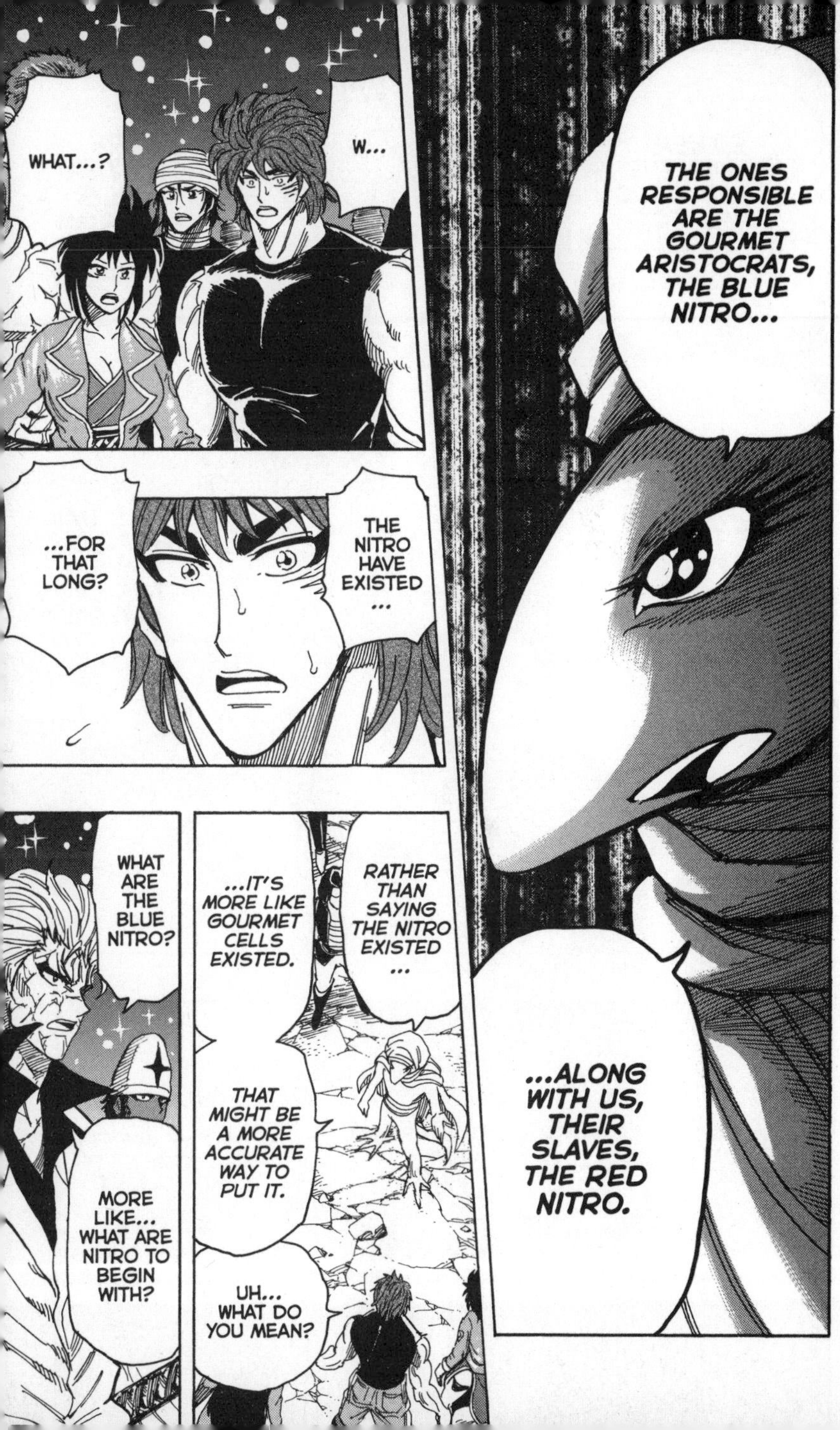
THE ONES RESPONSIBLE ARE THE GOURMET ARISTOCRATS, THE BLUE NITRO...
...ALONG WITH US, THEIR SLAVES, THE RED NITRO.
W...
WHAT...?
THE NITRO HAVE EXISTED...
...FOR THAT LONG?
RATHER THAN SAYING THE NITRO EXISTED...
...IT'S MORE LIKE GOURMET CELLS EXISTED.
THAT MIGHT BE A MORE ACCURATE WAY TO PUT IT.
UH... WHAT DO YOU MEAN?
WHAT ARE THE BLUE NITRO?
MORE LIKE... WHAT ARE NITRO TO BEGIN WITH?

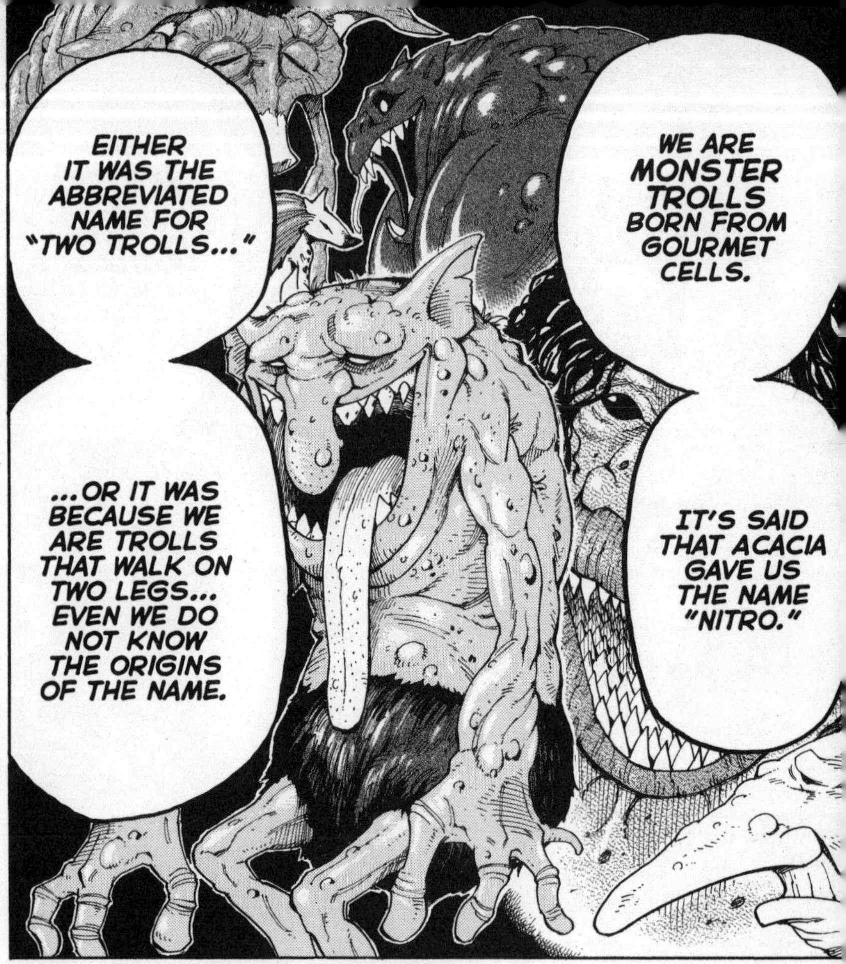
WE ARE MONSTER TROLLS BORN FROM GOURMET CELLS.
IT'S SAID THAT ACACIA GAVE US THE NAME "NITRO."
EITHER IT WAS THE ABBREVIATED NAME FOR "TWO TROLLS..."
...OR IT WAS BECAUSE WE ARE TROLLS THAT WALK ON TWO LEGS... EVEN WE DO NOT KNOW THE ORIGINS OF THE NAME.

*IN JAPANESE "NITRO" CAN BE READ AS TWO AND TROLL.

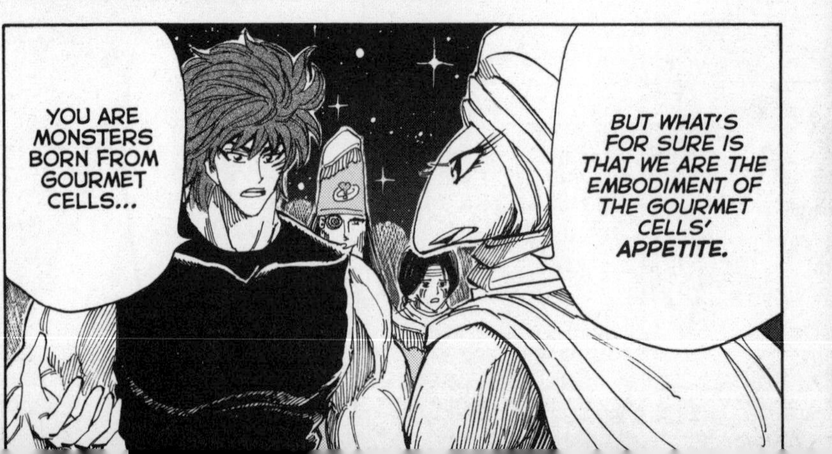
BUT WHAT'S FOR SURE IS THAT WE ARE THE EMBODIMENT OF THE GOURMET CELLS' APPETITE.
YOU ARE MONSTERS BORN FROM GOURMET CELLS...

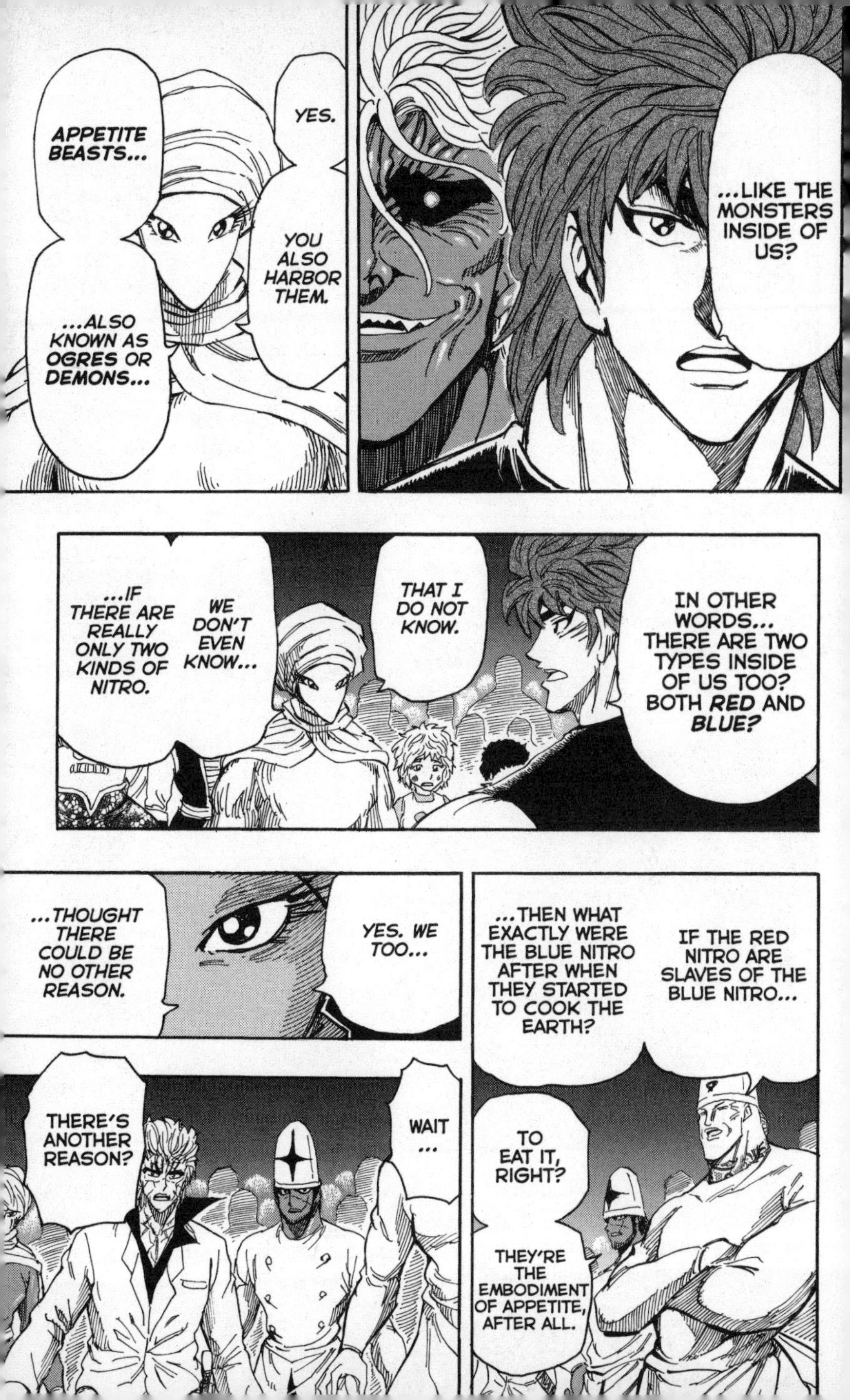
...LIKE THE MONSTERS INSIDE OF US?
YES.
YOU ALSO HARBOR THEM.
APPETITE BEASTS...
...ALSO KNOWN AS OGRES OR DEMONS...
IN OTHER WORDS... THERE ARE TWO TYPES INSIDE OF US TOO? BOTH RED AND BLUE?
THAT I DO NOT KNOW.
WE DON'T EVEN KNOW...
...IF THERE ARE REALLY ONLY TWO KINDS OF NITRO.
IF THE RED NITRO ARE SLAVES OF THE BLUE NITRO...
...THEN WHAT EXACTLY WERE THE BLUE NITRO AFTER WHEN THEY STARTED TO COOK THE EARTH?
TO EAT IT, RIGHT?
THEY'RE THE EMBODIMENT OF APPETITE, AFTER ALL.
YES. WE TOO...
...THOUGHT THERE COULD BE NO OTHER REASON.
WAIT...
THERE'S ANOTHER REASON?

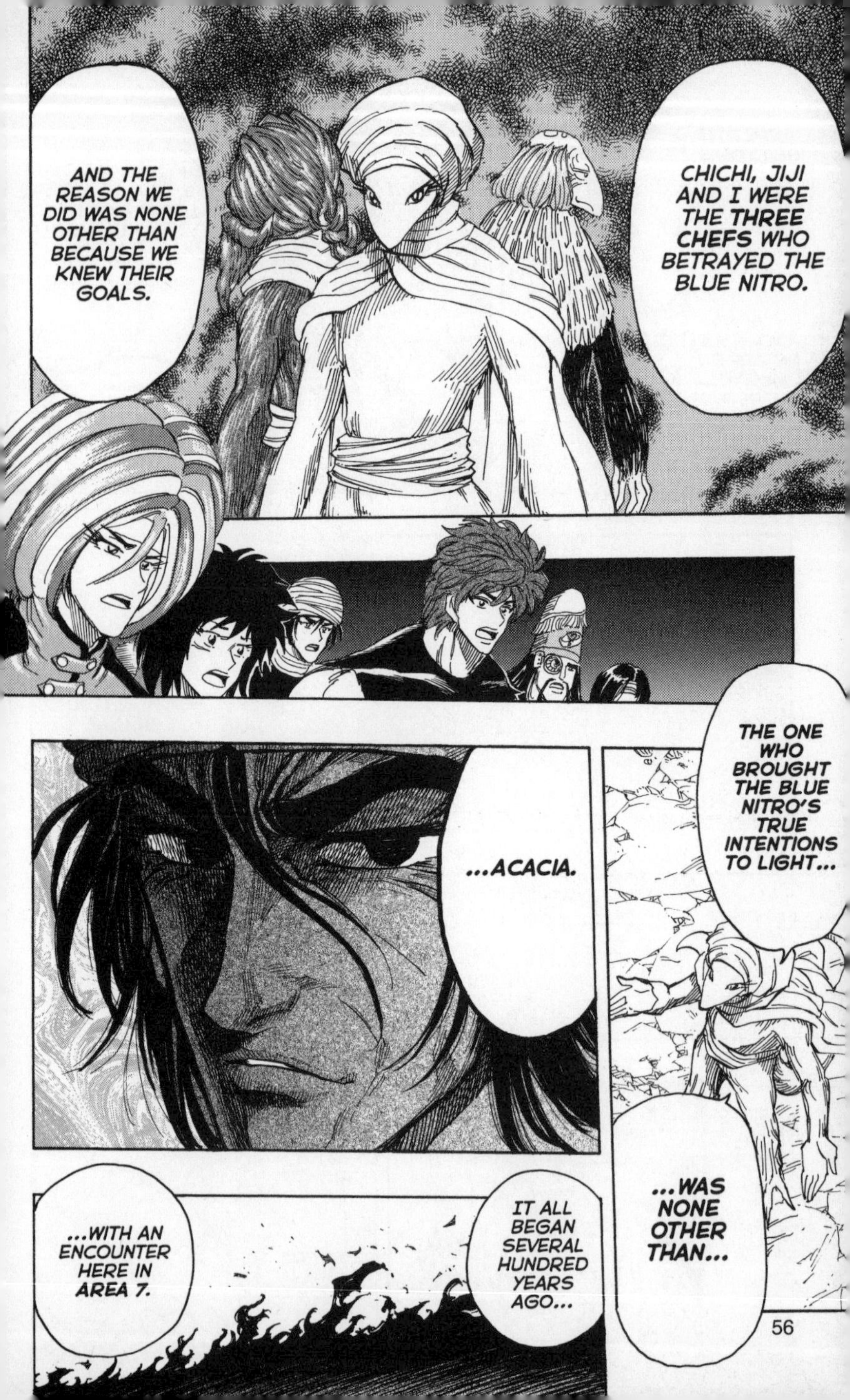
CHICHI, JIJI AND I WERE THE THREE CHEFS WHO BETRAYED THE BLUE NITRO.
AND THE REASON WE DID WAS NONE OTHER THAN BECAUSE WE KNEW THEIR GOALS.
THE ONE WHO BROUGHT THE BLUE NITRO'S TRUE INTENTIONS TO LIGHT...
...WAS NONE OTHER THAN...
...ACACIA.
IT ALL BEGAN SEVERAL HUNDRED YEARS AGO...
...WITH AN ENCOUNTER HERE IN AREA 7.

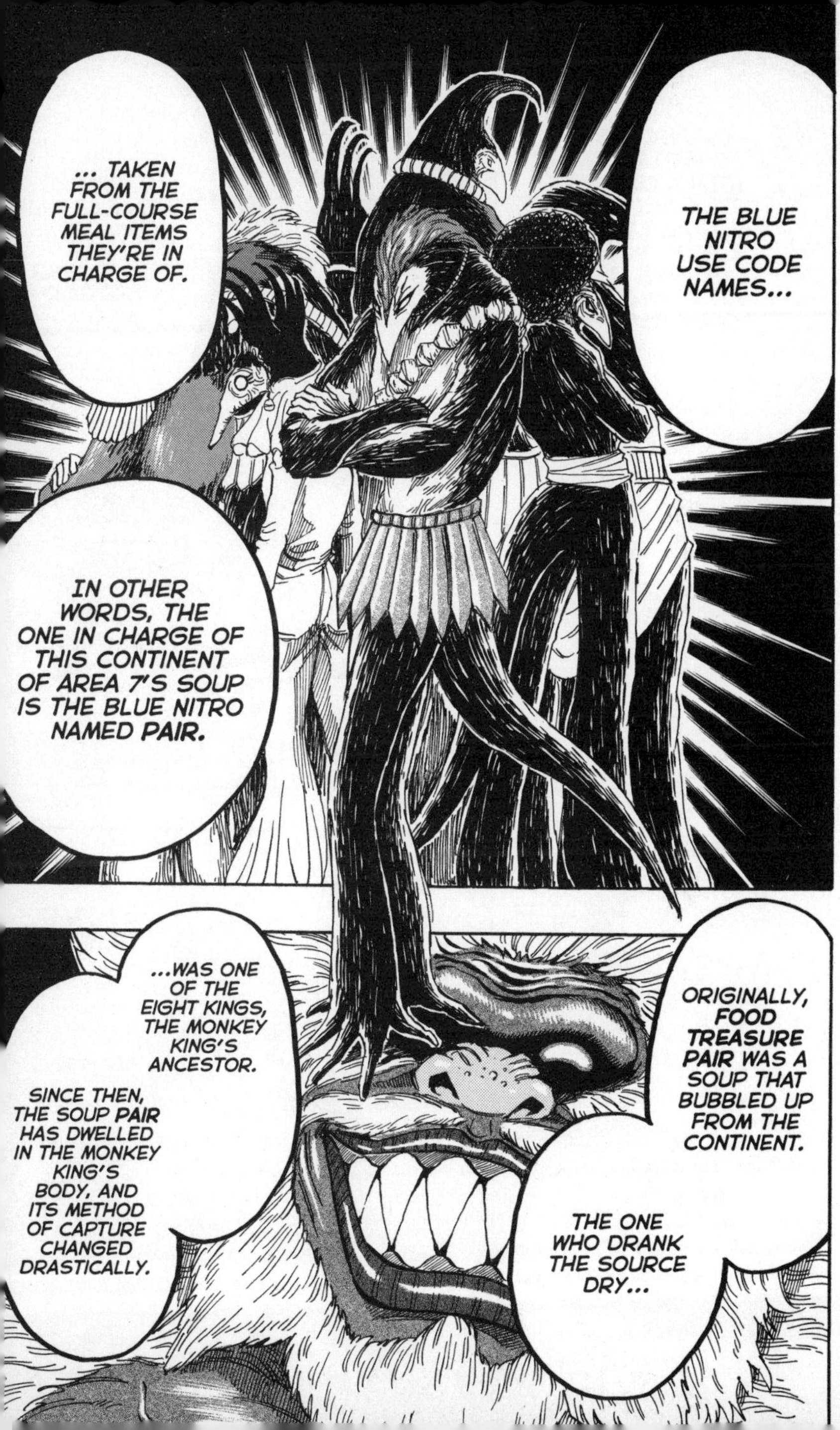
THE BLUE NITRO USE CODE NAMES...
... TAKEN FROM THE FULL-COURSE MEAL ITEMS THEY'RE IN CHARGE OF.
IN OTHER WORDS, THE ONE IN CHARGE OF THIS CONTINENT OF AREA 7'S SOUP IS THE BLUE NITRO NAMED PAIR.
ORIGINALLY, FOOD TREASURE PAIR WAS A SOUP THAT BUBBLED UP FROM THE CONTINENT.
THE ONE WHO DRANK THE SOURCE DRY...
...WAS ONE OF THE EIGHT KINGS, THE MONKEY KING'S ANCESTOR.
SINCE THEN, THE SOUP PAIR HAS DWELLED IN THE MONKEY KING'S BODY, AND ITS METHOD OF CAPTURE CHANGED DRASTICALLY.

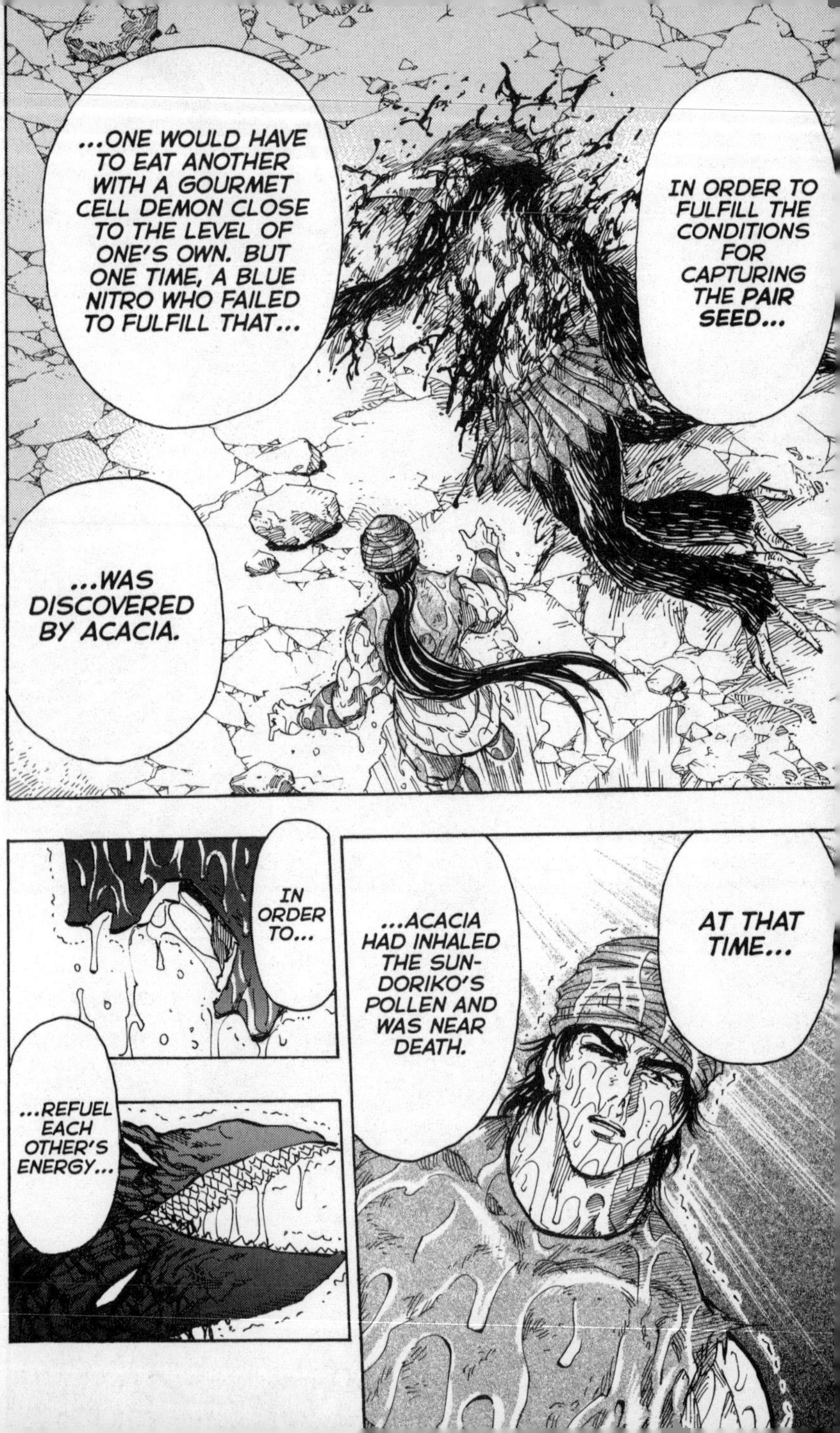
IN ORDER TO FULFILL THE CONDITIONS FOR CAPTURING THE PAIR SEED...
...ONE WOULD HAVE TO EAT ANOTHER WITH A GOURMET CELL DEMON CLOSE TO THE LEVEL OF ONE'S OWN. BUT ONE TIME, A BLUE NITRO WHO FAILED TO FULFILL THAT...
...WAS DISCOVERED BY ACACIA.
AT THAT TIME...
...ACACIA HAD INHALED THE SUN-DORIKO'S POLLEN AND WAS NEAR DEATH.
IN ORDER TO...
...REFUEL EACH OTHER'S ENERGY...

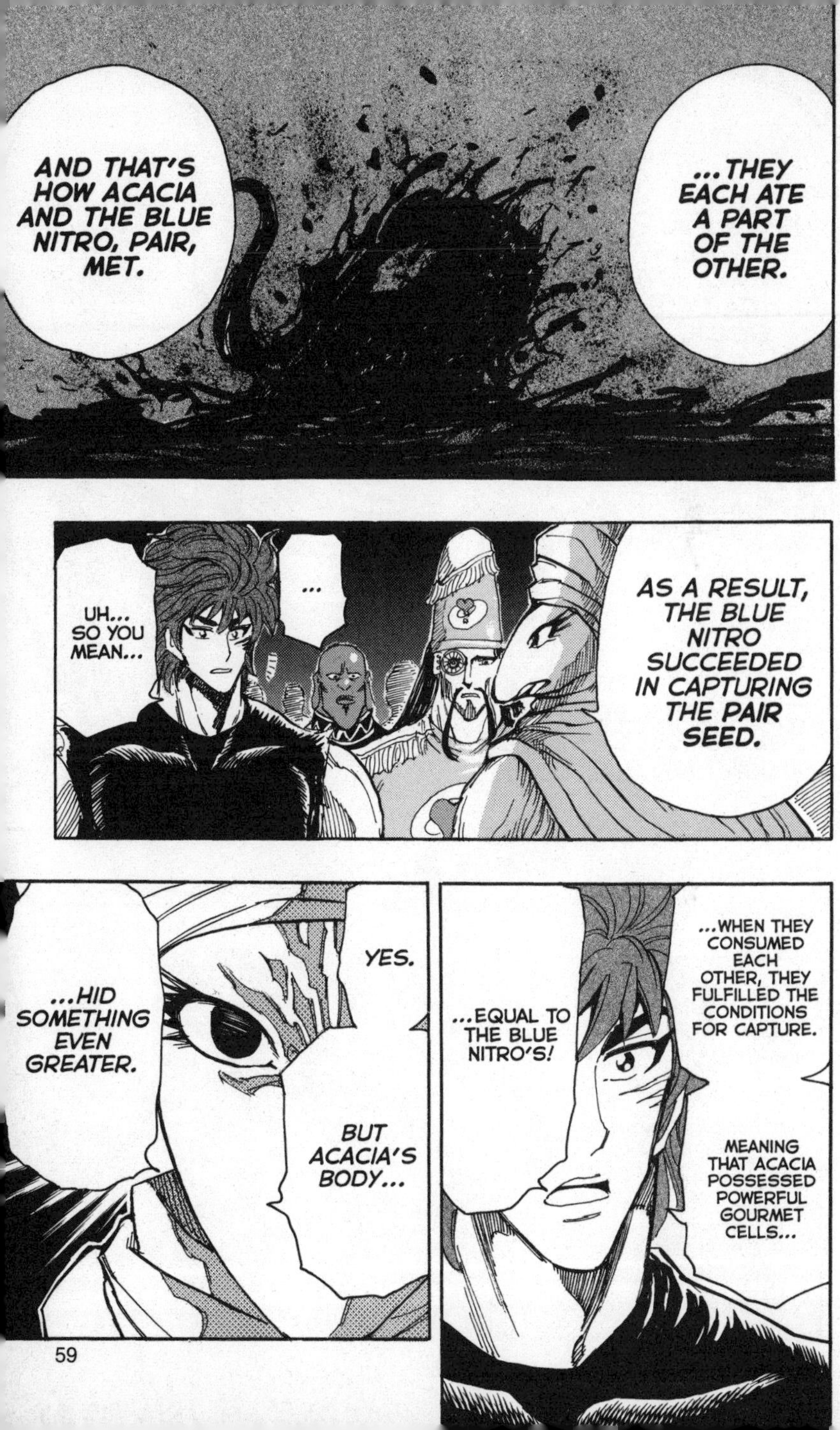
...THEY EACH ATE A PART OF THE OTHER.
AND THAT'S HOW ACACIA AND THE BLUE NITRO, PAIR, MET.
AS A RESULT, THE BLUE NITRO SUCCEEDED IN CAPTURING THE PAIR SEED.
...
UH... SO YOU MEAN...
...WHEN THEY CONSUMED EACH OTHER, THEY FULFILLED THE CONDITIONS FOR CAPTURE.
MEANING THAT ACACIA POSSESSED POWERFUL GOURMET CELLS...
...EQUAL TO THE BLUE NITRO'S!
YES.
BUT ACACIA'S BODY...
...HID SOMETHING EVEN GREATER.

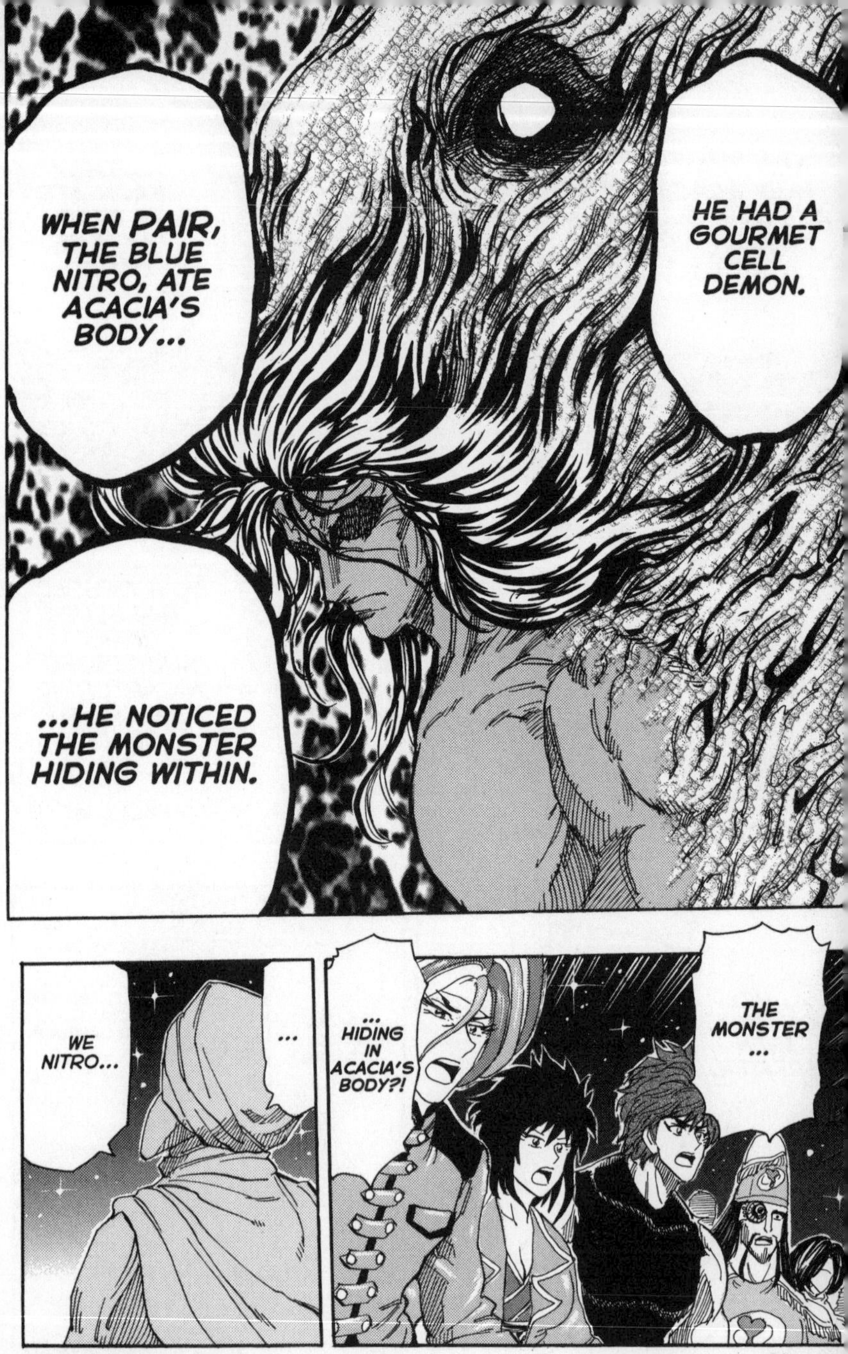

HE HAD A GOURMET CELL DEMON.
WHEN PAIR, THE BLUE NITRO, ATE ACACIA'S BODY...
...HE NOTICED THE MONSTER HIDING WITHIN.
THE MONSTER...
...HIDING IN ACACIA'S BODY?!
...
WE NITRO...

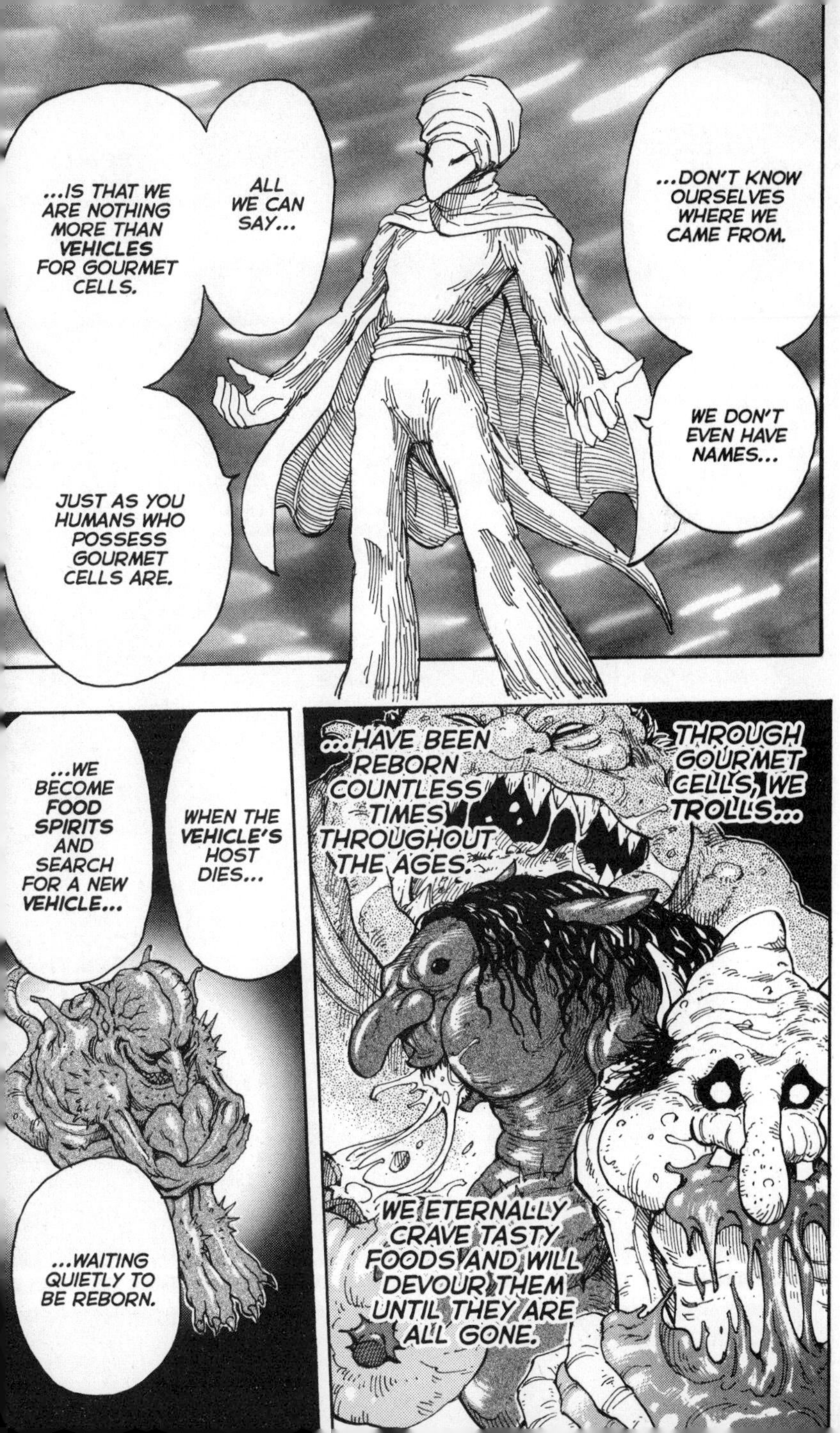
...DON'T KNOW OURSELVES WHERE WE CAME FROM.
WE DON'T EVEN HAVE NAMES...
ALL WE CAN SAY...
...IS THAT WE ARE NOTHING MORE THAN VEHICLES FOR GOURMET CELLS.
JUST AS YOU HUMANS WHO POSSESS GOURMET CELLS ARE.
THROUGH GOURMET CELLS, WE TROLLS...
...HAVE BEEN REBORN COUNTLESS TIMES THROUGHOUT THE AGES.
WE ETERNALLY CRAVE TASTY FOODS AND WILL DEVOUR THEM UNTIL THEY ARE ALL GONE.
WHEN THE VEHICLE'S HOST DIES...
...WE BECOME FOOD SPIRITS AND SEARCH FOR A NEW VEHICLE...
...WAITING QUIETLY TO BE REBORN.

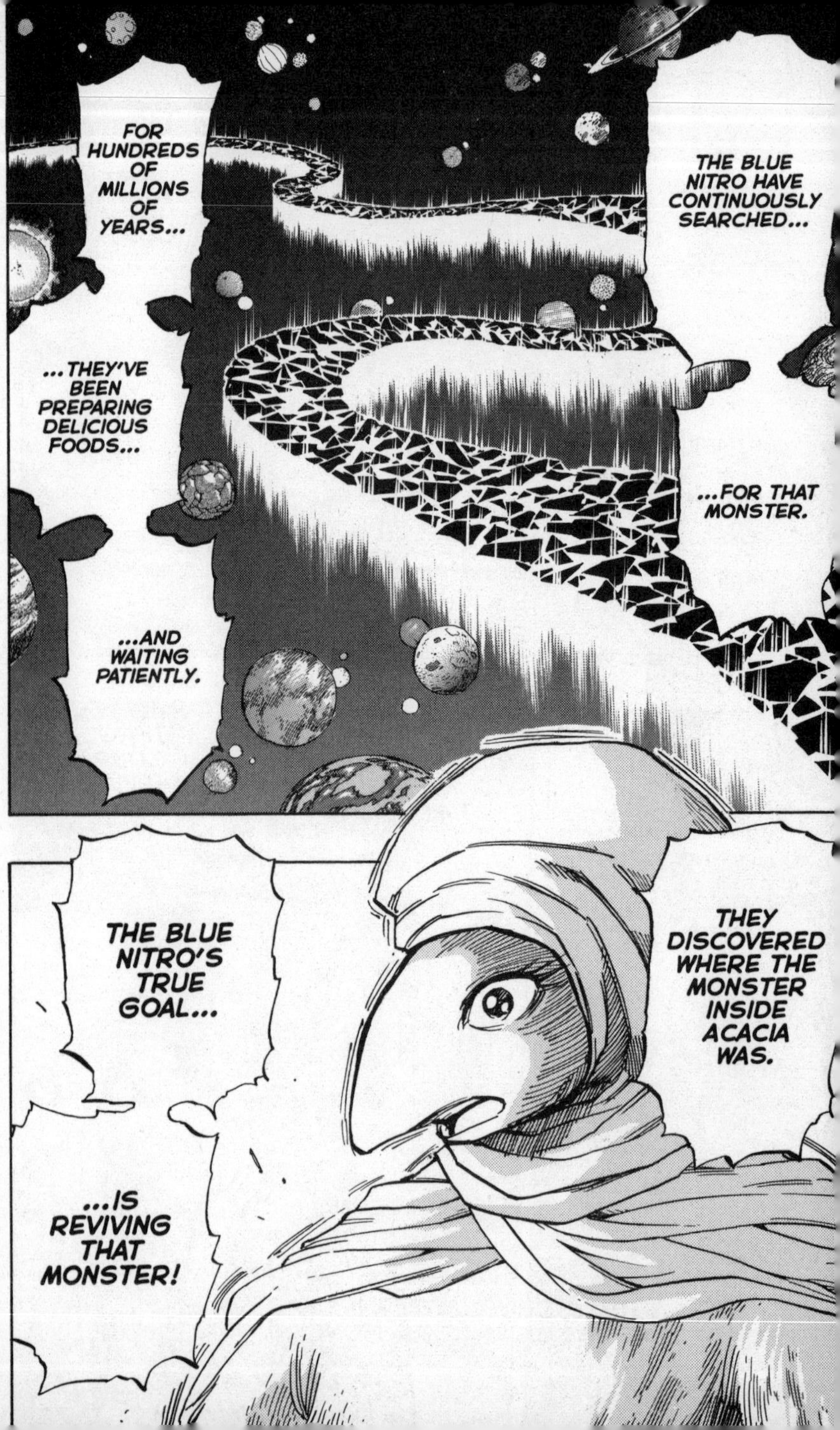
THE BLUE NITRO HAVE CONTINUOUSLY SEARCHED...
...FOR THAT MONSTER.
FOR HUNDREDS OF MILLIONS OF YEARS...
...THEY'VE BEEN PREPARING DELICIOUS FOODS...
...AND WAITING PATIENTLY.
THEY DISCOVERED WHERE THE MONSTER INSIDE ACACIA WAS.
THE BLUE NITRO'S TRUE GOAL...
...IS REVIVING THAT MONSTER!

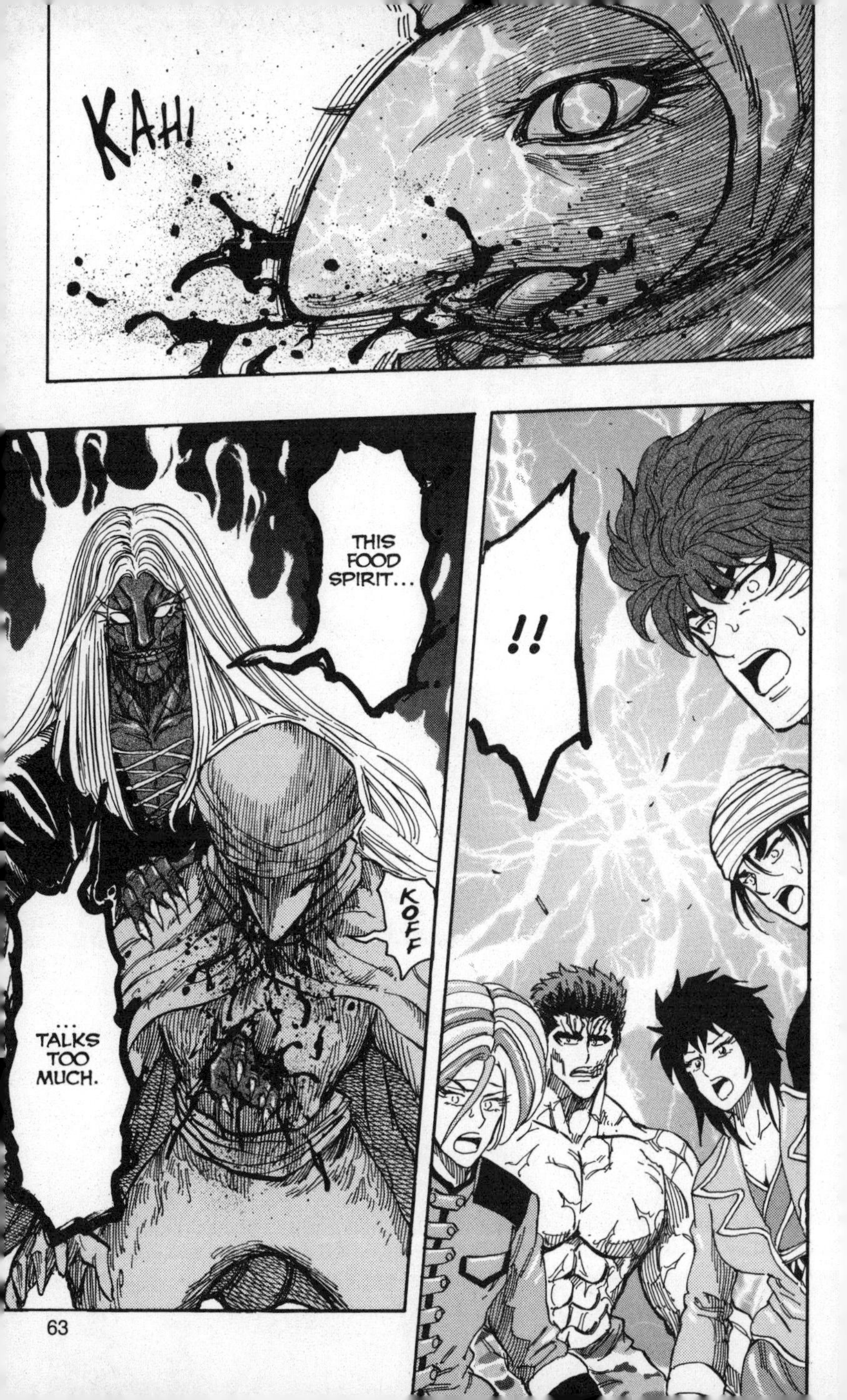
KAH!
!!
THIS FOOD SPIRIT...
KOFF
...TALKS TOO MUCH.

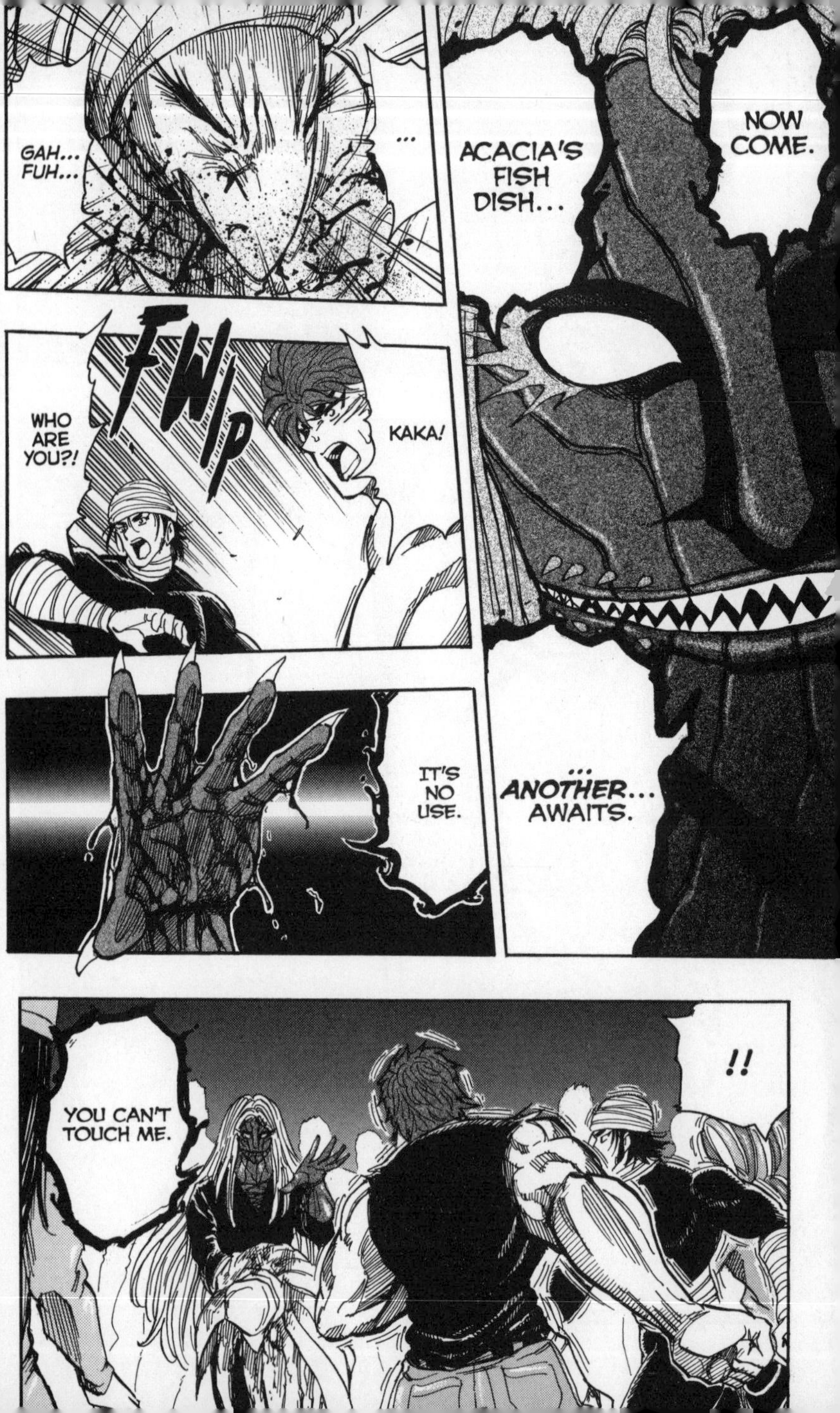
NOW COME.
ACACIA'S FISH DISH...
... ANOTHER... AWAITS.
...
GAH... FUH...
KAKA!
FWIP
WHO ARE YOU?!
IT'S NO USE.
!!
YOU CAN'T TOUCH ME.

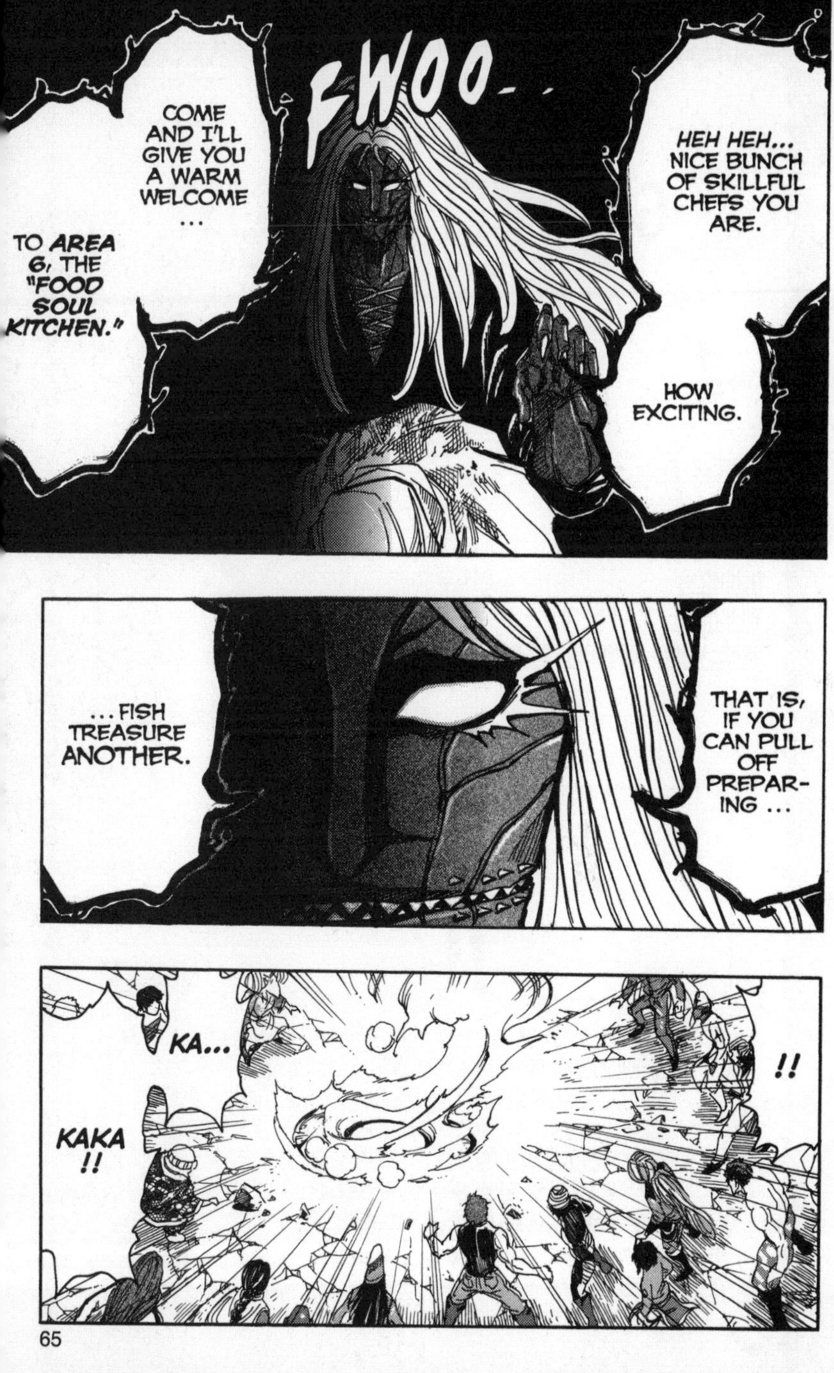
HEH HEH... NICE BUNCH OF SKILLFUL CHEFS YOU ARE.
HOW EXCITING.
FWOO...
COME AND I'LL GIVE YOU A WARM WELCOME ...
TO AREA 6, THE "FOOD SOUL KITCHEN."
THAT IS, IF YOU CAN PULL OFF PREPAR-ING ...
... FISH TREASURE ANOTHER.
!!
KA...
KAKA !!

TORIKO

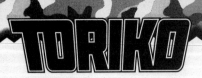

GOURMET CHECKLIST

Vol. 353

FOOD TABLET
(SUPPLEMENT)

CAPTURE LEVEL: ---
HABITAT: MAN-MADE
SIZE: ---
HEIGHT: ---
WEIGHT: ---
PRICE: VARIES DEPENDING ON TYPE

ALMOND CABBAGE
food tablet
No. 2029

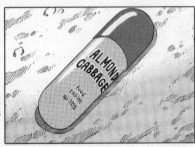

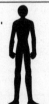

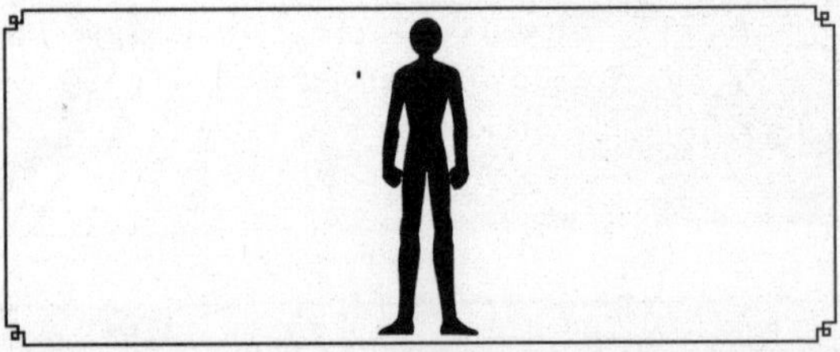

SCALE

THE DESTRUCTION FOLLOWING MIDORA'S METEOR SPICE PUT THE HUMAN WORLD IN A FOOD SHORTAGE CRISIS LIKE NEVER BEFORE. AS A LAST RESORT TO SAVE HUMANITY, THE IGO CREATED THESE TABLETS. A VARIETY OF FOOD TABLETS WERE DEVELOPED, BUT THEY LACKED FLAVOR, SCENT AND TEXTURE AND RETAINED ONLY THE BASE NUTRITIONAL CONTENT FROM THE ORIGINAL INGREDIENT. THOUGH DEPRIVED OF THE JOY OF EATING, MANKIND SURVIVED THANKS TO THESE TABLETS. THEY COULD EVEN BE CALLED A MINIMAL SUPPLEMENT INGREDIENT.

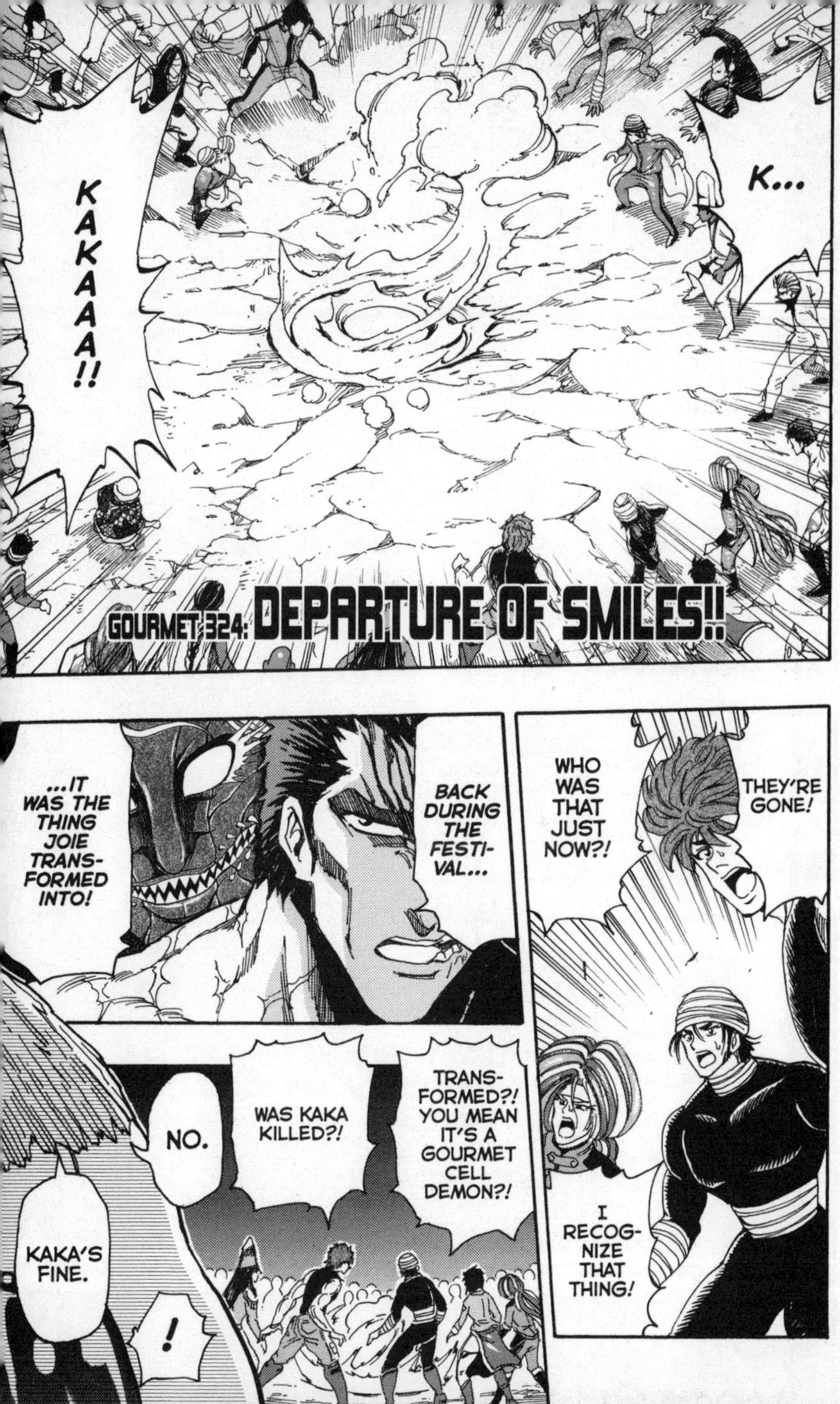
K...
KAKAAAA!!
GOURMET 324: DEPARTURE OF SMILES!!
THEY'RE GONE!
WHO WAS THAT JUST NOW?!
I RECOGNIZE THAT THING!
BACK DURING THE FESTIVAL...
...IT WAS THE THING JOIE TRANSFORMED INTO!
TRANSFORMED?! YOU MEAN IT'S A GOURMET CELL DEMON?!
WAS KAKA KILLED?!
NO.
KAKA'S FINE.
!

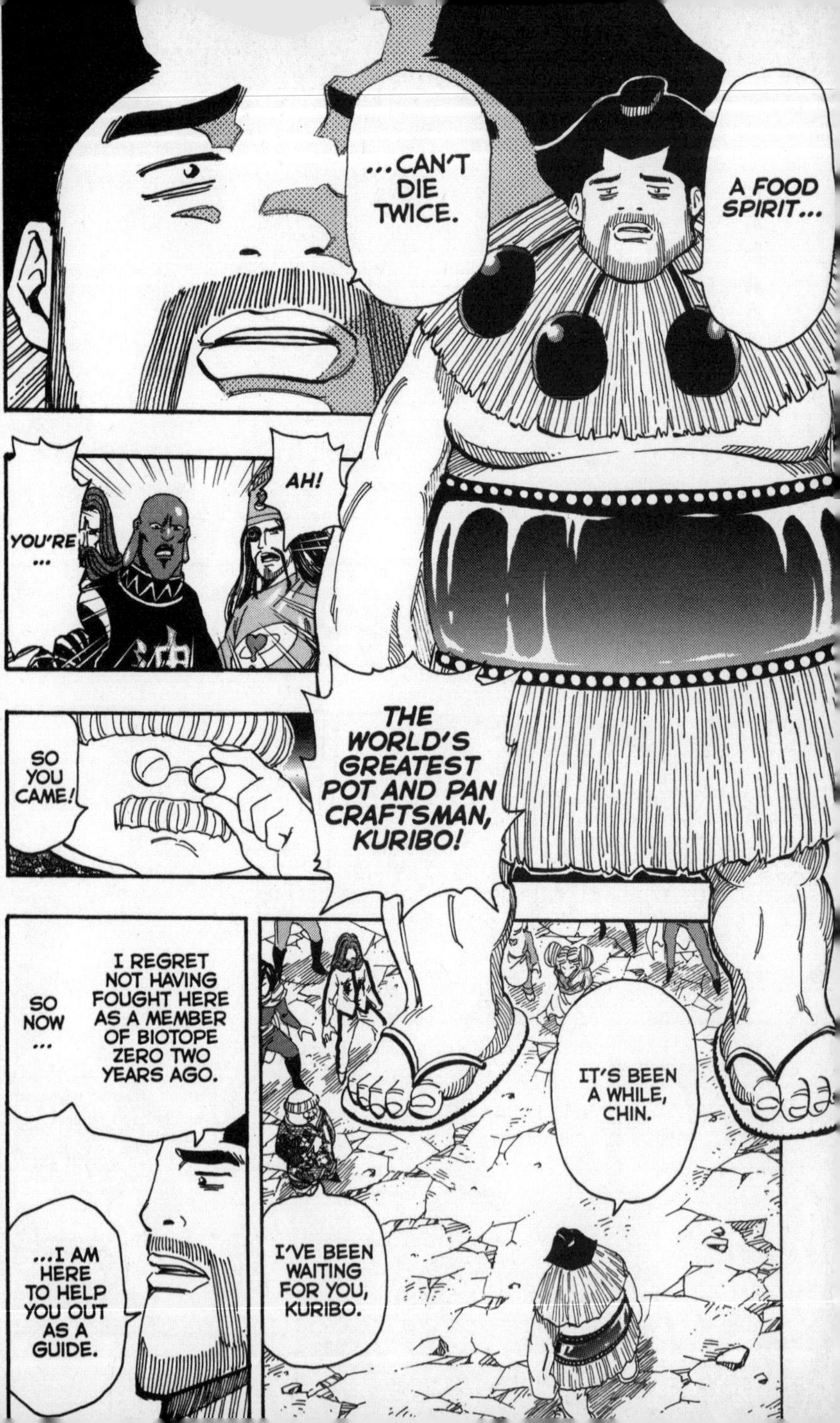

A FOOD SPIRIT...
...CAN'T DIE TWICE.
AH!
YOU'RE...
THE WORLD'S GREATEST POT AND PAN CRAFTSMAN, KURIBO!
SO YOU CAME!
IT'S BEEN A WHILE, CHIN.
I'VE BEEN WAITING FOR YOU, KURIBO.
I REGRET NOT HAVING FOUGHT HERE AS A MEMBER OF BIOTOPE ZERO TWO YEARS AGO.
SO NOW...
...I AM HERE TO HELP YOU OUT AS A GUIDE.

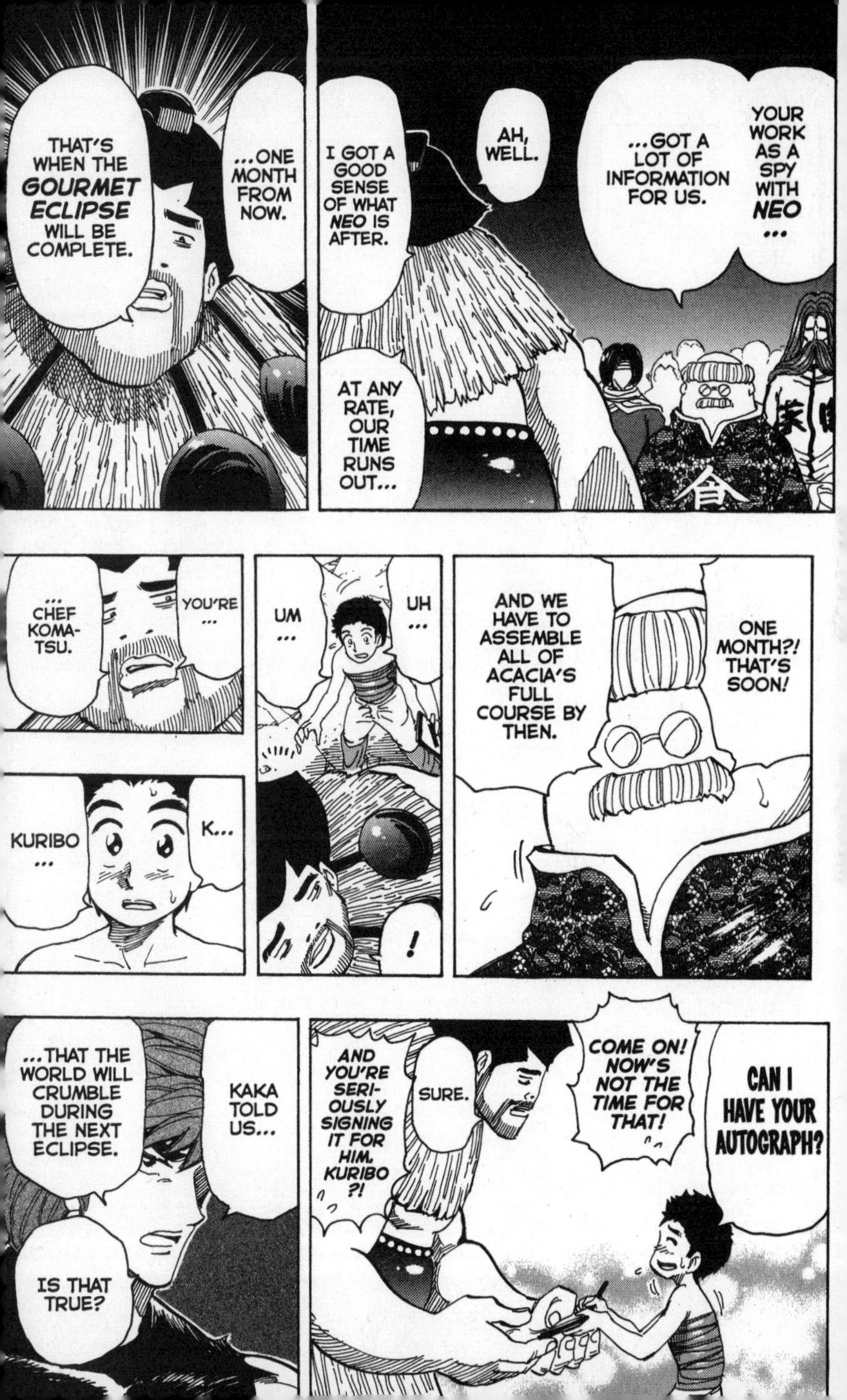
YOUR WORK AS A SPY WITH NEO ...
...GOT A LOT OF INFORMATION FOR US.
AH, WELL.
I GOT A GOOD SENSE OF WHAT NEO IS AFTER.
AT ANY RATE, OUR TIME RUNS OUT...
...ONE MONTH FROM NOW.
THAT'S WHEN THE GOURMET ECLIPSE WILL BE COMPLETE.
ONE MONTH?! THAT'S SOON!
AND WE HAVE TO ASSEMBLE ALL OF ACACIA'S FULL COURSE BY THEN.
UH ...
UM ...
!
YOU'RE ...
... CHEF KOMATSU.
K...
KURIBO ...
CAN I HAVE YOUR AUTOGRAPH?
COME ON! NOW'S NOT THE TIME FOR THAT!
SURE.
AND YOU'RE SERIOUSLY SIGNING IT FOR HIM. KURIBO ?!
KAKA TOLD US...
...THAT THE WORLD WILL CRUMBLE DURING THE NEXT ECLIPSE.
IS THAT TRUE?

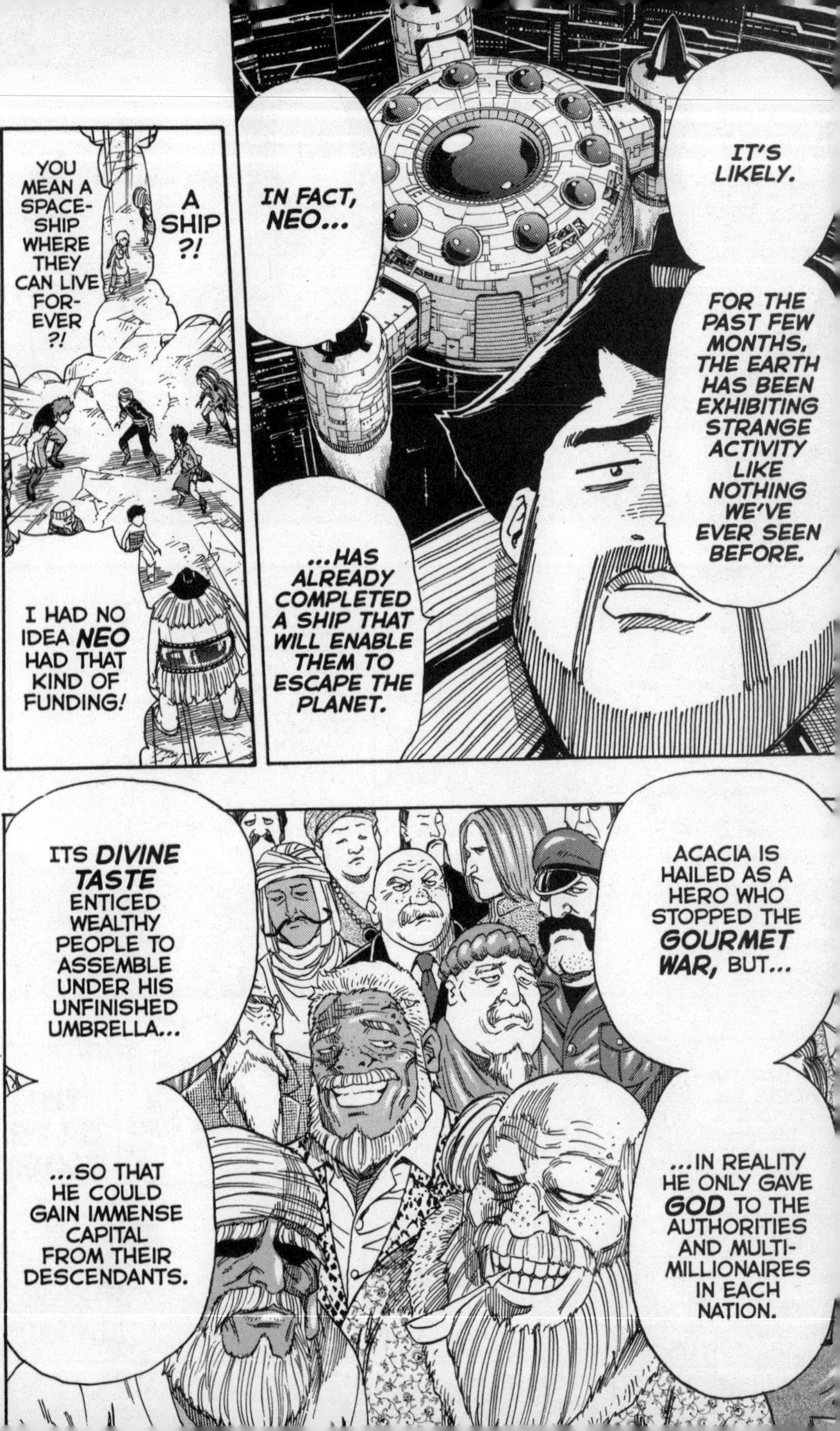
IT'S LIKELY.
FOR THE PAST FEW MONTHS, THE EARTH HAS BEEN EXHIBITING STRANGE ACTIVITY LIKE NOTHING WE'VE EVER SEEN BEFORE.
IN FACT, NEO...
...HAS ALREADY COMPLETED A SHIP THAT WILL ENABLE THEM TO ESCAPE THE PLANET.
A SHIP?!
YOU MEAN A SPACE-SHIP WHERE THEY CAN LIVE FOR-EVER?!
I HAD NO IDEA NEO HAD THAT KIND OF FUNDING!
ACACIA IS HAILED AS A HERO WHO STOPPED THE GOURMET WAR, BUT...
...IN REALITY HE ONLY GAVE GOD TO THE AUTHORITIES AND MULTI-MILLIONAIRES IN EACH NATION.
ITS DIVINE TASTE ENTICED WEALTHY PEOPLE TO ASSEMBLE UNDER HIS UNFINISHED UMBRELLA...
...SO THAT HE COULD GAIN IMMENSE CAPITAL FROM THEIR DESCENDANTS.

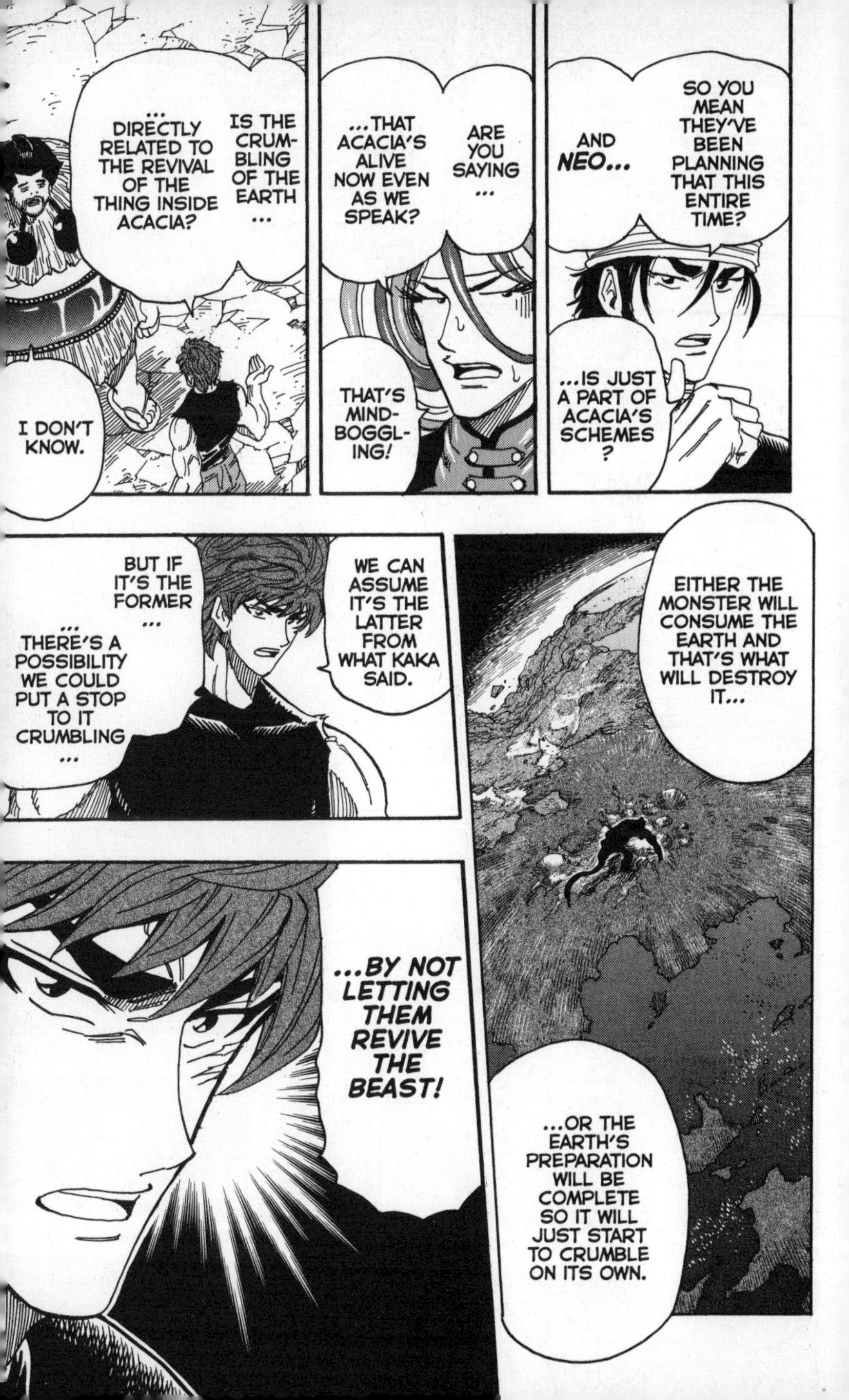
SO YOU MEAN THEY'VE BEEN PLANNING THAT THIS ENTIRE TIME?
AND NEO...
...IS JUST A PART OF ACACIA'S SCHEMES?
ARE YOU SAYING...
...THAT ACACIA'S ALIVE NOW EVEN AS WE SPEAK?
THAT'S MIND-BOGGLING!
IS THE CRUMBLING OF THE EARTH...
...DIRECTLY RELATED TO THE REVIVAL OF THE THING INSIDE ACACIA?
I DON'T KNOW.
EITHER THE MONSTER WILL CONSUME THE EARTH AND THAT'S WHAT WILL DESTROY IT...
...OR THE EARTH'S PREPARATION WILL BE COMPLETE SO IT WILL JUST START TO CRUMBLE ON ITS OWN.
WE CAN ASSUME IT'S THE LATTER FROM WHAT KAKA SAID.
BUT IF IT'S THE FORMER...
...THERE'S A POSSIBILITY WE COULD PUT A STOP TO IT CRUMBLING...
...BY NOT LETTING THEM REVIVE THE BEAST!

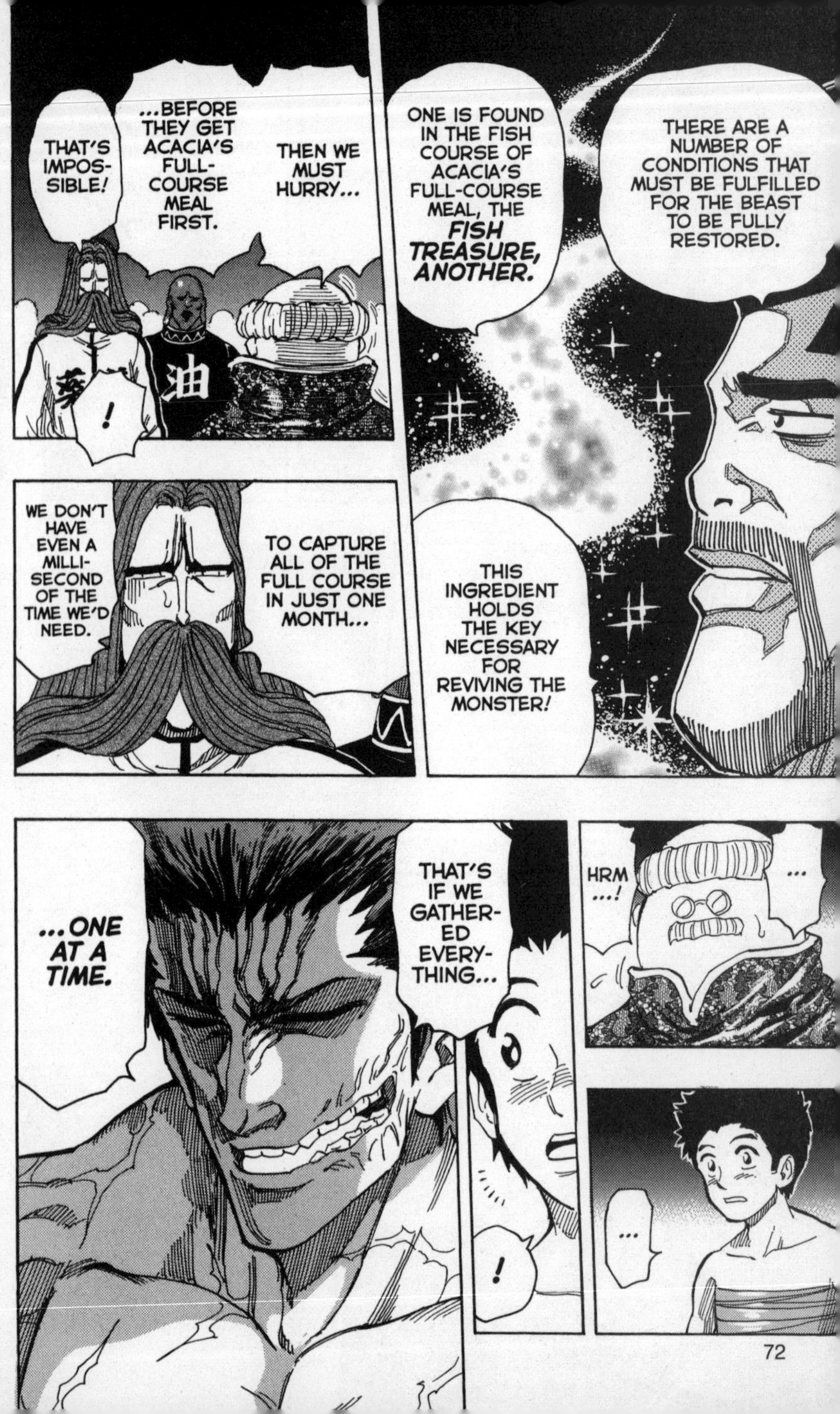
THERE ARE A NUMBER OF CONDITIONS THAT MUST BE FULFILLED FOR THE BEAST TO BE FULLY RESTORED.
ONE IS FOUND IN THE FISH COURSE OF ACACIA'S FULL-COURSE MEAL, THE *FISH TREASURE, ANOTHER.*
THIS INGREDIENT HOLDS THE KEY NECESSARY FOR REVIVING THE MONSTER!
THEN WE MUST HURRY...
...BEFORE THEY GET ACACIA'S FULL-COURSE MEAL FIRST.
THAT'S IMPOSSIBLE!
!
TO CAPTURE ALL OF THE FULL COURSE IN JUST ONE MONTH...
WE DON'T HAVE EVEN A MILLISECOND OF THE TIME WE'D NEED.
...
HRM ...!
...
THAT'S IF WE GATHERED EVERYTHING...
!
...ONE AT A TIME.

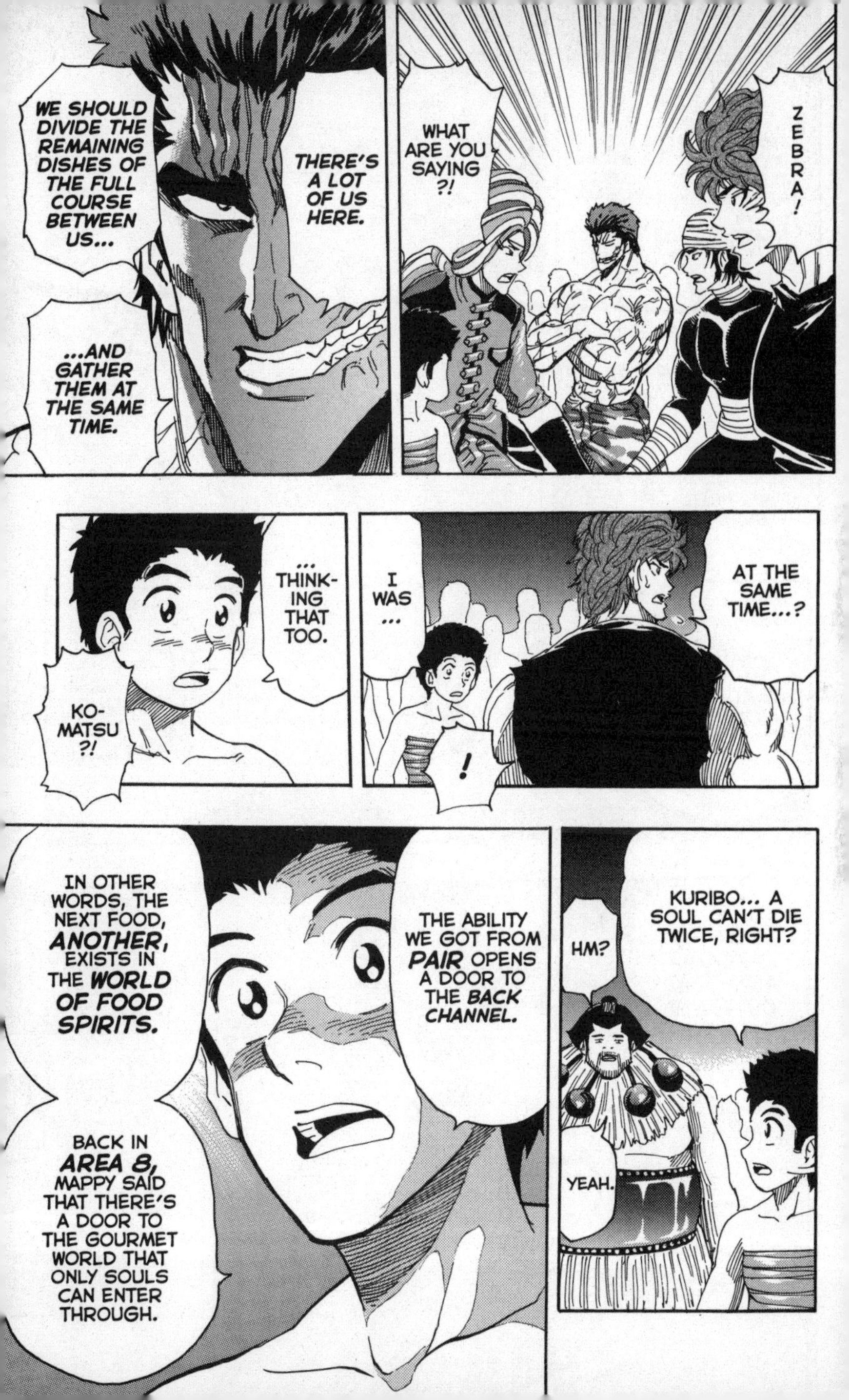
ZEBRA!
WHAT ARE YOU SAYING ?!
THERE'S A LOT OF US HERE.
WE SHOULD DIVIDE THE REMAINING DISHES OF THE FULL COURSE BETWEEN US...
...AND GATHER THEM AT THE SAME TIME.
AT THE SAME TIME...?
I WAS ...
!
... THINKING THAT TOO.
KO-MATSU ?!
KURIBO... A SOUL CAN'T DIE TWICE, RIGHT?
HM?
YEAH.
THE ABILITY WE GOT FROM PAIR OPENS A DOOR TO THE BACK CHANNEL.
IN OTHER WORDS, THE NEXT FOOD, ANOTHER, EXISTS IN THE WORLD OF FOOD SPIRITS.
BACK IN AREA 8, MAPPY SAID THAT THERE'S A DOOR TO THE GOURMET WORLD THAT ONLY SOULS CAN ENTER THROUGH.

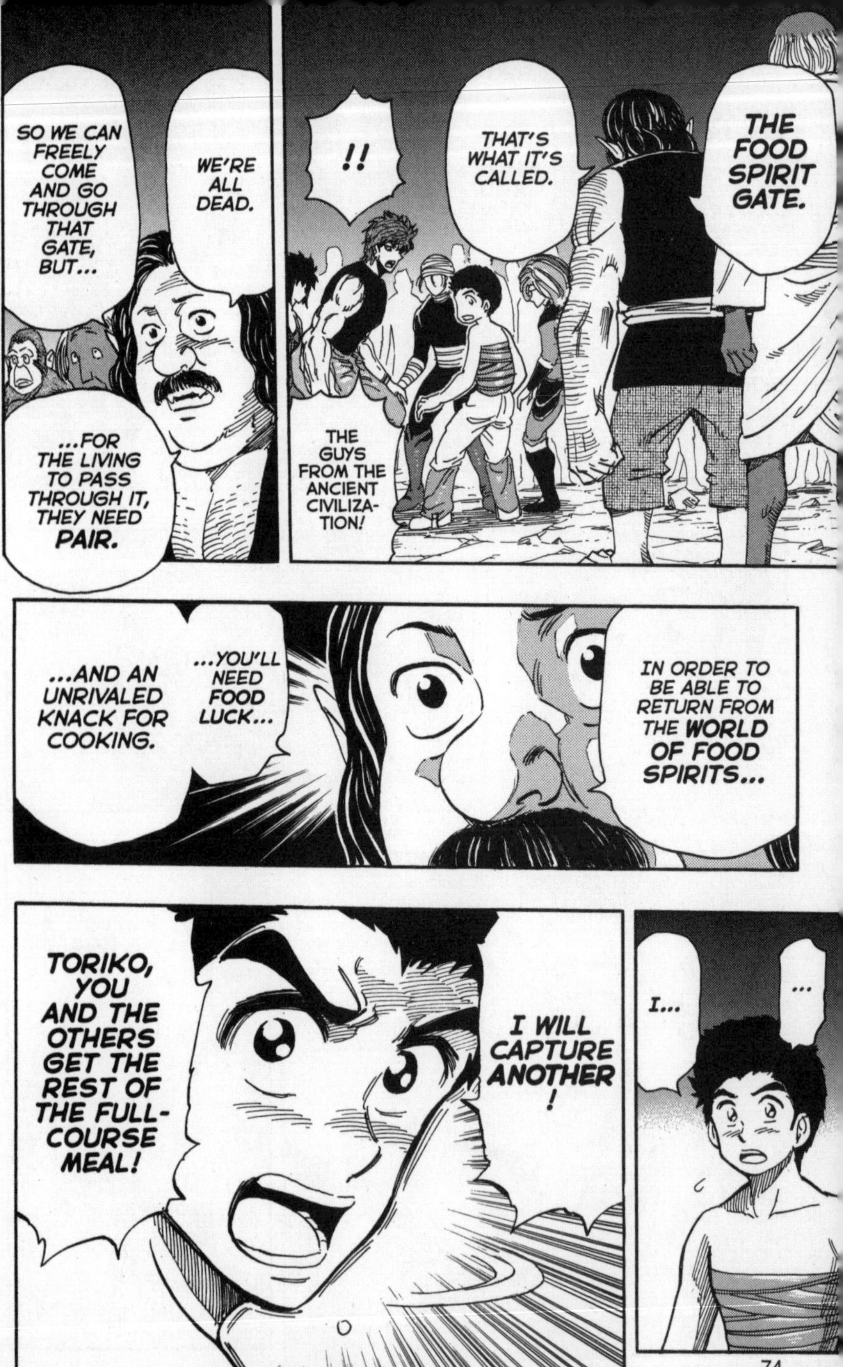
THE FOOD SPIRIT GATE.
THAT'S WHAT IT'S CALLED.
!!
THE GUYS FROM THE ANCIENT CIVILIZATION!
WE'RE ALL DEAD.
SO WE CAN FREELY COME AND GO THROUGH THAT GATE, BUT...
...FOR THE LIVING TO PASS THROUGH IT, THEY NEED PAIR.
IN ORDER TO BE ABLE TO RETURN FROM THE WORLD OF FOOD SPIRITS...
...YOU'LL NEED FOOD LUCK...
...AND AN UNRIVALED KNACK FOR COOKING.
...
I...
I WILL CAPTURE ANOTHER!
TORIKO, YOU AND THE OTHERS GET THE REST OF THE FULL-COURSE MEAL!

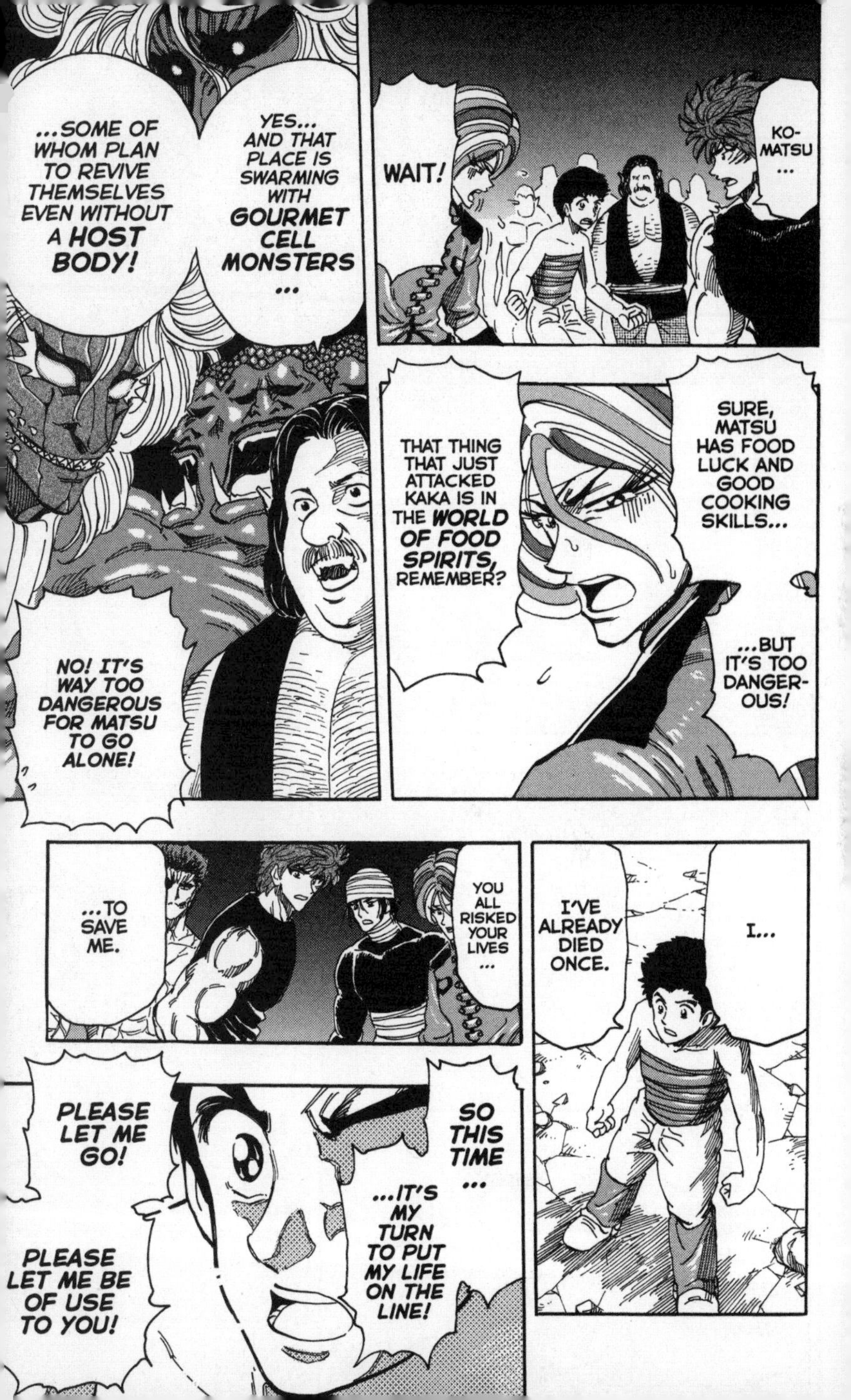
KO-MATSU...
WAIT!
SURE, MATSU HAS FOOD LUCK AND GOOD COOKING SKILLS...
THAT THING THAT JUST ATTACKED KAKA IS IN THE WORLD OF FOOD SPIRITS, REMEMBER?
...BUT IT'S TOO DANGER-OUS!
YES... AND THAT PLACE IS SWARMING WITH GOURMET CELL MONSTERS...
...SOME OF WHOM PLAN TO REVIVE THEMSELVES EVEN WITHOUT A HOST BODY!
NO! IT'S WAY TOO DANGEROUS FOR MATSU TO GO ALONE!
I...
I'VE ALREADY DIED ONCE.
YOU ALL RISKED YOUR LIVES...
...TO SAVE ME.
SO THIS TIME...
...IT'S MY TURN TO PUT MY LIFE ON THE LINE!
PLEASE LET ME GO!
PLEASE LET ME BE OF USE TO YOU!

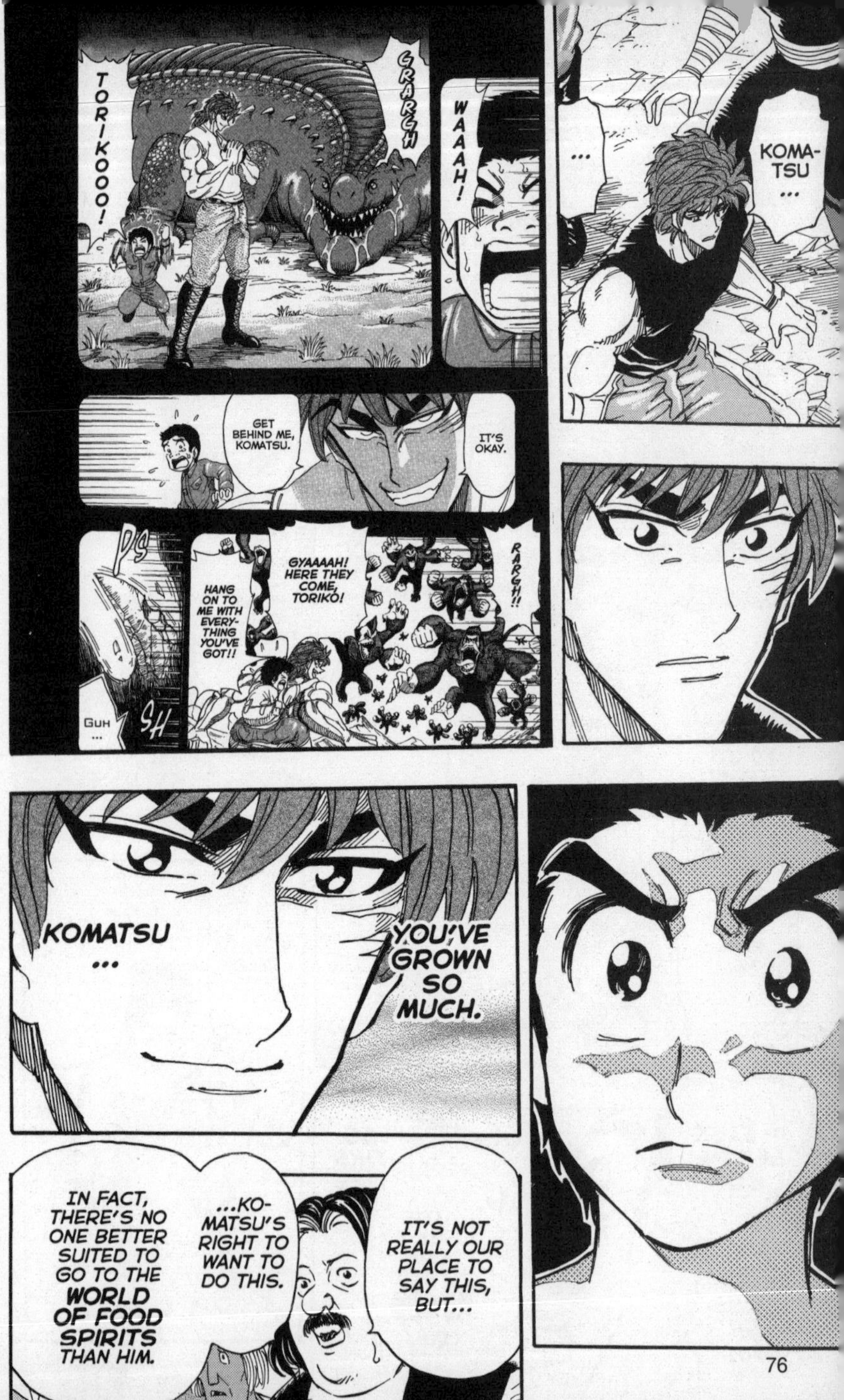

KOMA-TSU ...
...
WAAAAH!
GRARGH
TORIKOOO!
IT'S OKAY.
GET BEHIND ME, KOMATSU.
RARGH!!
GYAAAAH! HERE THEY COME, TORIKO!
HANG ON TO ME WITH EVERY-THING YOU'VE GOT!!
P'S
SH
GUH ...
KOMATSU ...
YOU'VE GROWN SO MUCH.
IT'S NOT REALLY OUR PLACE TO SAY THIS, BUT...
...KO-MATSU'S RIGHT TO WANT TO DO THIS.
IN FACT, THERE'S NO ONE BETTER SUITED TO GO TO THE WORLD OF FOOD SPIRITS THAN HIM.

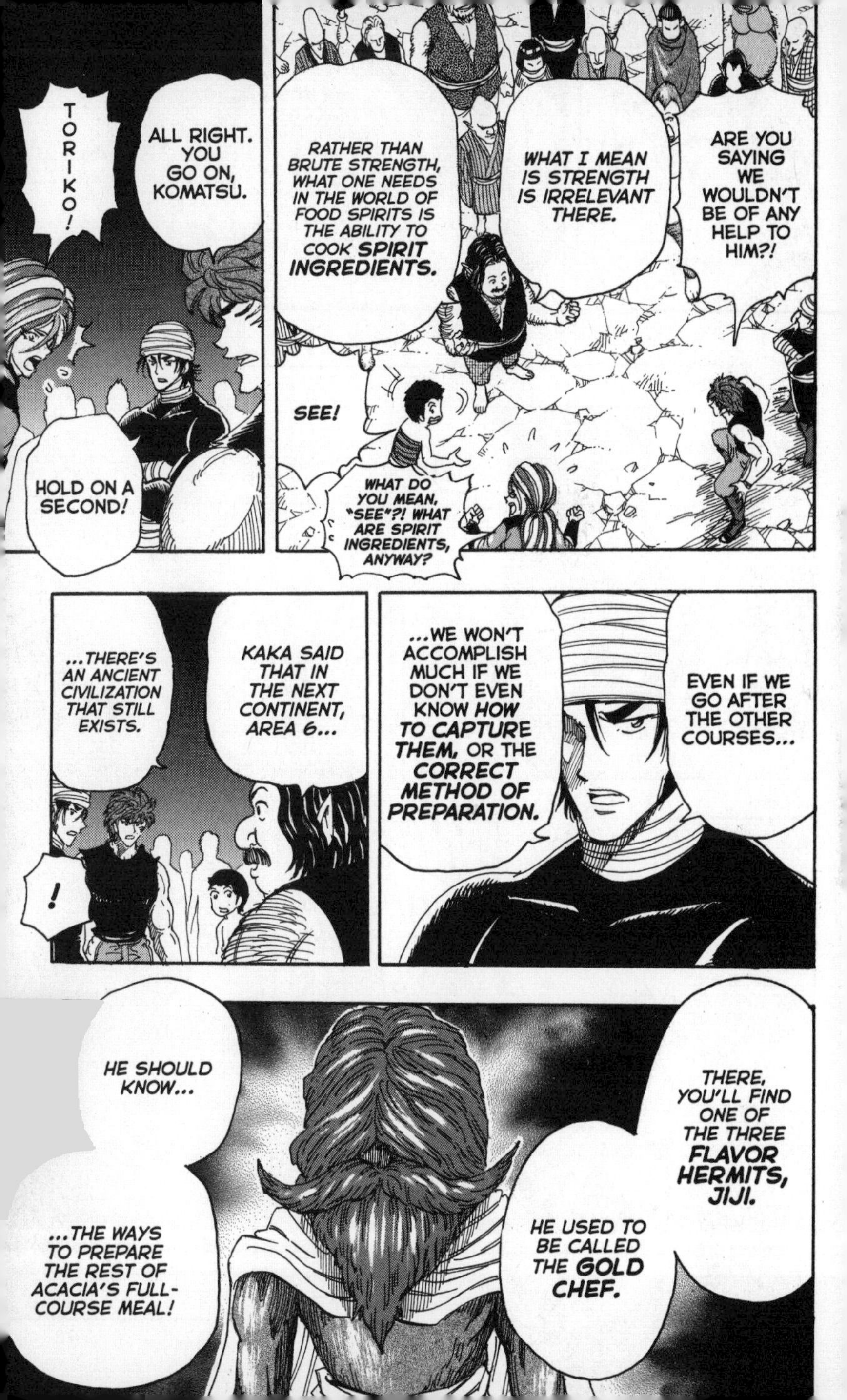
ARE YOU SAYING WE WOULDN'T BE OF ANY HELP TO HIM?!
WHAT I MEAN IS STRENGTH IS IRRELEVANT THERE.
RATHER THAN BRUTE STRENGTH, WHAT ONE NEEDS IN THE WORLD OF FOOD SPIRITS IS THE ABILITY TO COOK SPIRIT INGREDIENTS.
SEE!
WHAT DO YOU MEAN, "SEE"?! WHAT ARE SPIRIT INGREDIENTS, ANYWAY?
ALL RIGHT. YOU GO ON, KOMATSU.
TORIKO!
HOLD ON A SECOND!
EVEN IF WE GO AFTER THE OTHER COURSES...
...WE WON'T ACCOMPLISH MUCH IF WE DON'T EVEN KNOW HOW TO CAPTURE THEM, OR THE CORRECT METHOD OF PREPARATION.
KAKA SAID THAT IN THE NEXT CONTINENT, AREA 6...
...THERE'S AN ANCIENT CIVILIZATION THAT STILL EXISTS.
!
THERE, YOU'LL FIND ONE OF THE THREE FLAVOR HERMITS, JIJI.
HE USED TO BE CALLED THE GOLD CHEF.
HE SHOULD KNOW...
...THE WAYS TO PREPARE THE REST OF ACACIA'S FULL-COURSE MEAL!

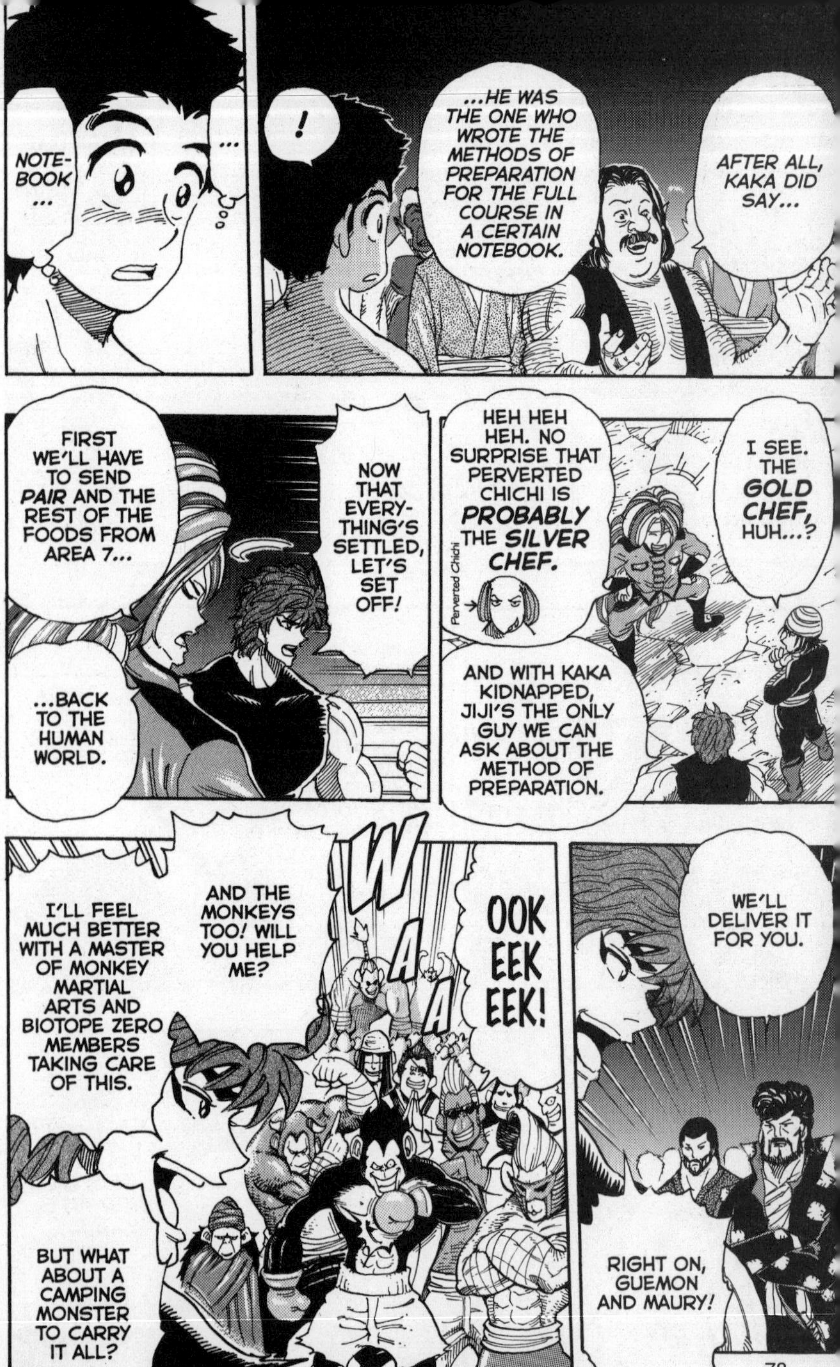
AFTER ALL, KAKA DID SAY...
...HE WAS THE ONE WHO WROTE THE METHODS OF PREPARATION FOR THE FULL COURSE IN A CERTAIN NOTEBOOK.
!
...
NOTE-BOOK ...
I SEE. THE GOLD CHEF, HUH...?
HEH HEH HEH. NO SURPRISE THAT PERVERTED CHICHI IS PROBABLY THE SILVER CHEF.
Perverted Chichi
AND WITH KAKA KIDNAPPED, JIJI'S THE ONLY GUY WE CAN ASK ABOUT THE METHOD OF PREPARATION.
NOW THAT EVERY-THING'S SETTLED, LET'S SET OFF!
FIRST WE'LL HAVE TO SEND PAIR AND THE REST OF THE FOODS FROM AREA 7...
...BACK TO THE HUMAN WORLD.
WE'LL DELIVER IT FOR YOU.
RIGHT ON, GUEMON AND MAURY!
OOK EEK EEK!
WAA
AND THE MONKEYS TOO! WILL YOU HELP ME?
I'LL FEEL MUCH BETTER WITH A MASTER OF MONKEY MARTIAL ARTS AND BIOTOPE ZERO MEMBERS TAKING CARE OF THIS.
BUT WHAT ABOUT A CAMPING MONSTER TO CARRY IT ALL?

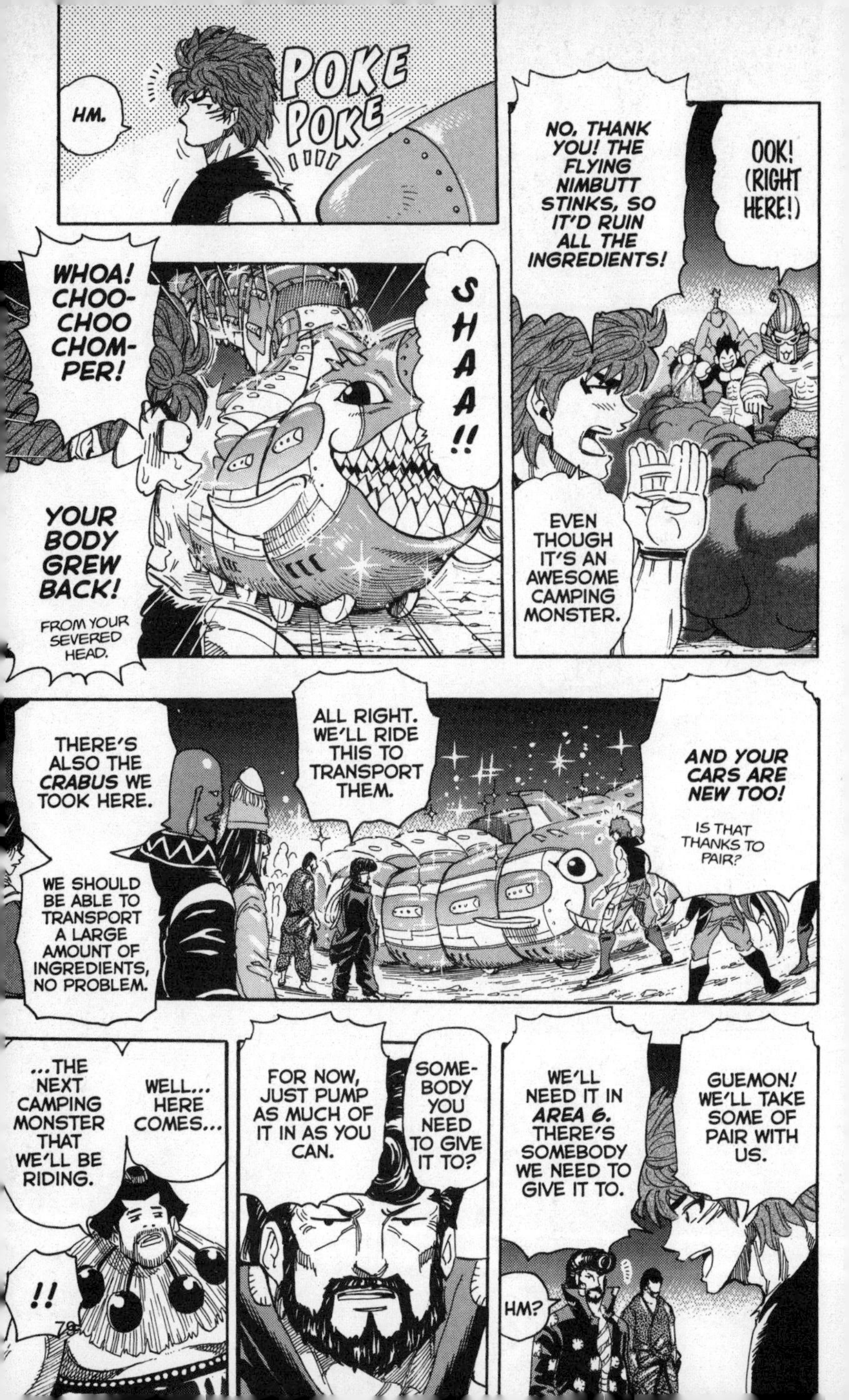
OOK! (RIGHT HERE!)
NO, THANK YOU! THE FLYING NIMBUTT STINKS, SO IT'D RUIN ALL THE INGREDIENTS!
EVEN THOUGH IT'S AN AWESOME CAMPING MONSTER.
POKE POKE
HM.
SHAAA!!
WHOA! CHOO-CHOO CHOMPER!
YOUR BODY GREW BACK!
FROM YOUR SEVERED HEAD.
AND YOUR CARS ARE NEW TOO!
IS THAT THANKS TO PAIR?
ALL RIGHT. WE'LL RIDE THIS TO TRANSPORT THEM.
THERE'S ALSO THE CRABUS WE TOOK HERE.
WE SHOULD BE ABLE TO TRANSPORT A LARGE AMOUNT OF INGREDIENTS, NO PROBLEM.
GUEMON! WE'LL TAKE SOME OF PAIR WITH US.
HM?
WE'LL NEED IT IN AREA 6. THERE'S SOMEBODY WE NEED TO GIVE IT TO.
SOMEBODY YOU NEED TO GIVE IT TO?
FOR NOW, JUST PUMP AS MUCH OF IT IN AS YOU CAN.
WELL... HERE COMES...
...THE NEXT CAMPING MONSTER THAT WE'LL BE RIDING.
!!

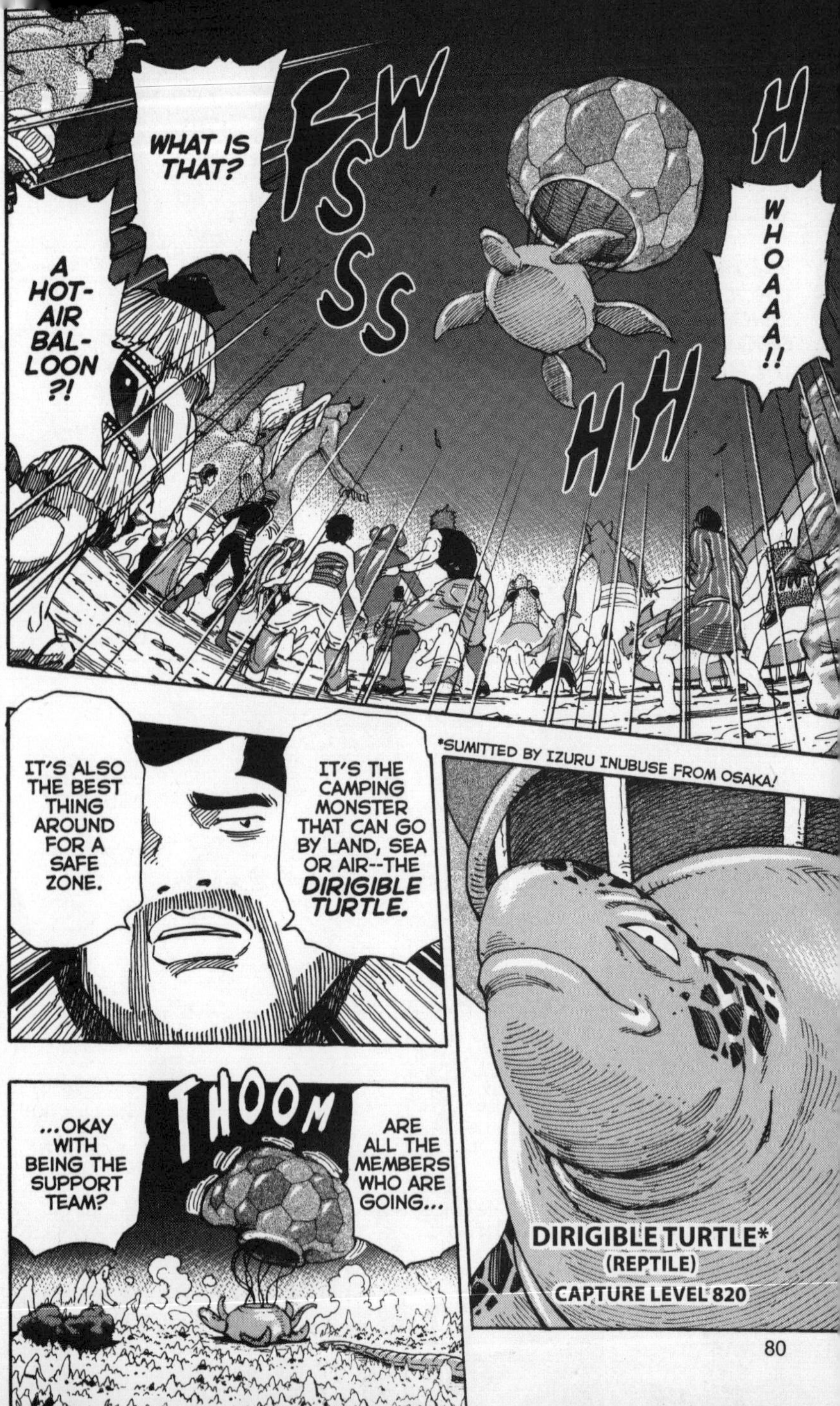
WHOAAAA!!
HHHH
FSWSSS
WHAT IS THAT?
A HOT-AIR BALLOON?!
*SUMITTED BY IZURU INUBUSE FROM OSAKA!
DIRIGIBLE TURTLE*
(REPTILE)
CAPTURE LEVEL 820
IT'S THE CAMPING MONSTER THAT CAN GO BY LAND, SEA OR AIR--THE *DIRIGIBLE TURTLE.*
IT'S ALSO THE BEST THING AROUND FOR A SAFE ZONE.
ARE ALL THE MEMBERS WHO ARE GOING...
THOOM
...OKAY WITH BEING THE SUPPORT TEAM?

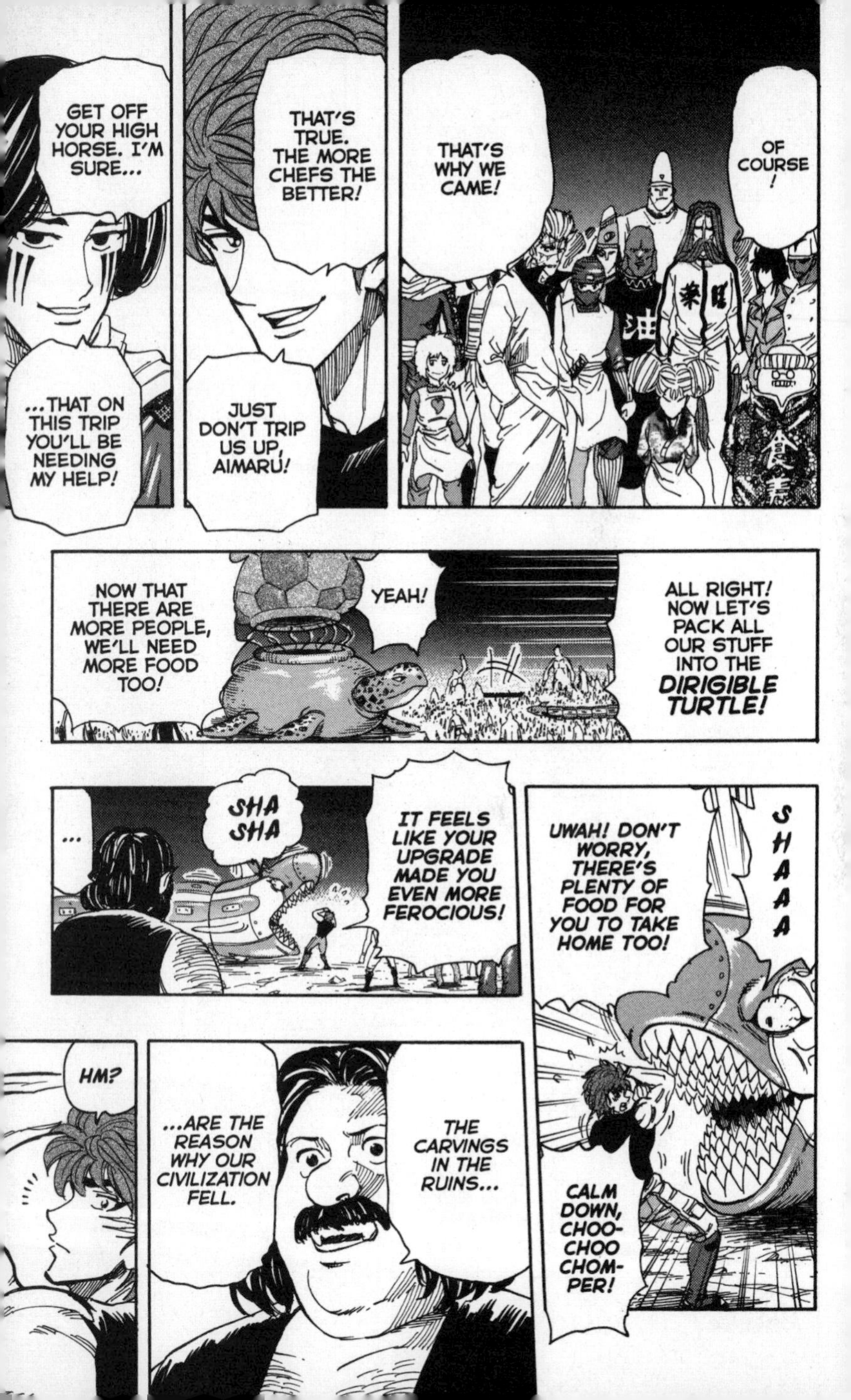
OF COURSE!
THAT'S WHY WE CAME!
THAT'S TRUE. THE MORE CHEFS THE BETTER!
JUST DON'T TRIP US UP, AIMARU!
GET OFF YOUR HIGH HORSE. I'M SURE...
...THAT ON THIS TRIP YOU'LL BE NEEDING MY HELP!
ALL RIGHT! NOW LET'S PACK ALL OUR STUFF INTO THE DIRIGIBLE TURTLE!
YEAH!
NOW THAT THERE ARE MORE PEOPLE, WE'LL NEED MORE FOOD TOO!
SHAAAA
UWAH! DON'T WORRY, THERE'S PLENTY OF FOOD FOR YOU TO TAKE HOME TOO!
CALM DOWN, CHOO-CHOO CHOMPER!
IT FEELS LIKE YOUR UPGRADE MADE YOU EVEN MORE FEROCIOUS!
SHA SHA
...
THE CARVINGS IN THE RUINS...
...ARE THE REASON WHY OUR CIVILIZATION FELL.
HM?

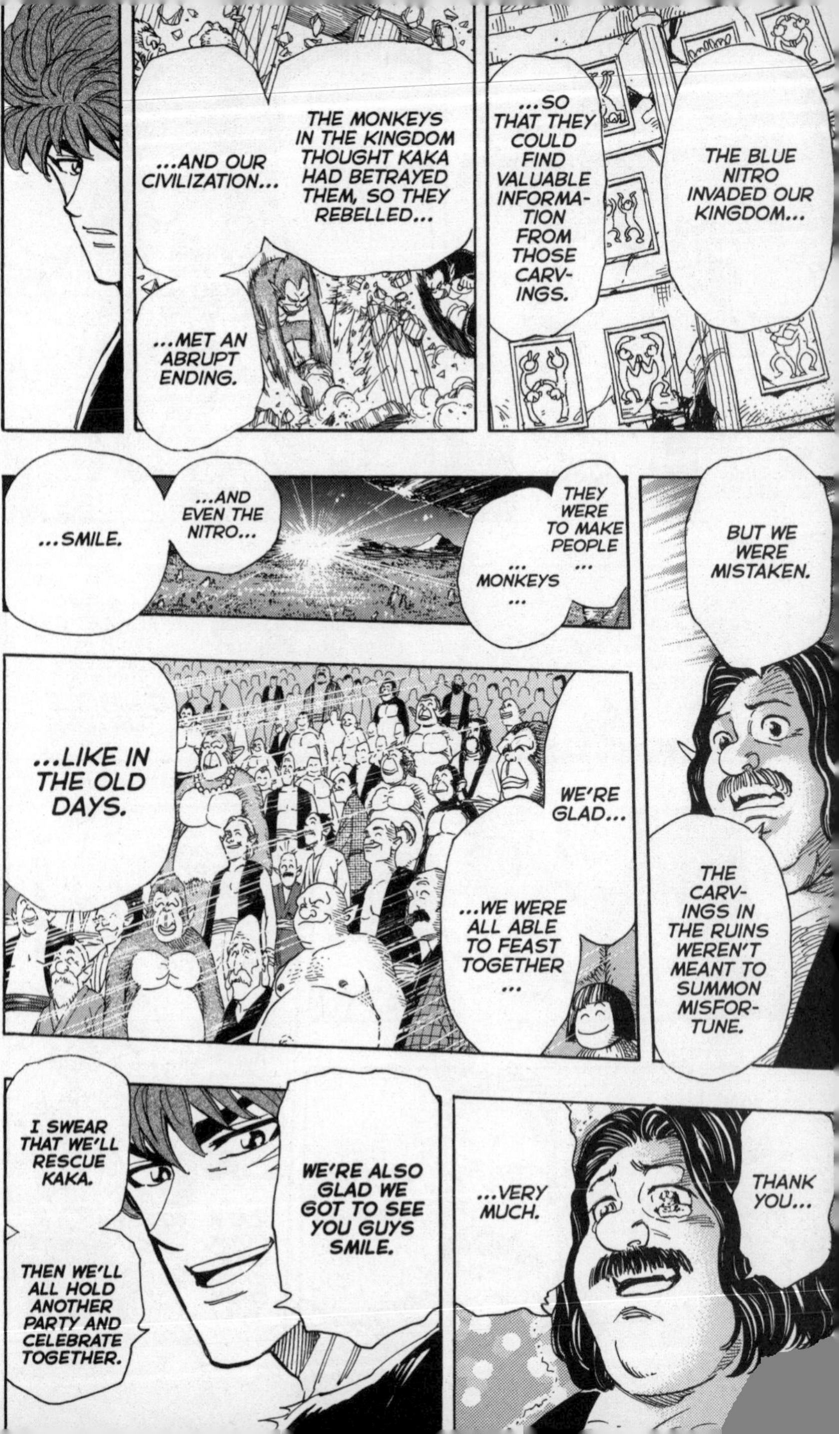
THE BLUE NITRO INVADED OUR KINGDOM...
...SO THAT THEY COULD FIND VALUABLE INFORMATION FROM THOSE CARVINGS.
THE MONKEYS IN THE KINGDOM THOUGHT KAKA HAD BETRAYED THEM, SO THEY REBELLED...
...AND OUR CIVILIZATION...
...MET AN ABRUPT ENDING.
BUT WE WERE MISTAKEN.
THE CARVINGS IN THE RUINS WEREN'T MEANT TO SUMMON MISFORTUNE.
THEY WERE TO MAKE PEOPLE ... ... MONKEYS ...
...AND EVEN THE NITRO...
...SMILE.
WE'RE GLAD...
...WE WERE ALL ABLE TO FEAST TOGETHER ...
...LIKE IN THE OLD DAYS.
THANK YOU...
...VERY MUCH.
WE'RE ALSO GLAD WE GOT TO SEE YOU GUYS SMILE.
I SWEAR THAT WE'LL RESCUE KAKA.
THEN WE'LL ALL HOLD ANOTHER PARTY AND CELEBRATE TOGETHER.

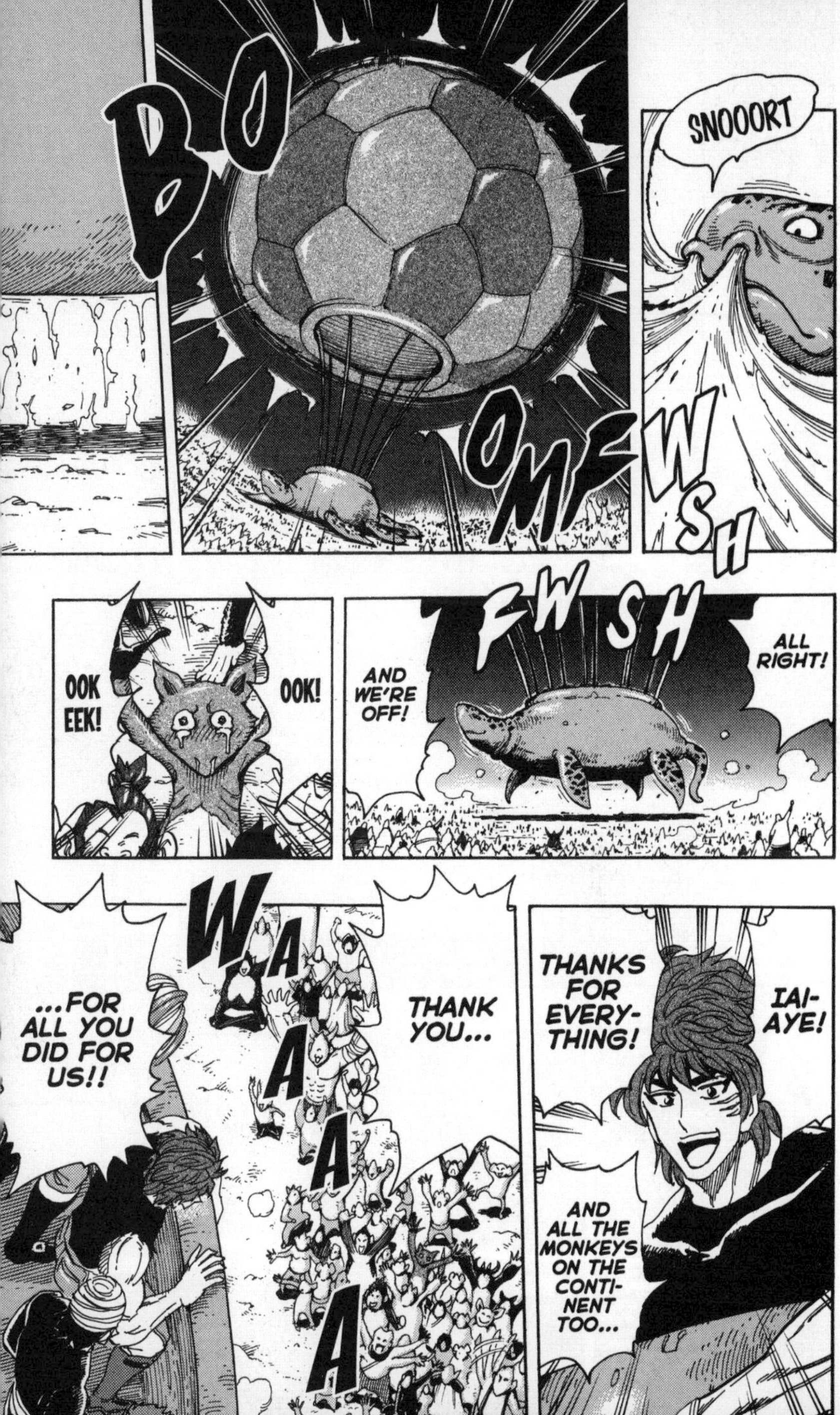
SNOOORT
WSH
BO
OMF
FWSH
ALL RIGHT!
AND WE'RE OFF!
OOK!
OOK EEK!
IAI-AYE!
THANKS FOR EVERY-THING!
AND ALL THE MONKEYS ON THE CONTI-NENT TOO...
THANK YOU...
WAAAAA
...FOR ALL YOU DID FOR US!!

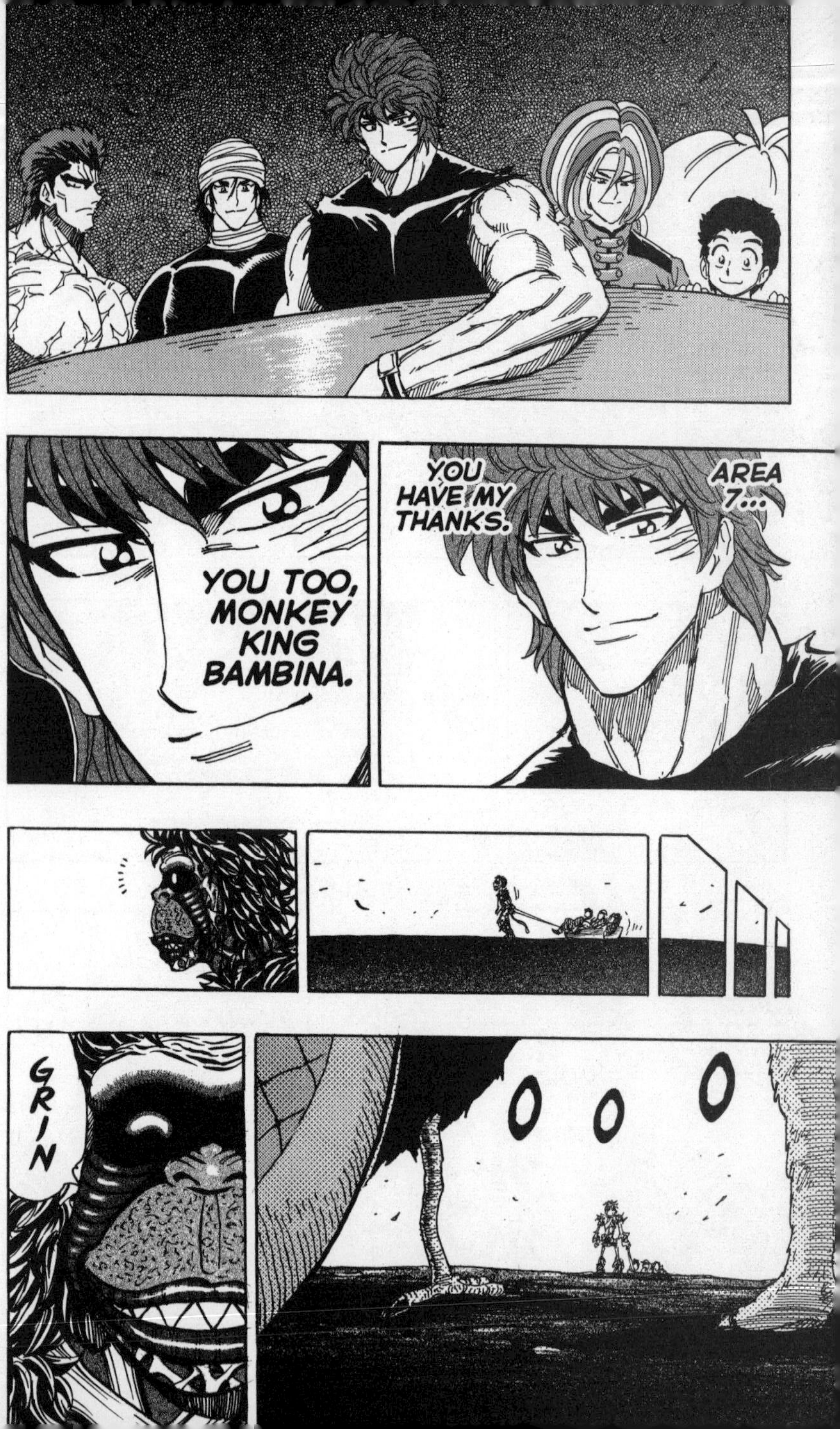
AREA 7...
YOU HAVE MY THANKS.
YOU TOO, MONKEY KING BAMBINA.
GRIN

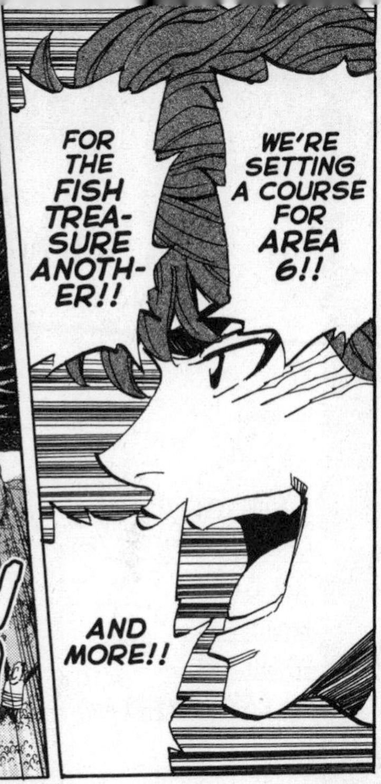
WE'RE SETTING A COURSE FOR AREA 6!!
FOR THE FISH TREA-SURE ANOTH-ER!!
AND MORE!!

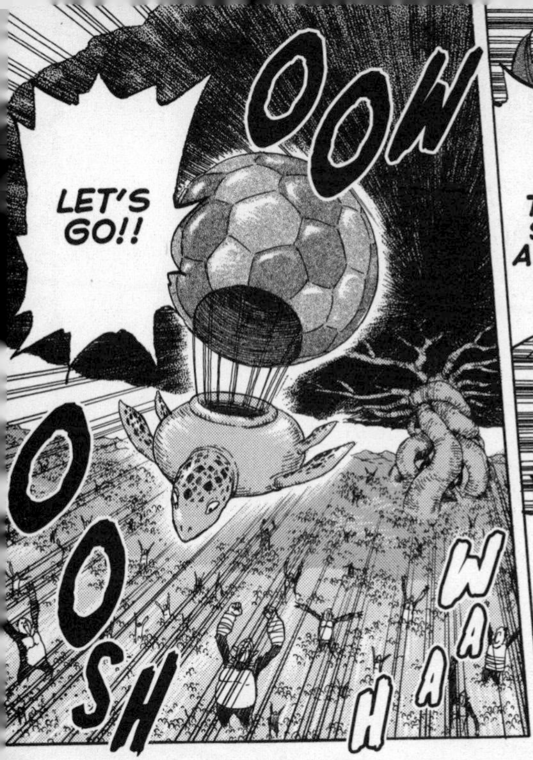
OOOW
LET'S GO!!
OOOSH
WAAH

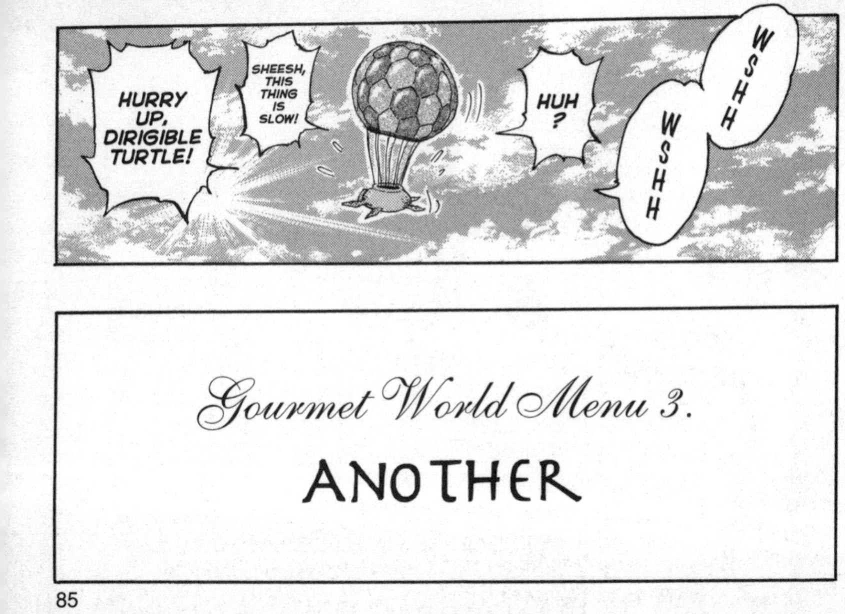
WSHH
WSHH
HUH?
SHEESH, THIS THING IS SLOW!
HURRY UP, DIRIGIBLE TURTLE!

Gourmet World Menu 3.

ANOTHER

TORIKO

GOURMET CHECKLIST

Vol. 354

BILLION BIRD
(UNLIMITED BIRD)

CAPTURE LEVEL: LESS THAN 1

HABITAT: EXTINCT

SIZE: 45 CM

HEIGHT: ---

WEIGHT: 8 KG

PRICE: 5 YEN PER BIRD

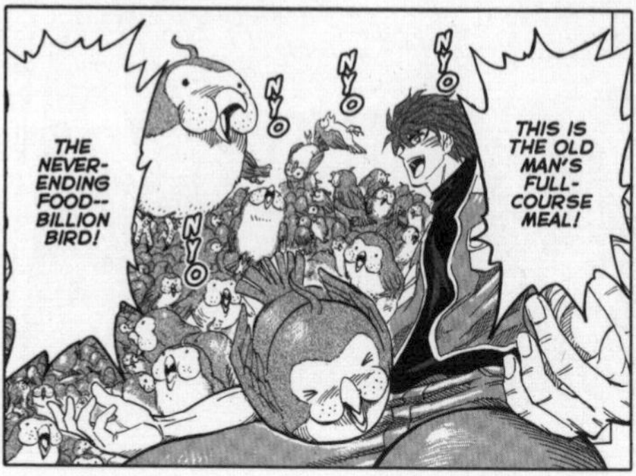
THIS IS THE OLD MAN'S FULL-COURSE MEAL!
NYO
NYO
NYO
NYO
THE NEVER-ENDING FOOD-- BILLION BIRD!

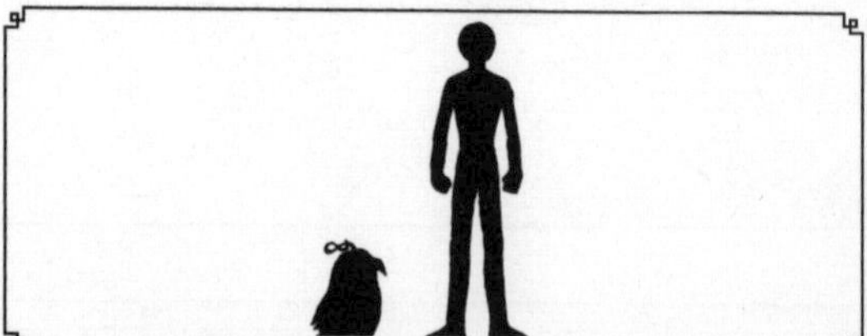

SCALE

THIS IS A MYSTERIOUS BIRD THAT INHABITED THE GOURMET WORLD LONG AGO AND WAS THE MAIN DISH OF IGO PRESIDENT ICHIRYU'S FULL COURSE. ITS ENTIRE BODY IS EDIBLE, AND ONCE IT HAS HATCHED, IT WILL REPRODUCE NO MATTER WHAT THE ENVIRONMENT WITH INFINITE EGGS THAT HAVE BEEN FERTILIZED THROUGH APOGAMY. IT'S ALSO SAID TO HAVE A LIFESPAN OF SEVERAL THOUSAND IF NOT HUNDREDS OF THOUSANDS OF YEARS AND IS KNOWN AS THE "BIRD YOU CAN EAT FOR EONS," MAKING IT PRIZED LONG AGO AS THE KING OF LIVESTOCK. IN THE AGE OF GOURMET, WHERE EVERYONE WAS ALREADY VERY SATIATED, IT WAS FORGOTTEN DUE TO ITS BLAND FLAVOR, BUT ONCE THE FOOD SHORTAGE HIT, IT WAS THE INGREDIENT THAT BROUGHT THE JOY OF EATING BACK TO MANKIND.

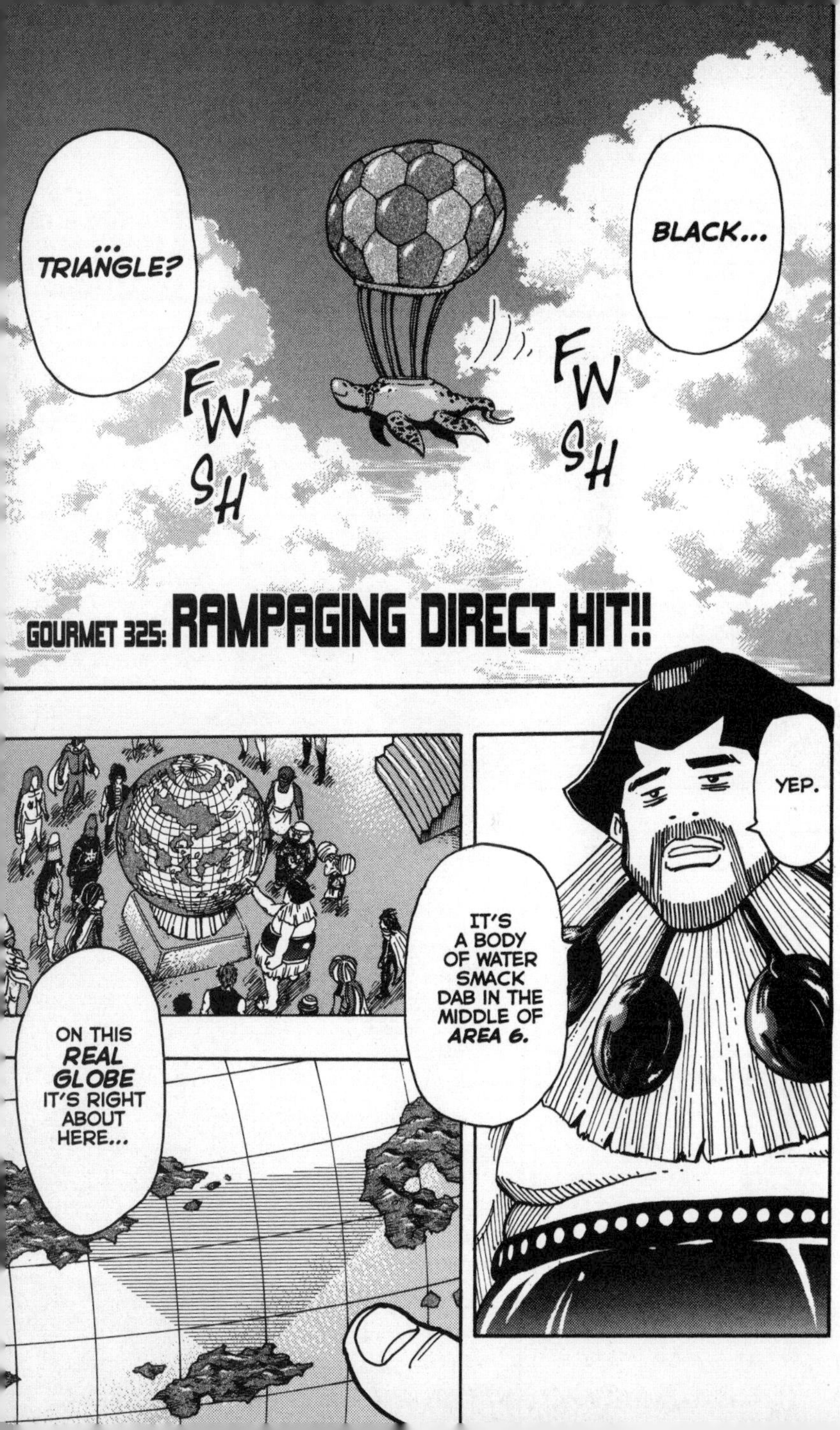
BLACK...
...TRIANGLE?
FWSH
FWSH
GOURMET 325: RAMPAGING DIRECT HIT!!
YEP.
IT'S A BODY OF WATER SMACK DAB IN THE MIDDLE OF AREA 6.
ON THIS REAL GLOBE IT'S RIGHT ABOUT HERE...

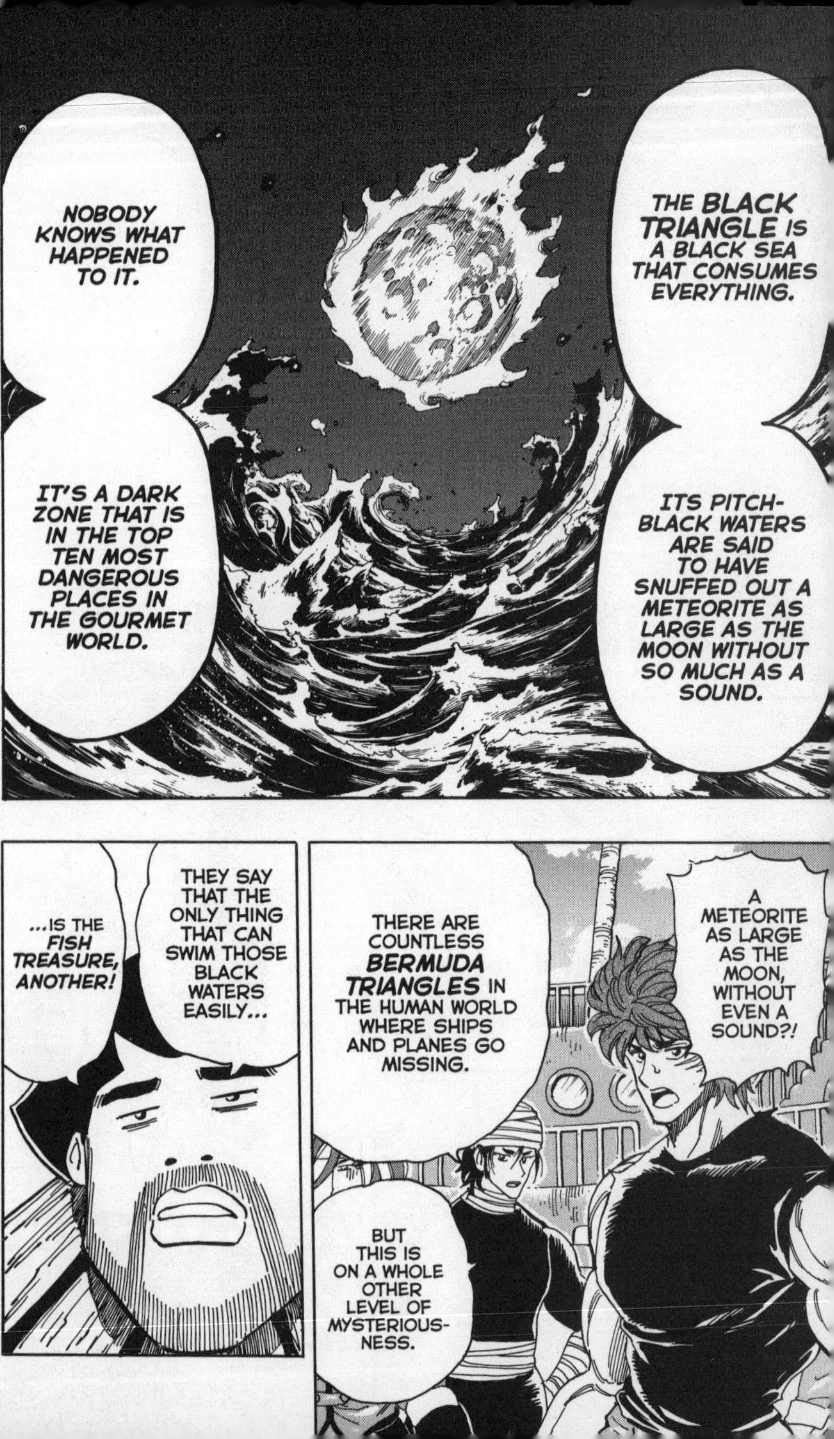

THE BLACK TRIANGLE IS A BLACK SEA THAT CONSUMES EVERYTHING.
ITS PITCH-BLACK WATERS ARE SAID TO HAVE SNUFFED OUT A METEORITE AS LARGE AS THE MOON WITHOUT SO MUCH AS A SOUND.
NOBODY KNOWS WHAT HAPPENED TO IT.
IT'S A DARK ZONE THAT IS IN THE TOP TEN MOST DANGEROUS PLACES IN THE GOURMET WORLD.
A METEORITE AS LARGE AS THE MOON, WITHOUT EVEN A SOUND?!
THERE ARE COUNTLESS BERMUDA TRIANGLES IN THE HUMAN WORLD WHERE SHIPS AND PLANES GO MISSING.
BUT THIS IS ON A WHOLE OTHER LEVEL OF MYSTERIOUS-NESS.
THEY SAY THAT THE ONLY THING THAT CAN SWIM THOSE BLACK WATERS EASILY...
...IS THE FISH TREASURE, ANOTHER!

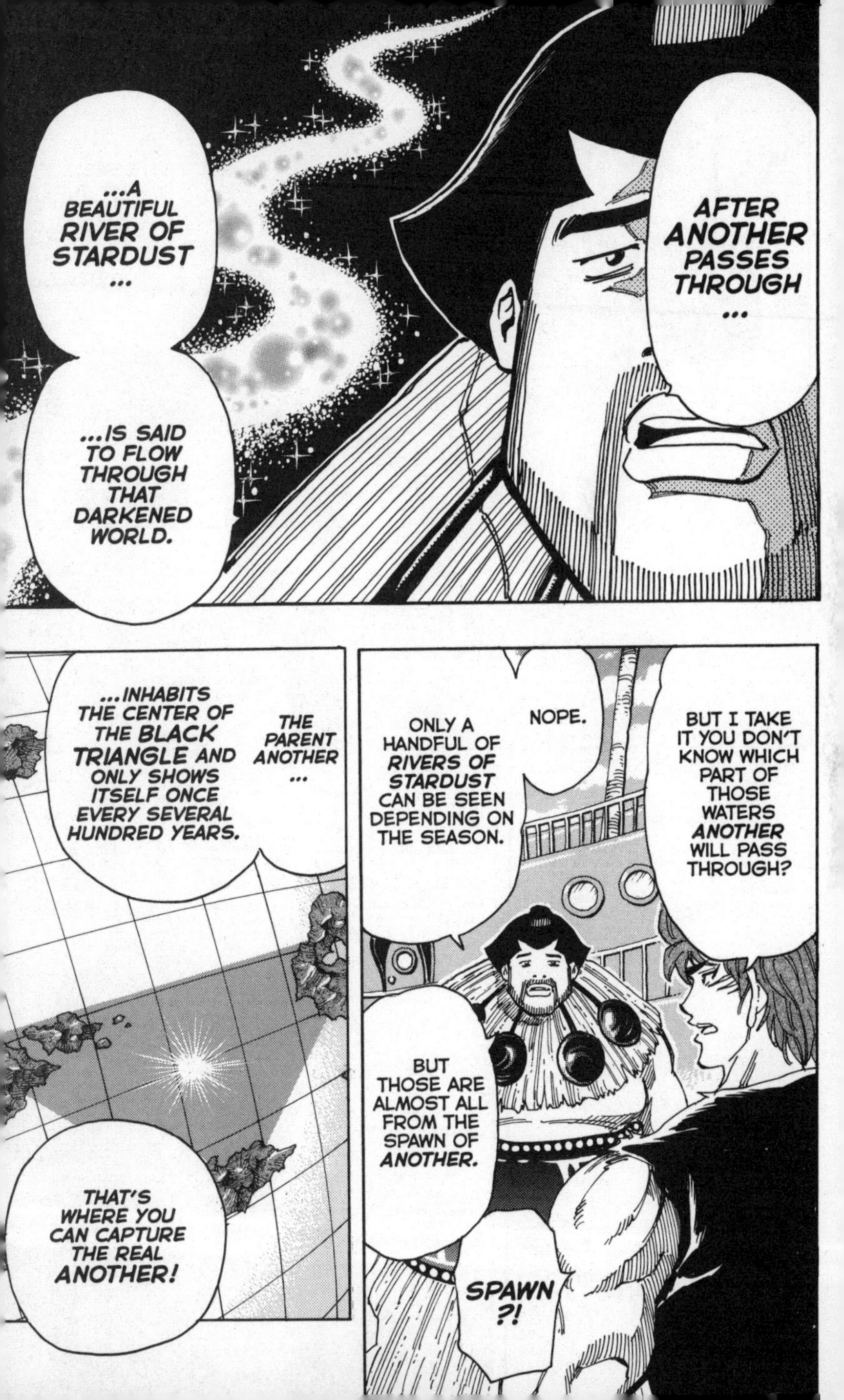
AFTER ANOTHER PASSES THROUGH...
...A BEAUTIFUL RIVER OF STARDUST...
...IS SAID TO FLOW THROUGH THAT DARKENED WORLD.
BUT I TAKE IT YOU DON'T KNOW WHICH PART OF THOSE WATERS ANOTHER WILL PASS THROUGH?
NOPE.
ONLY A HANDFUL OF RIVERS OF STARDUST CAN BE SEEN DEPENDING ON THE SEASON.
BUT THOSE ARE ALMOST ALL FROM THE SPAWN OF ANOTHER.
SPAWN?!
THE PARENT ANOTHER...
...INHABITS THE CENTER OF THE BLACK TRIANGLE AND ONLY SHOWS ITSELF ONCE EVERY SEVERAL HUNDRED YEARS.
THAT'S WHERE YOU CAN CAPTURE THE REAL ANOTHER!

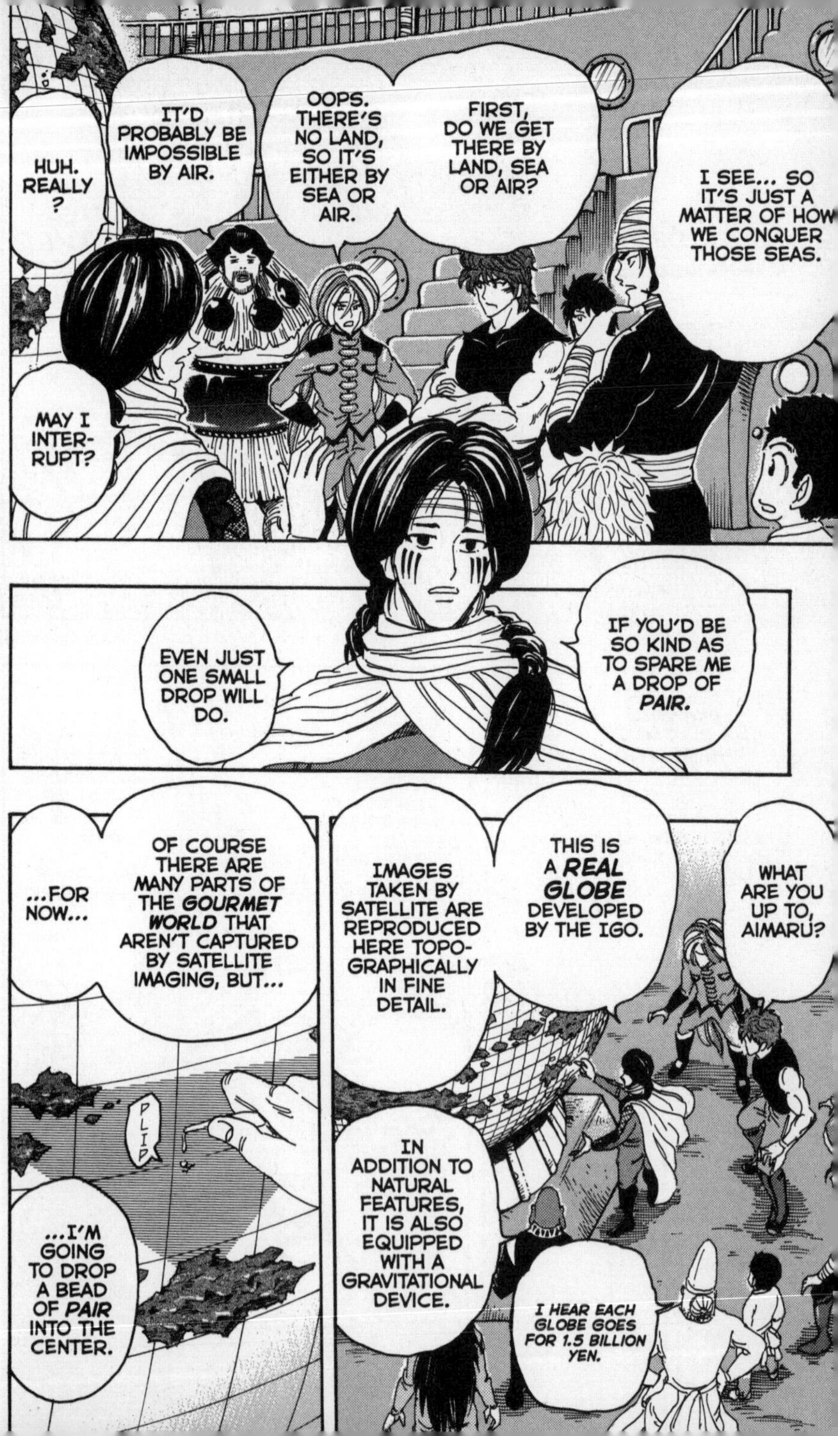

I SEE... SO IT'S JUST A MATTER OF HOW WE CONQUER THOSE SEAS.
FIRST, DO WE GET THERE BY LAND, SEA OR AIR?
OOPS. THERE'S NO LAND, SO IT'S EITHER BY SEA OR AIR.
IT'D PROBABLY BE IMPOSSIBLE BY AIR.
HUH. REALLY?
MAY I INTERRUPT?
IF YOU'D BE SO KIND AS TO SPARE ME A DROP OF *PAIR.*
EVEN JUST ONE SMALL DROP WILL DO.
WHAT ARE YOU UP TO, AIMARU?
THIS IS A *REAL GLOBE* DEVELOPED BY THE IGO.
IMAGES TAKEN BY SATELLITE ARE REPRODUCED HERE TOPOGRAPHICALLY IN FINE DETAIL.
IN ADDITION TO NATURAL FEATURES, IT IS ALSO EQUIPPED WITH A GRAVITATIONAL DEVICE.
I HEAR EACH GLOBE GOES FOR 1.5 BILLION YEN.
OF COURSE THERE ARE MANY PARTS OF THE *GOURMET WORLD* THAT AREN'T CAPTURED BY SATELLITE IMAGING, BUT...
...FOR NOW...
PLIP
...I'M GOING TO DROP A BEAD OF *PAIR* INTO THE CENTER.

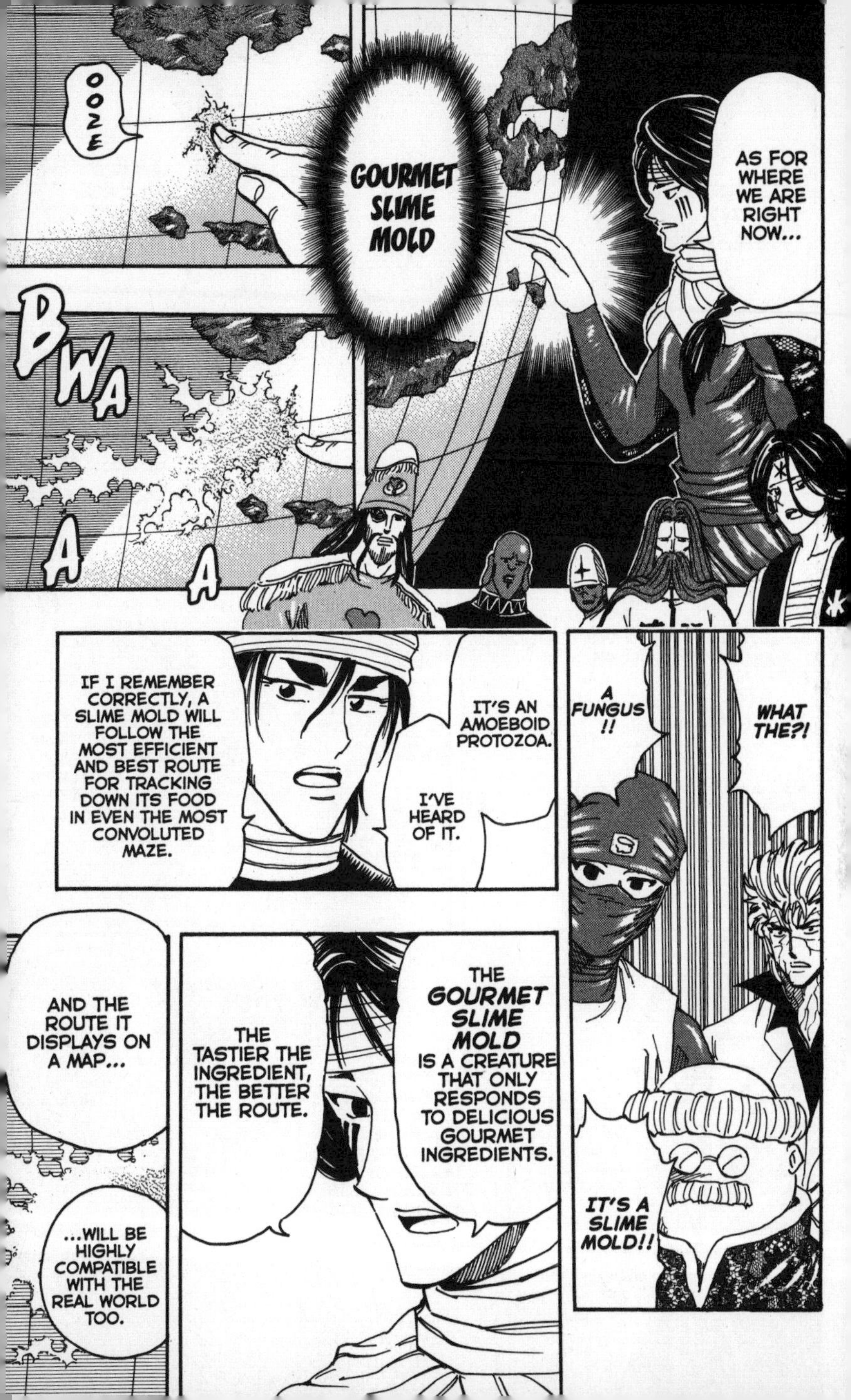
AS FOR WHERE WE ARE RIGHT NOW...
GOURMET SLIME MOLD
OOZE
BWAAA
WHAT THE?!
A FUNGUS!!
IT'S A SLIME MOLD!!
IT'S AN AMOEBOID PROTOZOA.
I'VE HEARD OF IT.
IF I REMEMBER CORRECTLY, A SLIME MOLD WILL FOLLOW THE MOST EFFICIENT AND BEST ROUTE FOR TRACKING DOWN ITS FOOD IN EVEN THE MOST CONVOLUTED MAZE.
THE GOURMET SLIME MOLD IS A CREATURE THAT ONLY RESPONDS TO DELICIOUS GOURMET INGREDIENTS.
THE TASTIER THE INGREDIENT, THE BETTER THE ROUTE.
AND THE ROUTE IT DISPLAYS ON A MAP...
...WILL BE HIGHLY COMPATIBLE WITH THE REAL WORLD TOO.

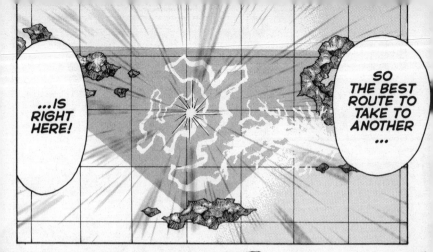

SO THE BEST ROUTE TO TAKE TO ANOTHER ...
...IS RIGHT HERE!
FOR REAL ?!
IF WE KNEW THE EXACT LOCATION OF THE OTHER ITEMS IN THE FULL COURSE MEAL, COULDN'T WE USE THIS TO MAP A ROUTE TO THEM?
IF THIS IS TRUE, THEN THAT'S AMAZING, AIMARU!
OF COURSE! IF WE KNEW WHERE THEY WERE, THAT IS.
MANIPULATING FUNGUS IS A MYSTERIOUS ABILITY.
IT PROBABLY HAS LOTS OF USES IN THE PREPARATION OF NONPERISHABLE INGREDIENTS TOO.
WHAT A FITTING ABILITY FOR A GOURMET KNIGHT WHO PREACHES A SIMPLE DIET.
THERE ARE ALSO SOME FUNGI THAT CAN HAVE AN EFFECT ON THE BRAINS OF LIVING THINGS.
THERE'S A TYPE OF MUSHROOM THAT CAN PARASITIZE THE HEADS OF ANTS, TAKING OVER THEIR NERVOUS SYSTEMS TO CONTROL THEM.
THERE EXISTS A DARK ART THAT USES THAT ABILITY IN COOKING.

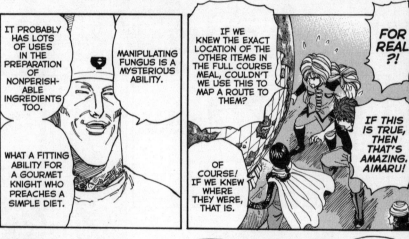

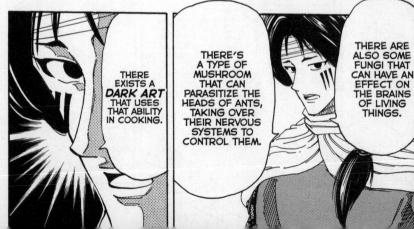

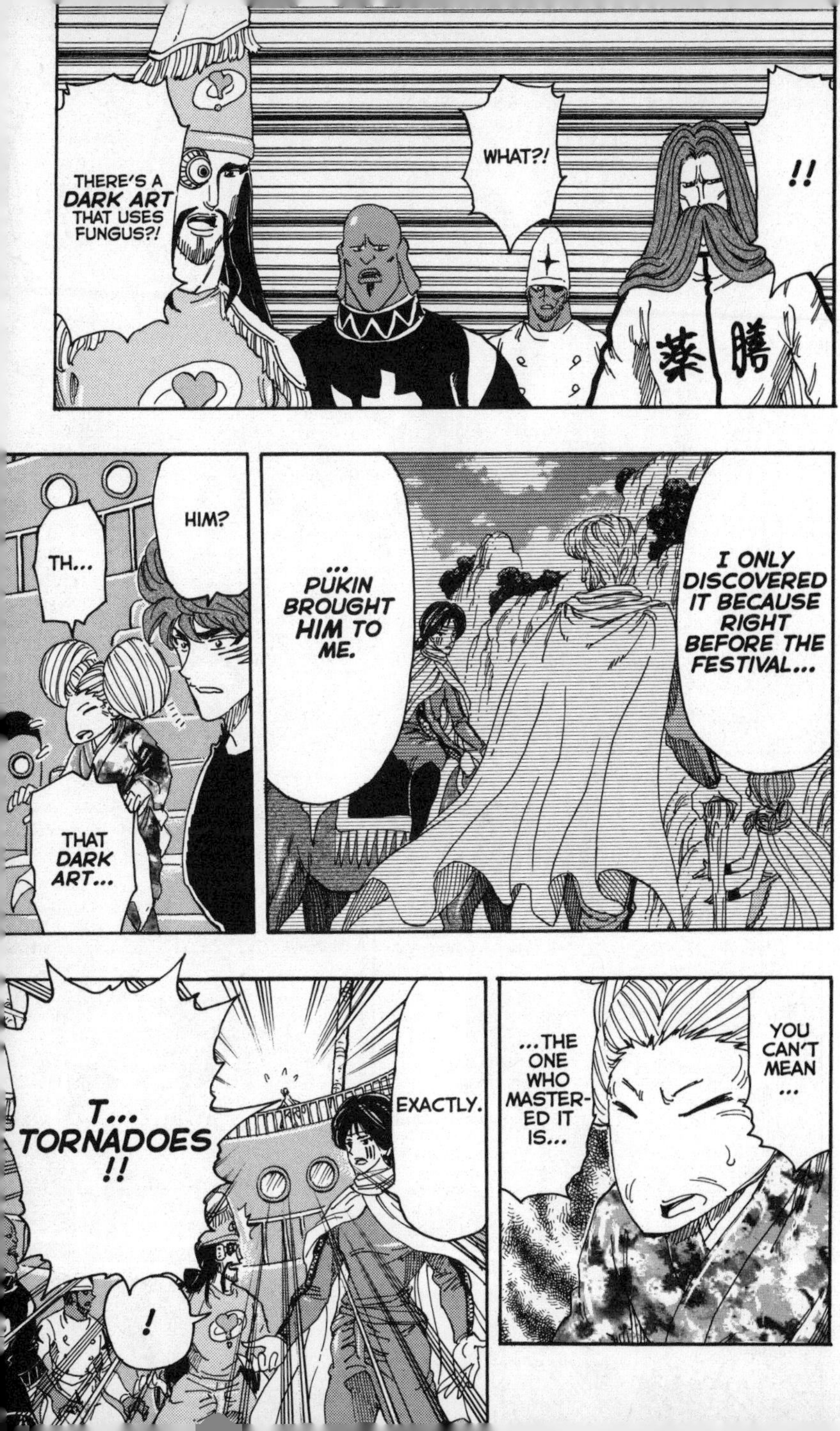
!!
WHAT?!
THERE'S A DARK ART THAT USES FUNGUS?!
I ONLY DISCOVERED IT BECAUSE RIGHT BEFORE THE FESTIVAL...
...PŪKIN BROUGHT HIM TO ME.
HIM?
TH...
THAT DARK ART...
YOU CAN'T MEAN ...
...THE ONE WHO MASTERED IT IS...
EXACTLY.
T... TORNADOES !!
!

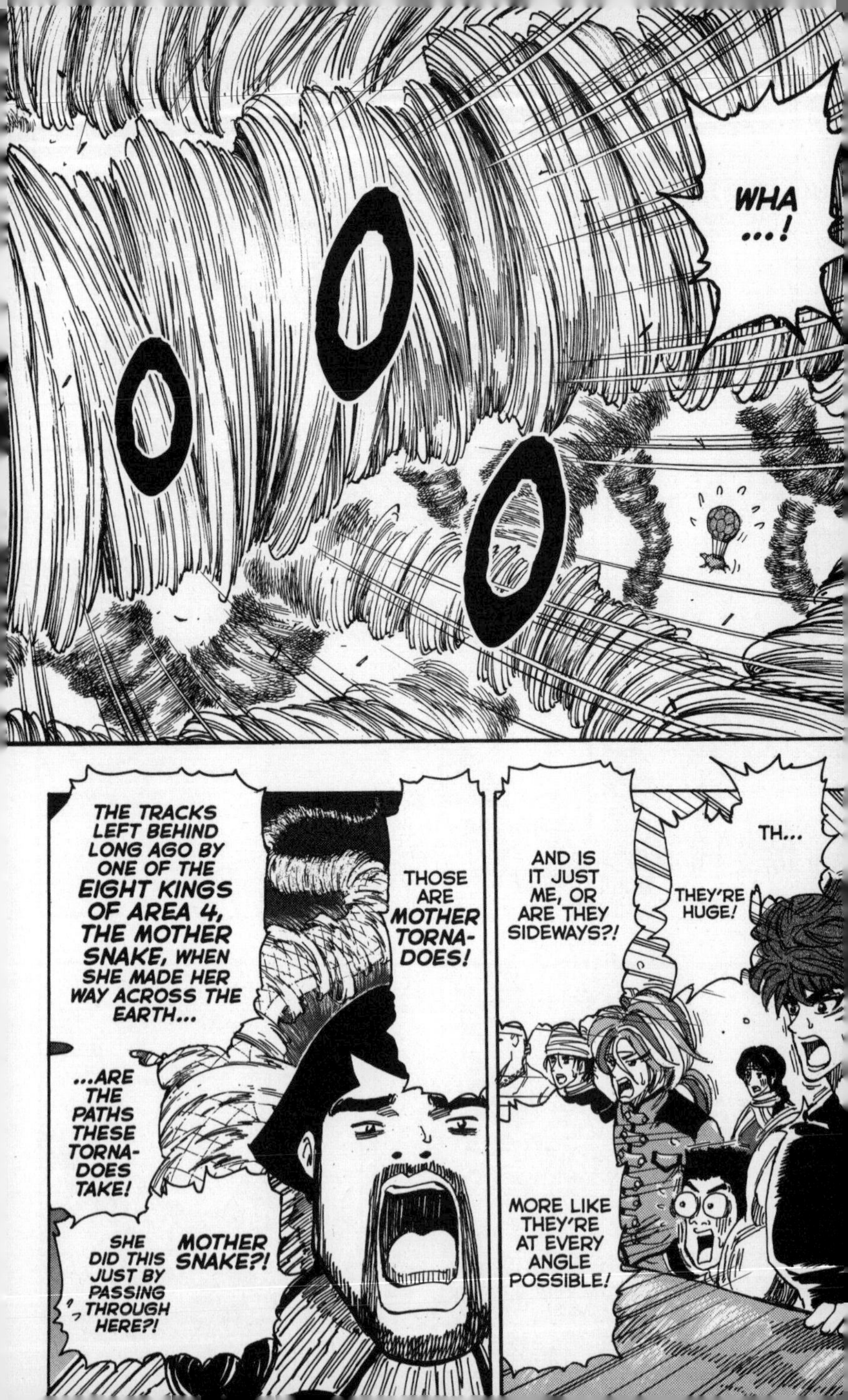
WHA...!
TH...
THEY'RE HUGE!
AND IS IT JUST ME, OR ARE THEY SIDEWAYS?!
MORE LIKE THEY'RE AT EVERY ANGLE POSSIBLE!
THOSE ARE MOTHER TORNADOES!
THE TRACKS LEFT BEHIND LONG AGO BY ONE OF THE EIGHT KINGS OF AREA 4, THE MOTHER SNAKE, WHEN SHE MADE HER WAY ACROSS THE EARTH...
...ARE THE PATHS THESE TORNADOES TAKE!
MOTHER SNAKE?!
SHE DID THIS JUST BY PASSING THROUGH HERE?!

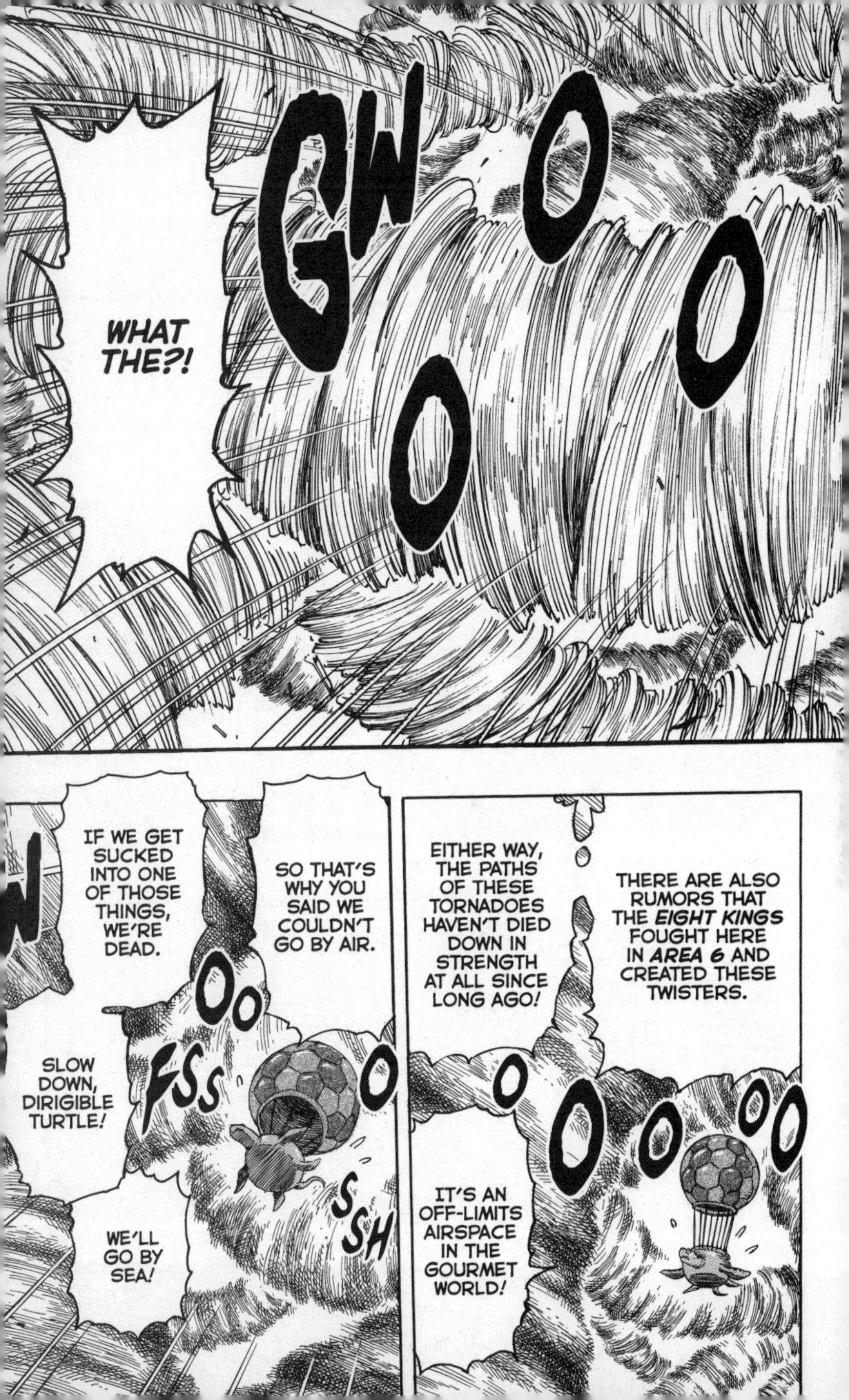
GWOOOO
WHAT THE?!
THERE ARE ALSO RUMORS THAT THE *EIGHT KINGS* FOUGHT HERE IN *AREA 6* AND CREATED THESE TWISTERS.
EITHER WAY, THE PATHS OF THESE TORNADOES HAVEN'T DIED DOWN IN STRENGTH AT ALL SINCE LONG AGO!
OOOOOO
IT'S AN OFF-LIMITS AIRSPACE IN THE GOURMET WORLD!
SO THAT'S WHY YOU SAID WE COULDN'T GO BY AIR.
IF WE GET SUCKED INTO ONE OF THOSE THINGS, WE'RE DEAD.
OOO
FSSSSH
SLOW DOWN, DIRIGIBLE TURTLE!
WE'LL GO BY SEA!

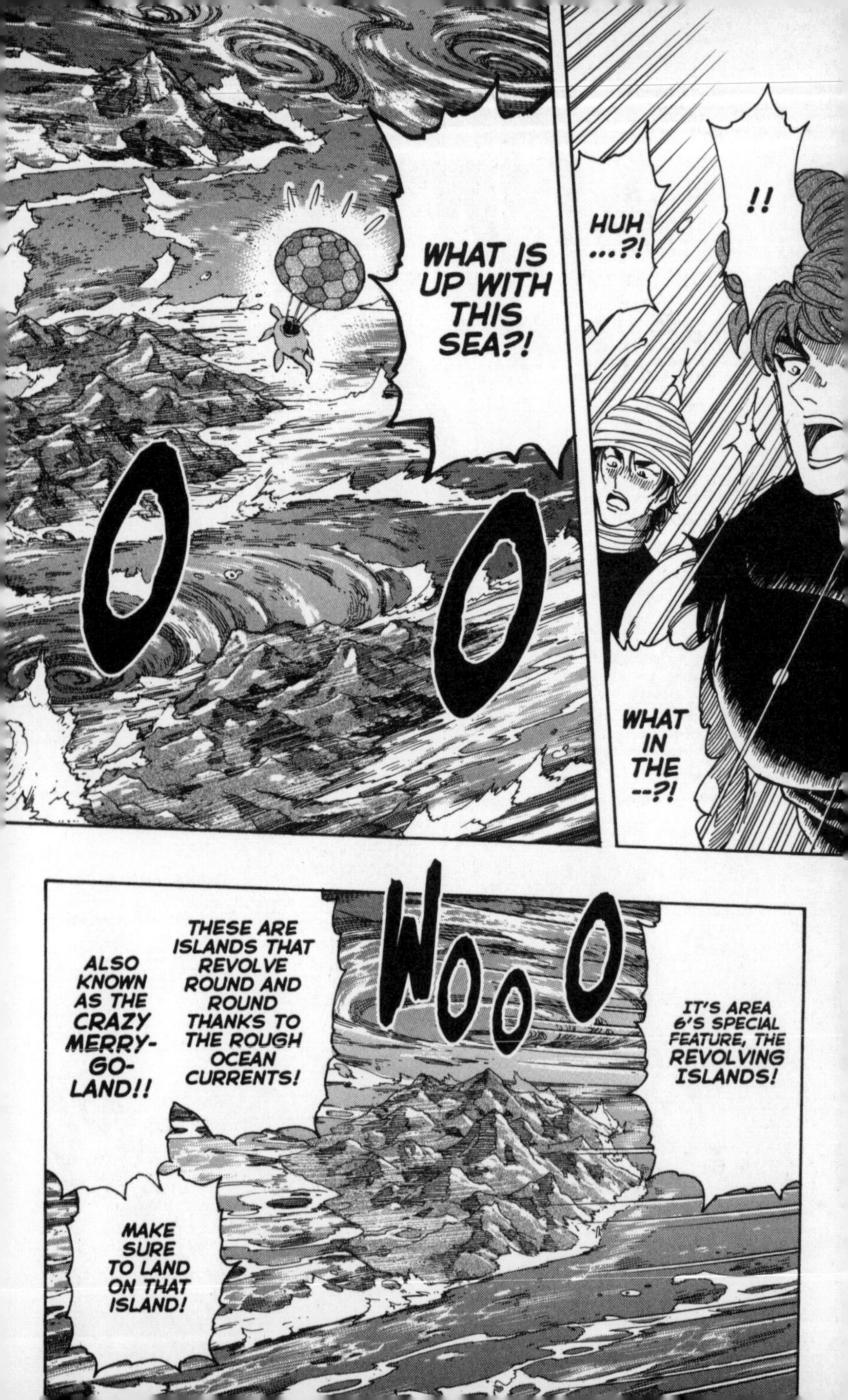
!!
HUH ...?!
WHAT IN THE --?!
WHAT IS UP WITH THIS SEA?!
OO
IT'S AREA 6'S SPECIAL FEATURE, THE REVOLVING ISLANDS!
WOOOO
THESE ARE ISLANDS THAT REVOLVE ROUND AND ROUND THANKS TO THE ROUGH OCEAN CURRENTS!
ALSO KNOWN AS THE CRAZY MERRY-GO-LAND!!
MAKE SURE TO LAND ON THAT ISLAND!

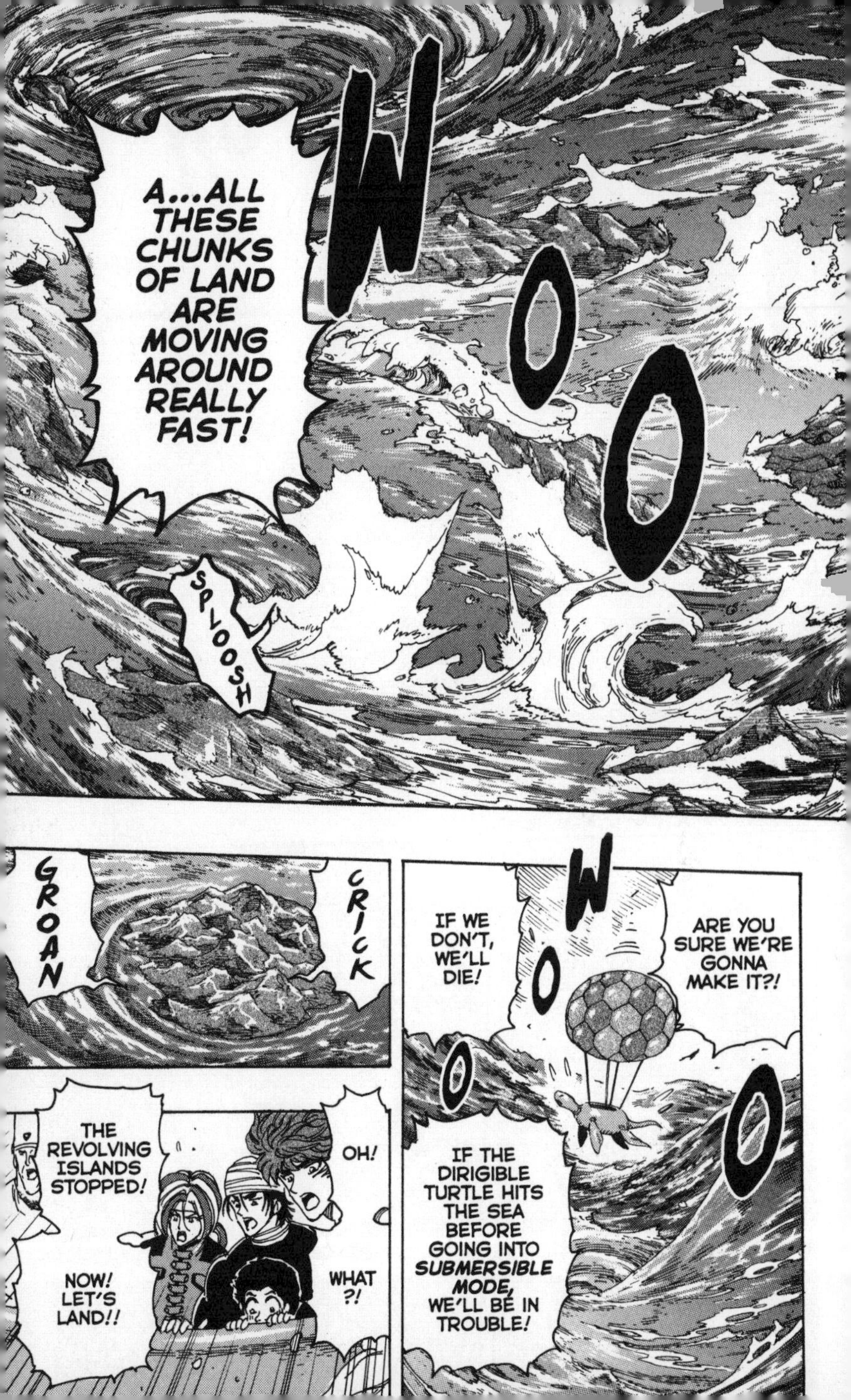
A...ALL THESE CHUNKS OF LAND ARE MOVING AROUND REALLY FAST!
WOOO
SPLOOSH
WOOOO
ARE YOU SURE WE'RE GONNA MAKE IT?!
IF WE DON'T, WE'LL DIE!
IF THE DIRIGIBLE TURTLE HITS THE SEA BEFORE GOING INTO *SUBMERSIBLE MODE,* WE'LL BE IN TROUBLE!
CRICK
GROAN
OH!
THE REVOLVING ISLANDS STOPPED!
WHAT?!
NOW! LET'S LAND!!

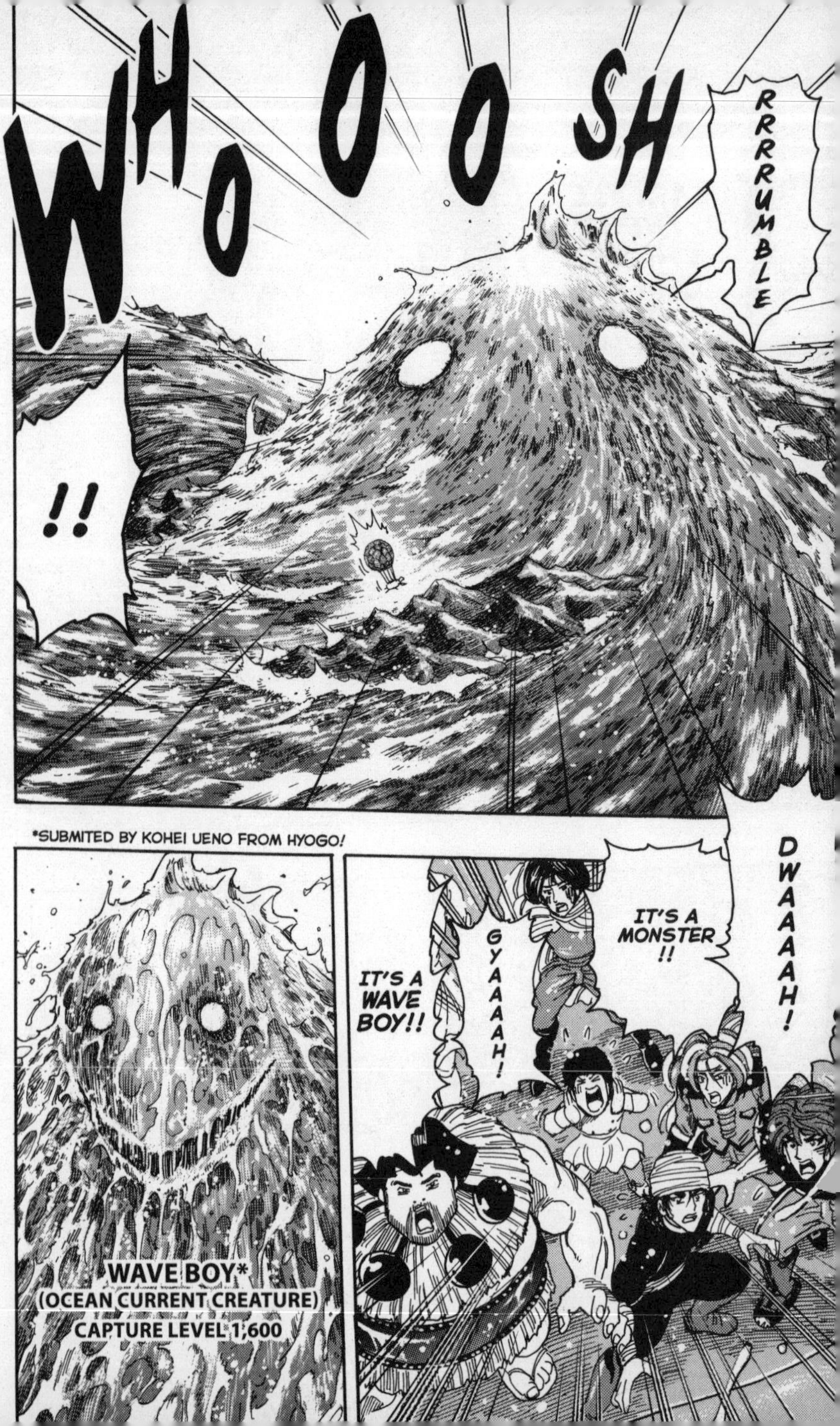

RRRRUMBLE
WHOOOSH
!!
DWAAAAAAH!
IT'S A MONSTER!!
GYAAAAAH!
IT'S A WAVE BOY!!
WAVE BOY*
(OCEAN CURRENT CREATURE)
CAPTURE LEVEL 1,600
*SUBMITED BY KOHEI UENO FROM HYOGO!

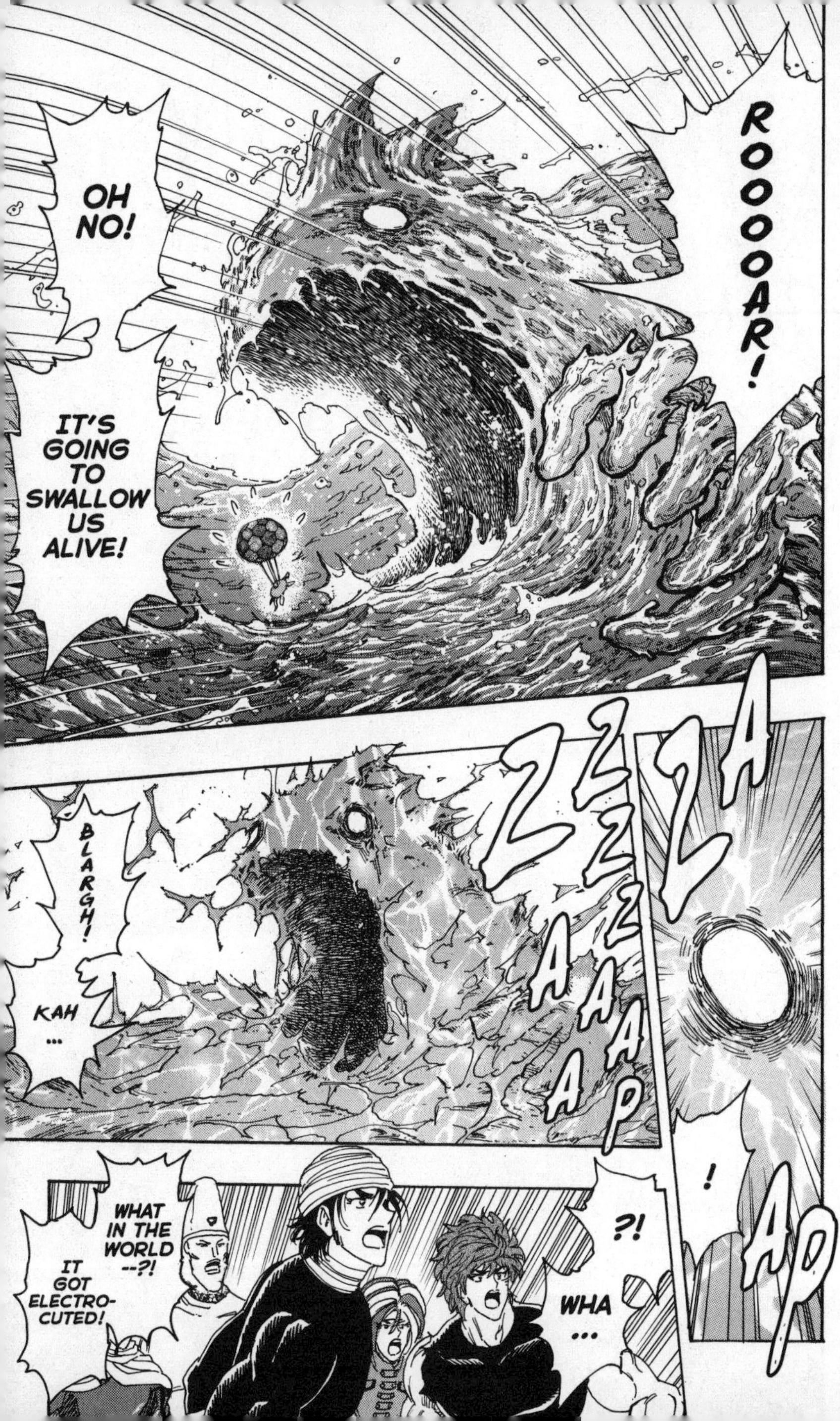
ROOOOOAR!
OH NO!
IT'S GOING TO SWALLOW US ALIVE!
ZZA
ZZZZZAAAAAP
BLARGH!
KAH...
!
AP
?!
WHA...
WHAT IN THE WORLD--?!
IT GOT ELECTROCUTED!

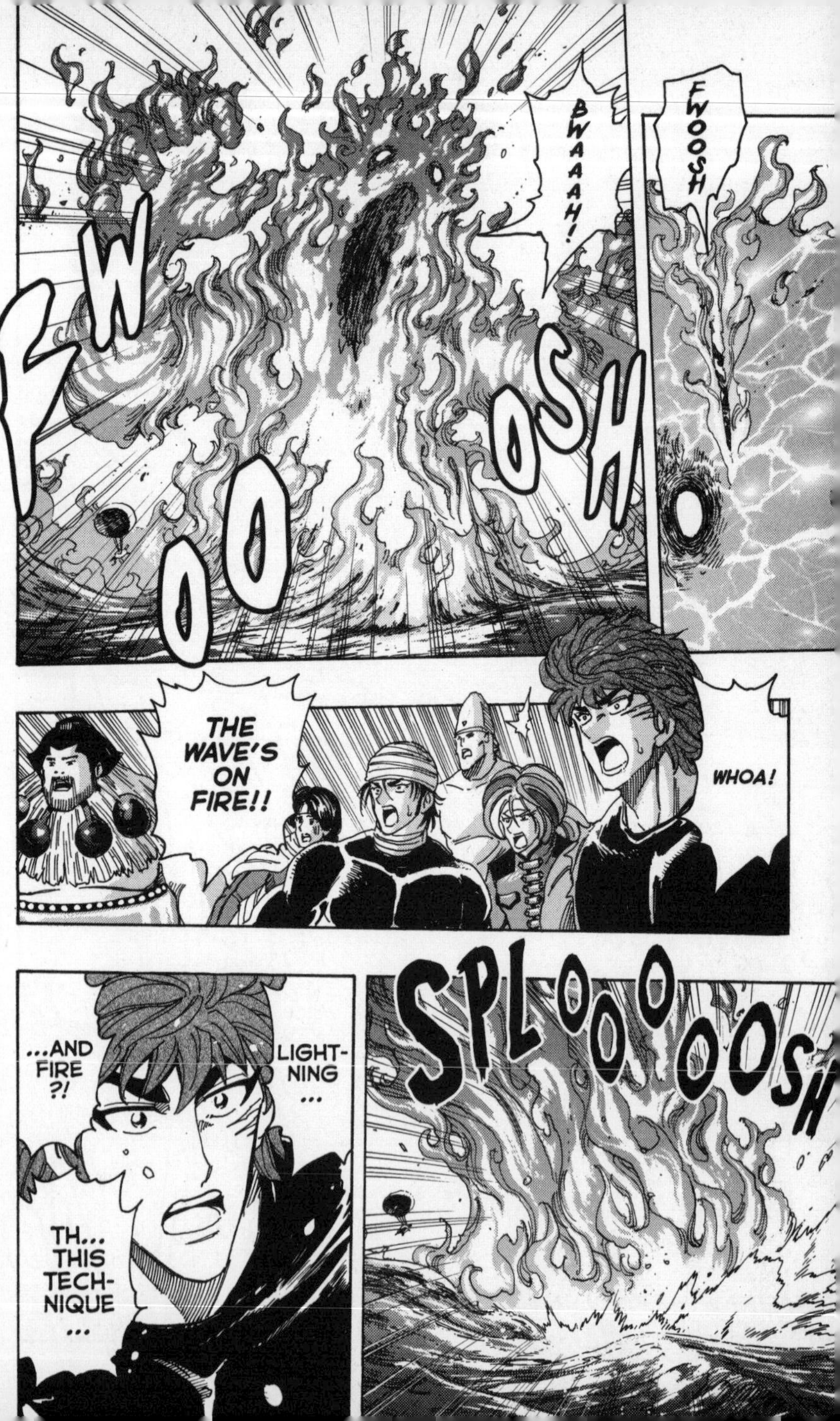
FWOOSH
BWAAAAH!
FWOOOSH
WHOA!
THE WAVE'S ON FIRE!!
SPLOOOOOSH
LIGHT-NING...
...AND FIRE?!
TH... THIS TECH-NIQUE...

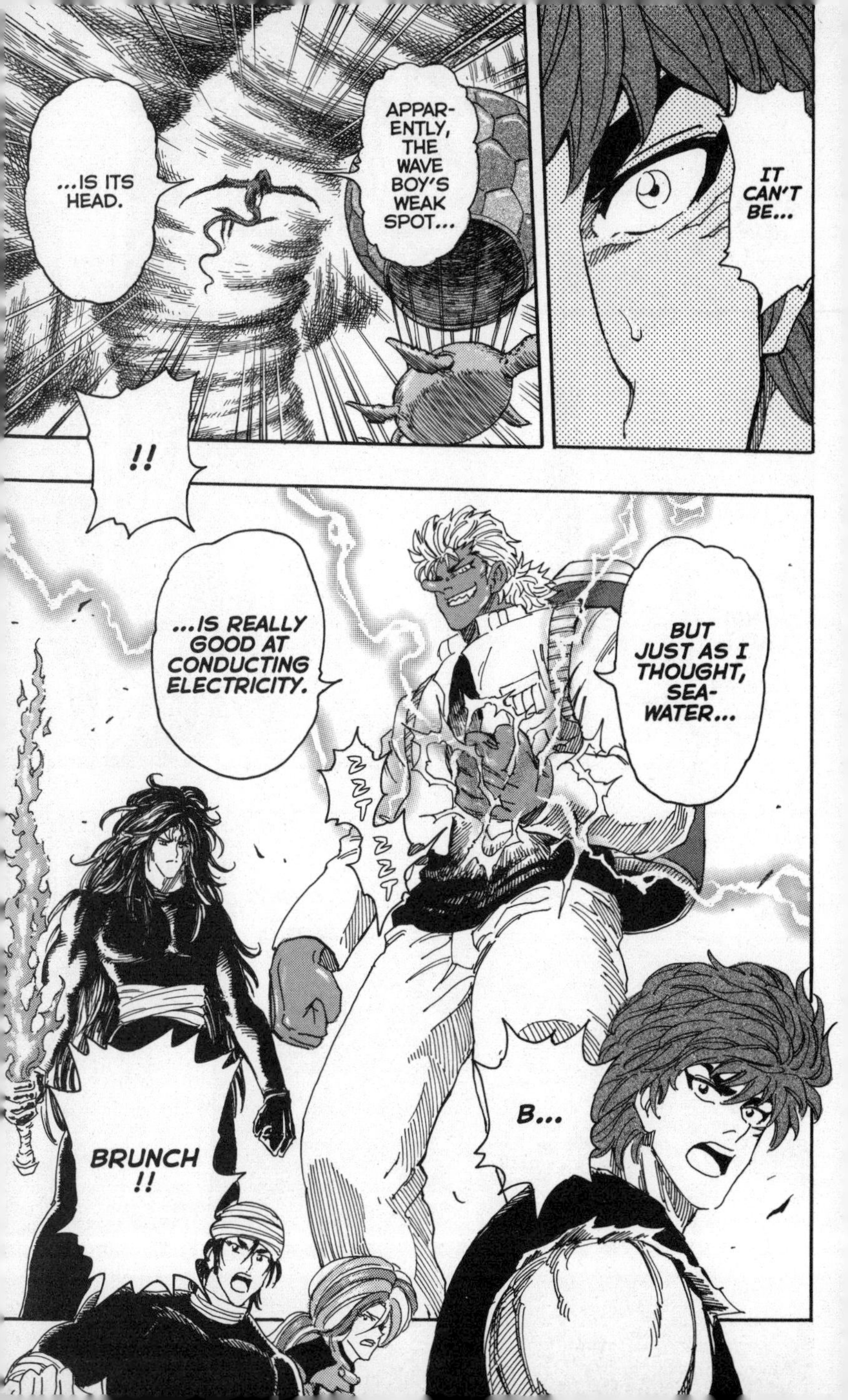

IT CAN'T BE...
APPARENTLY, THE WAVE BOY'S WEAK SPOT...
...IS ITS HEAD.
!!
BUT JUST AS I THOUGHT, SEA-WATER...
...IS REALLY GOOD AT CONDUCTING ELECTRICITY.
ZZZT
ZZZT
B...
BRUNCH !!

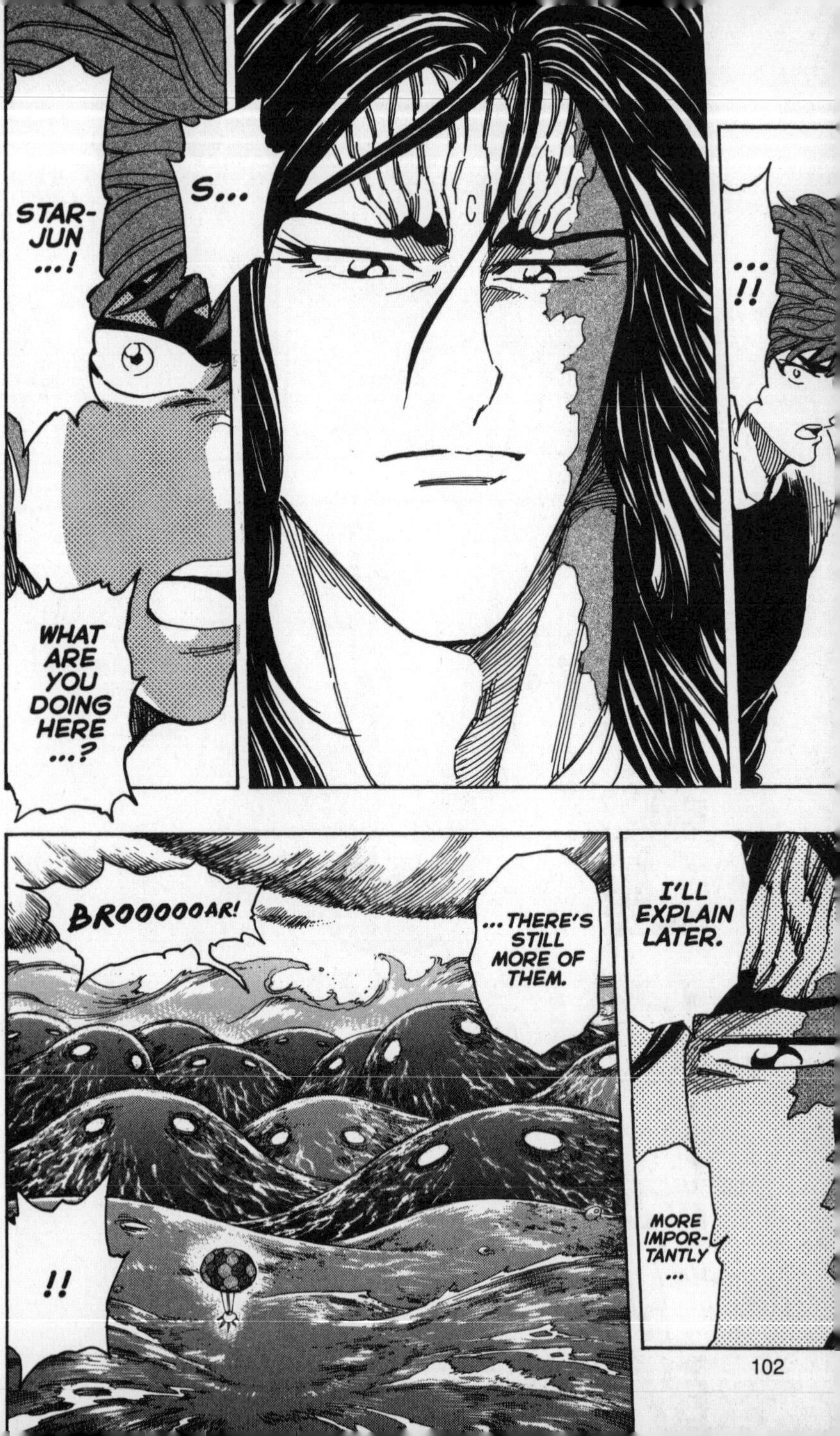
...!!
S...
STAR-JUN...!
WHAT ARE YOU DOING HERE...?
I'LL EXPLAIN LATER.
MORE IMPORTANTLY...
...THERE'S STILL MORE OF THEM.
BROOOOOAR!
!!

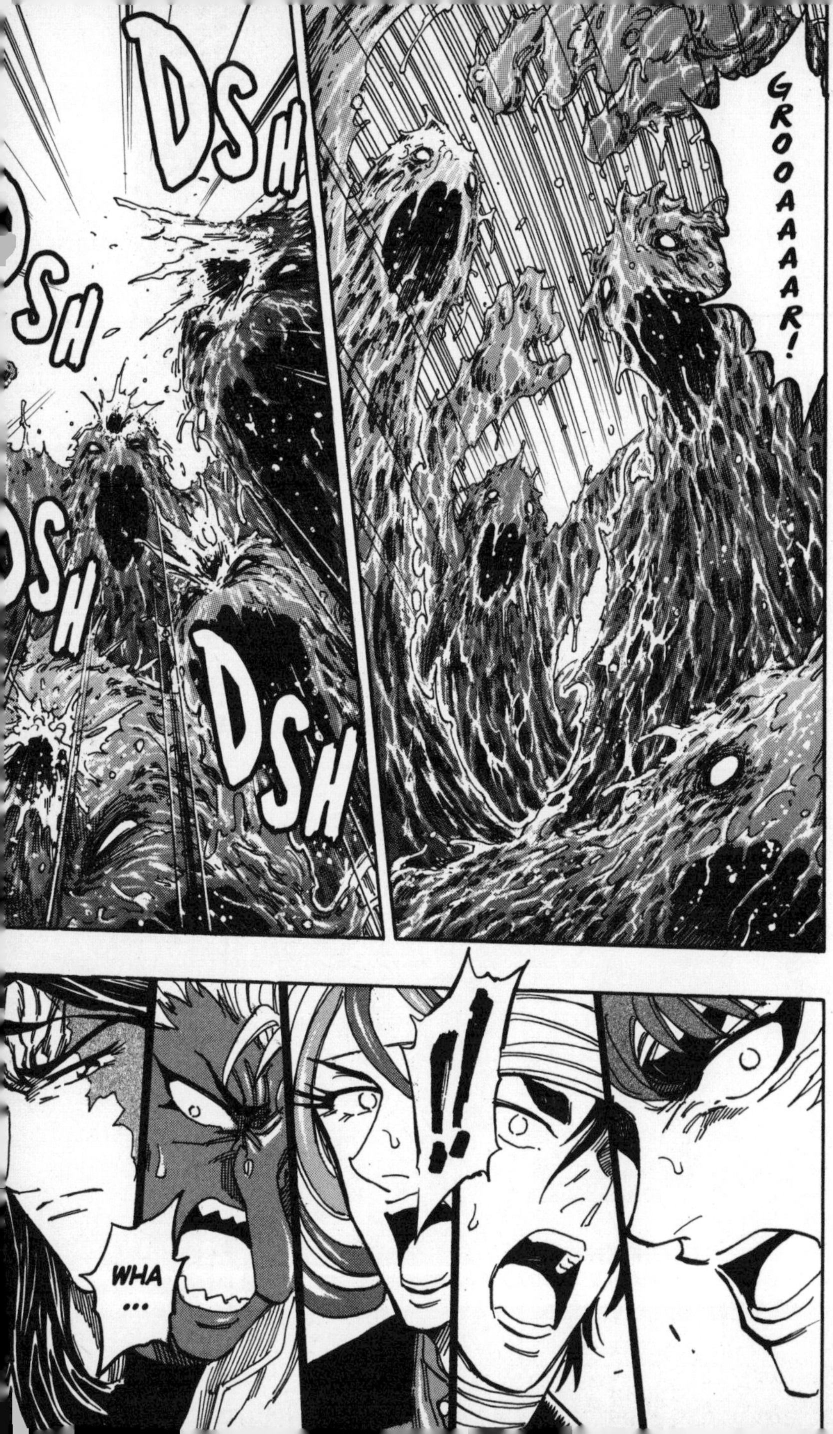
GROOOAAAAR!
DSH
DSH
DSH
DSH
!!
WHA ...

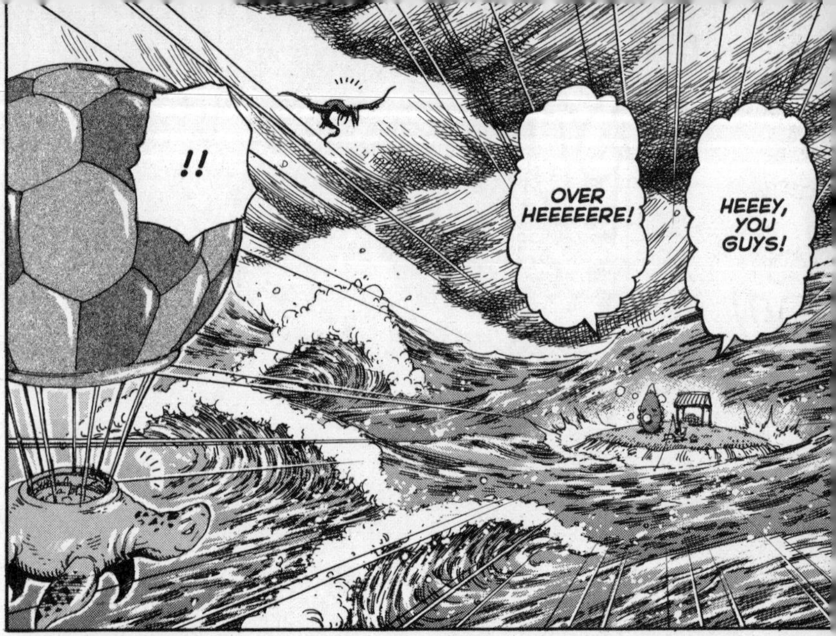
HEEEY, YOU GUYS!
OVER HEEEEERE!
!!

*SUBMITTED BY YUTARO ABE FROM YAMAGATA!

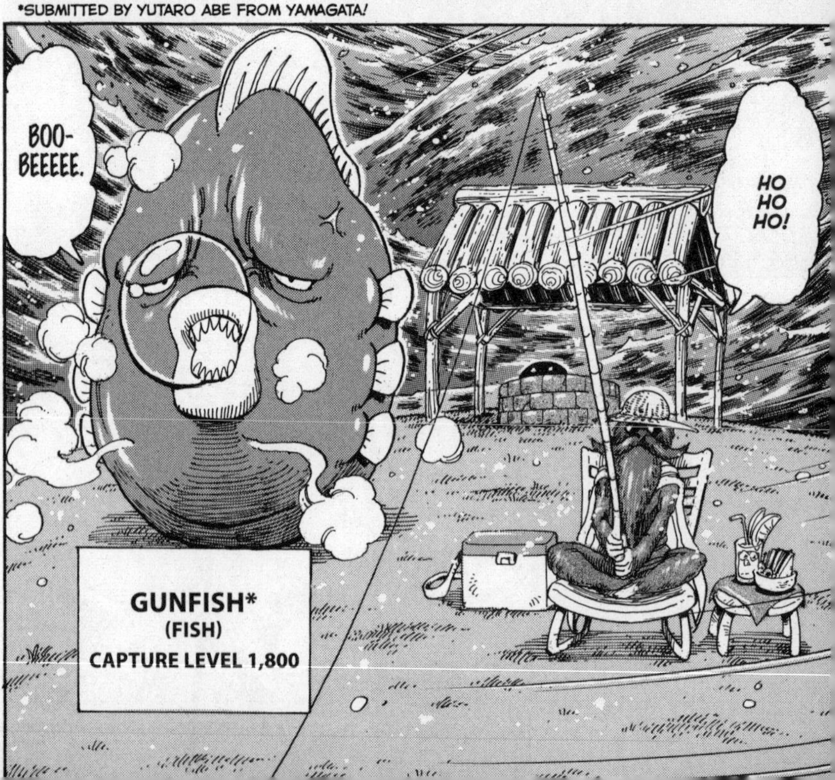
HO HO HO!
BOO-BEEEEE.
GUNFISH* (FISH) CAPTURE LEVEL 1,800

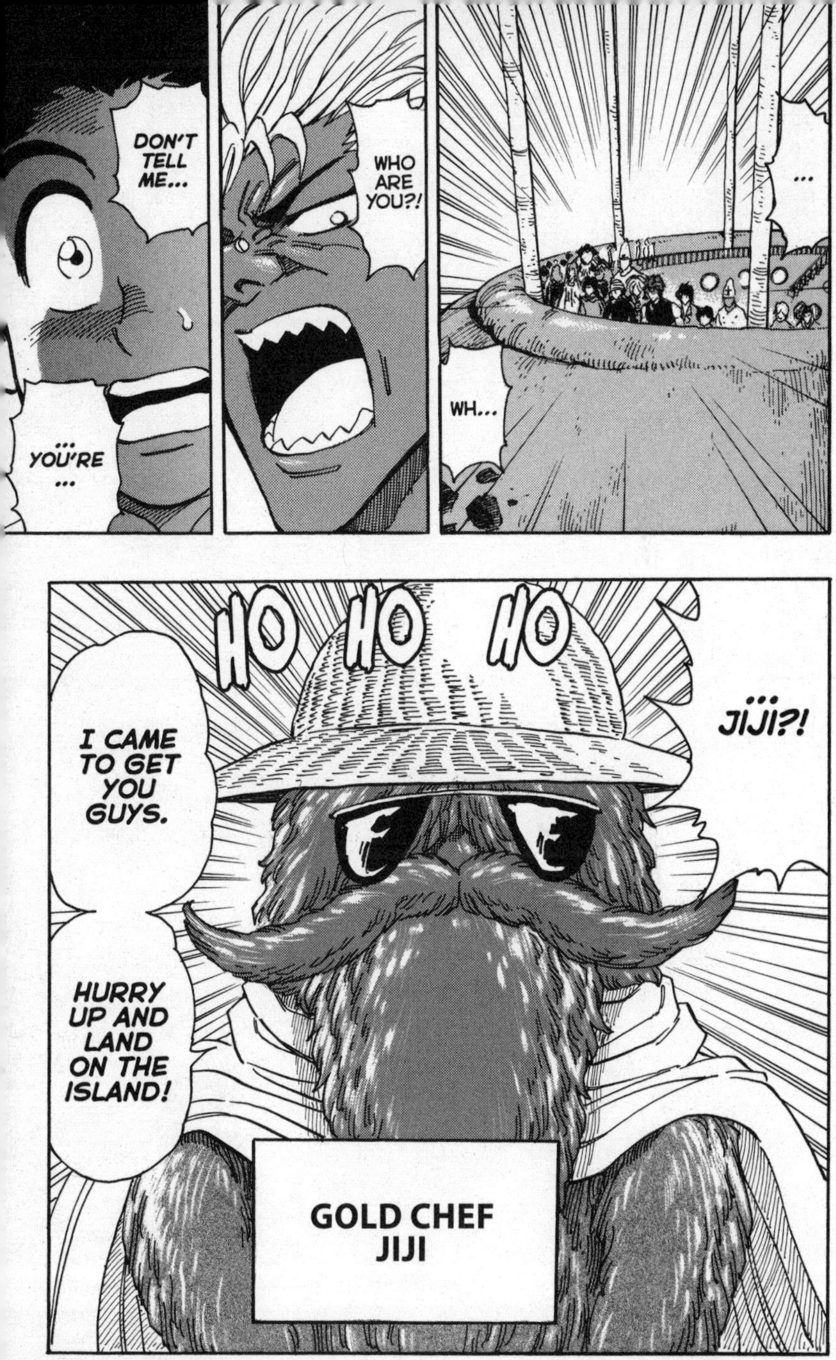
...
WH...
WHO ARE YOU?!
DON'T TELL ME...
... YOU'RE ...
HO HO HO
... JIJI?!
I CAME TO GET YOU GUYS.
HURRY UP AND LAND ON THE ISLAND!
GOLD CHEF JIJI

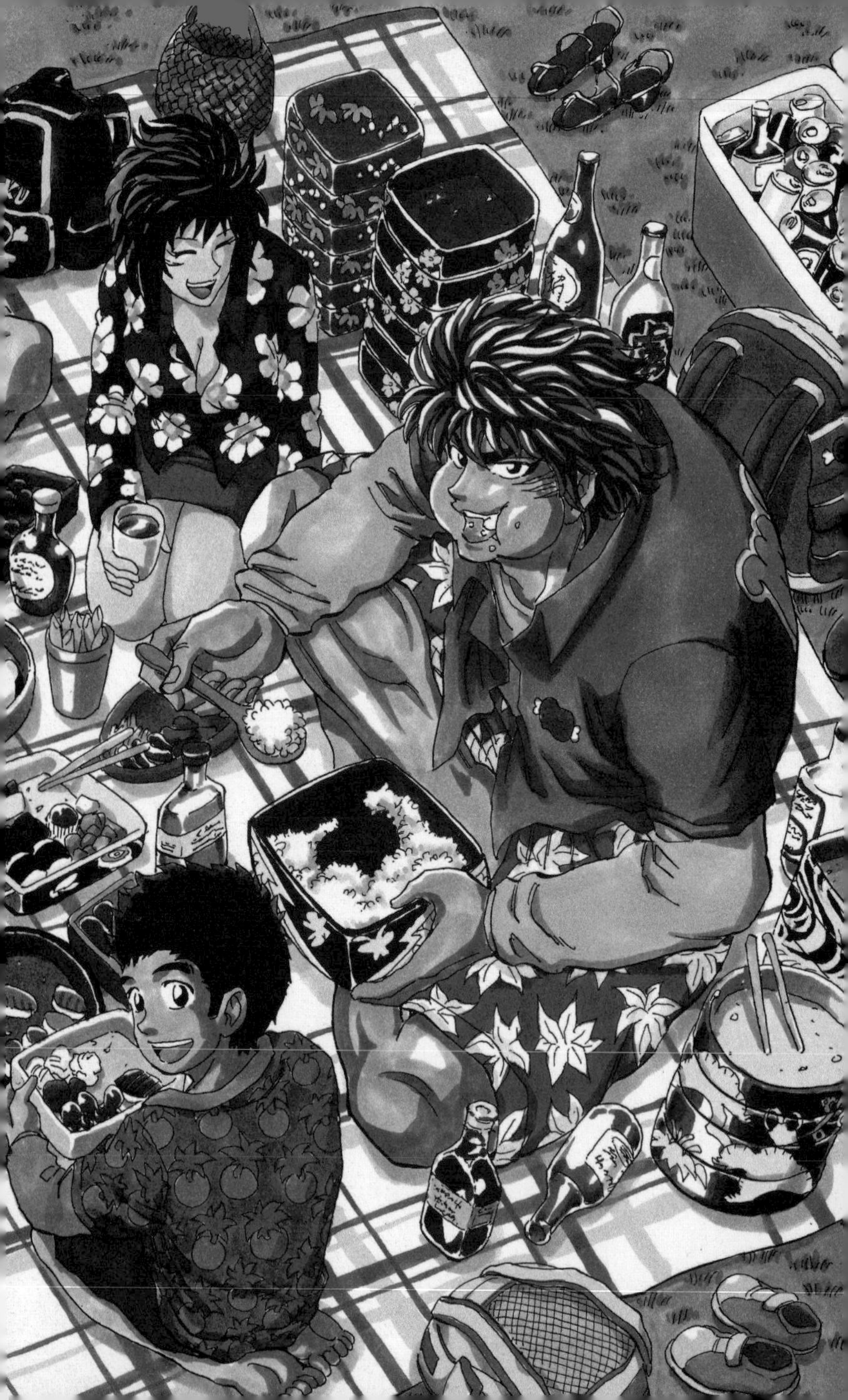

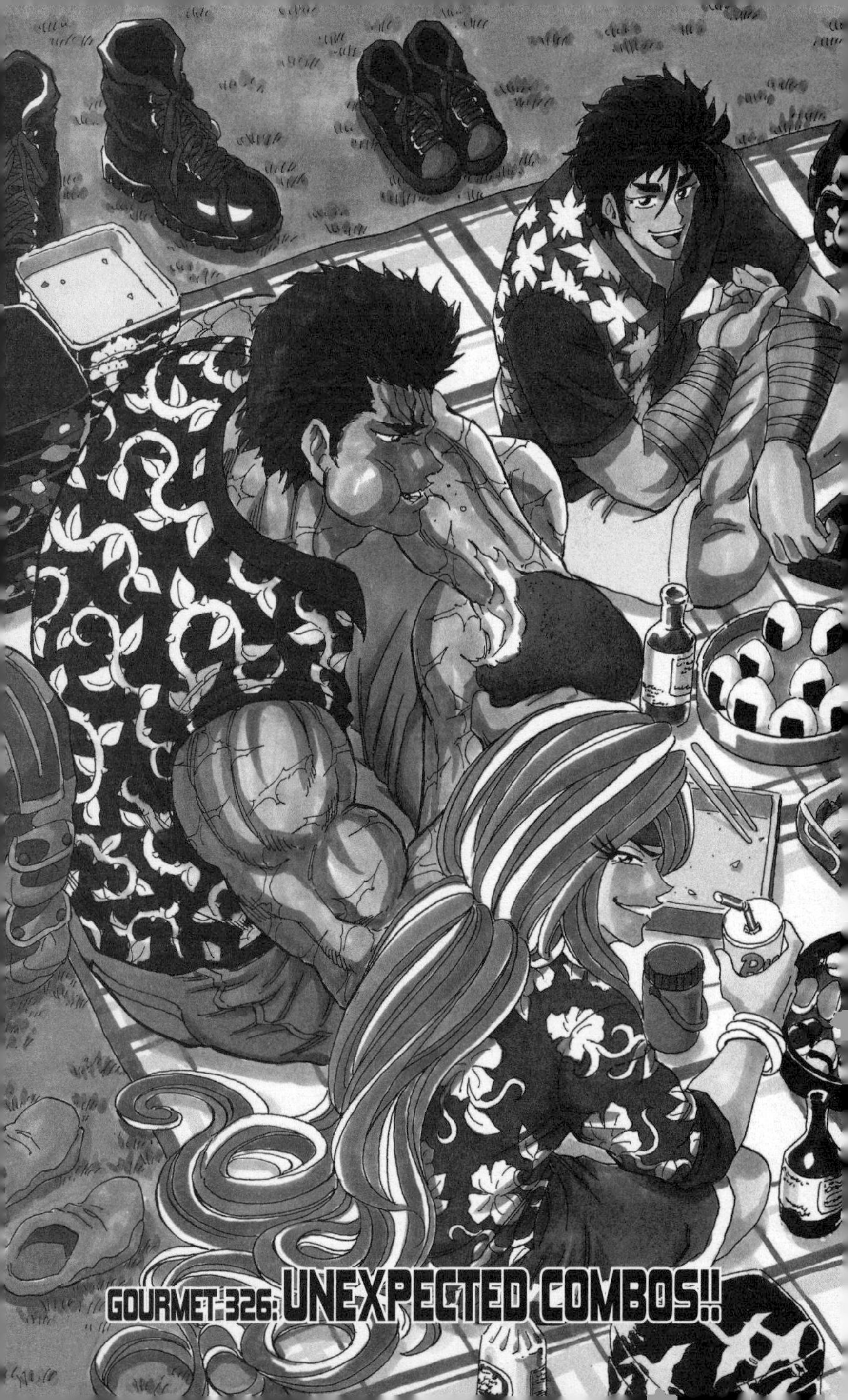
GOURMET 326: UNEXPECTED COMBOS!!

TORIKO

GOURMET CHECKLIST

Vol. 355

BILLION BIRD EGG
(EGG)

CAPTURE LEVEL: LESS THAN 1
HABITAT: EXTINCT
SIZE: 25 CM
HEIGHT: ---
WEIGHT: 500 G
PRICE: 10,000 YEN PER EGG

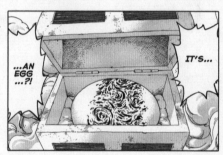

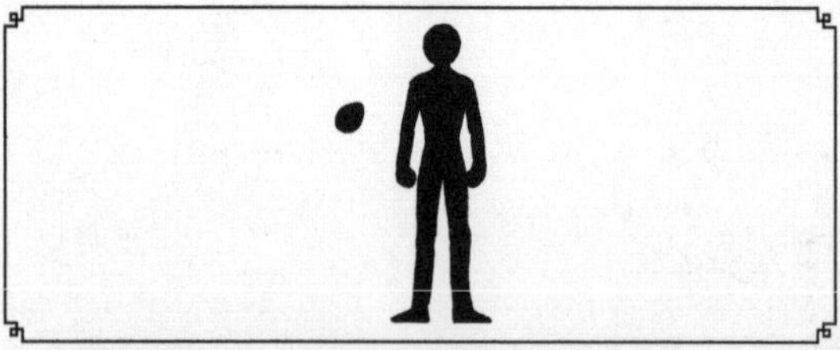

...AN EGG...?!

IT'S...

SCALE

THIS IS THE EGG OF THE LEGENDARY BILLION BIRD THAT USED TO INHABIT THE GOURMET
WORLD, WHICH IS ONLY LAID UNDER SPECIAL PREPARATION CONDITIONS. AN EGG LAID
BY A BILLION BIRD THAT'S BEEN SPOOKED WILL MATURE IMMEDIATELY AND MULTIPLY
WITHOUT END. BUT WHEN THE BILLION BIRD IS SHOWN AFFECTION AND PREPARED IN A
HEARTFELT WAY, IT IS SAID TO LAY A SPECIAL KIND OF EGG. LIKE THE THICK STRATUM
OF THE THOUSANDS OF YEARS THE BILLION BIRD LIVES, THE LAYERED FLAVORS COURSE
THROUGH THE BODY IN ONE GO, AWAKENING A FRESH AND YOUTHFUL SENSATION OF
LIFE, WHICH IS WHY TORIKO DECIDED TO MAKE IT HIS FULL COURSE'S DRINK.

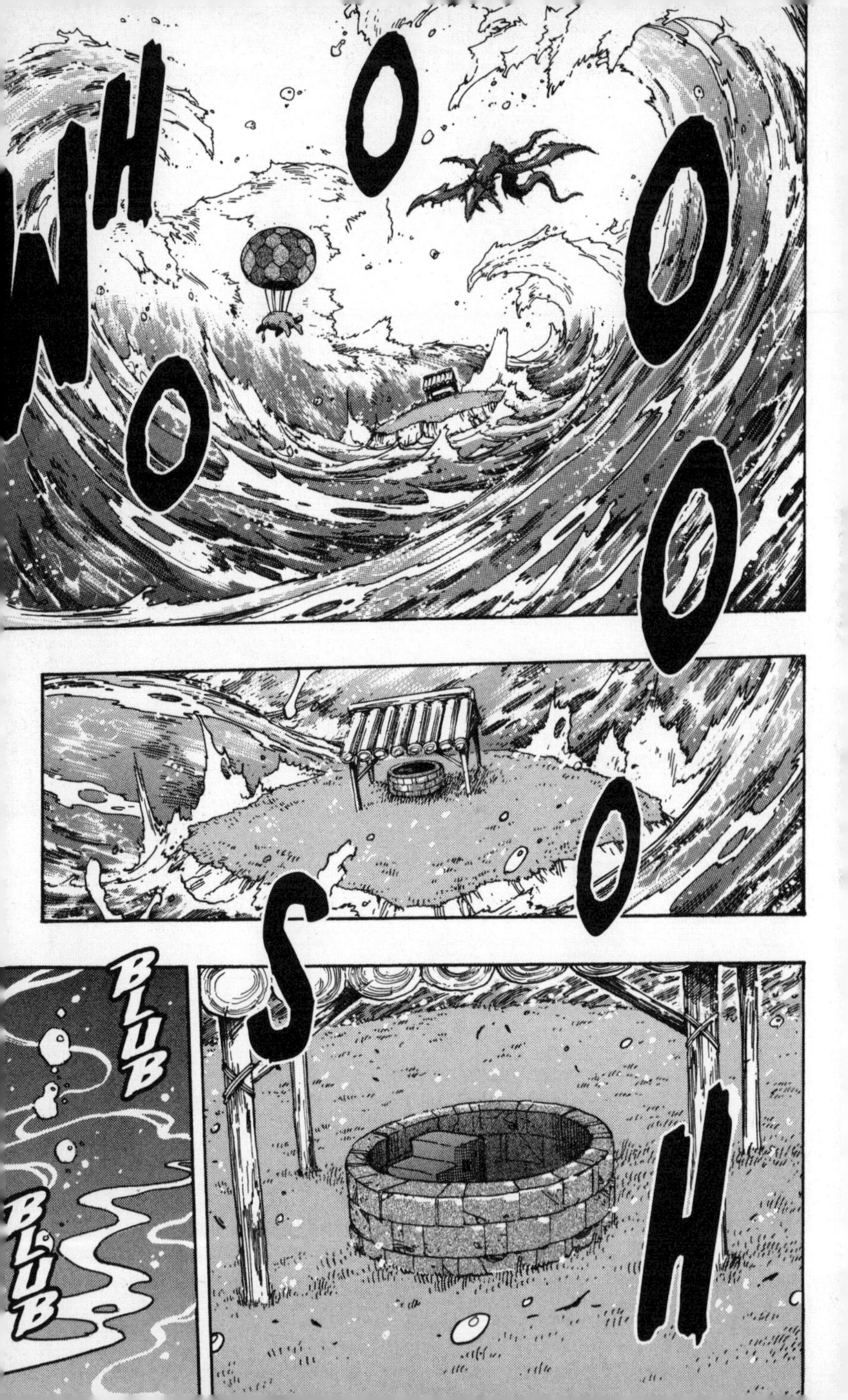
WHOOOOOSH
BLUB
BLUB

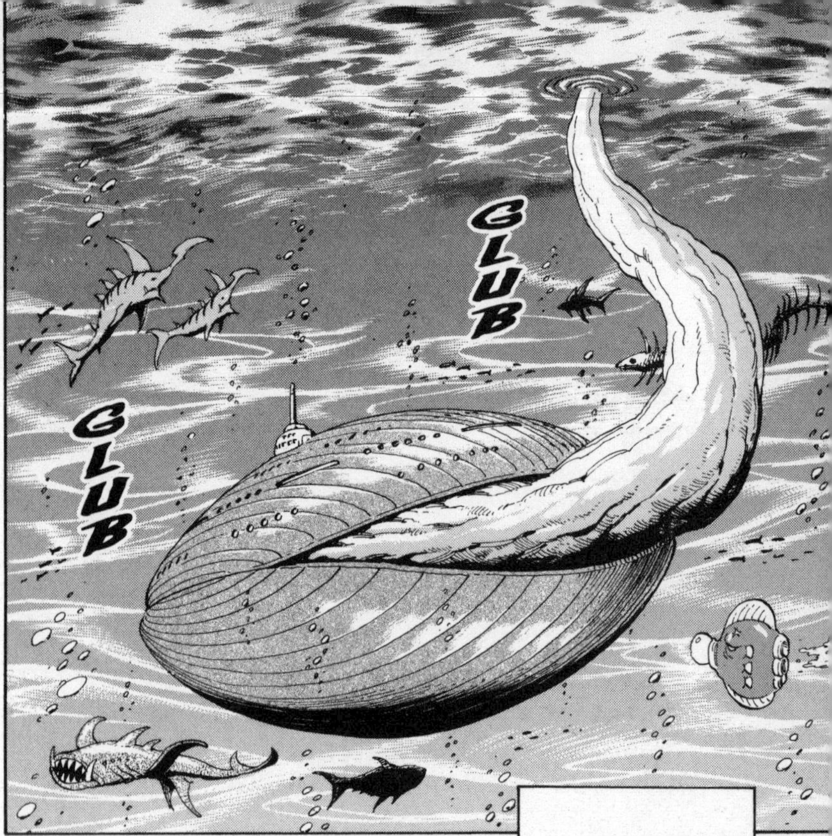
GLUB
GLUB

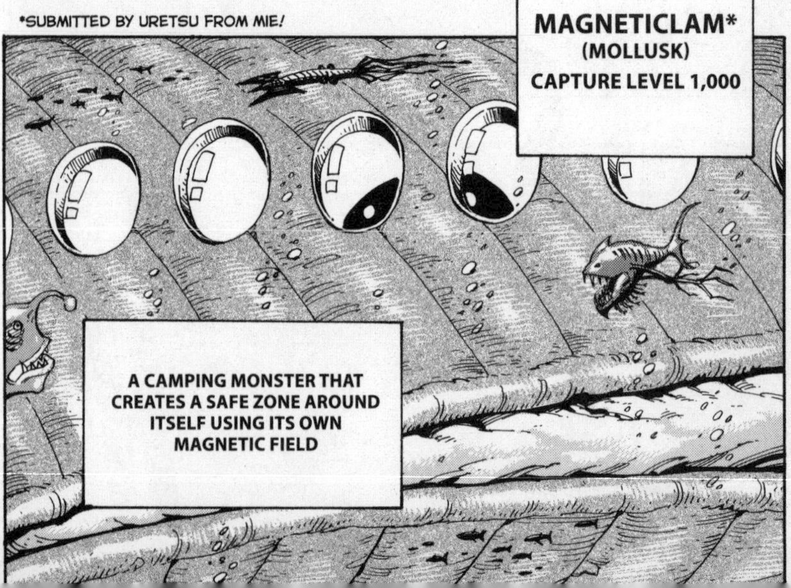
MAGNETICLAM*
(MOLLUSK)
CAPTURE LEVEL 1,000
A CAMPING MONSTER THAT CREATES A SAFE ZONE AROUND ITSELF USING ITS OWN MAGNETIC FIELD

*SUBMITTED BY URETSU FROM MIE!

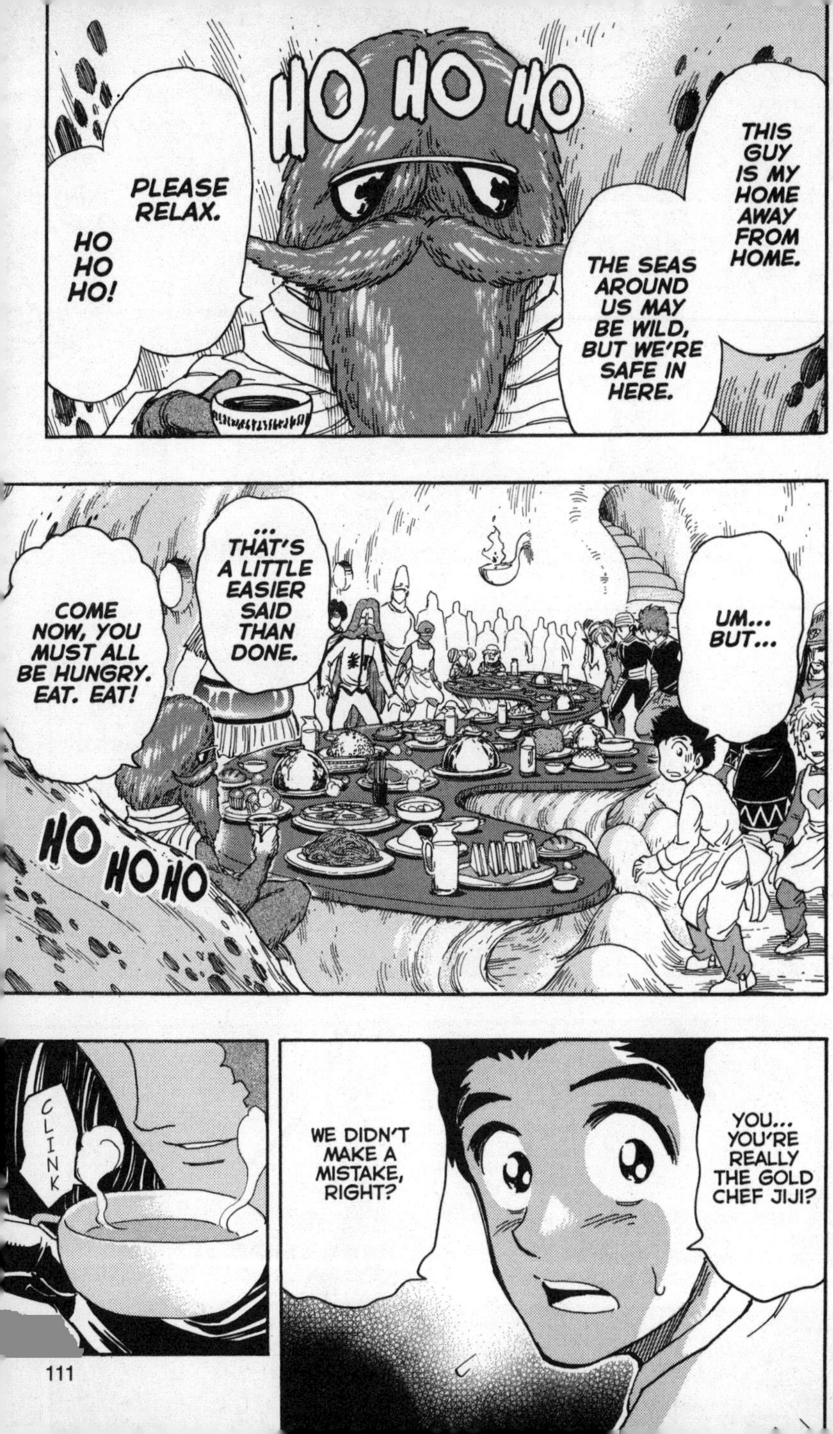
THIS GUY IS MY HOME AWAY FROM HOME.
THE SEAS AROUND US MAY BE WILD, BUT WE'RE SAFE IN HERE.
HO HO HO
PLEASE RELAX.
HO HO HO!
UM... BUT...
...THAT'S A LITTLE EASIER SAID THAN DONE.
COME NOW, YOU MUST ALL BE HUNGRY. EAT. EAT!
HO HO HO
YOU... YOU'RE REALLY THE GOLD CHEF JIJI?
WE DIDN'T MAKE A MISTAKE, RIGHT?
CLINK

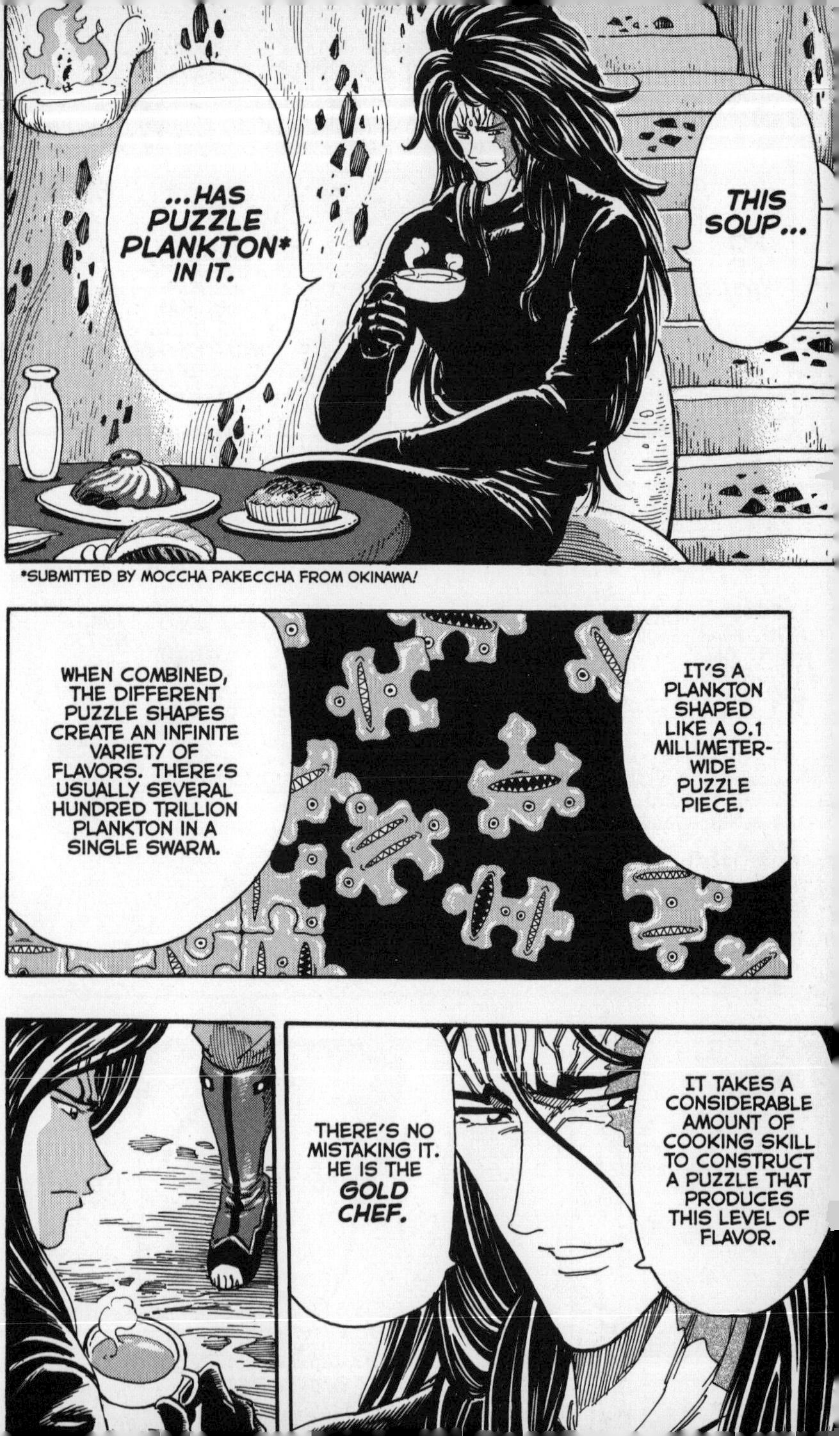
THIS SOUP...
...HAS PUZZLE PLANKTON* IN IT.
*SUBMITTED BY MOCCHA PAKECCHA FROM OKINAWA!
IT'S A PLANKTON SHAPED LIKE A 0.1 MILLIMETER-WIDE PUZZLE PIECE.
WHEN COMBINED, THE DIFFERENT PUZZLE SHAPES CREATE AN INFINITE VARIETY OF FLAVORS. THERE'S USUALLY SEVERAL HUNDRED TRILLION PLANKTON IN A SINGLE SWARM.
IT TAKES A CONSIDERABLE AMOUNT OF COOKING SKILL TO CONSTRUCT A PUZZLE THAT PRODUCES THIS LEVEL OF FLAVOR.
THERE'S NO MISTAKING IT. HE IS THE GOLD CHEF.

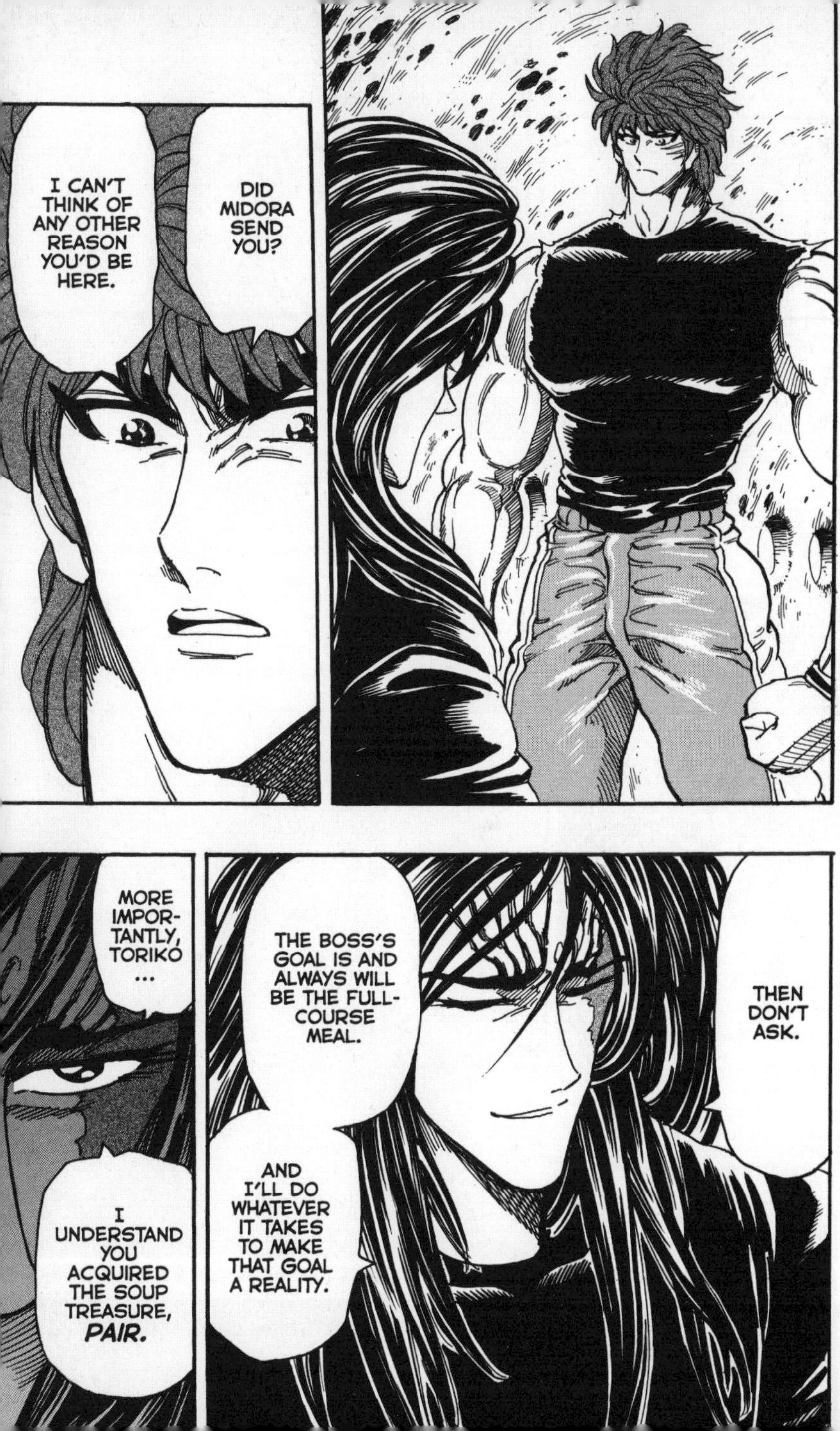
DID MIDORA SEND YOU?
I CAN'T THINK OF ANY OTHER REASON YOU'D BE HERE.
THEN DON'T ASK.
THE BOSS'S GOAL IS AND ALWAYS WILL BE THE FULL-COURSE MEAL.
AND I'LL DO WHATEVER IT TAKES TO MAKE THAT GOAL A REALITY.
MORE IMPOR-TANTLY, TORIKO ...
I UNDERSTAND YOU ACQUIRED THE SOUP TREASURE, PAIR.

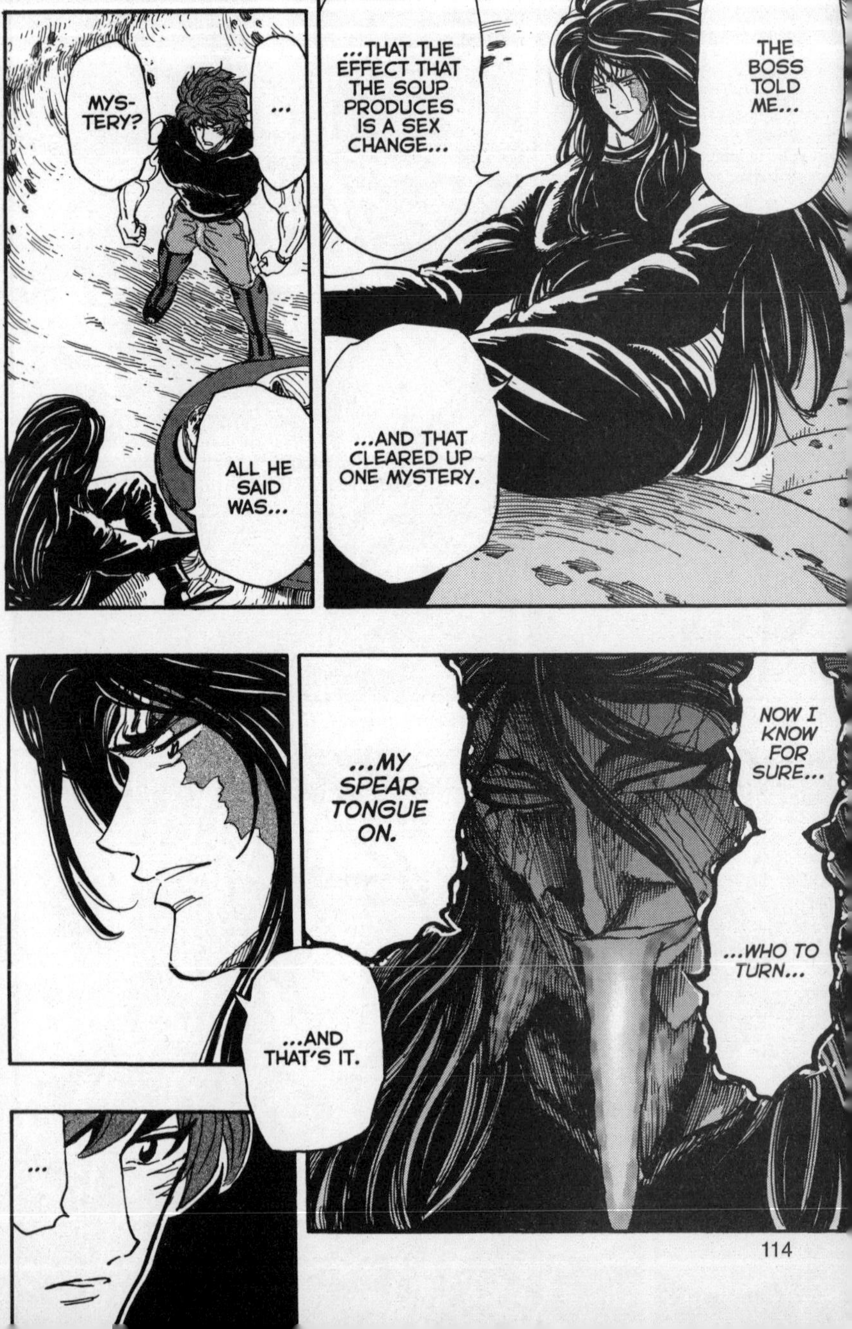
THE BOSS TOLD ME...
...THAT THE EFFECT THAT THE SOUP PRODUCES IS A SEX CHANGE...
...AND THAT CLEARED UP ONE MYSTERY.
...
MYS-TERY?
ALL HE SAID WAS...
NOW I KNOW FOR SURE...
...WHO TO TURN...
...MY SPEAR TONGUE ON.
...AND THAT'S IT.
...

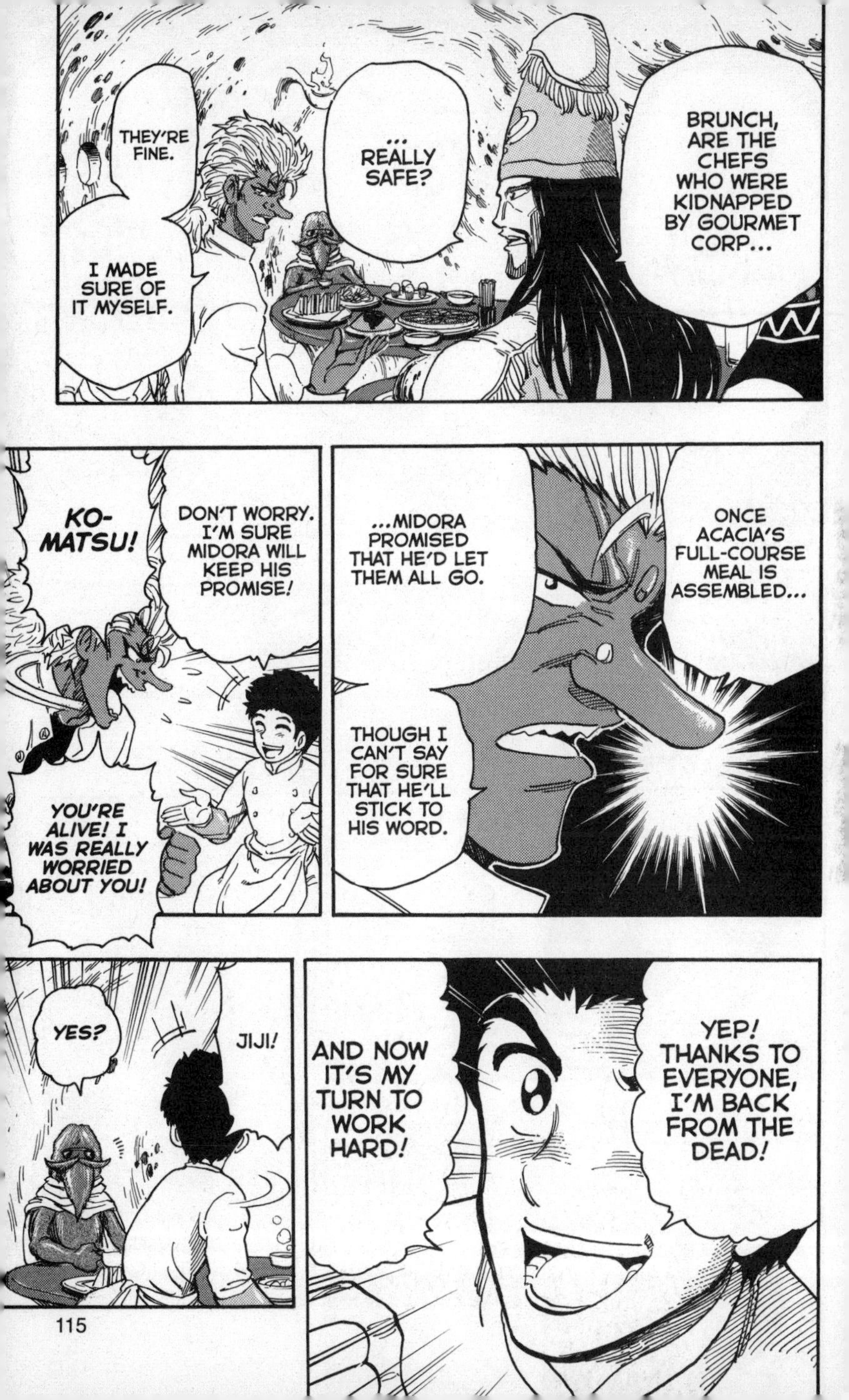
BRUNCH, ARE THE CHEFS WHO WERE KIDNAPPED BY GOURMET CORP...
... REALLY SAFE?
THEY'RE FINE.
I MADE SURE OF IT MYSELF.
ONCE ACACIA'S FULL-COURSE MEAL IS ASSEMBLED...
...MIDORA PROMISED THAT HE'D LET THEM ALL GO.
THOUGH I CAN'T SAY FOR SURE THAT HE'LL STICK TO HIS WORD.
DON'T WORRY. I'M SURE MIDORA WILL KEEP HIS PROMISE!
KO-MATSU!
YOU'RE ALIVE! I WAS REALLY WORRIED ABOUT YOU!
YEP! THANKS TO EVERYONE, I'M BACK FROM THE DEAD!
AND NOW IT'S MY TURN TO WORK HARD!
JIJI!
YES?

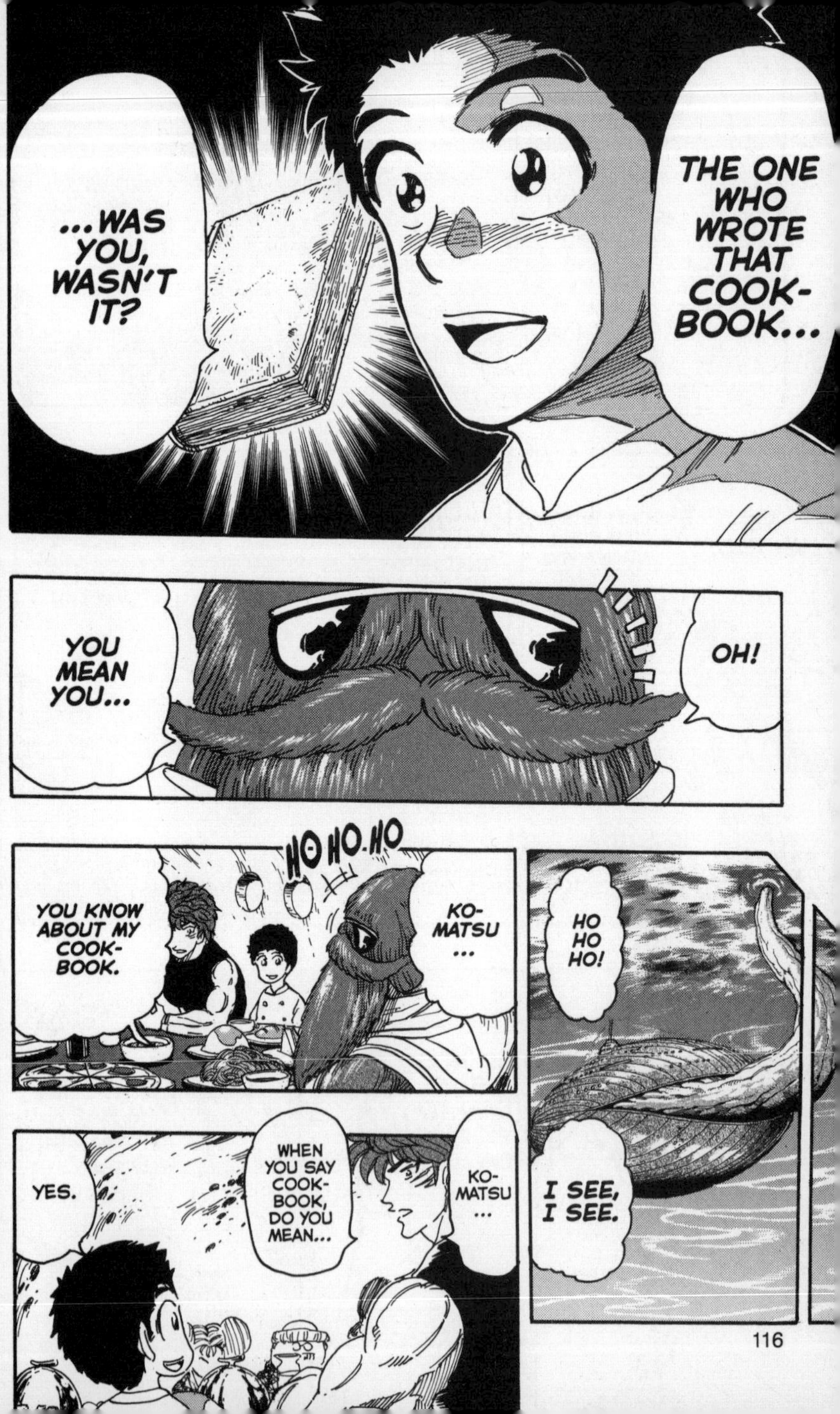
THE ONE WHO WROTE THAT COOK-BOOK...
...WAS YOU, WASN'T IT?
OH!
YOU MEAN YOU...
HO HO HO!
I SEE, I SEE.
HO HO HO
KO-MATSU ...
YOU KNOW ABOUT MY COOK-BOOK.
KO-MATSU ...
WHEN YOU SAY COOK-BOOK, DO YOU MEAN...
YES.

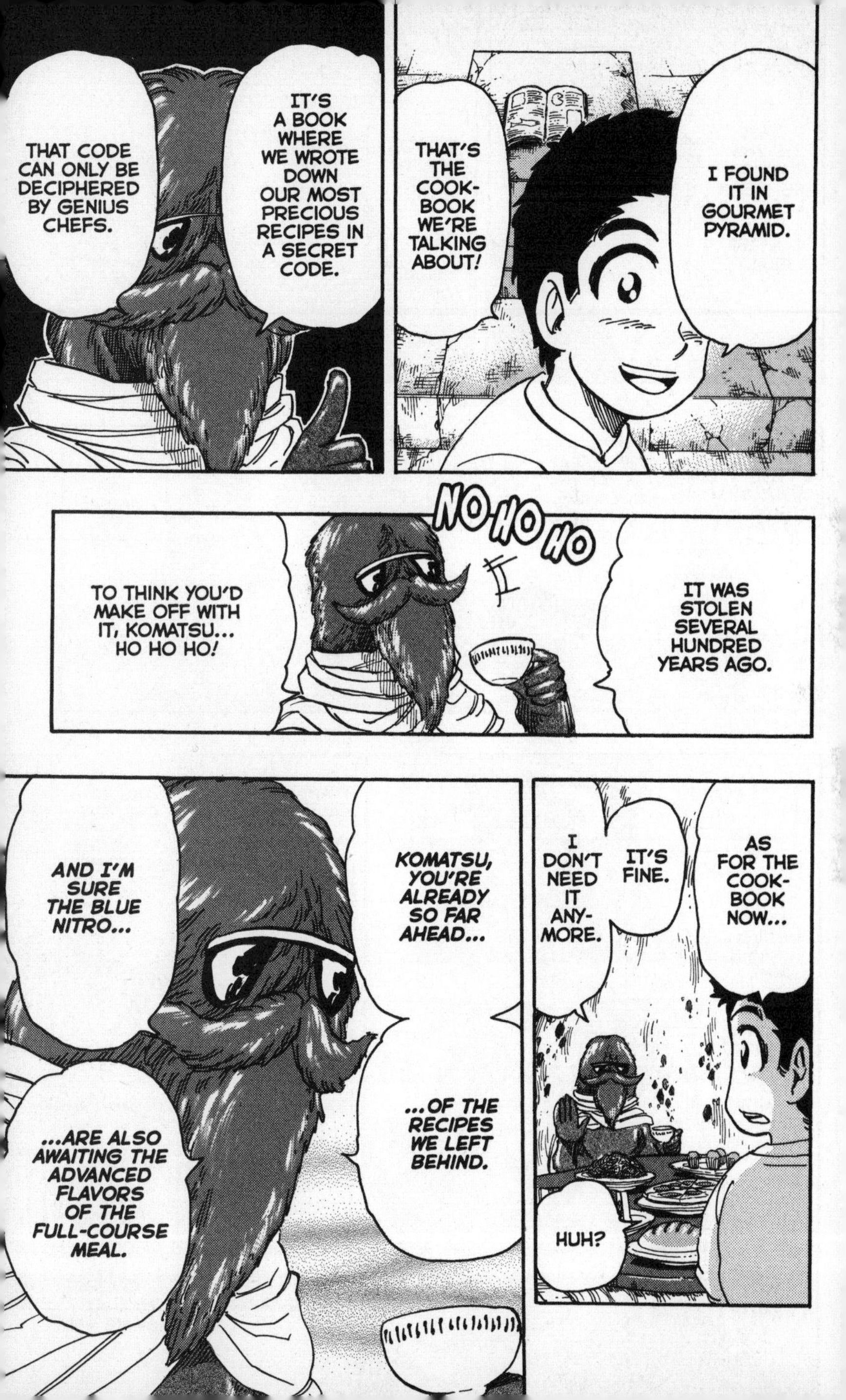
I FOUND IT IN GOURMET PYRAMID.
THAT'S THE COOKBOOK WE'RE TALKING ABOUT!
IT'S A BOOK WHERE WE WROTE DOWN OUR MOST PRECIOUS RECIPES IN A SECRET CODE.
THAT CODE CAN ONLY BE DECIPHERED BY GENIUS CHEFS.
NO HO HO HO
IT WAS STOLEN SEVERAL HUNDRED YEARS AGO.
TO THINK YOU'D MAKE OFF WITH IT, KOMATSU... HO HO HO!
AS FOR THE COOKBOOK NOW...
IT'S FINE.
I DON'T NEED IT ANYMORE.
HUH?
KOMATSU, YOU'RE ALREADY SO FAR AHEAD...
...OF THE RECIPES WE LEFT BEHIND.
AND I'M SURE THE BLUE NITRO...
...ARE ALSO AWAITING THE ADVANCED FLAVORS OF THE FULL-COURSE MEAL.

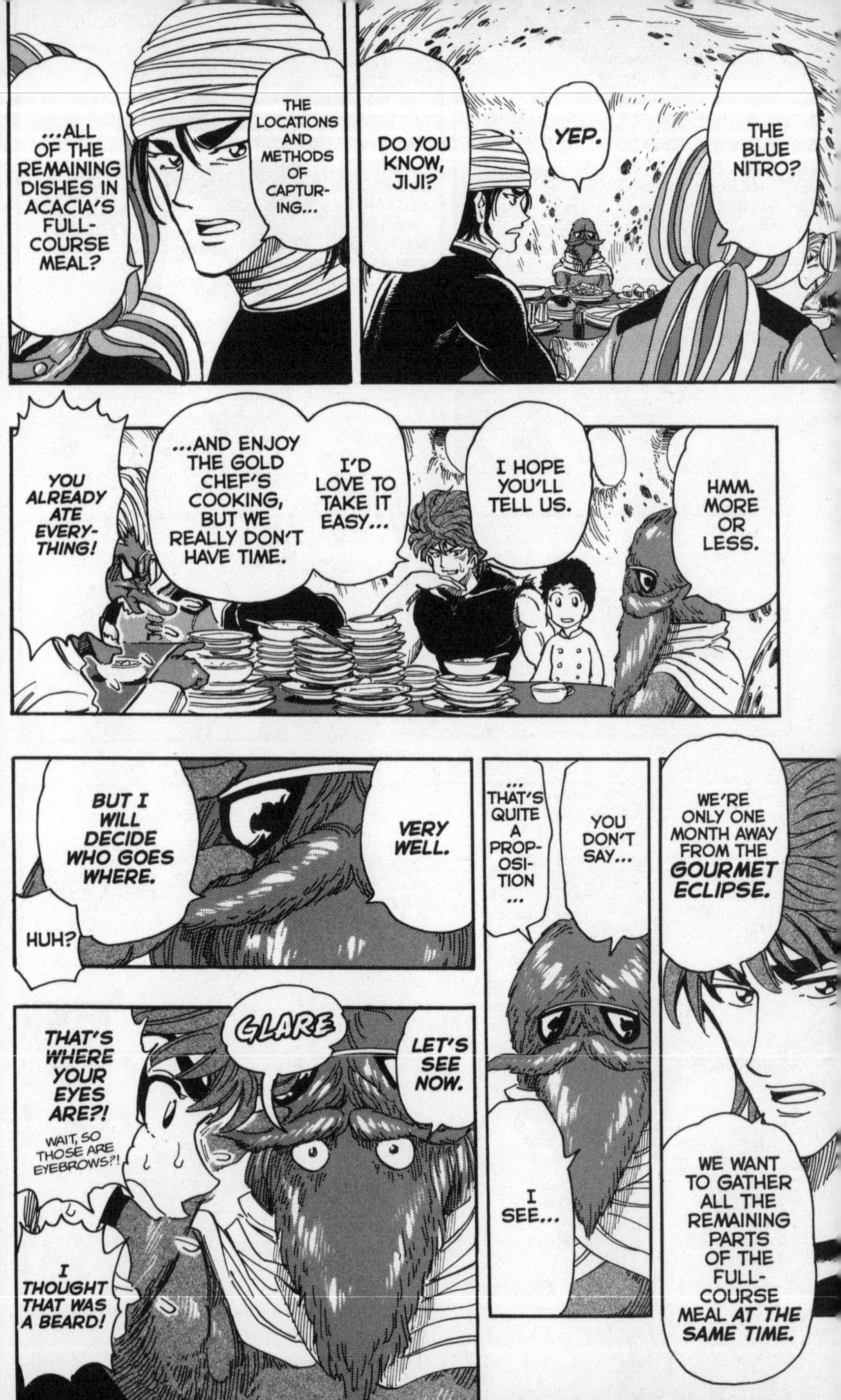
THE BLUE NITRO?
YEP.
DO YOU KNOW, JIJI?
THE LOCATIONS AND METHODS OF CAPTURING...
...ALL OF THE REMAINING DISHES IN ACACIA'S FULL-COURSE MEAL?
HMM. MORE OR LESS.
I HOPE YOU'LL TELL US.
I'D LOVE TO TAKE IT EASY...
...AND ENJOY THE GOLD CHEF'S COOKING, BUT WE REALLY DON'T HAVE TIME.
YOU ALREADY ATE EVERYTHING!
WE'RE ONLY ONE MONTH AWAY FROM THE GOURMET ECLIPSE.
WE WANT TO GATHER ALL THE REMAINING PARTS OF THE FULL-COURSE MEAL AT THE SAME TIME.
YOU DON'T SAY...
...THAT'S QUITE A PROPOSITION...
I SEE...
VERY WELL.
BUT I WILL DECIDE WHO GOES WHERE.
HUH?
LET'S SEE NOW.
GLARE
THAT'S WHERE YOUR EYES ARE?!
WAIT, SO THOSE ARE EYEBROWS?!
I THOUGHT THAT WAS A BEARD!

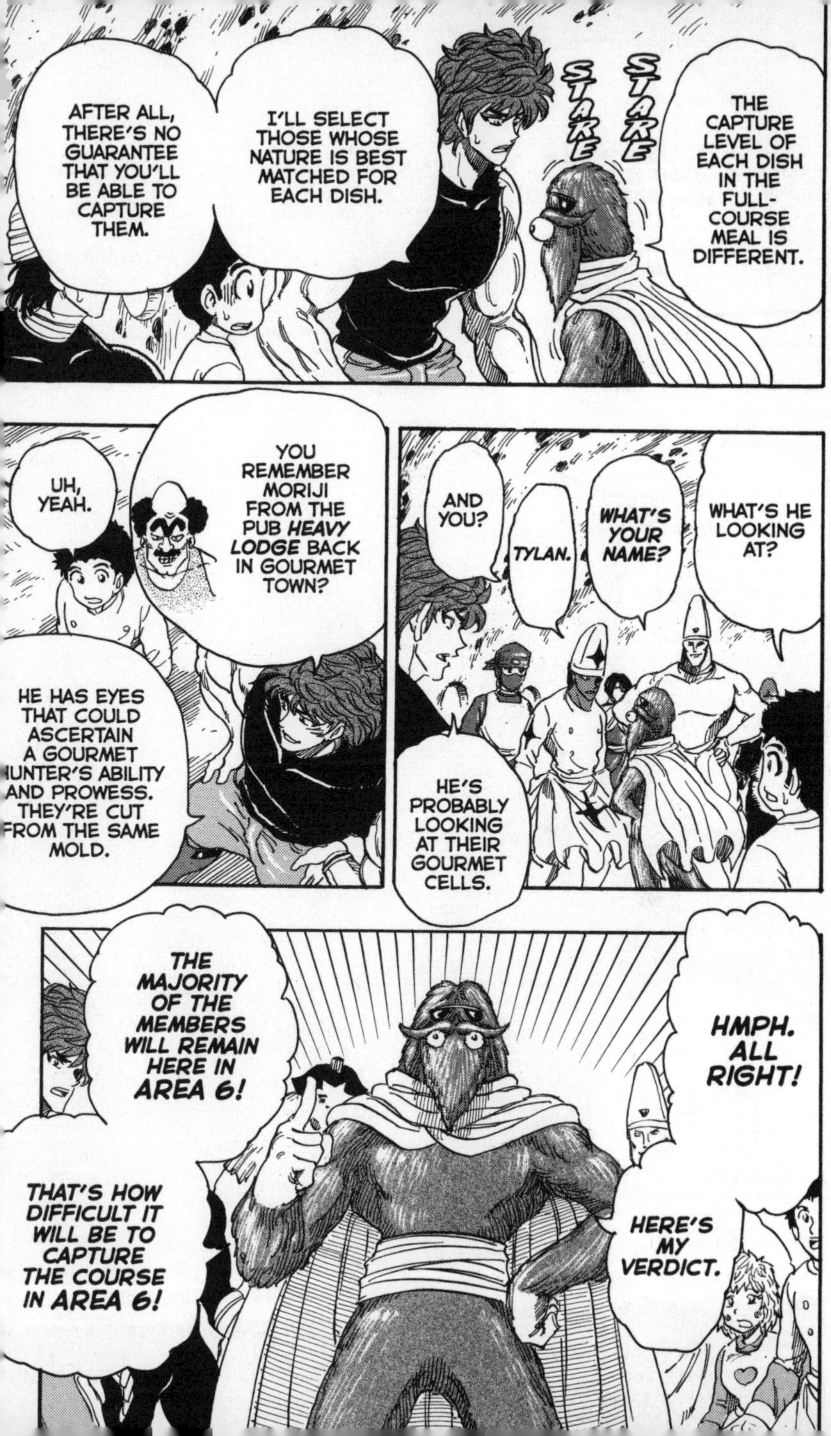
THE CAPTURE LEVEL OF EACH DISH IN THE FULL-COURSE MEAL IS DIFFERENT.
STARE
STARE
I'LL SELECT THOSE WHOSE NATURE IS BEST MATCHED FOR EACH DISH.
AFTER ALL, THERE'S NO GUARANTEE THAT YOU'LL BE ABLE TO CAPTURE THEM.
WHAT'S HE LOOKING AT?
WHAT'S YOUR NAME?
TYLAN.
AND YOU?
HE'S PROBABLY LOOKING AT THEIR GOURMET CELLS.
YOU REMEMBER MORIJI FROM THE PUB *HEAVY LODGE* BACK IN GOURMET TOWN?
UH, YEAH.
HE HAS EYES THAT COULD ASCERTAIN A GOURMET HUNTER'S ABILITY AND PROWESS. THEY'RE CUT FROM THE SAME MOLD.
HMPH. ALL RIGHT!
HERE'S MY VERDICT.
THE MAJORITY OF THE MEMBERS WILL REMAIN HERE IN AREA 6!
THAT'S HOW DIFFICULT IT WILL BE TO CAPTURE THE COURSE IN AREA 6!

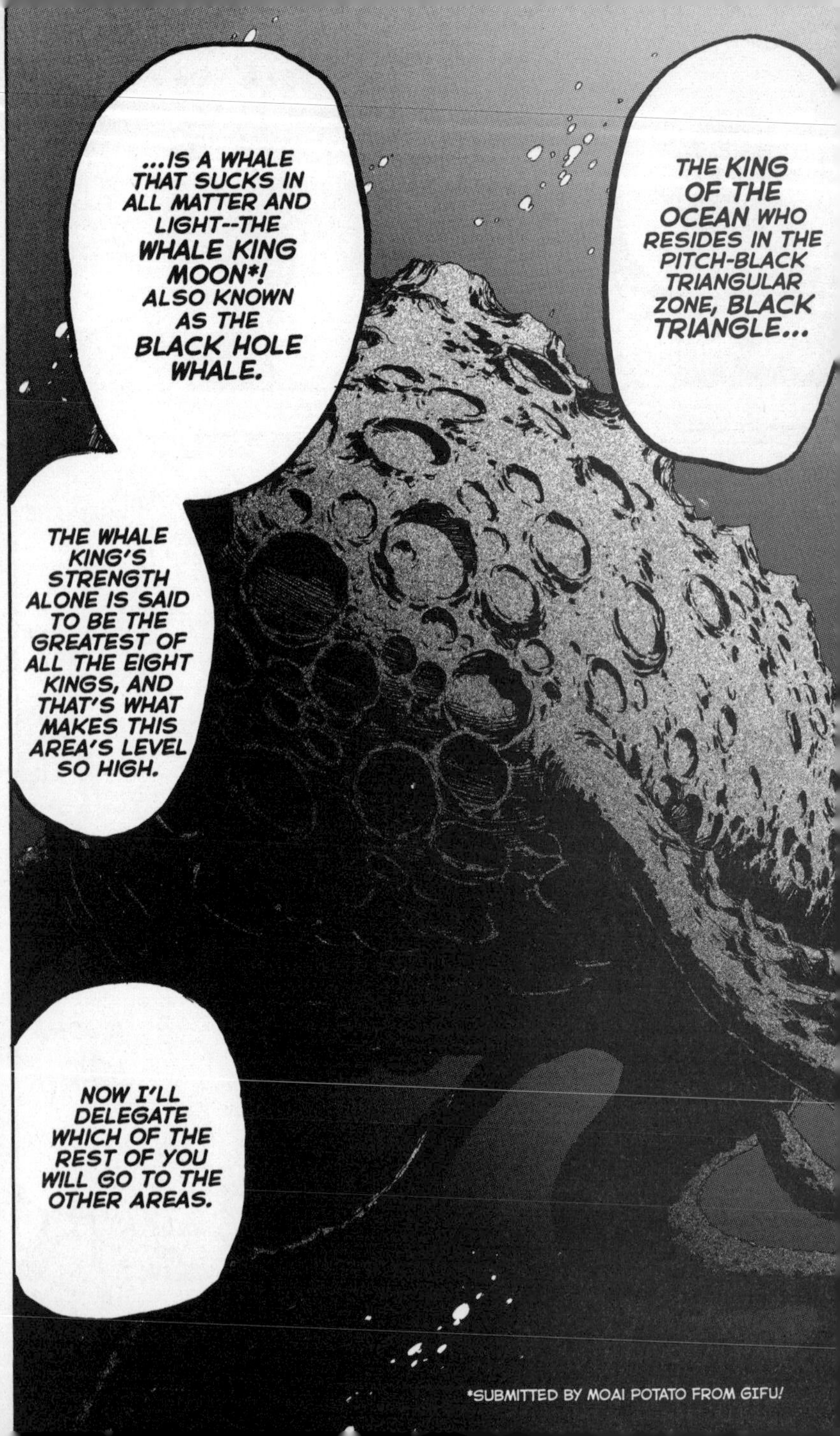
THE KING OF THE OCEAN WHO RESIDES IN THE PITCH-BLACK TRIANGULAR ZONE, BLACK TRIANGLE...
...IS A WHALE THAT SUCKS IN ALL MATTER AND LIGHT--THE WHALE KING MOON*! ALSO KNOWN AS THE BLACK HOLE WHALE.
THE WHALE KING'S STRENGTH ALONE IS SAID TO BE THE GREATEST OF ALL THE EIGHT KINGS, AND THAT'S WHAT MAKES THIS AREA'S LEVEL SO HIGH.
NOW I'LL DELEGATE WHICH OF THE REST OF YOU WILL GO TO THE OTHER AREAS.
*SUBMITTED BY MOAI POTATO FROM GIFU!

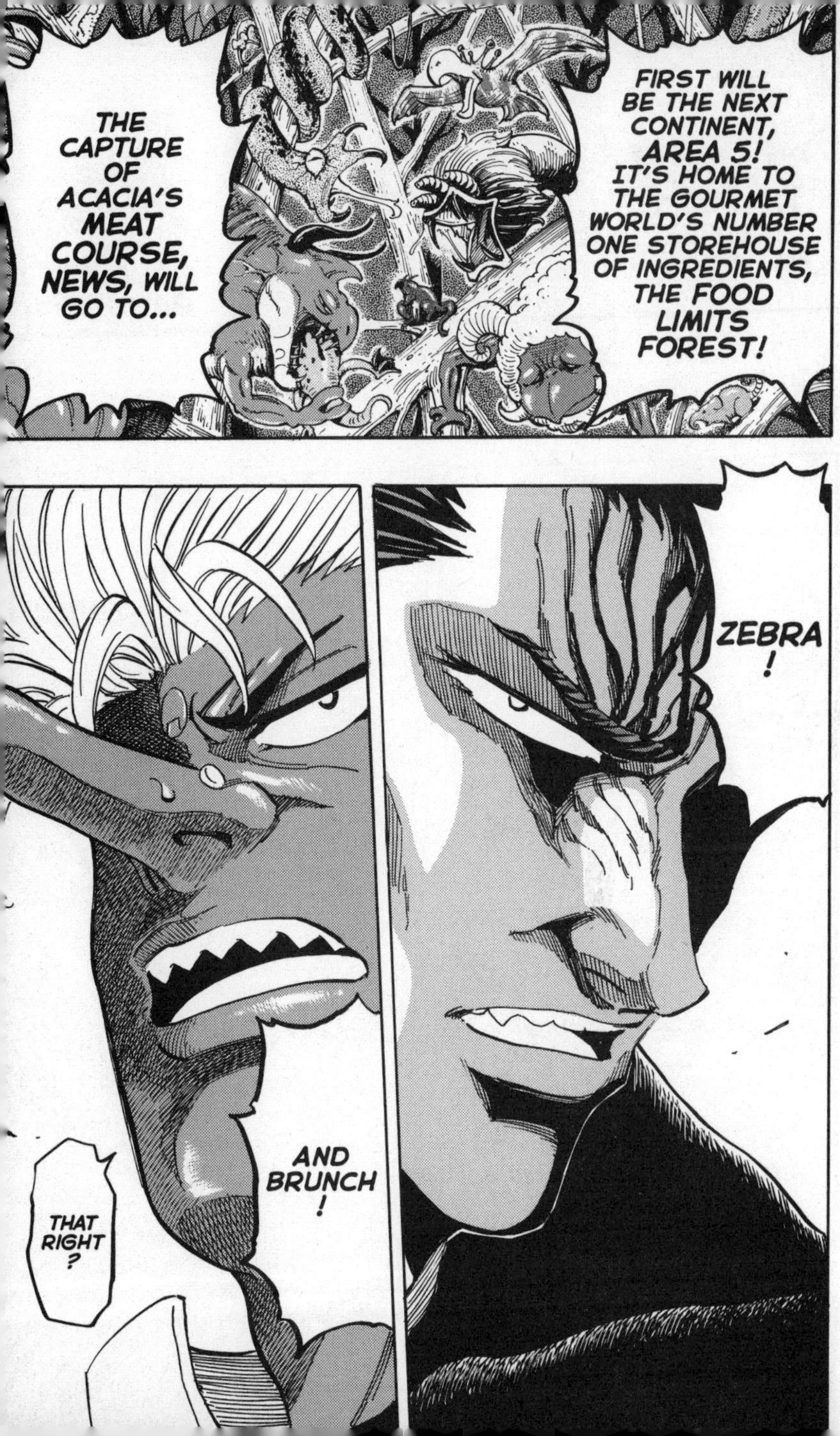
FIRST WILL BE THE NEXT CONTINENT, AREA 5! IT'S HOME TO THE GOURMET WORLD'S NUMBER ONE STOREHOUSE OF INGREDIENTS, THE FOOD LIMITS FOREST!
THE CAPTURE OF ACACIA'S MEAT COURSE, NEWS, WILL GO TO...
ZEBRA!
AND BRUNCH!
THAT RIGHT?

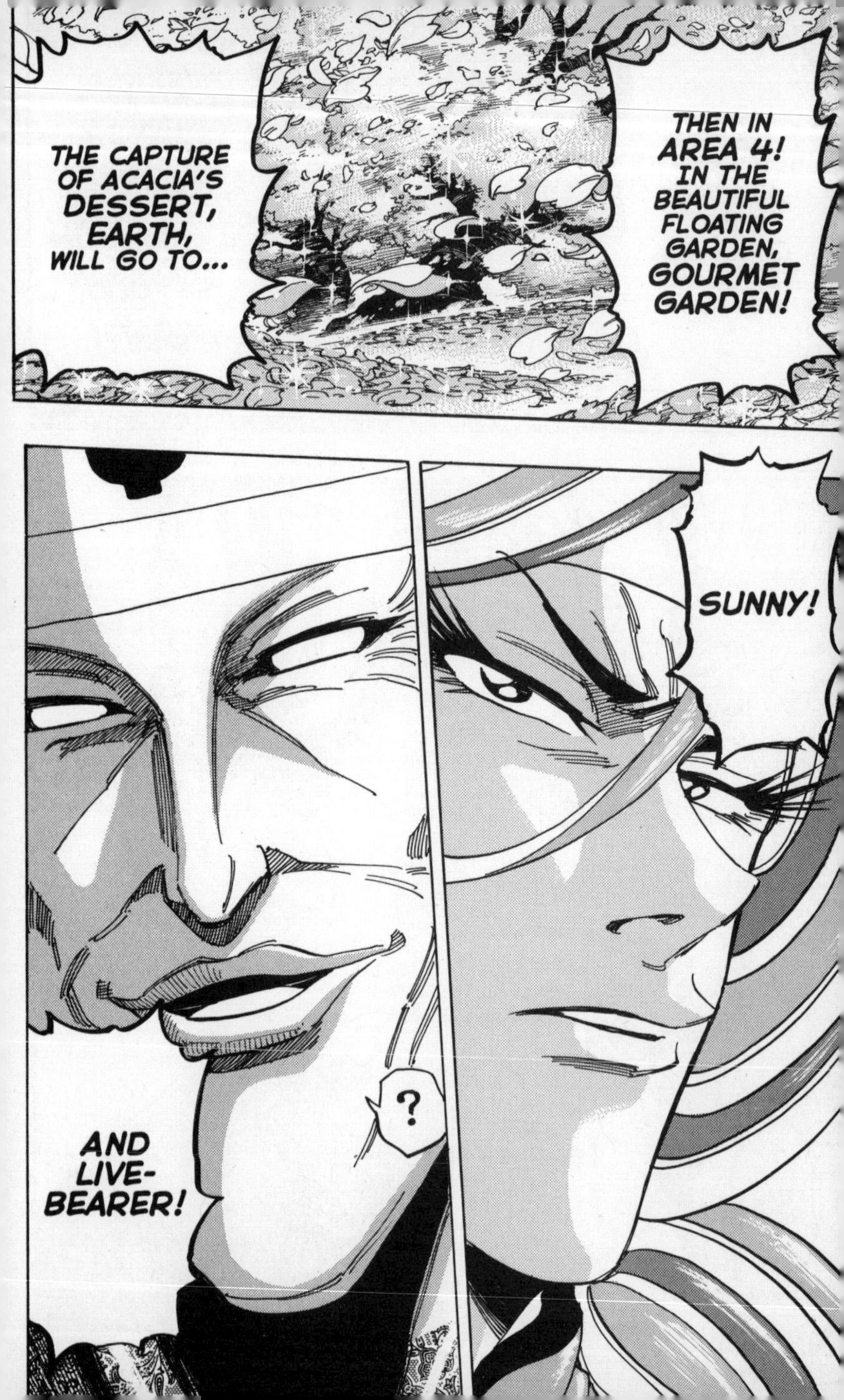
THEN IN AREA 4! IN THE BEAUTIFUL FLOATING GARDEN, GOURMET GARDEN!
THE CAPTURE OF ACACIA'S DESSERT, EARTH, WILL GO TO...
SUNNY!
?
AND LIVE-BEARER!

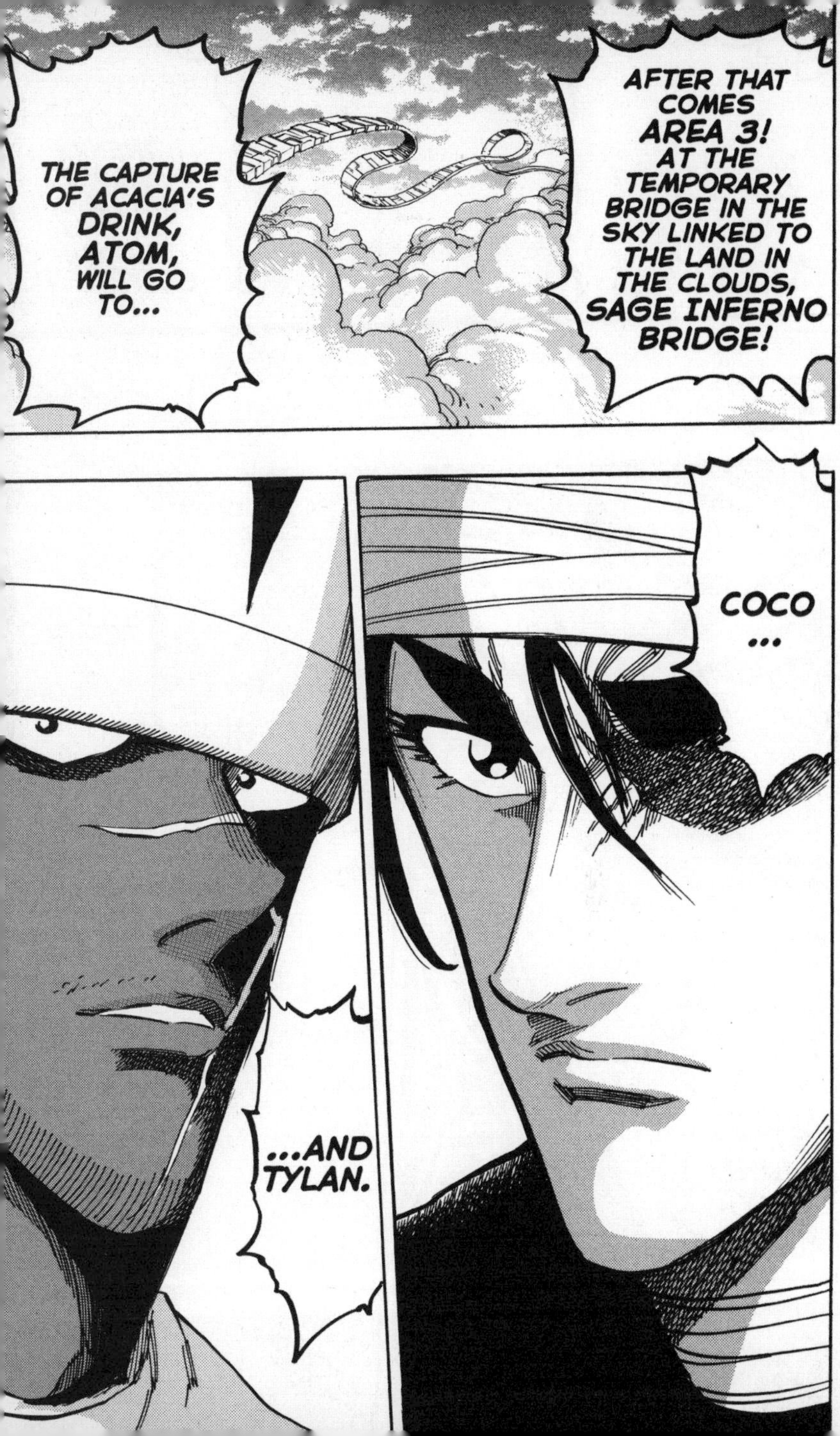
AFTER THAT COMES AREA 3! AT THE TEMPORARY BRIDGE IN THE SKY LINKED TO THE LAND IN THE CLOUDS, SAGE INFERNO BRIDGE!
THE CAPTURE OF ACACIA'S DRINK, ATOM, WILL GO TO...
COCO ...
...AND TYLAN.

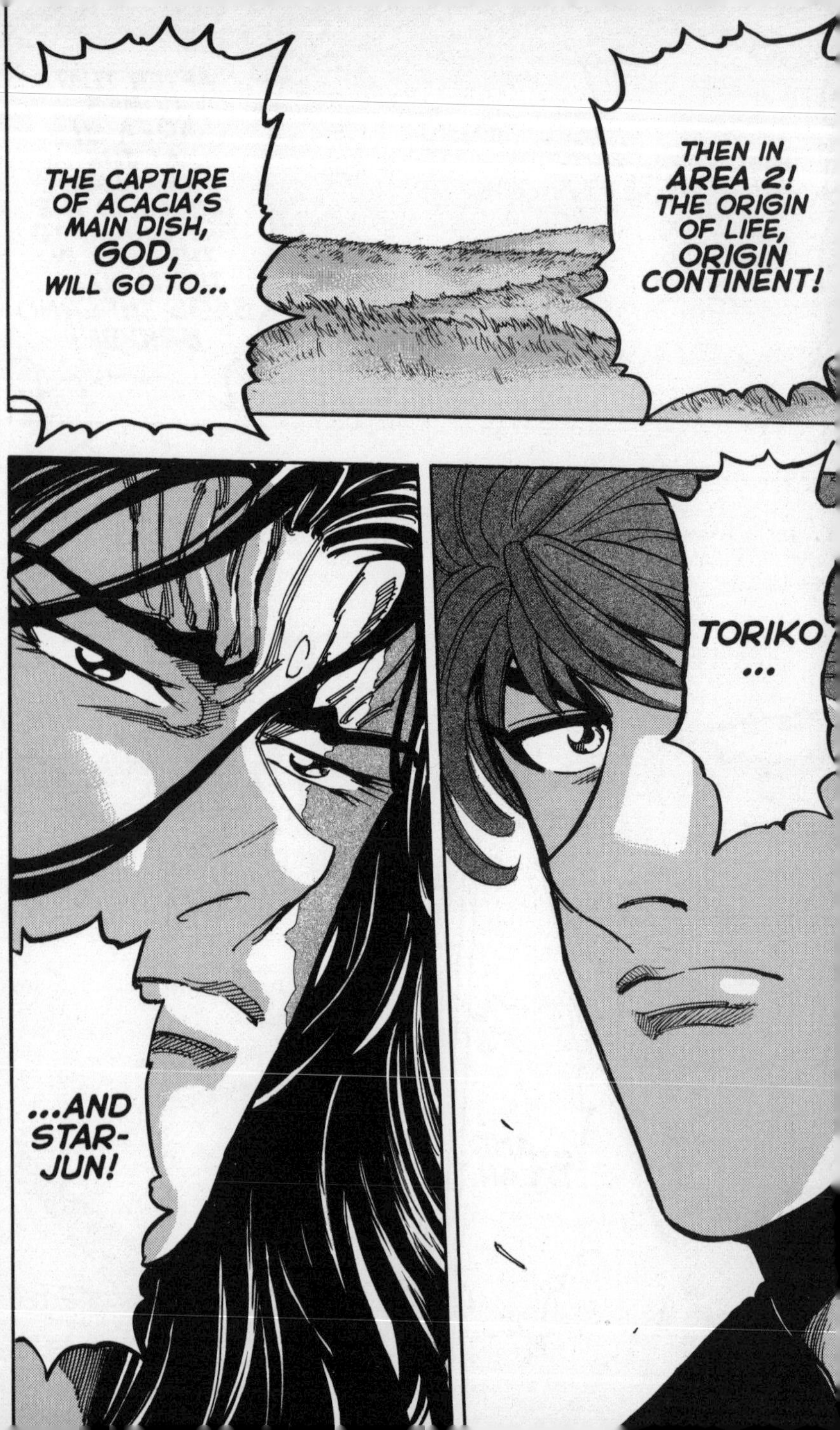
THEN IN AREA 2! THE ORIGIN OF LIFE, ORIGIN CONTINENT!
THE CAPTURE OF ACACIA'S MAIN DISH, GOD, WILL GO TO...
TORIKO ...
...AND STAR-JUN!

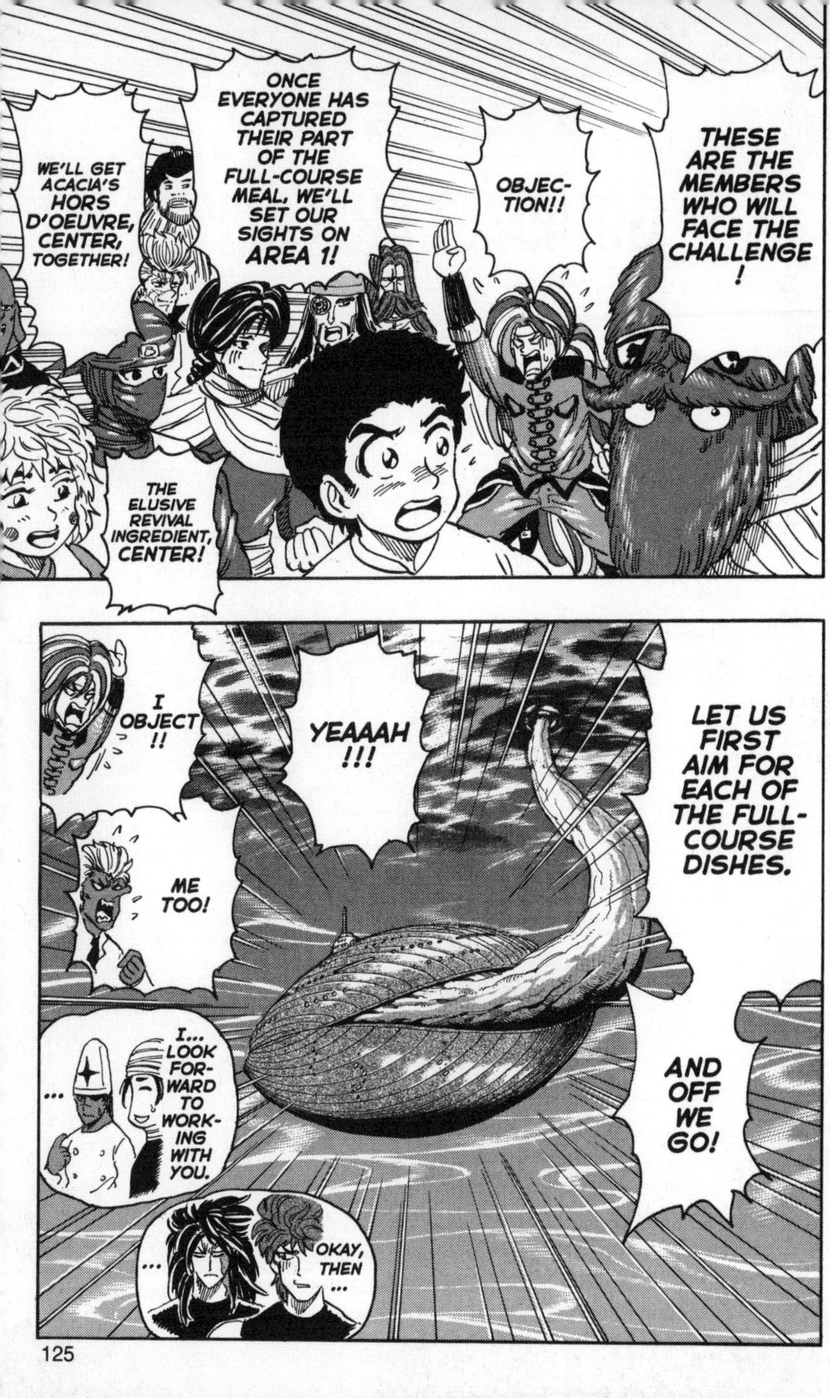
THESE ARE THE MEMBERS WHO WILL FACE THE CHALLENGE!
OBJECTION!!
ONCE EVERYONE HAS CAPTURED THEIR PART OF THE FULL-COURSE MEAL, WE'LL SET OUR SIGHTS ON AREA 1!
WE'LL GET ACACIA'S HORS D'OEUVRE, CENTER, TOGETHER!
THE ELUSIVE REVIVAL INGREDIENT, CENTER!
LET US FIRST AIM FOR EACH OF THE FULL-COURSE DISHES.
YEAAAH!!!
I OBJECT!!
ME TOO!
AND OFF WE GO!
I... LOOK FORWARD TO WORKING WITH YOU.
...
OKAY, THEN...
...

GOURMET CHECKLIST

Vol. 356

OCTOMELON
(MOLLUSK FRUIT)

CAPTURE LEVEL: 265

HABITAT: IGO'S BIOTOPE 1

SIZE: 3,500 M

HEIGHT: ---

WEIGHT: 50 BILLION TONS

PRICE: 50 YEN PER KILOGRAM

SCALE

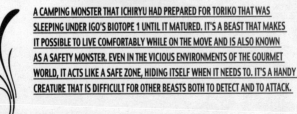

A CAMPING MONSTER THAT ICHIRYU HAD PREPARED FOR TORIKO THAT WAS SLEEPING UNDER IGO'S BIOTOPE 1 UNTIL IT MATURED. IT'S A BEAST THAT MAKES IT POSSIBLE TO LIVE COMFORTABLY WHILE ON THE MOVE AND IS ALSO KNOWN AS A SAFETY MONSTER. EVEN IN THE VICIOUS ENVIRONMENTS OF THE GOURMET WORLD, IT ACTS LIKE A SAFE ZONE, HIDING ITSELF WHEN IT NEEDS TO. IT'S A HANDY CREATURE THAT IS DIFFICULT FOR OTHER BEASTS BOTH TO DETECT AND TO ATTACK.

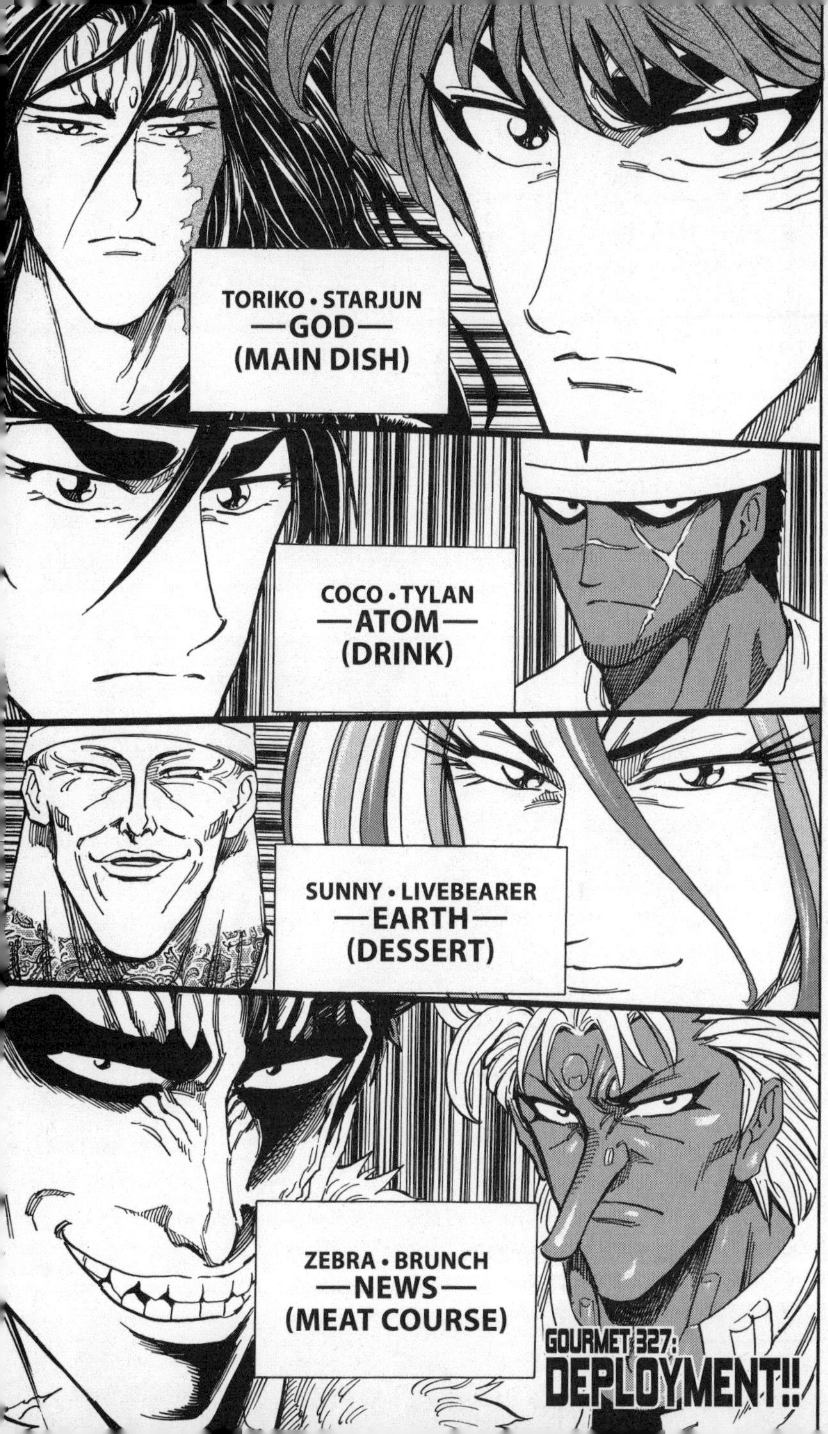
TORIKO • STARJUN
—GOD—
(MAIN DISH)
COCO • TYLAN
—ATOM—
(DRINK)
SUNNY • LIVEBEARER
—EARTH—
(DESSERT)
ZEBRA • BRUNCH
—NEWS—
(MEAT COURSE)
GOURMET 327:
DEPLOYMENT!!

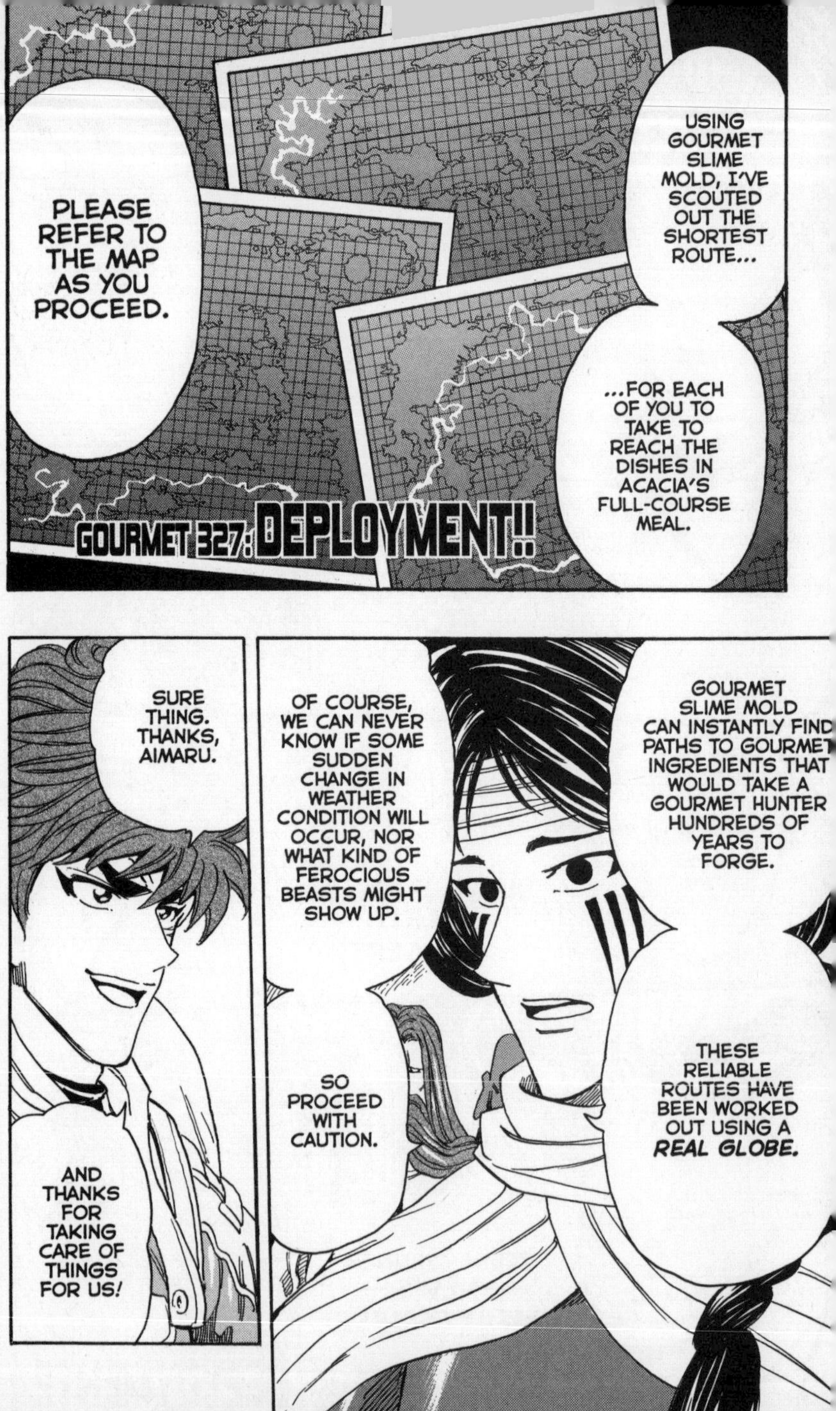
USING GOURMET SLIME MOLD, I'VE SCOUTED OUT THE SHORTEST ROUTE...
...FOR EACH OF YOU TO TAKE TO REACH THE DISHES IN ACACIA'S FULL-COURSE MEAL.
GOURMET 327: DEPLOYMENT!!
PLEASE REFER TO THE MAP AS YOU PROCEED.
GOURMET SLIME MOLD CAN INSTANTLY FIND PATHS TO GOURMET INGREDIENTS THAT WOULD TAKE A GOURMET HUNTER HUNDREDS OF YEARS TO FORGE.
THESE RELIABLE ROUTES HAVE BEEN WORKED OUT USING A *REAL GLOBE.*
OF COURSE, WE CAN NEVER KNOW IF SOME SUDDEN CHANGE IN WEATHER CONDITION WILL OCCUR, NOR WHAT KIND OF FEROCIOUS BEASTS MIGHT SHOW UP.
SO PROCEED WITH CAUTION.
SURE THING. THANKS, AIMARU.
AND THANKS FOR TAKING CARE OF THINGS FOR US!

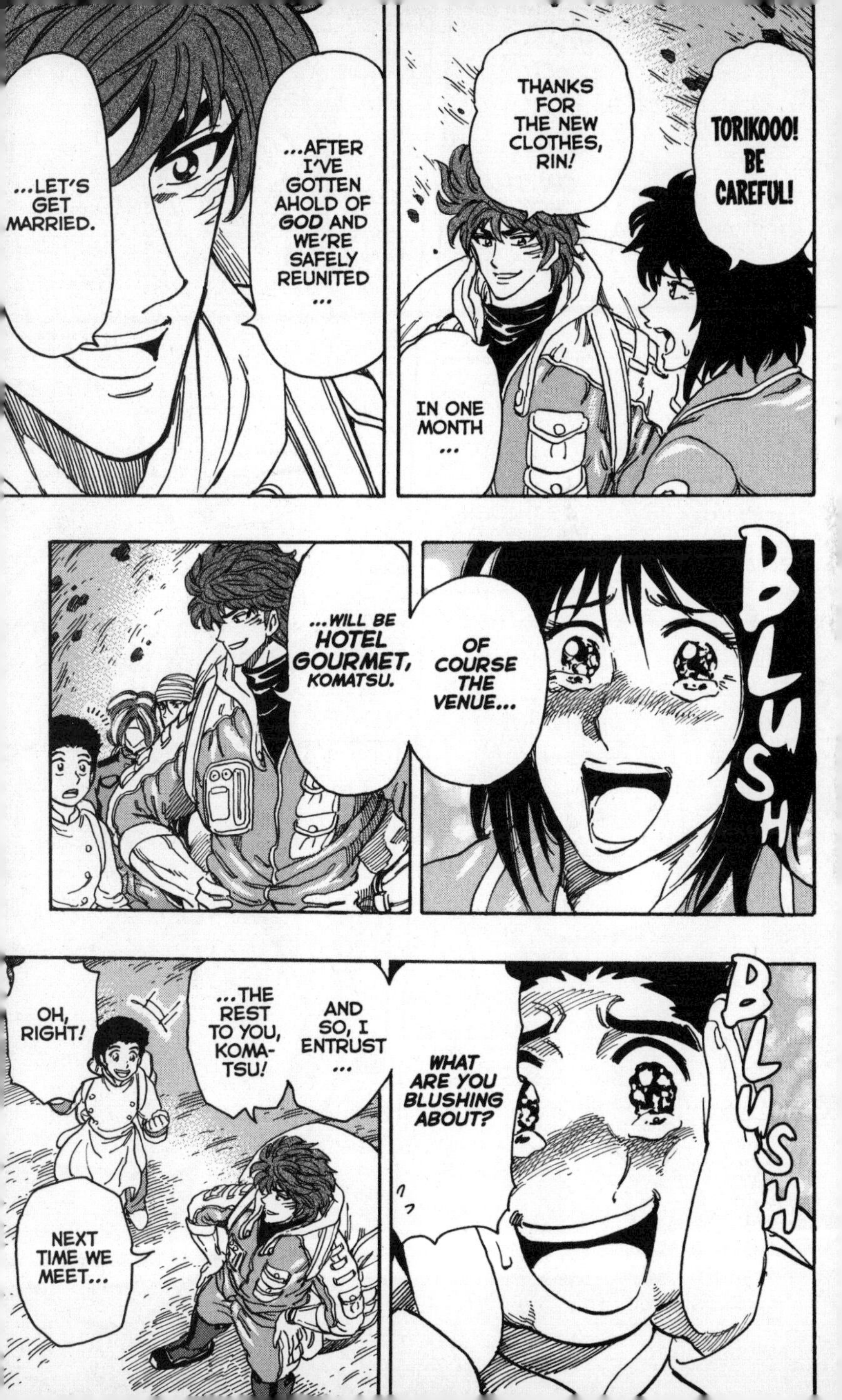
TORIKOOO! BE CAREFUL!
THANKS FOR THE NEW CLOTHES, RIN!
IN ONE MONTH...
...AFTER I'VE GOTTEN AHOLD OF GOD AND WE'RE SAFELY REUNITED...
...LET'S GET MARRIED.
BLUSH
OF COURSE THE VENUE...
...WILL BE HOTEL GOURMET, KOMATSU.
BLUSH
WHAT ARE YOU BLUSHING ABOUT?
AND SO, I ENTRUST...
...THE REST TO YOU, KOMATSU!
OH, RIGHT!
NEXT TIME WE MEET...

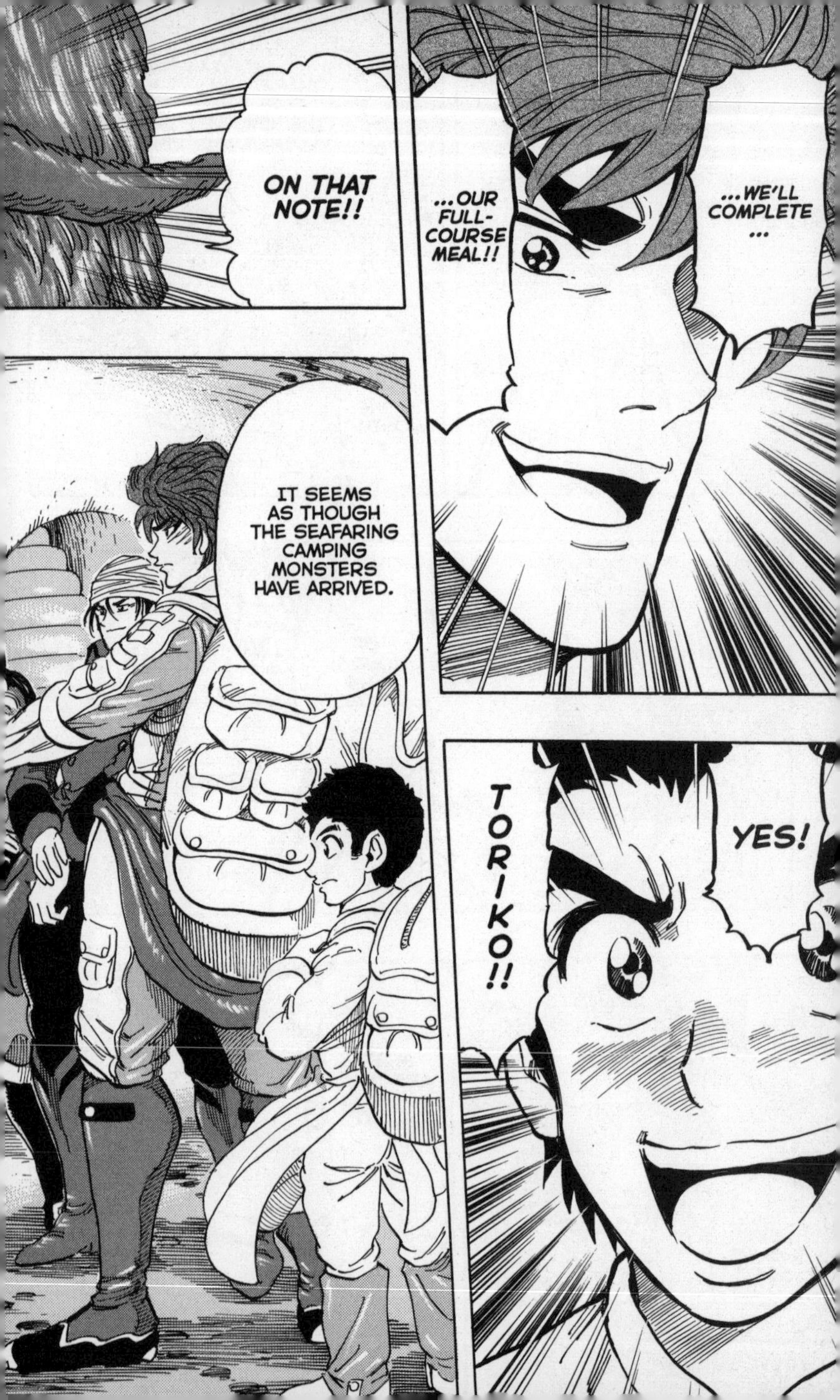
...WE'LL COMPLETE ...
...OUR FULL-COURSE MEAL!!
ON THAT NOTE!!
YES!
TORIKO!!
IT SEEMS AS THOUGH THE SEAFARING CAMPING MONSTERS HAVE ARRIVED.

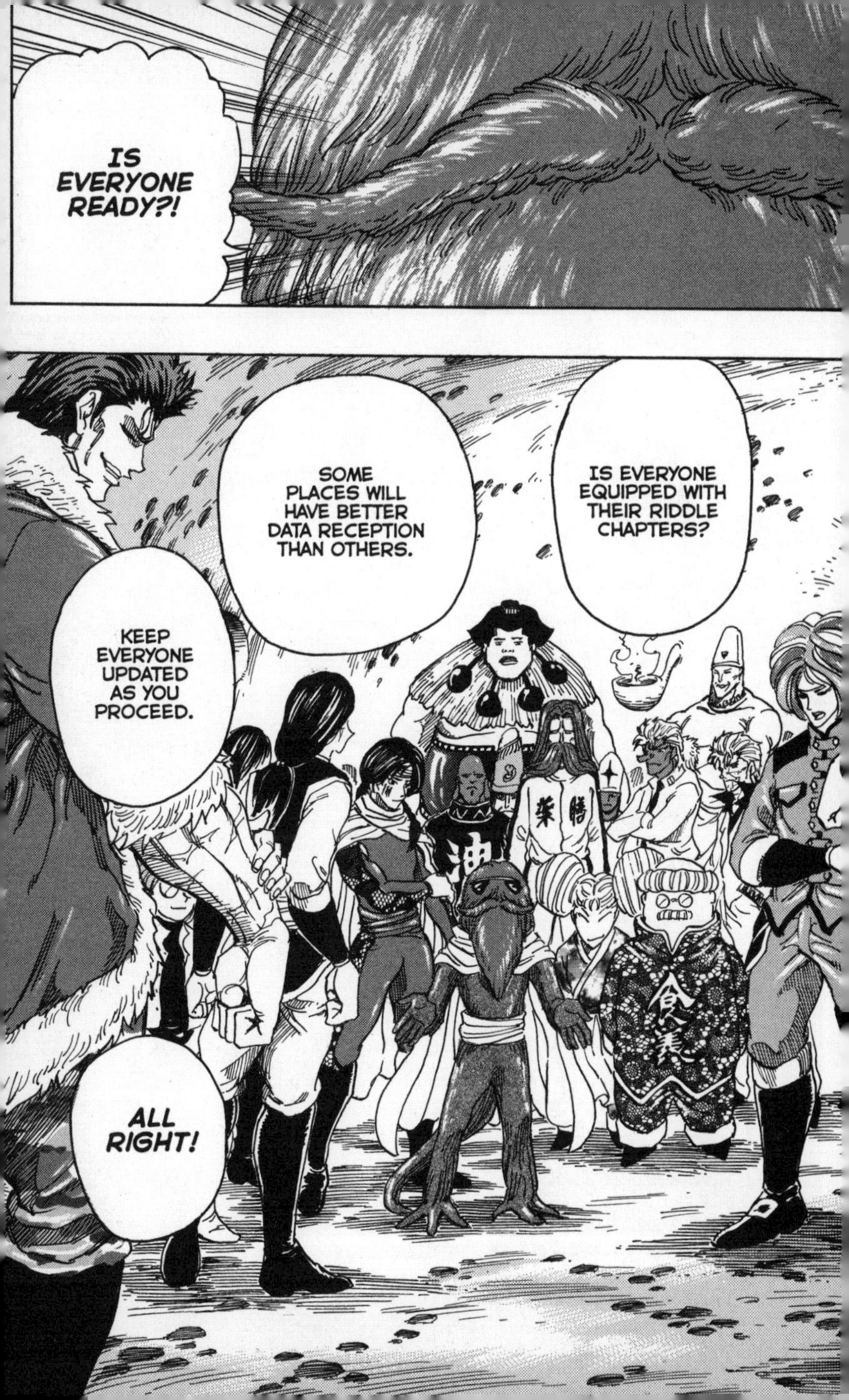
IS EVERYONE READY?!
IS EVERYONE EQUIPPED WITH THEIR RIDDLE CHAPTERS?
SOME PLACES WILL HAVE BETTER DATA RECEPTION THAN OTHERS.
KEEP EVERYONE UPDATED AS YOU PROCEED.
ALL RIGHT!

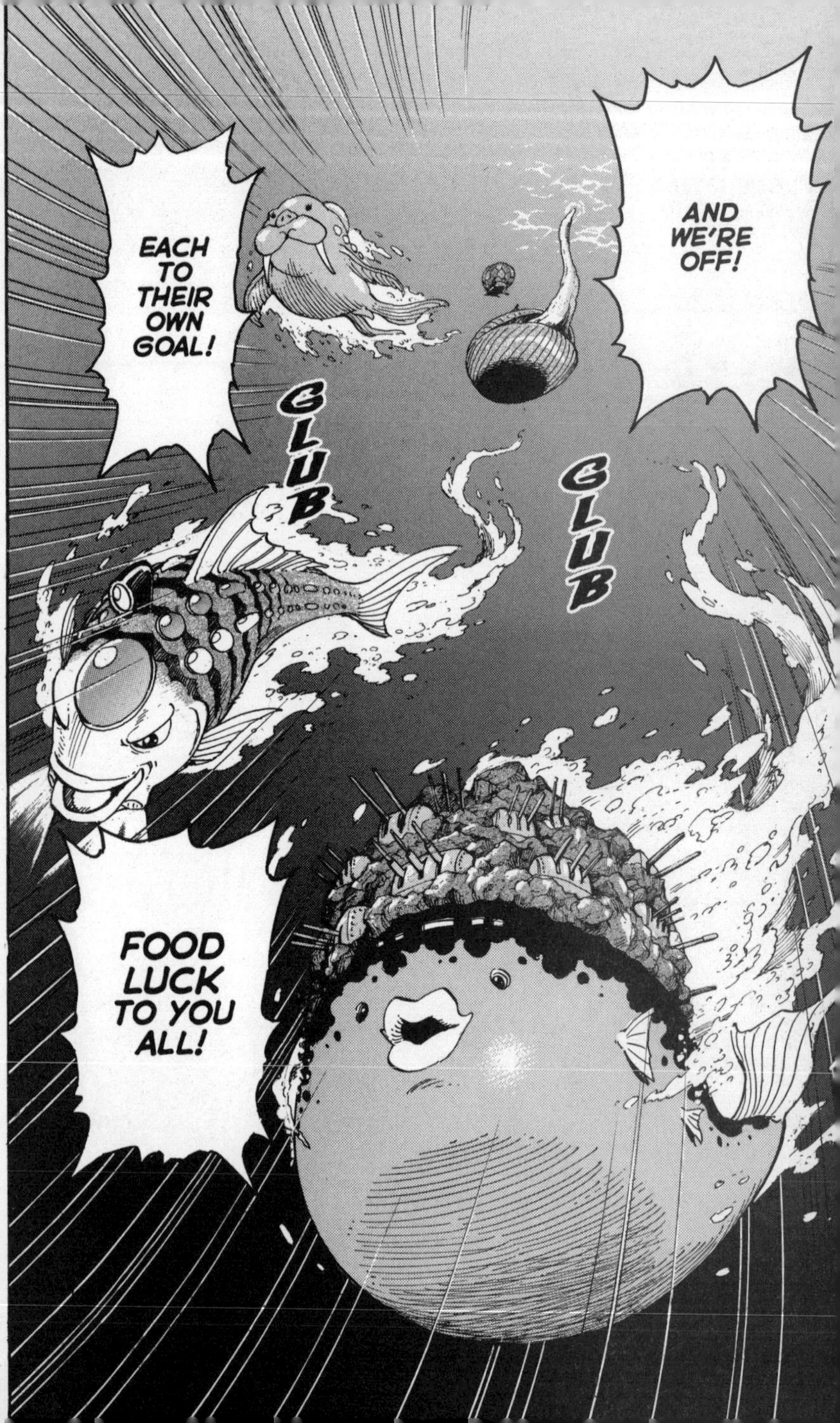
AND WE'RE OFF!
EACH TO THEIR OWN GOAL!
GLUB
GLUB
FOOD LUCK TO YOU ALL!

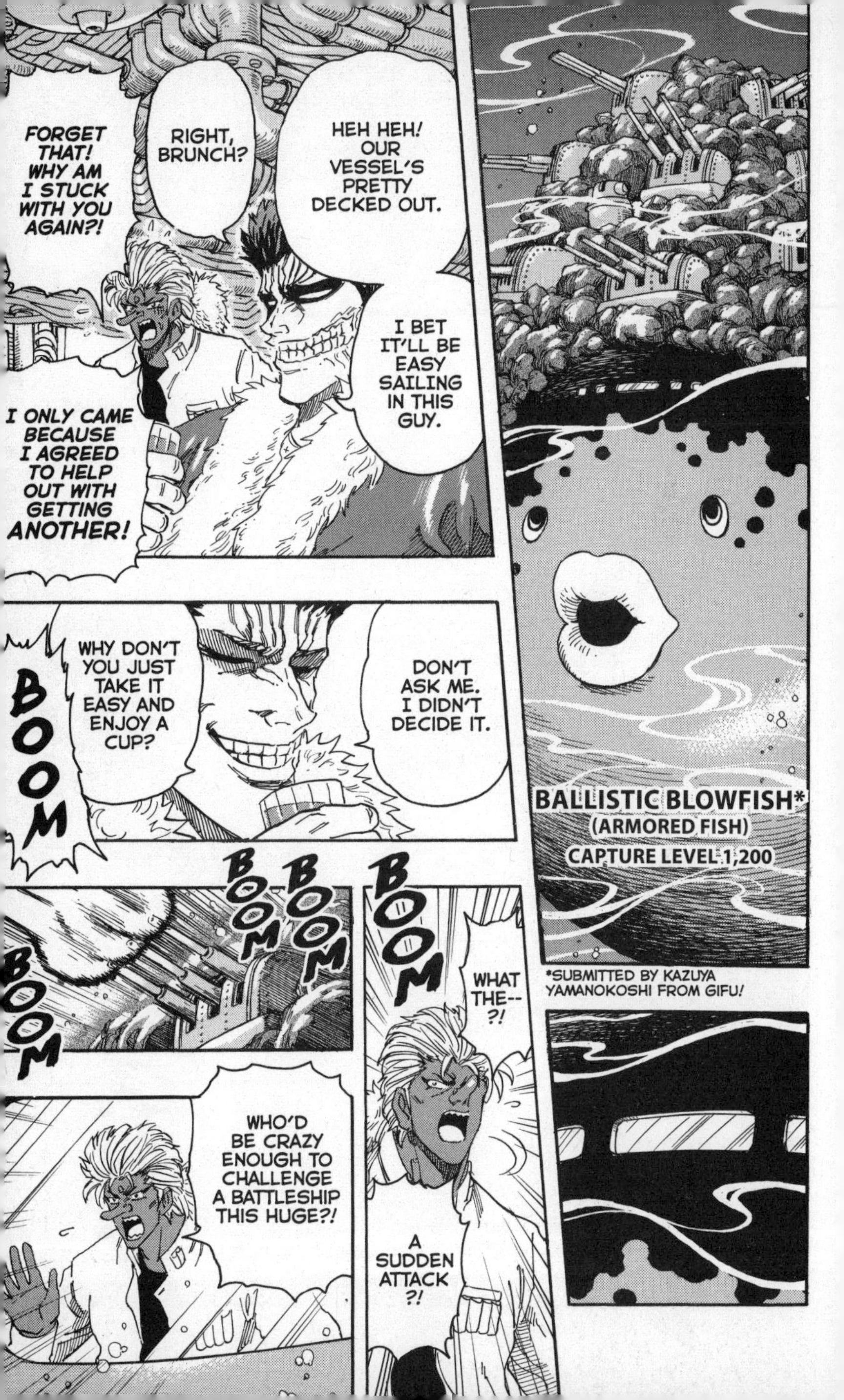
BALLISTIC BLOWFISH*
(ARMORED FISH)
CAPTURE LEVEL 1,200
*SUBMITTED BY KAZUYA YAMANOKOSHI FROM GIFU!
HEH HEH! OUR VESSEL'S PRETTY DECKED OUT.
I BET IT'LL BE EASY SAILING IN THIS GUY.
RIGHT, BRUNCH?
FORGET THAT! WHY AM I STUCK WITH YOU AGAIN?!
I ONLY CAME BECAUSE I AGREED TO HELP OUT WITH GETTING ANOTHER!
DON'T ASK ME. I DIDN'T DECIDE IT.
WHY DON'T YOU JUST TAKE IT EASY AND ENJOY A CUP?
BOOM
BOOM
WHAT THE--?!
A SUDDEN ATTACK?!
BOOM
BOOM
BOOM
WHO'D BE CRAZY ENOUGH TO CHALLENGE A BATTLESHIP THIS HUGE?!

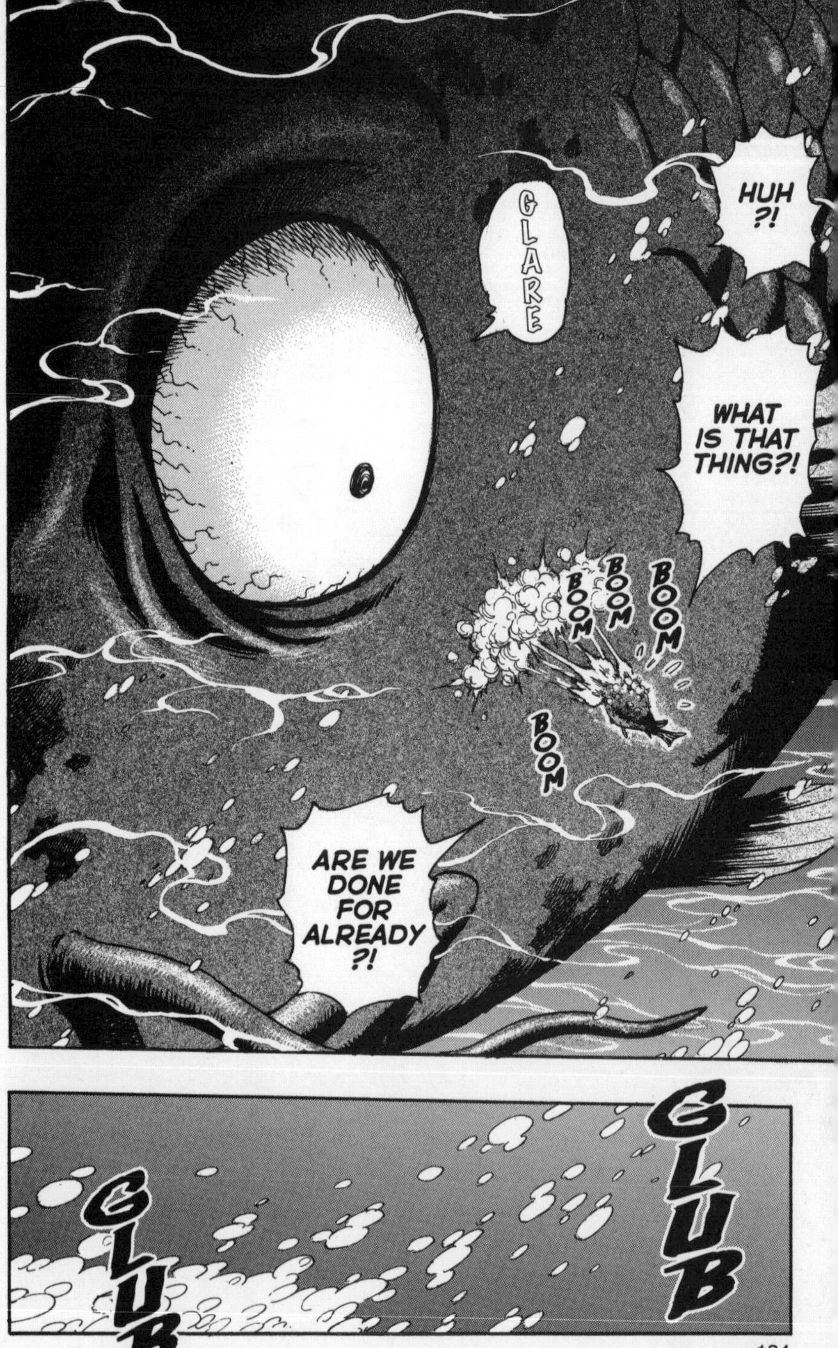
HUH ?!
WHAT IS THAT THING?!
GLARE
BOOM
BOOM
BOOM
BOOM
ARE WE DONE FOR ALREADY ?!
GLUB
GLUB

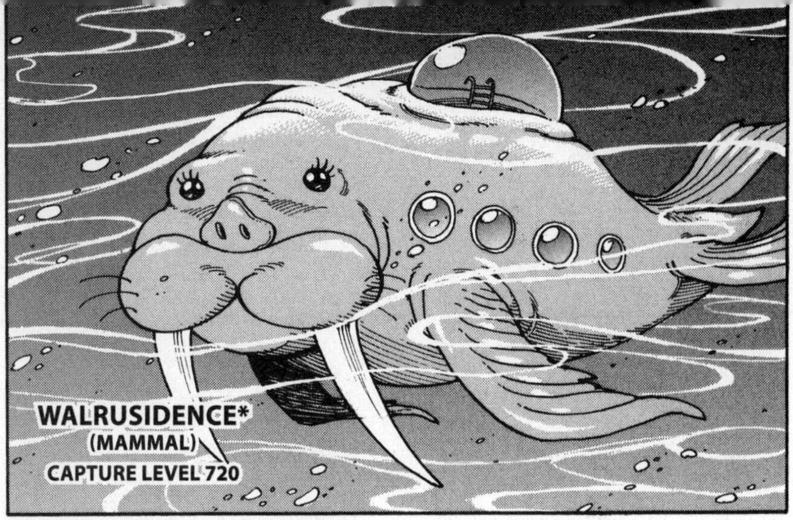
WALRUSIDENCE*
(MAMMAL)
CAPTURE LEVEL 720

*SUBMITTED BY KIYOSHI KURITA FROM TOKYO!

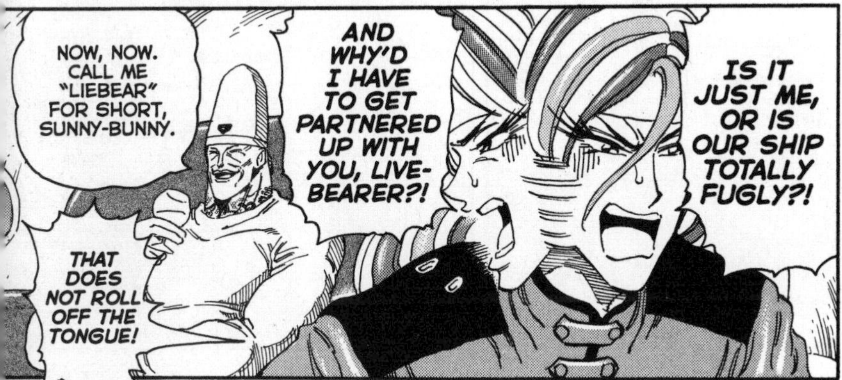
IS IT JUST ME, OR IS OUR SHIP TOTALLY FUGLY?!
AND WHY'D I HAVE TO GET PARTNERED UP WITH YOU, LIVE-BEARER?!
NOW, NOW. CALL ME "LIEBEAR" FOR SHORT, SUNNY-BUNNY.
THAT DOES NOT ROLL OFF THE TONGUE!

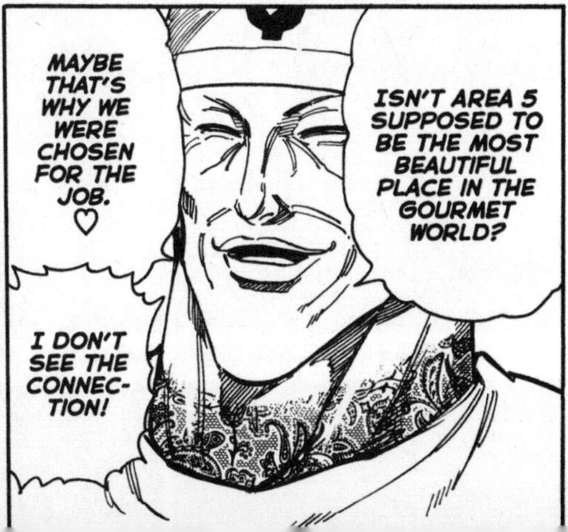
ISN'T AREA 5 SUPPOSED TO BE THE MOST BEAUTIFUL PLACE IN THE GOURMET WORLD?
MAYBE THAT'S WHY WE WERE CHOSEN FOR THE JOB. ♡
I DON'T SEE THE CONNECTION!

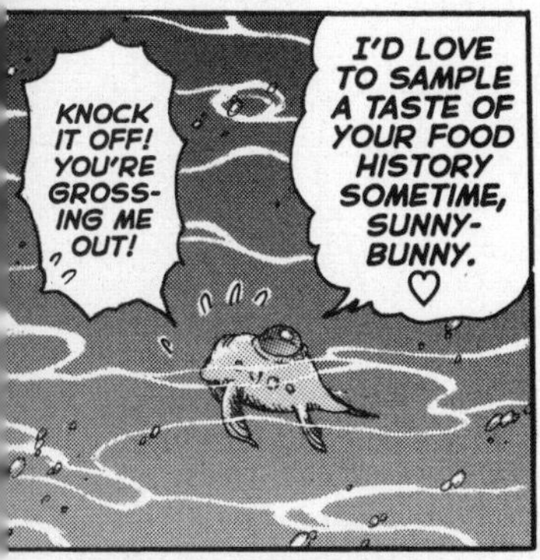
I'D LOVE TO SAMPLE A TASTE OF YOUR FOOD HISTORY SOMETIME, SUNNY-BUNNY. ♡
KNOCK IT OFF! YOU'RE GROSSING ME OUT!

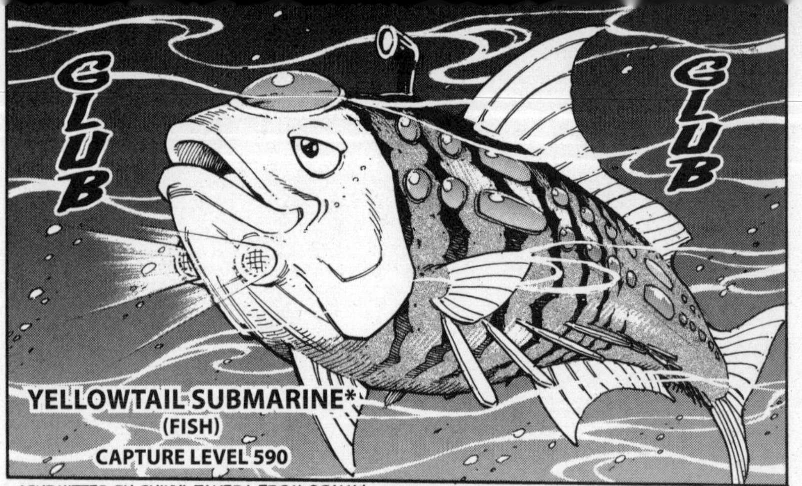
GLUB
GLUB
YELLOWTAIL SUBMARINE*
(FISH)
CAPTURE LEVEL 590

*SUBMITTED BY SHINYA TAKEDA FROM OSAKA!

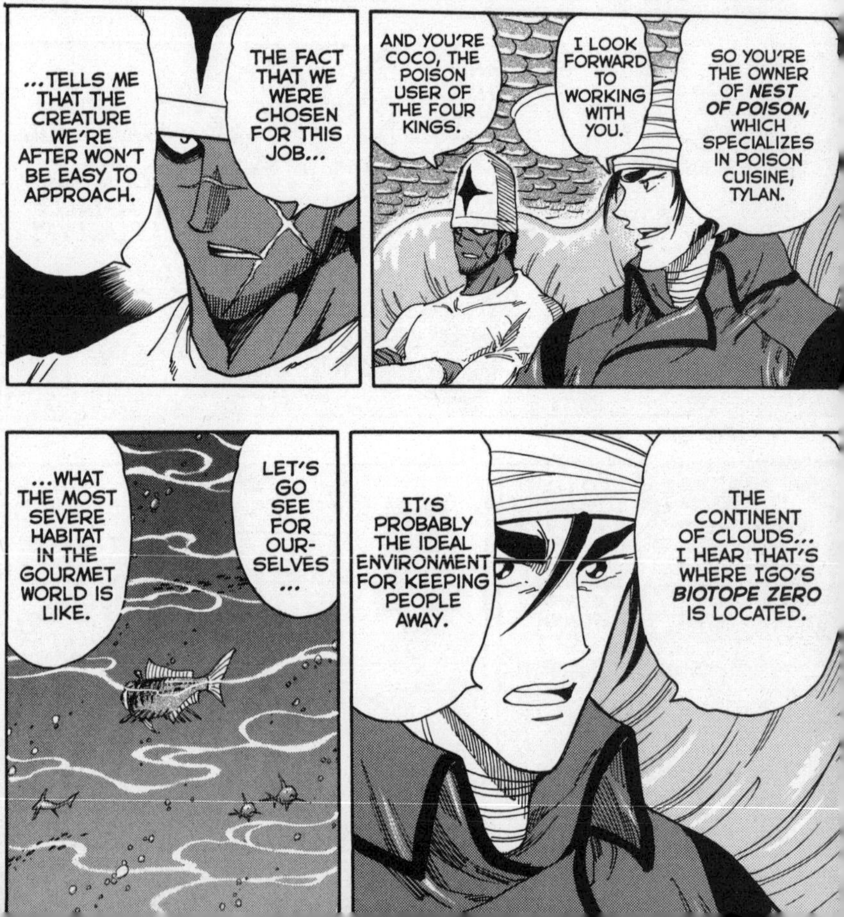
SO YOU'RE THE OWNER OF *NEST OF POISON,* WHICH SPECIALIZES IN POISON CUISINE, TYLAN.
I LOOK FORWARD TO WORKING WITH YOU.
AND YOU'RE COCO, THE POISON USER OF THE FOUR KINGS.
THE FACT THAT WE WERE CHOSEN FOR THIS JOB...
...TELLS ME THAT THE CREATURE WE'RE AFTER WON'T BE EASY TO APPROACH.
THE CONTINENT OF CLOUDS... I HEAR THAT'S WHERE IGO'S *BIOTOPE ZERO* IS LOCATED.
IT'S PROBABLY THE IDEAL ENVIRONMENT FOR KEEPING PEOPLE AWAY.
LET'S GO SEE FOR OUR-SELVES...
...WHAT THE MOST SEVERE HABITAT IN THE GOURMET WORLD IS LIKE.

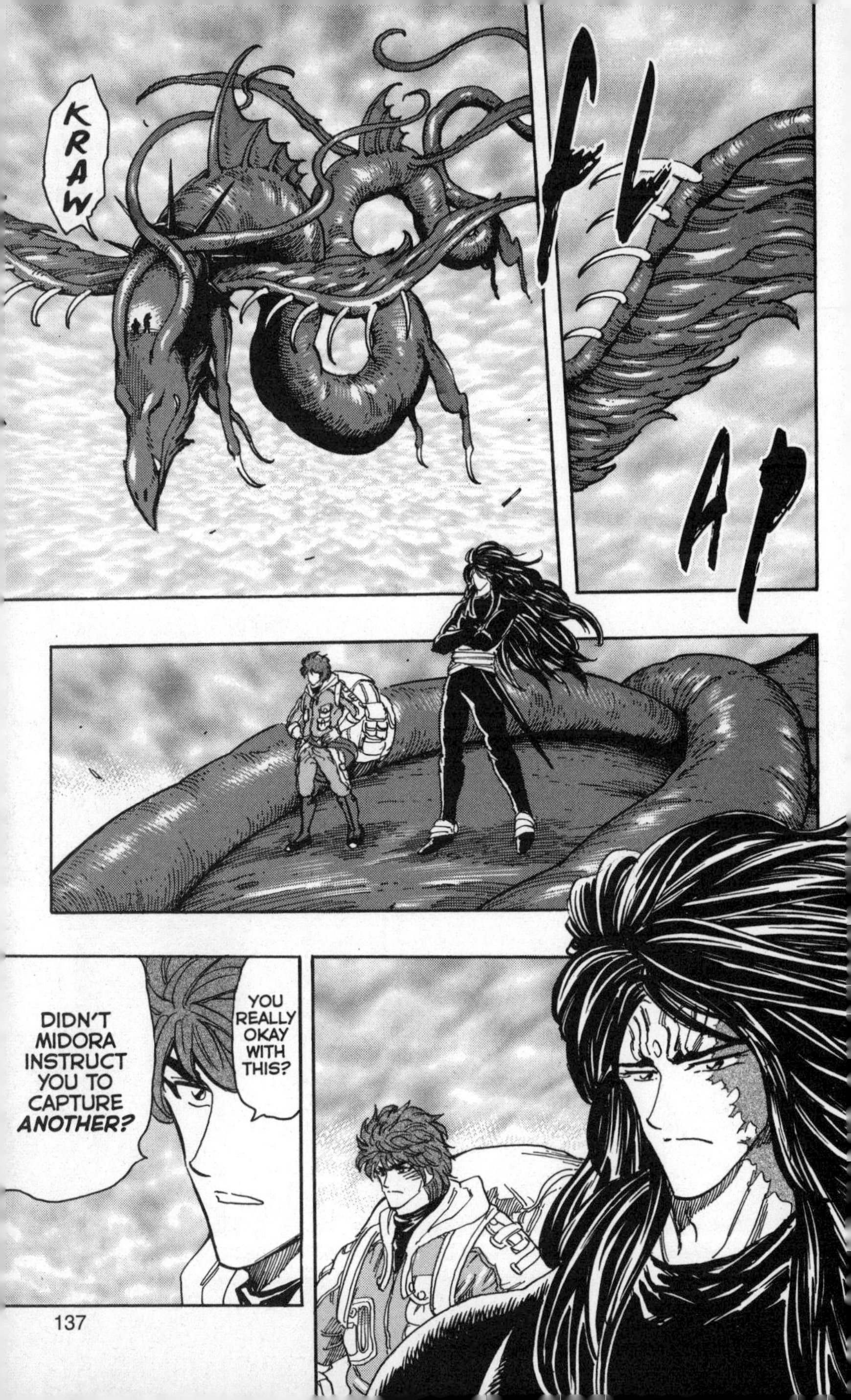
FLAP
KRAW
YOU REALLY OKAY WITH THIS?
DIDN'T MIDORA INSTRUCT YOU TO CAPTURE *ANOTHER?*

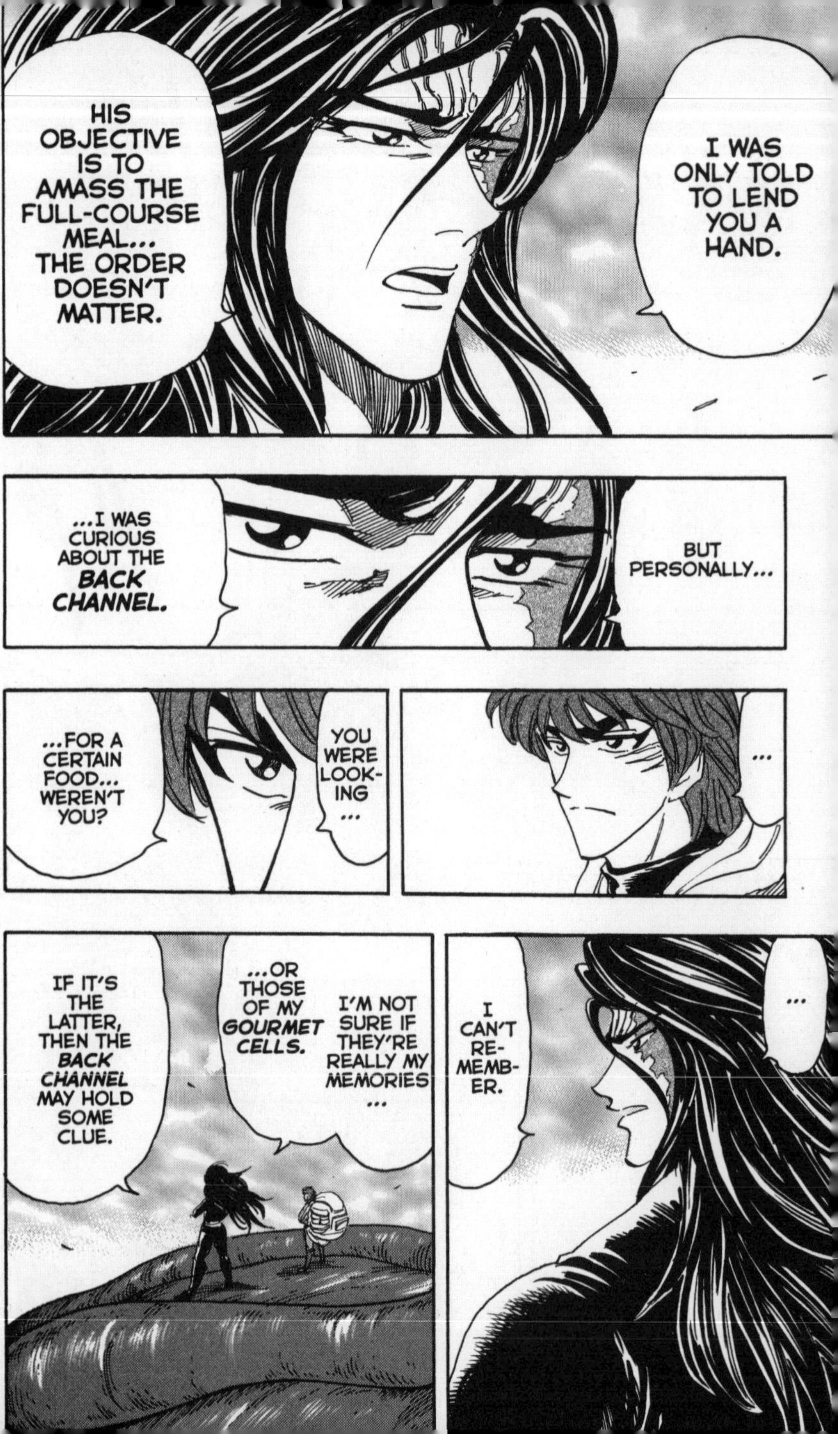
I WAS ONLY TOLD TO LEND YOU A HAND.
HIS OBJECTIVE IS TO AMASS THE FULL-COURSE MEAL... THE ORDER DOESN'T MATTER.
BUT PERSONALLY...
...I WAS CURIOUS ABOUT THE BACK CHANNEL.
...
YOU WERE LOOKING-ING...
...FOR A CERTAIN FOOD... WEREN'T YOU?
...
I CAN'T RE-MEMB-ER.
I'M NOT SURE IF THEY'RE REALLY MY MEMORIES...
...OR THOSE OF MY GOURMET CELLS.
IF IT'S THE LATTER, THEN THE BACK CHANNEL MAY HOLD SOME CLUE.

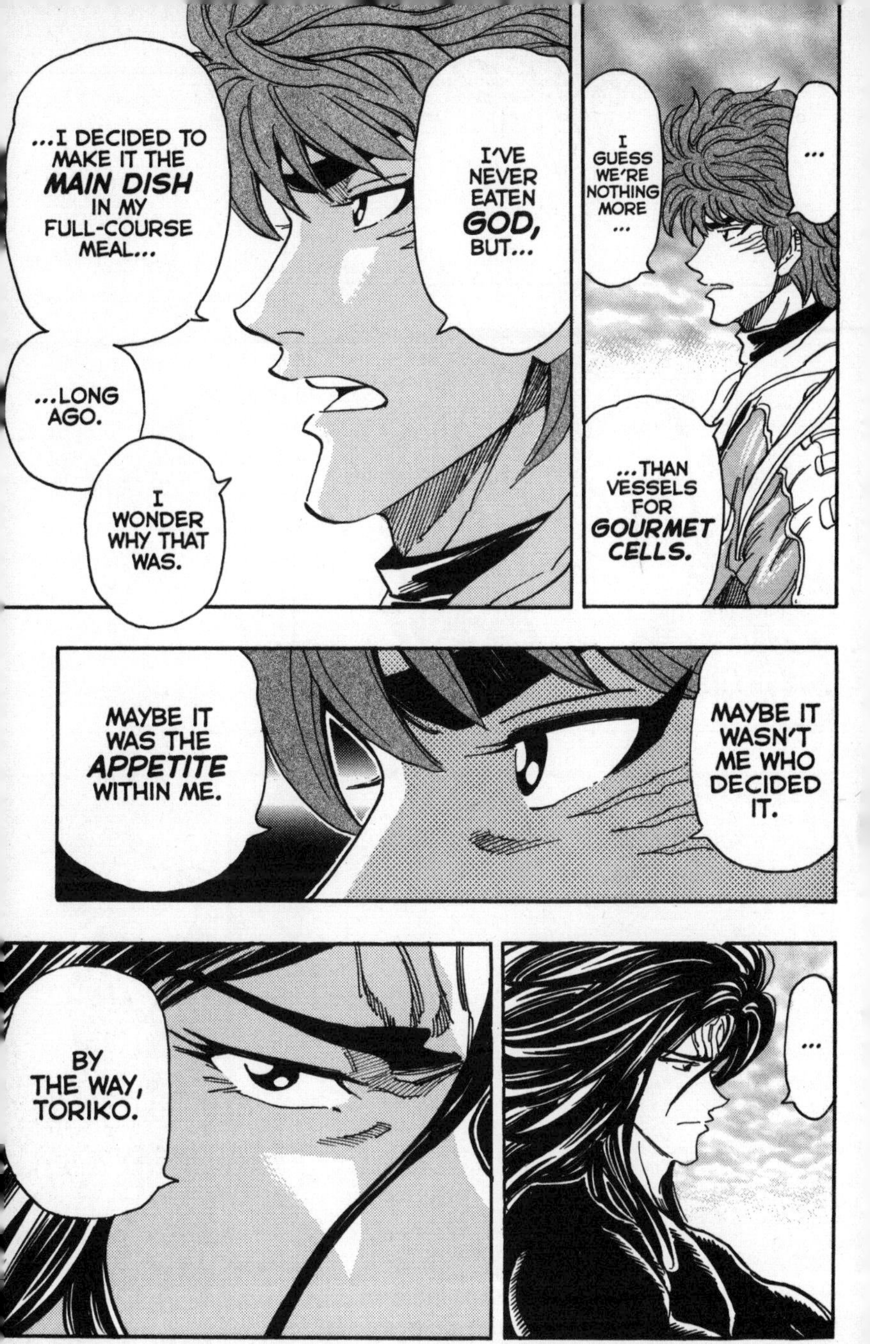
...
I GUESS WE'RE NOTHING MORE...
...THAN VESSELS FOR GOURMET CELLS.
I'VE NEVER EATEN GOD, BUT...
...I DECIDED TO MAKE IT THE MAIN DISH IN MY FULL-COURSE MEAL...
...LONG AGO.
I WONDER WHY THAT WAS.
MAYBE IT WASN'T ME WHO DECIDED IT.
MAYBE IT WAS THE APPETITE WITHIN ME.
...
BY THE WAY, TORIKO.

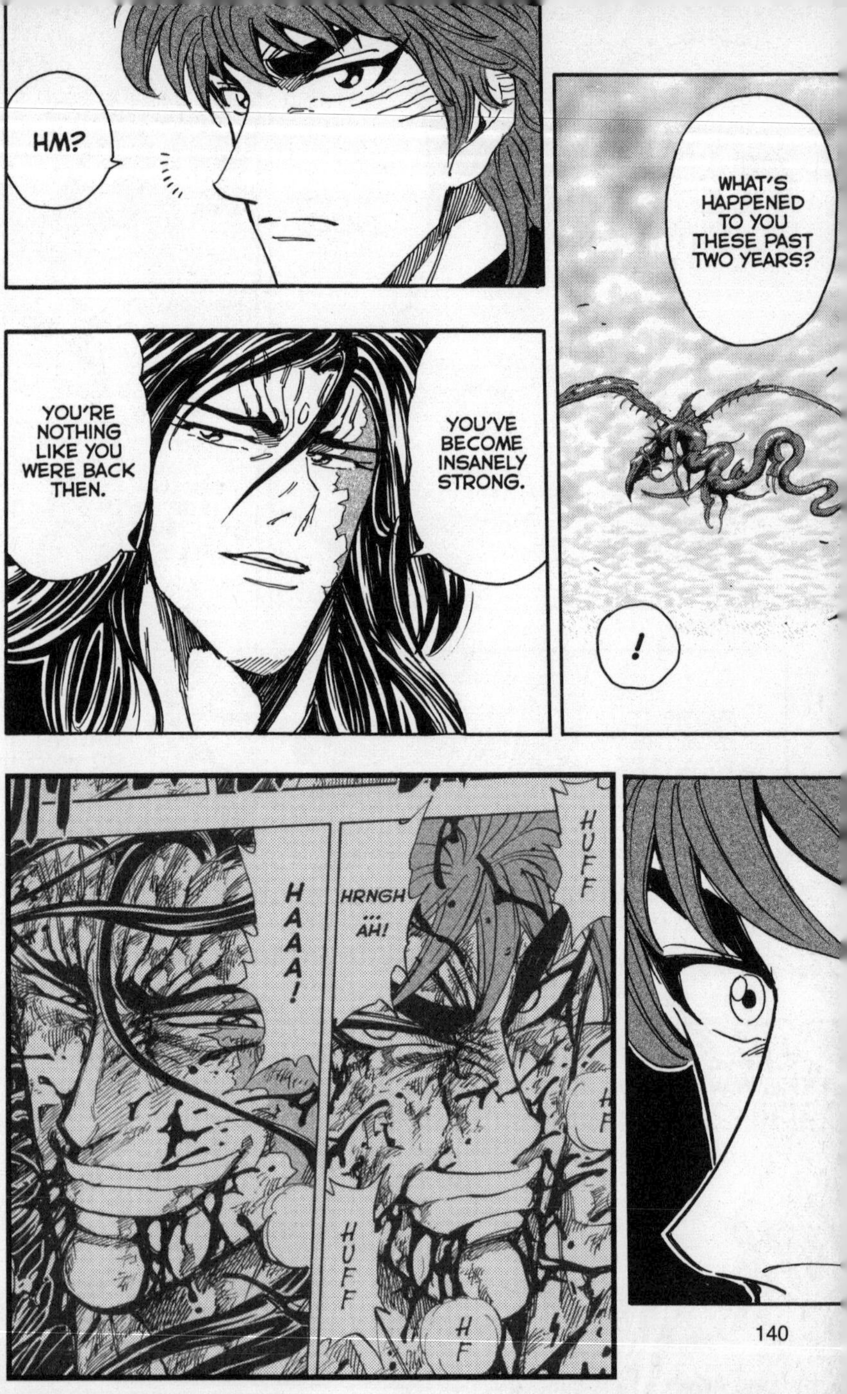
WHAT'S HAPPENED TO YOU THESE PAST TWO YEARS?
!
HM?
YOU'VE BECOME INSANELY STRONG.
YOU'RE NOTHING LIKE YOU WERE BACK THEN.
HUFF
HRNGH ... AH!
HF
HUFF
HF
HAAAA!

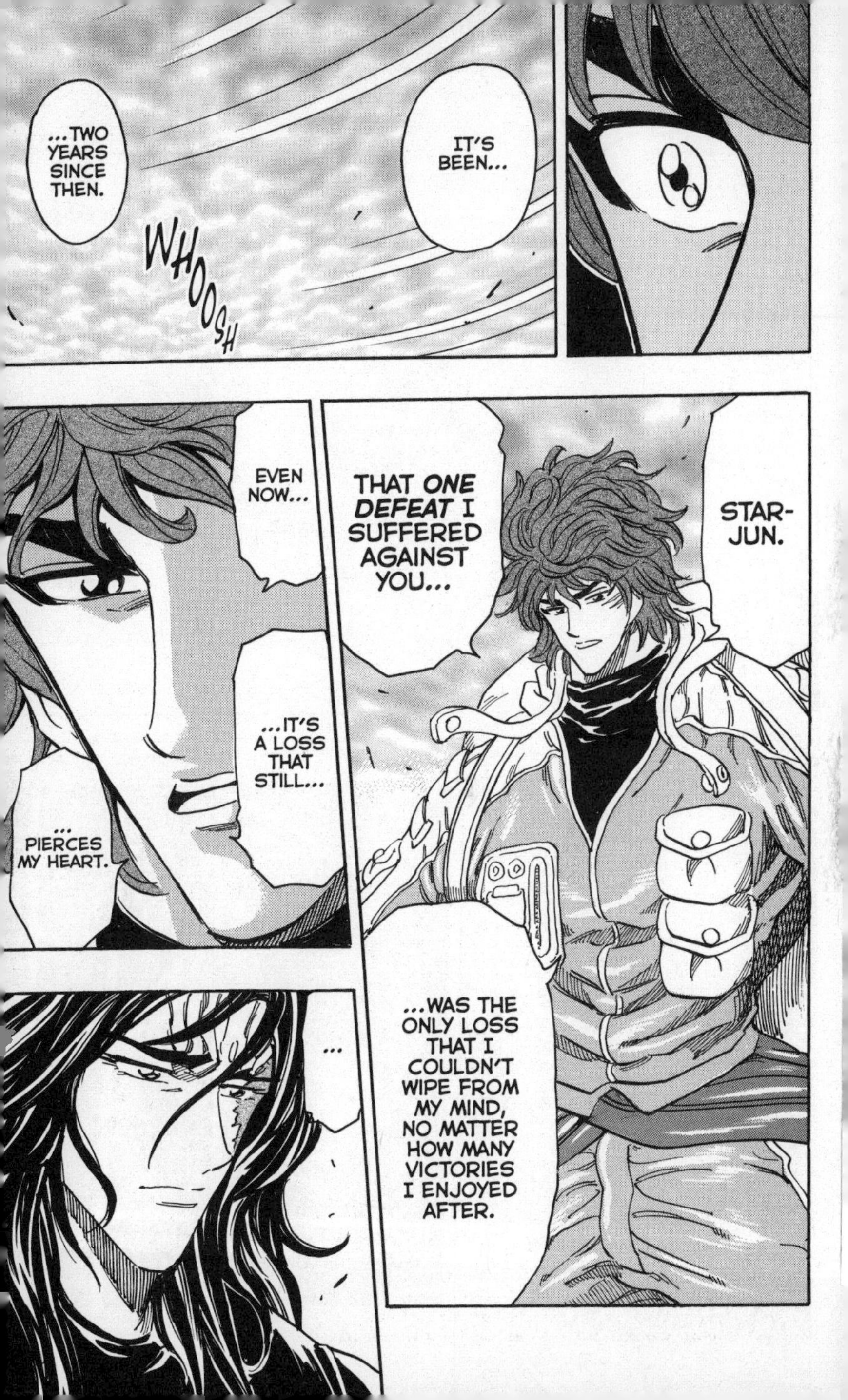
IT'S BEEN...
...TWO YEARS SINCE THEN.
WHOOSH
STAR-JUN.
THAT *ONE DEFEAT* I SUFFERED AGAINST YOU...
...WAS THE ONLY LOSS THAT I COULDN'T WIPE FROM MY MIND, NO MATTER HOW MANY VICTORIES I ENJOYED AFTER.
EVEN NOW...
...IT'S A LOSS THAT STILL...
...PIERCES MY HEART.
...

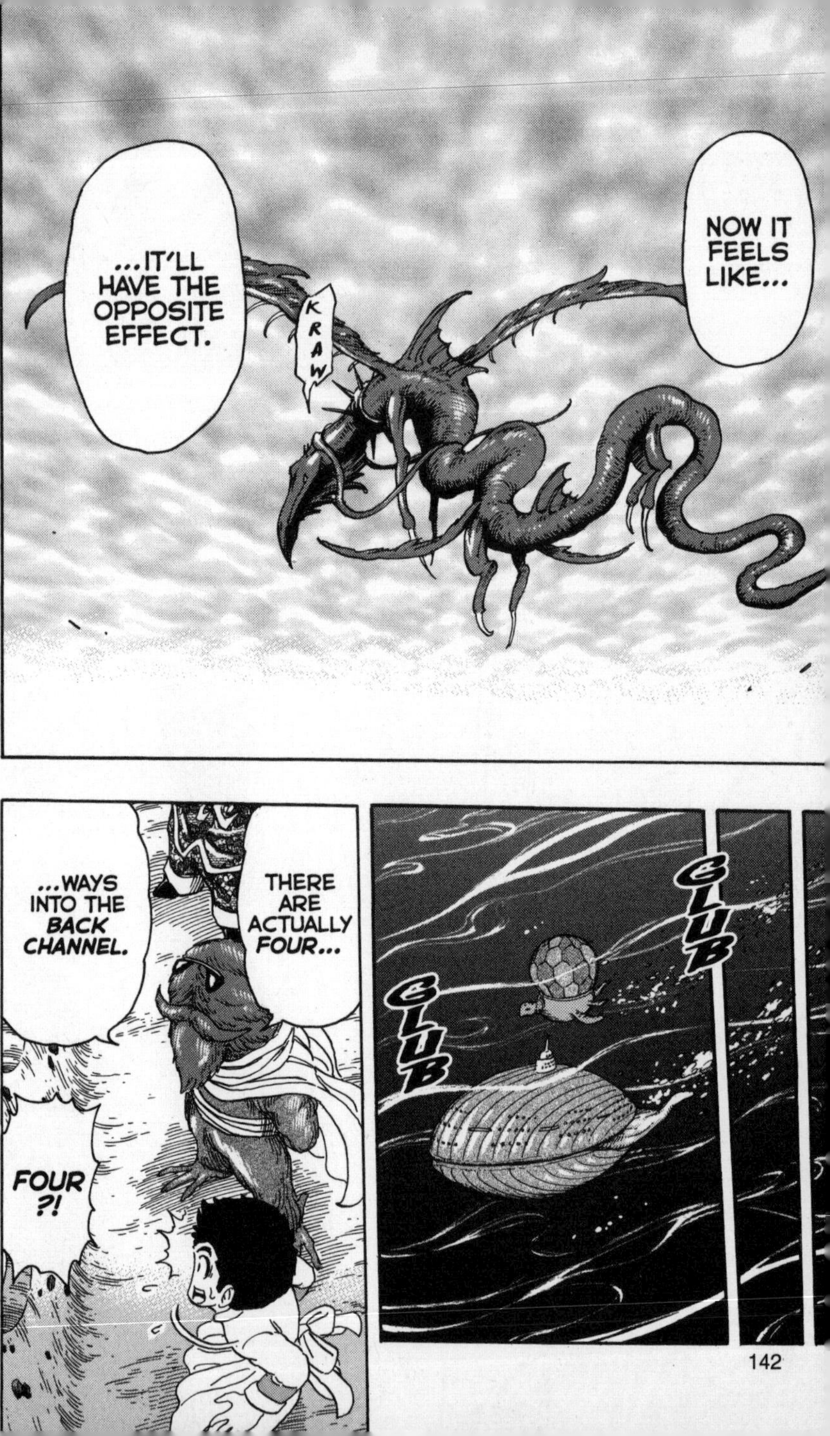
NOW IT FEELS LIKE...
KRAW
...IT'LL HAVE THE OPPOSITE EFFECT.
GLUB
GLUB
THERE ARE ACTUALLY *FOUR*...
...WAYS INTO THE *BACK CHANNEL.*
FOUR?!

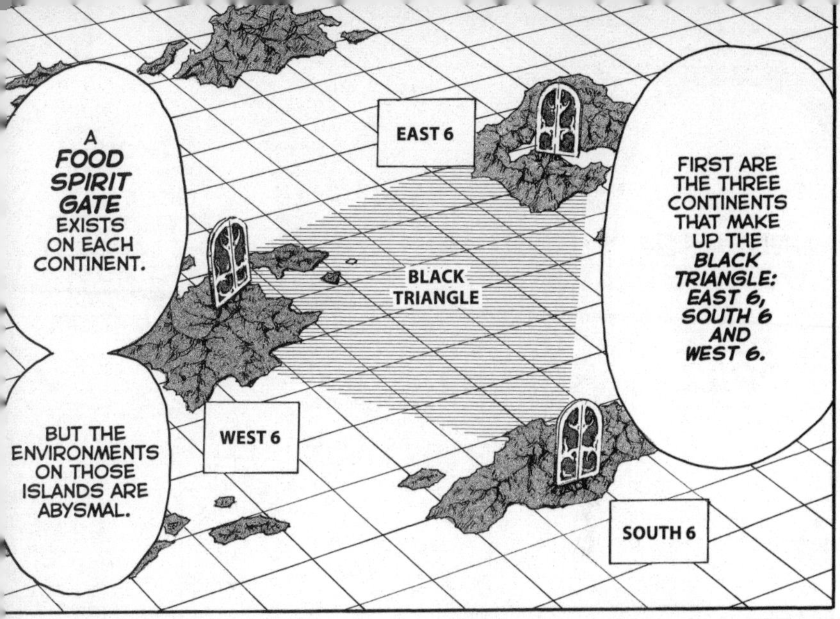
FIRST ARE THE THREE CONTINENTS THAT MAKE UP THE *BLACK TRIANGLE: EAST 6, SOUTH 6 AND WEST 6.*
EAST 6
BLACK TRIANGLE
SOUTH 6
WEST 6
A *FOOD SPIRIT GATE* EXISTS ON EACH CONTINENT.
BUT THE ENVIRONMENTS ON THOSE ISLANDS ARE ABYSMAL.

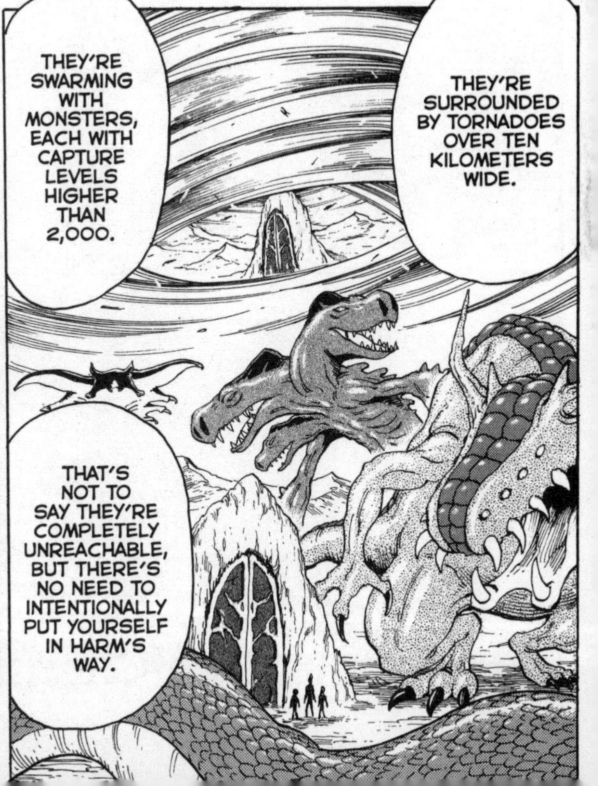
THEY'RE SURROUNDED BY TORNADOES OVER TEN KILOMETERS WIDE.
THEY'RE SWARMING WITH MONSTERS, EACH WITH CAPTURE LEVELS HIGHER THAN 2,000.
THAT'S NOT TO SAY THEY'RE COMPLETELY UNREACHABLE, BUT THERE'S NO NEED TO INTENTIONALLY PUT YOURSELF IN HARM'S WAY.

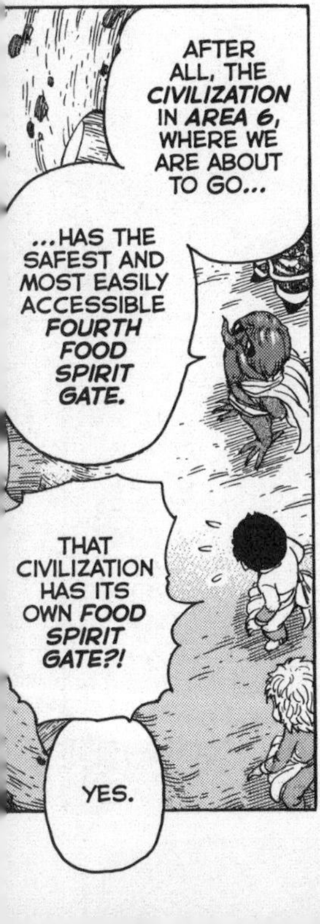
AFTER ALL, THE *CIVILIZATION* IN *AREA 6*, WHERE WE ARE ABOUT TO GO...
...HAS THE SAFEST AND MOST EASILY ACCESSIBLE *FOURTH FOOD SPIRIT GATE.*
THAT CIVILIZATION HAS ITS OWN *FOOD SPIRIT GATE?!*
YES.

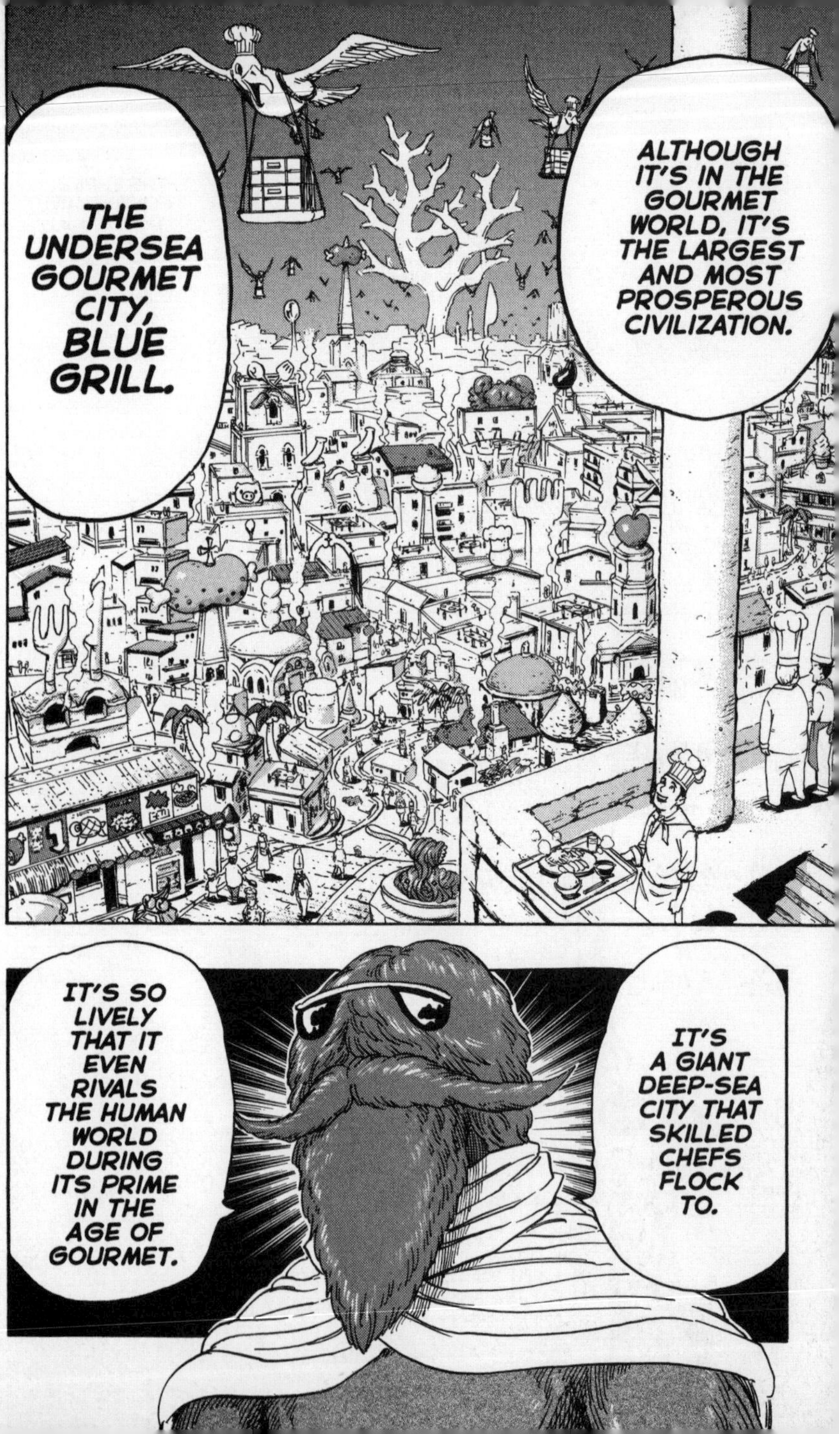
ALTHOUGH IT'S IN THE GOURMET WORLD, IT'S THE LARGEST AND MOST PROSPEROUS CIVILIZATION.
THE UNDERSEA GOURMET CITY, BLUE GRILL.
IT'S A GIANT DEEP-SEA CITY THAT SKILLED CHEFS FLOCK TO.
IT'S SO LIVELY THAT IT EVEN RIVALS THE HUMAN WORLD DURING ITS PRIME IN THE AGE OF GOURMET.

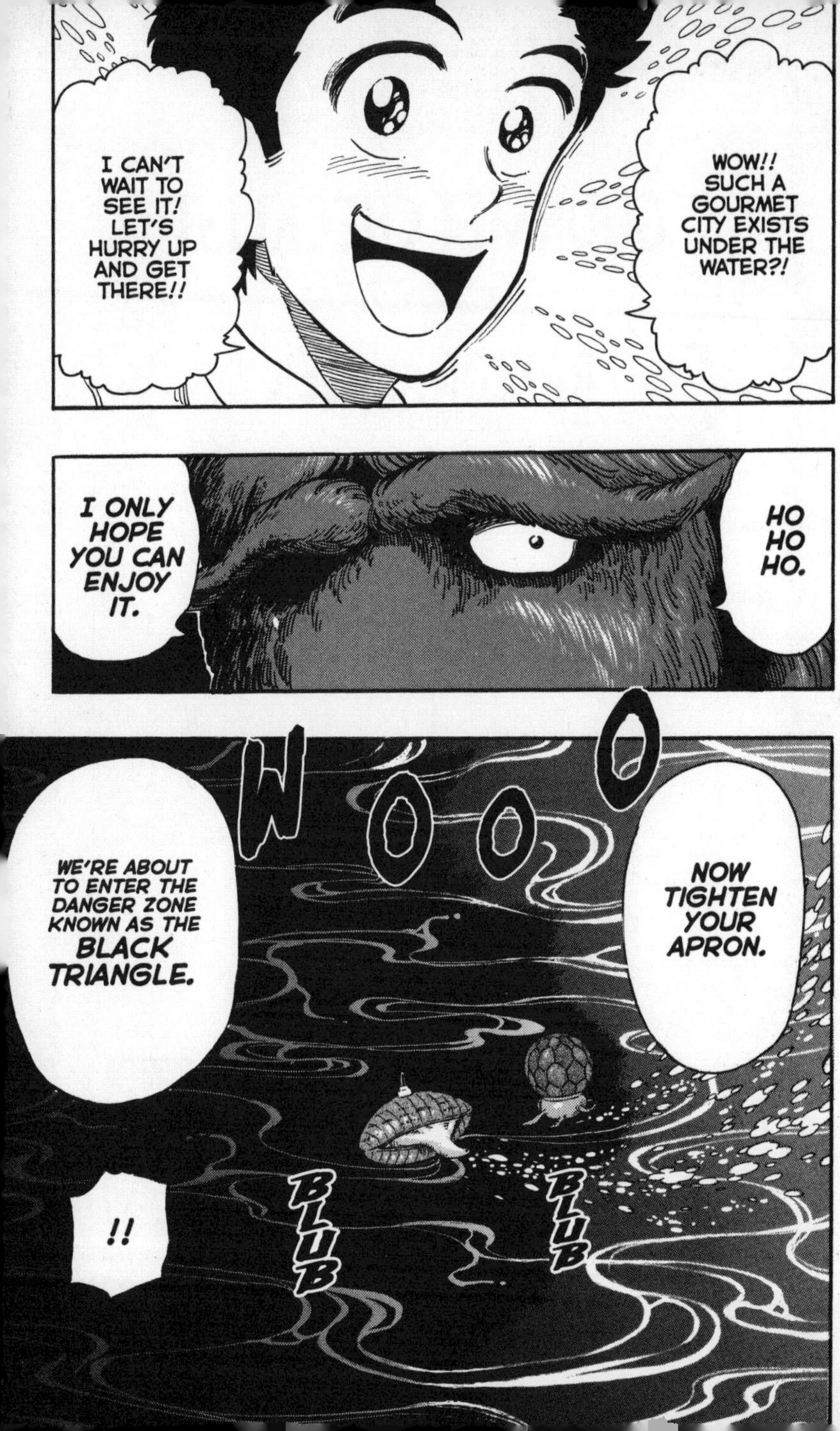
WOW!! SUCH A GOURMET CITY EXISTS UNDER THE WATER?!
I CAN'T WAIT TO SEE IT! LET'S HURRY UP AND GET THERE!!
HO HO HO.
I ONLY HOPE YOU CAN ENJOY IT.
WOOO
NOW TIGHTEN YOUR APRON.
WE'RE ABOUT TO ENTER THE DANGER ZONE KNOWN AS THE BLACK TRIANGLE.
BLUB
BLUB
!!

GOURMET CHECKLIST

Vol. 357

RAYZOR ANGLER
(HYBRID FISH)

CAPTURE LEVEL: 299

HABITAT: THE SEAS AROUND YUTO ISLAND

SIZE: 5,000 M

HEIGHT: ---

WEIGHT: 700 MILLION TONS

PRICE: 90,000 YEN PER KILOGRAM

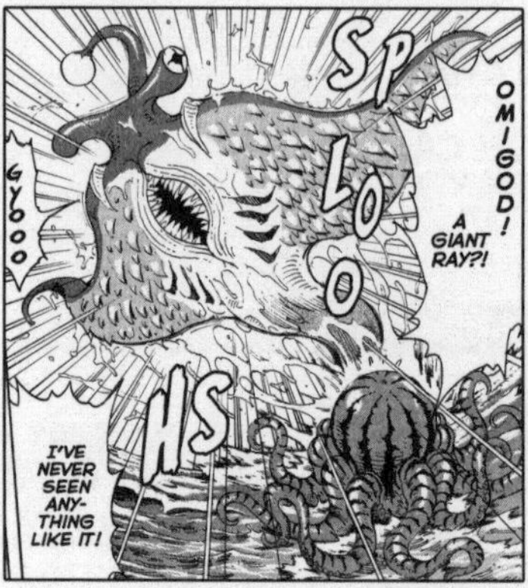
OMIGOD!
A GIANT RAY?!
SP
LO
O
HS
GYOOO
I'VE NEVER SEEN ANY-THING LIKE IT!

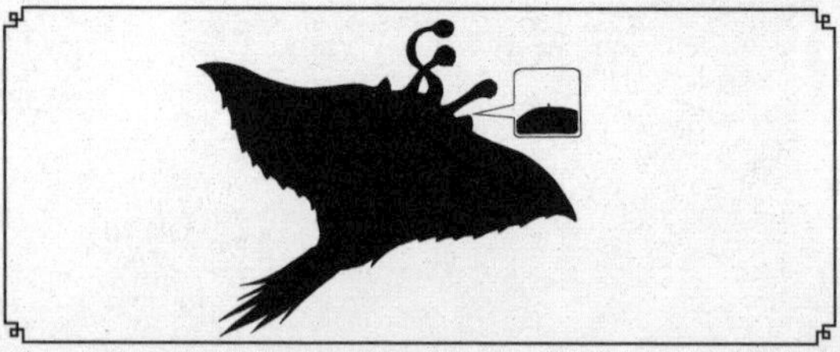

SCALE

A HYBRID BEAST THAT IS A CROSS BETWEEN A STINGRAY AND AN ANGLERFISH. IT INHABITS THE SEAS AROUND YUTO ISLAND IN THE GOURMET WORLD AND NOT ONLY CAN IT SURVIVE ON LAND, BUT IT CAN ALSO FLY. ITS FINS ARE VERY SHARP AND IT WILL FIRE OFF THE BLACK PARTS OF ITS POISONOUS TAIL TO ATTACK. ITS SHARP FINS ARE ALSO A DELICACY IN THE GOURMET WORLD WHILE THE RAYZOR ANGLER'S RAY FINS ARE THE ENVY OF EVERY BOOZE ENTHUSIAST.

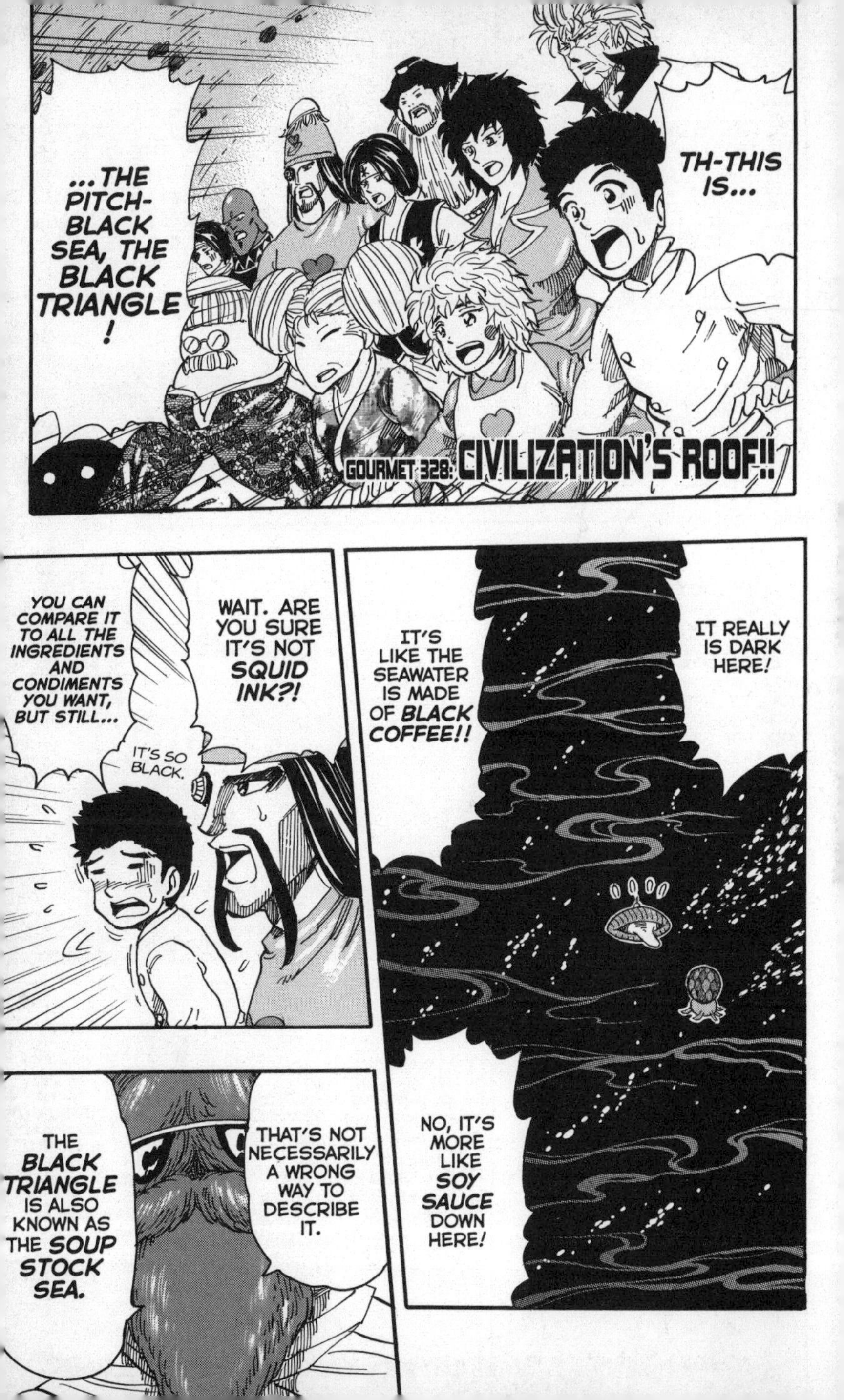
TH-THIS IS...
...THE PITCH-BLACK SEA, THE BLACK TRIANGLE!
GOURMET 328: CIVILIZATION'S ROOF!!
IT REALLY IS DARK HERE!
IT'S LIKE THE SEAWATER IS MADE OF BLACK COFFEE!!
NO, IT'S MORE LIKE SOY SAUCE DOWN HERE!
WAIT. ARE YOU SURE IT'S NOT SQUID INK?!
YOU CAN COMPARE IT TO ALL THE INGREDIENTS AND CONDIMENTS YOU WANT, BUT STILL...
IT'S SO BLACK.
THAT'S NOT NECESSARILY A WRONG WAY TO DESCRIBE IT.
THE BLACK TRIANGLE IS ALSO KNOWN AS THE SOUP STOCK SEA.

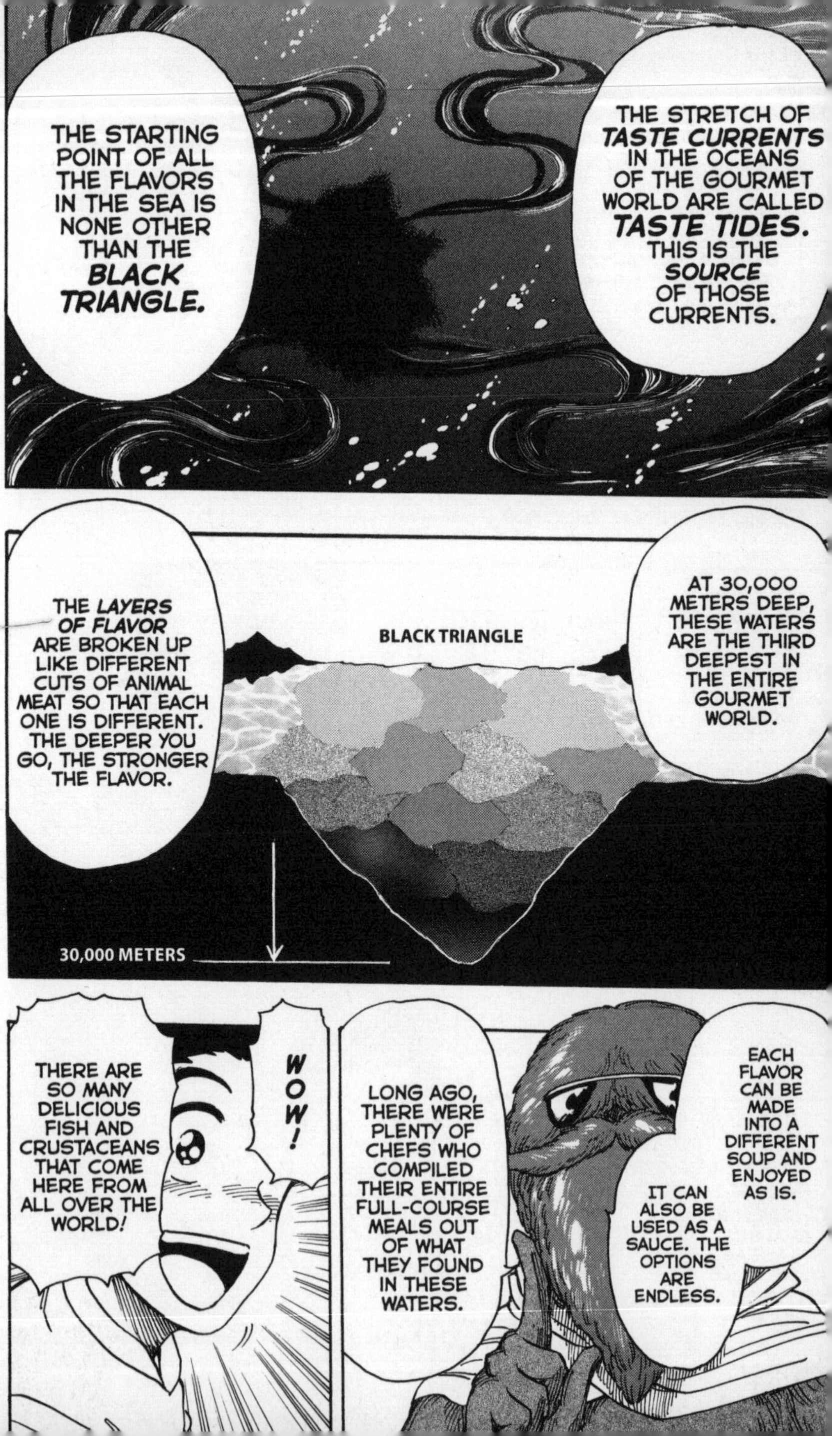
THE STRETCH OF *TASTE CURRENTS* IN THE OCEANS OF THE GOURMET WORLD ARE CALLED ***TASTE TIDES.*** THIS IS THE *SOURCE* OF THOSE CURRENTS.
THE STARTING POINT OF ALL THE FLAVORS IN THE SEA IS NONE OTHER THAN THE ***BLACK TRIANGLE.***
AT 30,000 METERS DEEP, THESE WATERS ARE THE THIRD DEEPEST IN THE ENTIRE GOURMET WORLD.
THE *LAYERS OF FLAVOR* ARE BROKEN UP LIKE DIFFERENT CUTS OF ANIMAL MEAT SO THAT EACH ONE IS DIFFERENT. THE DEEPER YOU GO, THE STRONGER THE FLAVOR.
BLACK TRIANGLE
30,000 METERS
EACH FLAVOR CAN BE MADE INTO A DIFFERENT SOUP AND ENJOYED AS IS.
IT CAN ALSO BE USED AS A SAUCE. THE OPTIONS ARE ENDLESS.
LONG AGO, THERE WERE PLENTY OF CHEFS WHO COMPILED THEIR ENTIRE FULL-COURSE MEALS OUT OF WHAT THEY FOUND IN THESE WATERS.
WOW!
THERE ARE SO *MANY* DELICIOUS FISH AND CRUSTACEANS THAT COME HERE FROM ALL OVER THE WORLD!

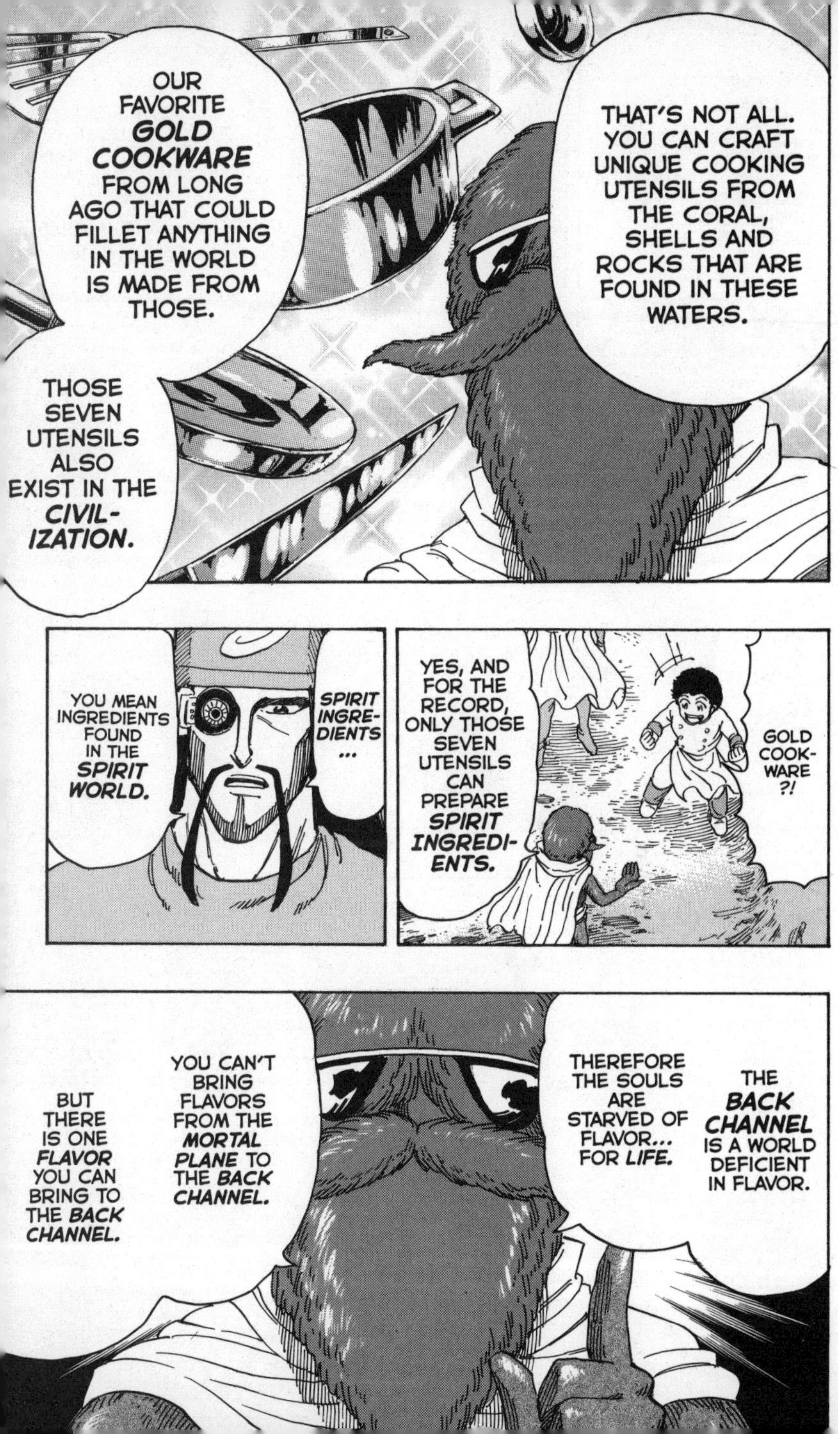
THAT'S NOT ALL. YOU CAN CRAFT UNIQUE COOKING UTENSILS FROM THE CORAL, SHELLS AND ROCKS THAT ARE FOUND IN THESE WATERS.
OUR FAVORITE GOLD COOKWARE FROM LONG AGO THAT COULD FILLET ANYTHING IN THE WORLD IS MADE FROM THOSE.
THOSE SEVEN UTENSILS ALSO EXIST IN THE CIVILIZATION.
GOLD COOKWARE?!
YES, AND FOR THE RECORD, ONLY THOSE SEVEN UTENSILS CAN PREPARE SPIRIT INGREDIENTS.
SPIRIT INGREDIENTS...
YOU MEAN INGREDIENTS FOUND IN THE SPIRIT WORLD.
THE BACK CHANNEL IS A WORLD DEFICIENT IN FLAVOR.
THEREFORE THE SOULS ARE STARVED OF FLAVOR... FOR LIFE.
YOU CAN'T BRING FLAVORS FROM THE MORTAL PLANE TO THE BACK CHANNEL.
BUT THERE IS ONE FLAVOR YOU CAN BRING TO THE BACK CHANNEL.

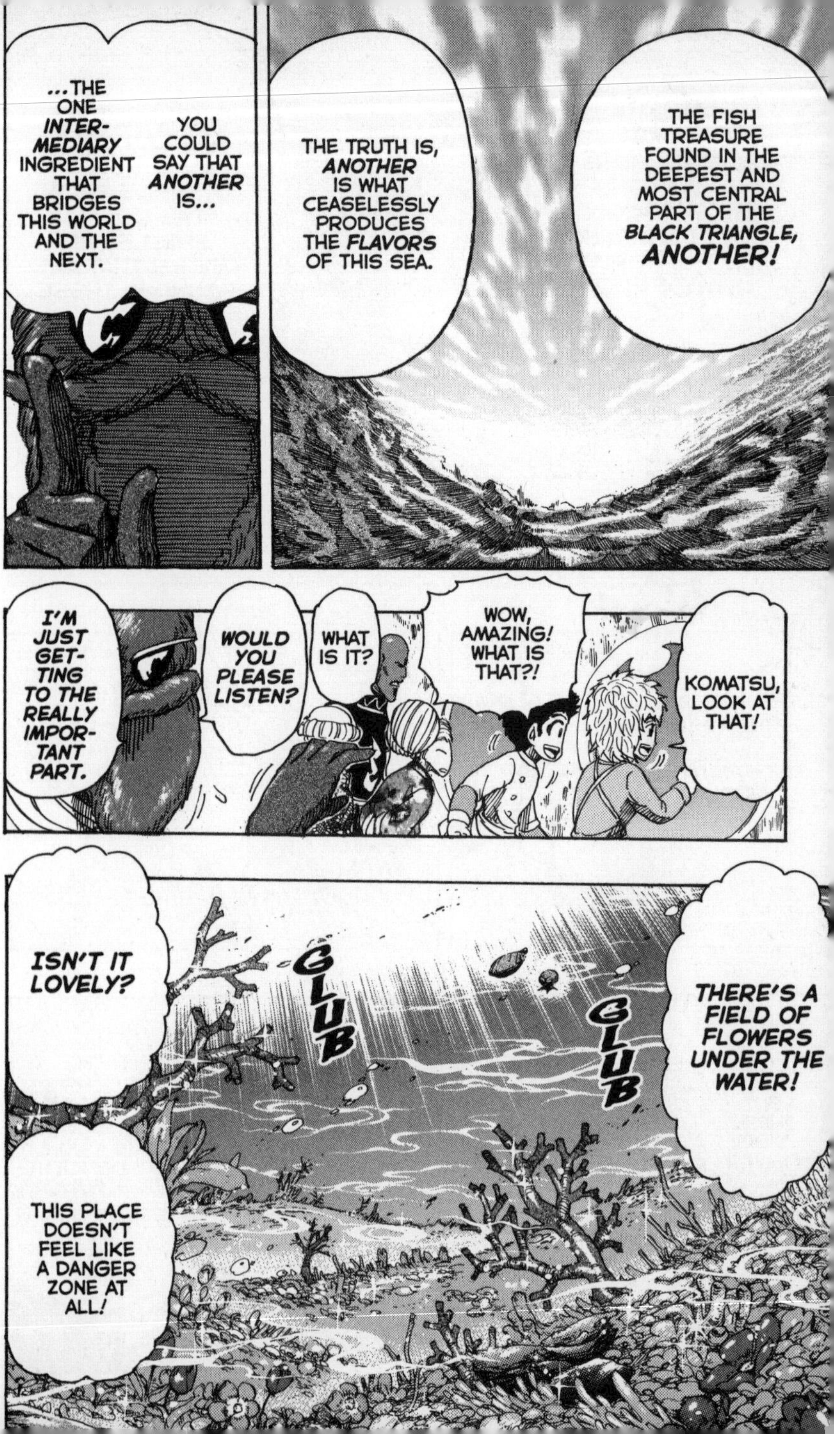
THE FISH TREASURE FOUND IN THE DEEPEST AND MOST CENTRAL PART OF THE BLACK TRIANGLE, ANOTHER!
THE TRUTH IS, ANOTHER IS WHAT CEASELESSLY PRODUCES THE FLAVORS OF THIS SEA.
YOU COULD SAY THAT ANOTHER IS...
...THE ONE INTERMEDIARY INGREDIENT THAT BRIDGES THIS WORLD AND THE NEXT.
KOMATSU, LOOK AT THAT!
WOW, AMAZING! WHAT IS THAT?!
WHAT IS IT?
WOULD YOU PLEASE LISTEN?
I'M JUST GETTING TO THE REALLY IMPORTANT PART.
THERE'S A FIELD OF FLOWERS UNDER THE WATER!
GLUB
GLUB
ISN'T IT LOVELY?
THIS PLACE DOESN'T FEEL LIKE A DANGER ZONE AT ALL!

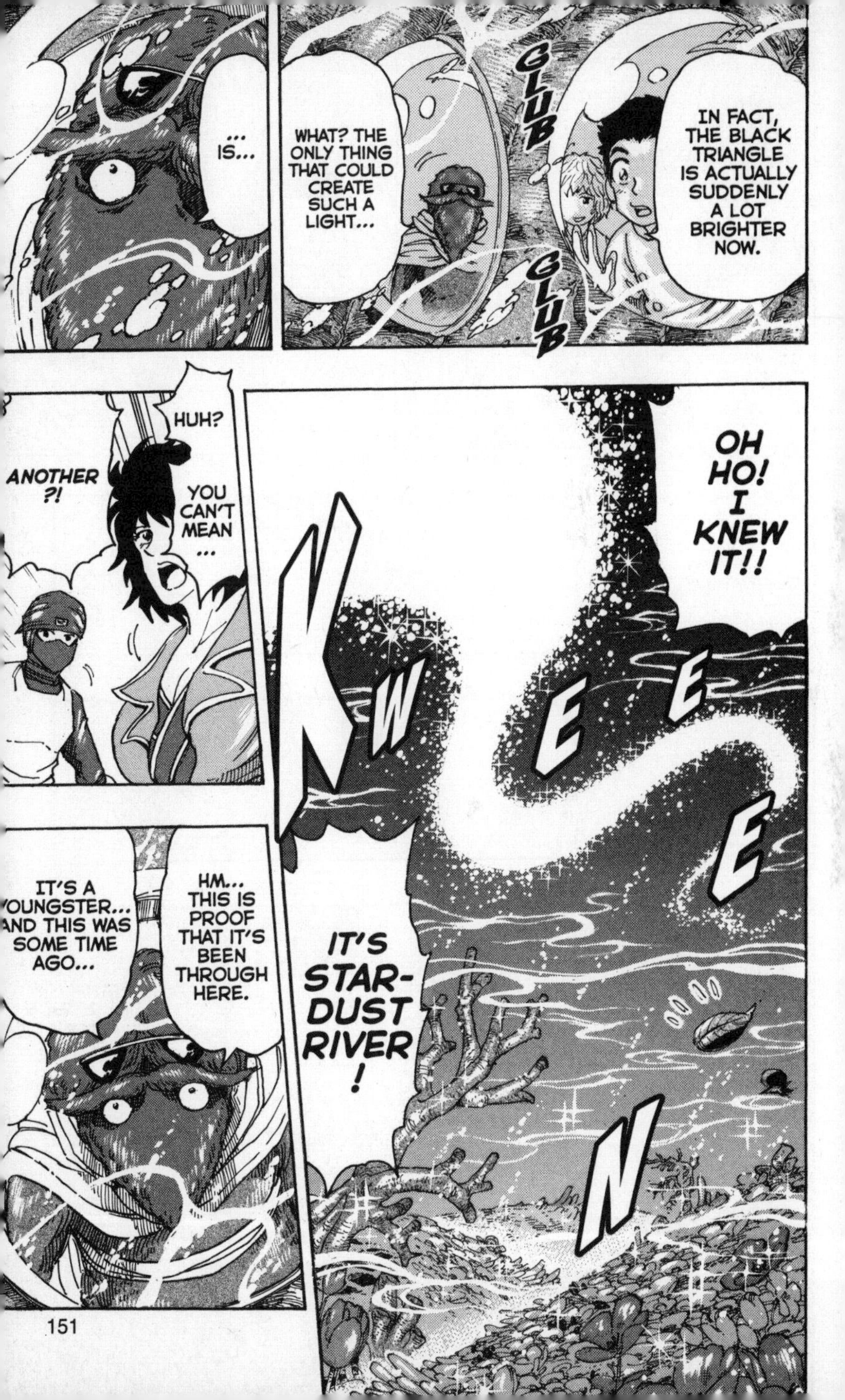

IN FACT, THE BLACK TRIANGLE IS ACTUALLY SUDDENLY A LOT BRIGHTER NOW.
GLUB
GLUB
WHAT? THE ONLY THING THAT COULD CREATE SUCH A LIGHT...
... IS...
OH HO! I KNEW IT!!
KWEEEEN
IT'S STAR-DUST RIVER!
HUH?
YOU CAN'T MEAN...
ANOTHER?!
HM... THIS IS PROOF THAT IT'S BEEN THROUGH HERE.
IT'S A YOUNGSTER... AND THIS WAS SOME TIME AGO...

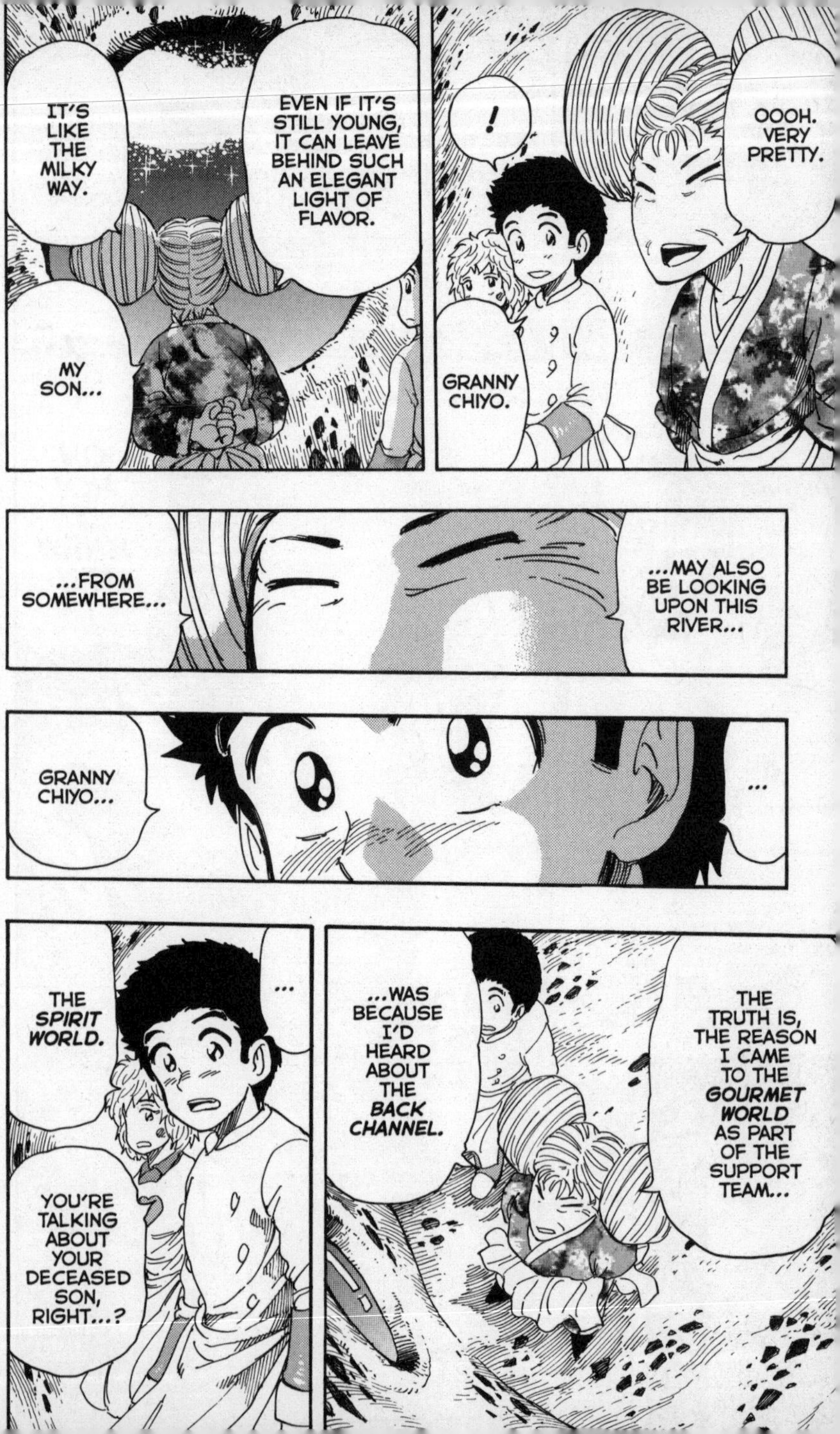
OOOH. VERY PRETTY.
!
GRANNY CHIYO.
EVEN IF IT'S STILL YOUNG, IT CAN LEAVE BEHIND SUCH AN ELEGANT LIGHT OF FLAVOR.
IT'S LIKE THE MILKY WAY.
MY SON...
...MAY ALSO BE LOOKING UPON THIS RIVER...
...FROM SOMEWHERE...
...
GRANNY CHIYO...
THE TRUTH IS, THE REASON I CAME TO THE *GOURMET WORLD* AS PART OF THE SUPPORT TEAM...
...WAS BECAUSE I'D HEARD ABOUT THE *BACK CHANNEL*.
...
THE *SPIRIT WORLD*.
YOU'RE TALKING ABOUT YOUR DECEASED SON, RIGHT...?

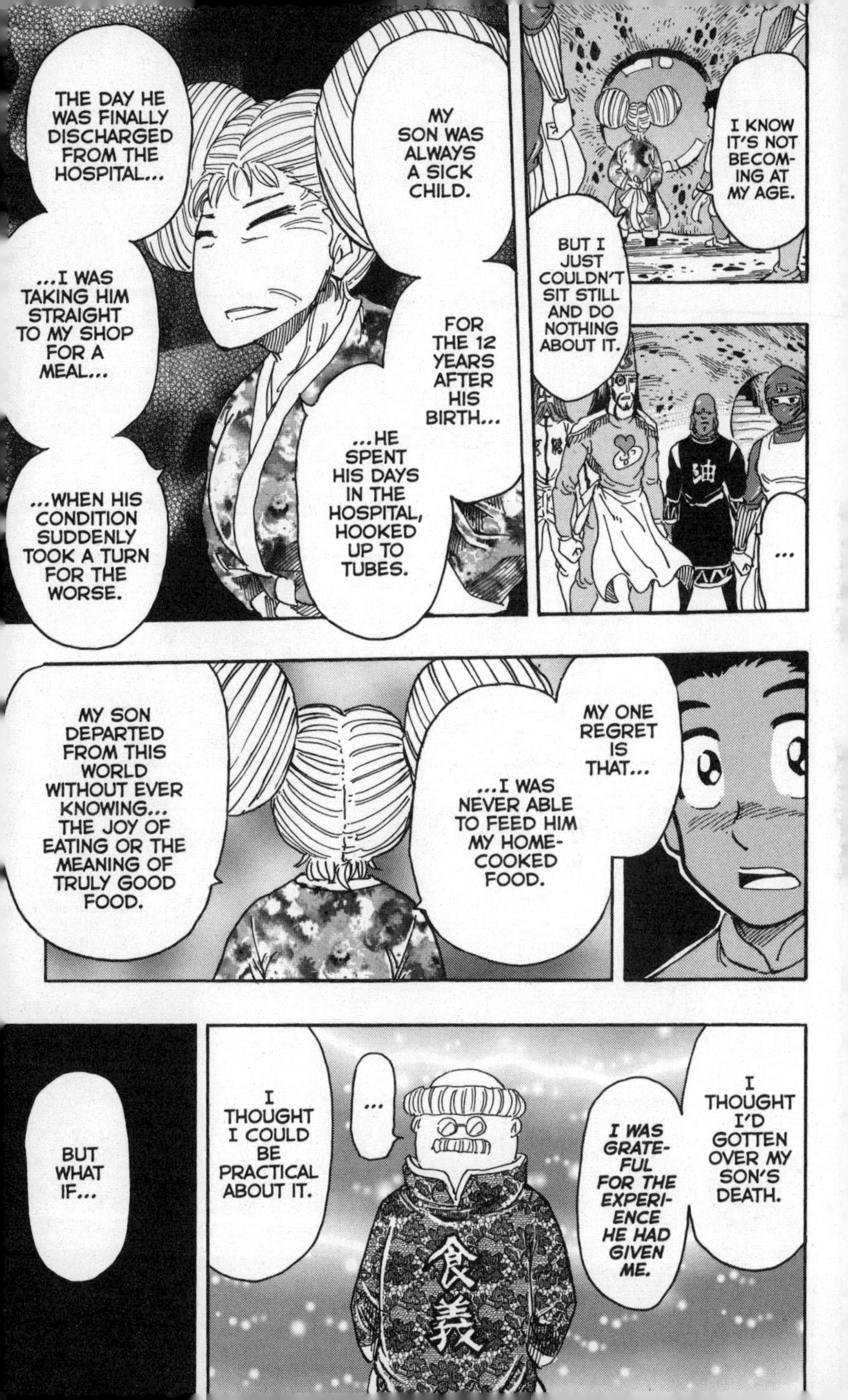
I KNOW IT'S NOT BECOMING AT MY AGE.
BUT I JUST COULDN'T SIT STILL AND DO NOTHING ABOUT IT.
...
MY SON WAS ALWAYS A SICK CHILD.
FOR THE 12 YEARS AFTER HIS BIRTH...
...HE SPENT HIS DAYS IN THE HOSPITAL, HOOKED UP TO TUBES.
THE DAY HE WAS FINALLY DISCHARGED FROM THE HOSPITAL...
...I WAS TAKING HIM STRAIGHT TO MY SHOP FOR A MEAL...
...WHEN HIS CONDITION SUDDENLY TOOK A TURN FOR THE WORSE.
MY ONE REGRET IS THAT...
...I WAS NEVER ABLE TO FEED HIM MY HOME-COOKED FOOD.
MY SON DEPARTED FROM THIS WORLD WITHOUT EVER KNOWING... THE JOY OF EATING OR THE MEANING OF TRULY GOOD FOOD.
I THOUGHT I'D GOTTEN OVER MY SON'S DEATH.
I WAS GRATEFUL FOR THE EXPERIENCE HE HAD GIVEN ME.
...
I THOUGHT I COULD BE PRACTICAL ABOUT IT.
BUT WHAT IF...

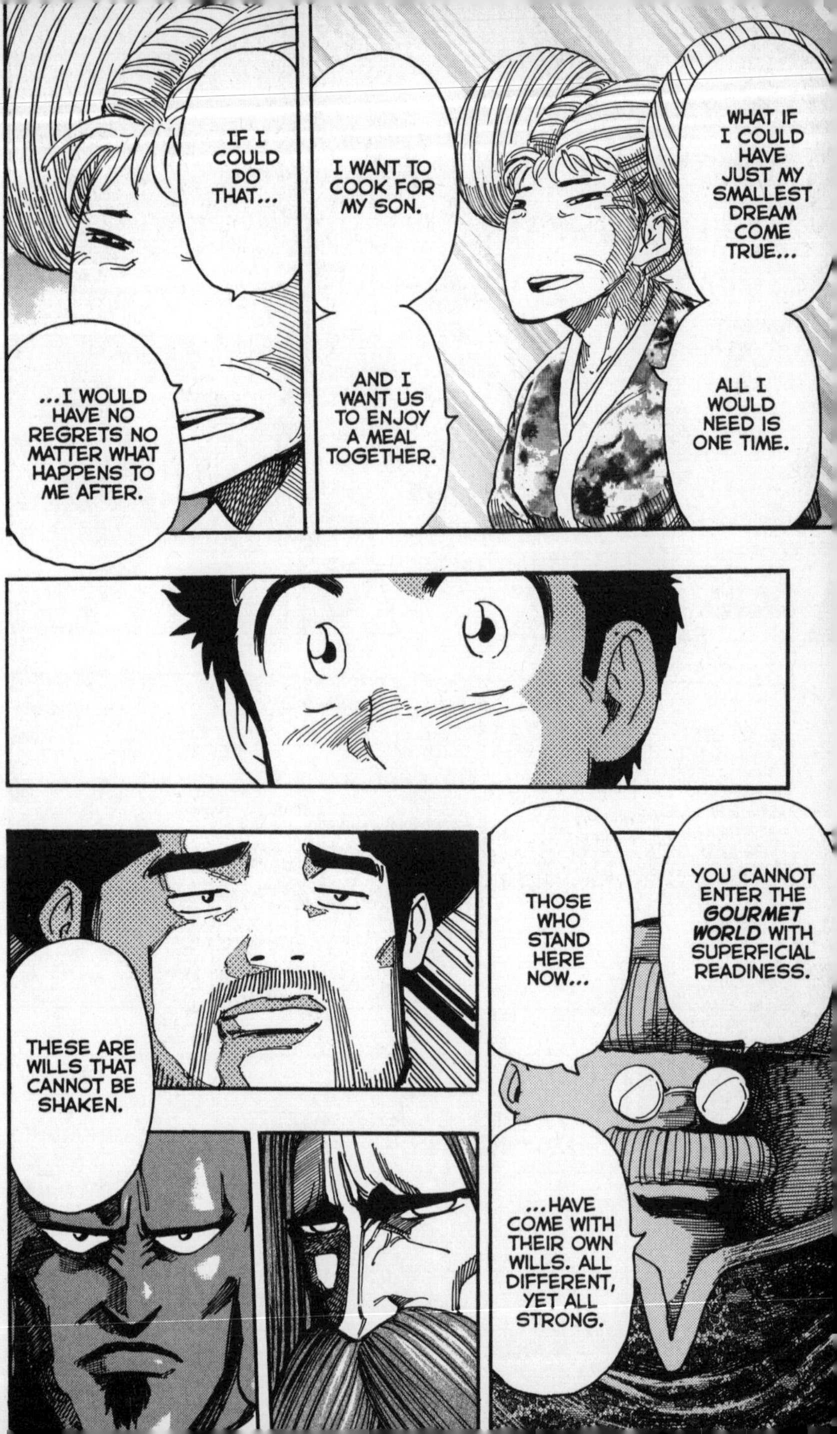
WHAT IF I COULD HAVE JUST MY SMALLEST DREAM COME TRUE...
ALL I WOULD NEED IS ONE TIME.
I WANT TO COOK FOR MY SON.
AND I WANT US TO ENJOY A MEAL TOGETHER.
IF I COULD DO THAT...
...I WOULD HAVE NO REGRETS NO MATTER WHAT HAPPENS TO ME AFTER.
YOU CANNOT ENTER THE *GOURMET WORLD* WITH SUPERFICIAL READINESS.
THOSE WHO STAND HERE NOW...
...HAVE COME WITH THEIR OWN WILLS. ALL DIFFERENT, YET ALL STRONG.
THESE ARE WILLS THAT CANNOT BE SHAKEN.

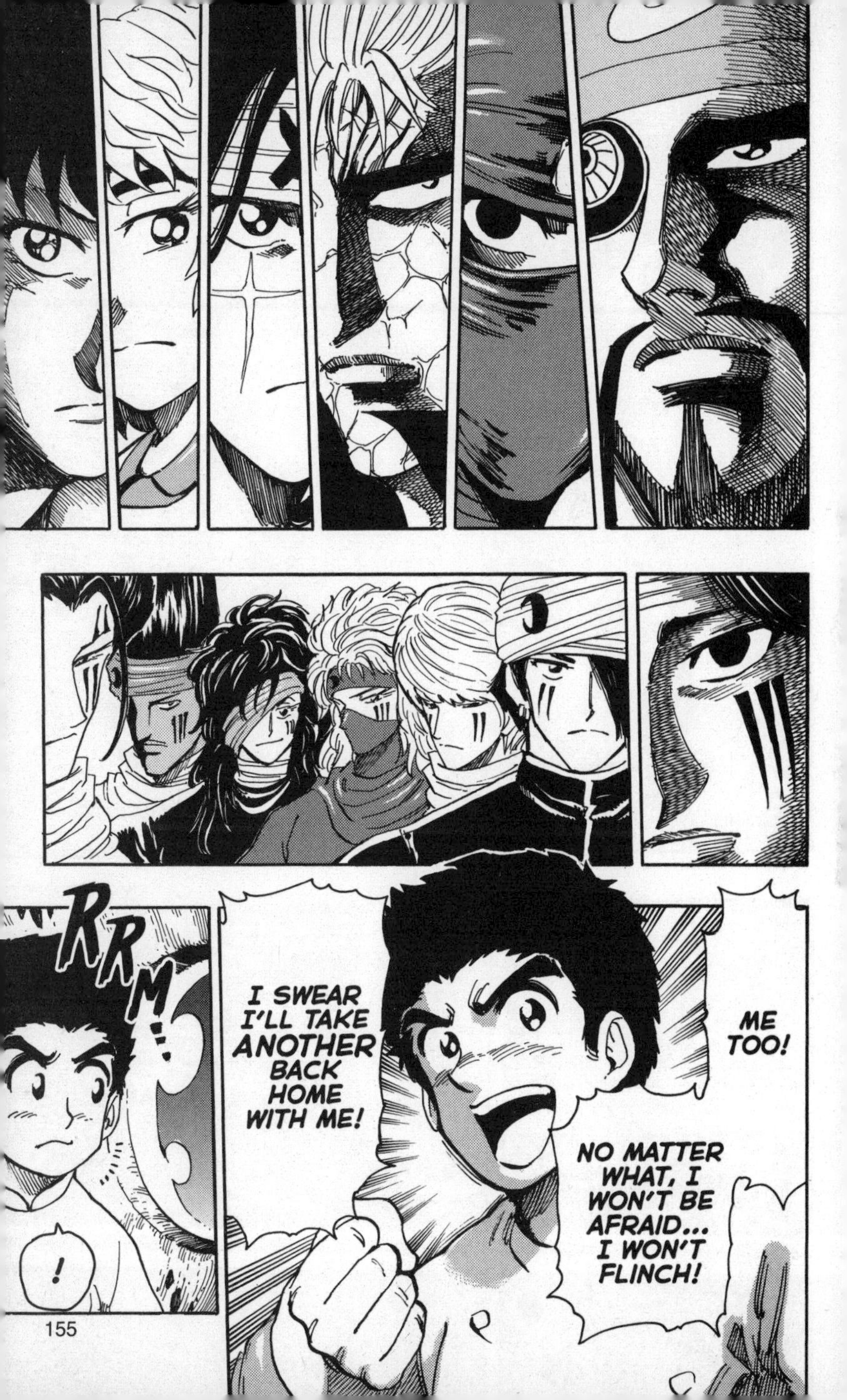
ME TOO!
I SWEAR I'LL TAKE ANOTHER BACK HOME WITH ME!
NO MATTER WHAT, I WON'T BE AFRAID... I WON'T FLINCH!
RRRM
!

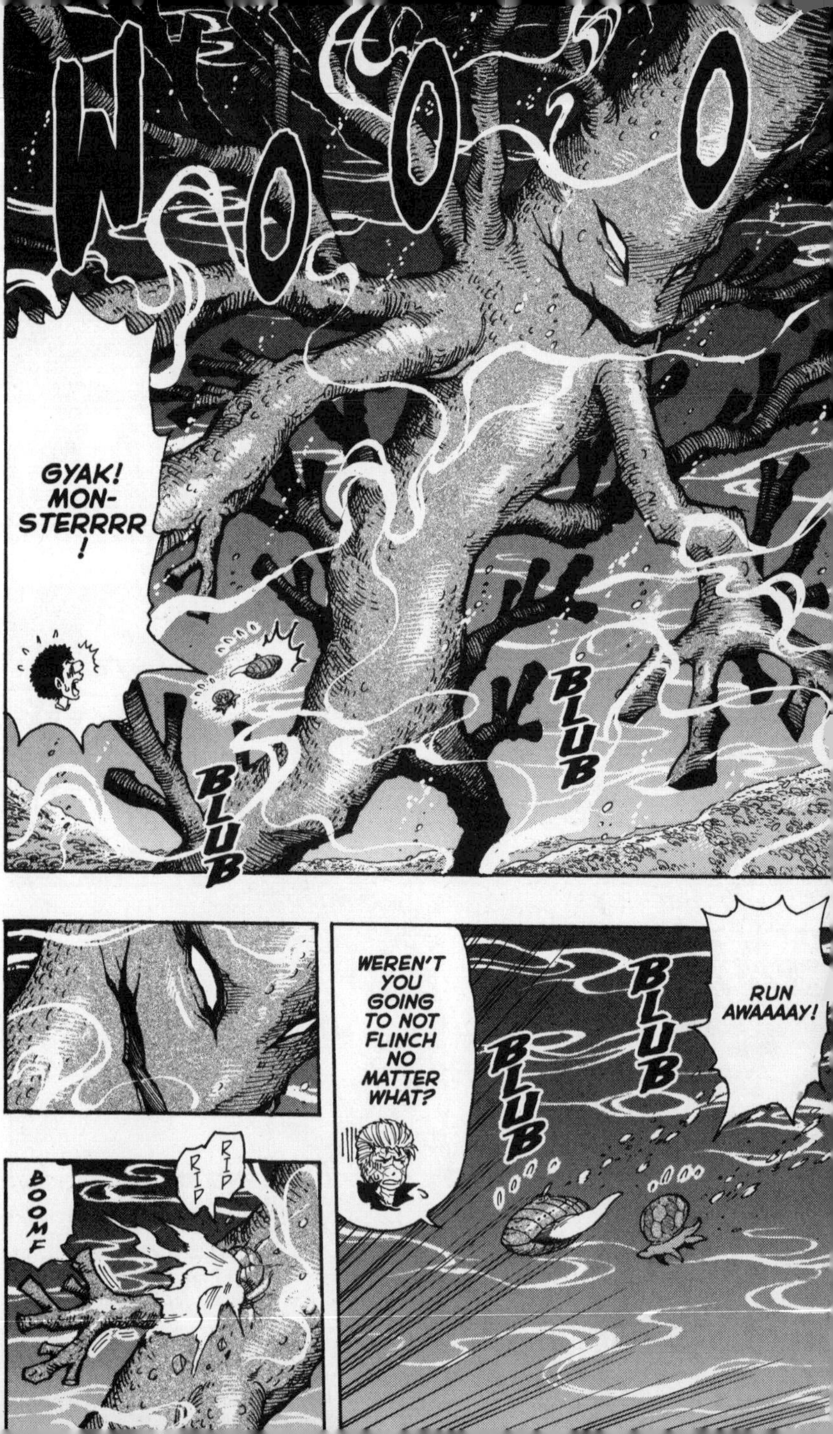
WOOOO
GYAK! MON-STERRRR!
BLUB
BLUB
RUN AWAAAAY!
BLUB
BLUB
WEREN'T YOU GOING TO NOT FLINCH NO MATTER WHAT?
RIP RIP
BOOMF

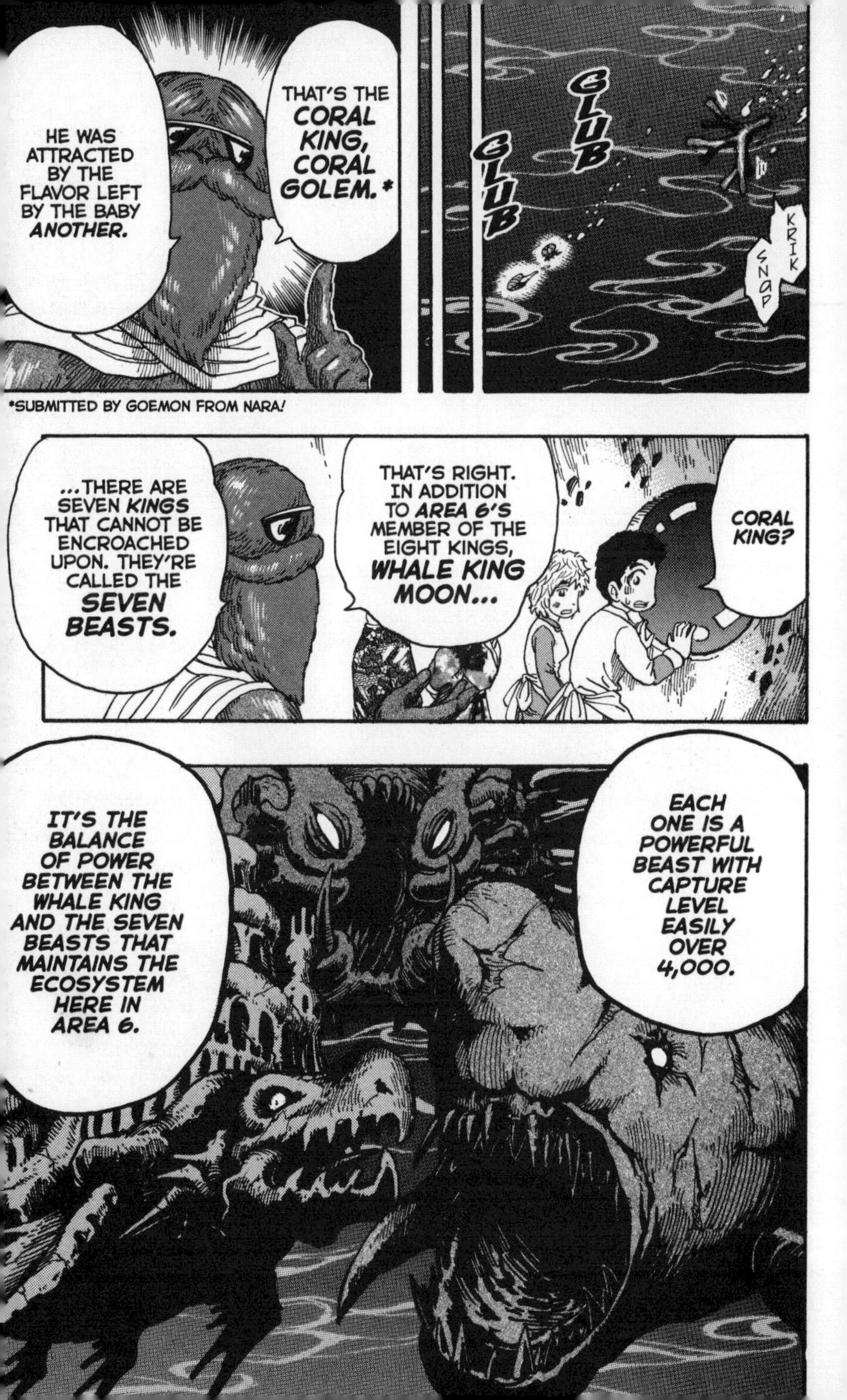
GLUB
GLUB
KRIK
SNAP
THAT'S THE CORAL KING, CORAL GOLEM.*
HE WAS ATTRACTED BY THE FLAVOR LEFT BY THE BABY ANOTHER.
*SUBMITTED BY GOEMON FROM NARA!
CORAL KING?
THAT'S RIGHT. IN ADDITION TO AREA 6'S MEMBER OF THE EIGHT KINGS, WHALE KING MOON...
...THERE ARE SEVEN KINGS THAT CANNOT BE ENCROACHED UPON. THEY'RE CALLED THE SEVEN BEASTS.
EACH ONE IS A POWERFUL BEAST WITH CAPTURE LEVEL EASILY OVER 4,000.
IT'S THE BALANCE OF POWER BETWEEN THE WHALE KING AND THE SEVEN BEASTS THAT MAINTAINS THE ECOSYSTEM HERE IN AREA 6.

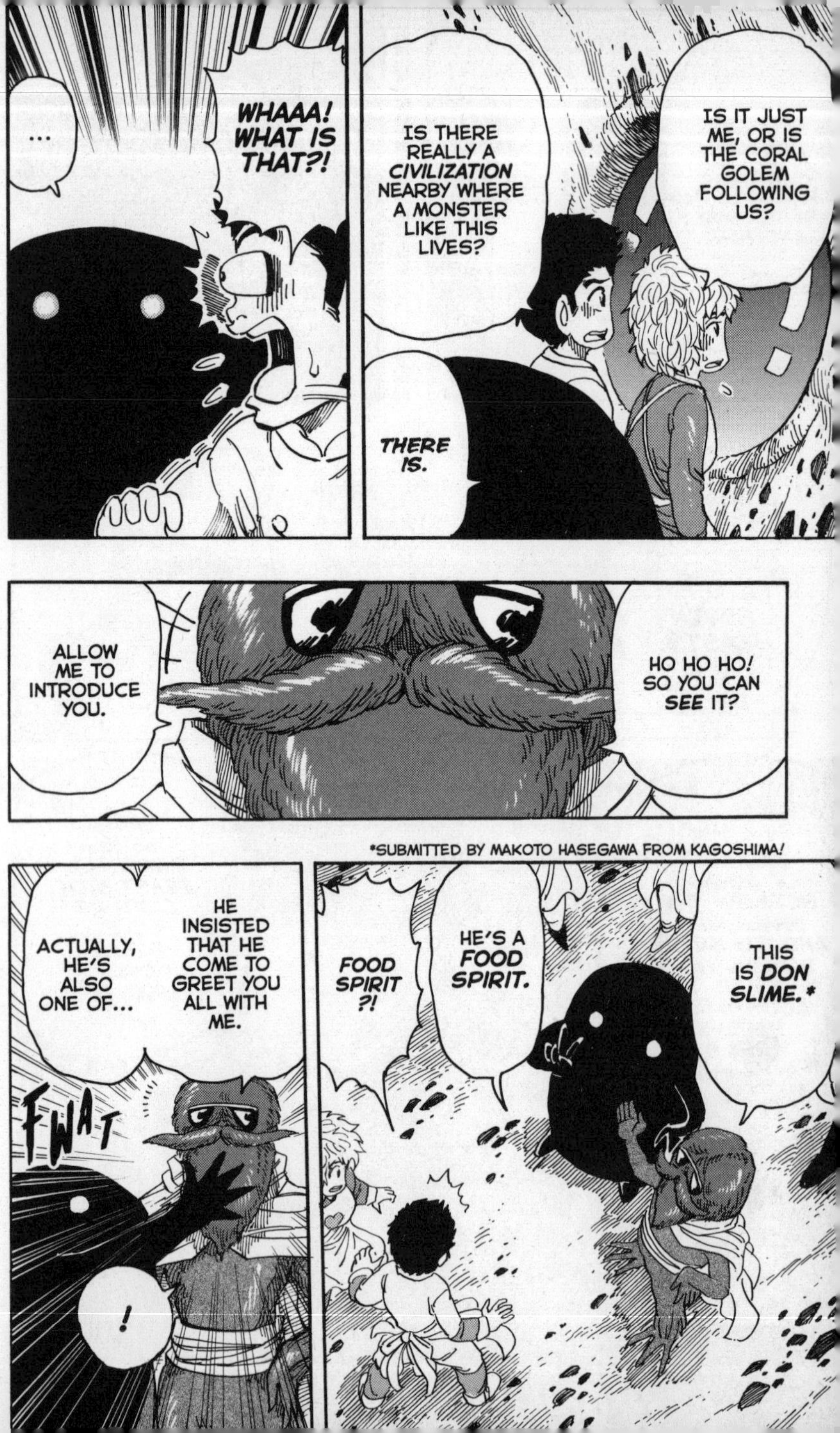
IS IT JUST ME, OR IS THE CORAL GOLEM FOLLOWING US?
IS THERE REALLY A CIVILIZATION NEARBY WHERE A MONSTER LIKE THIS LIVES?
THERE IS.
WHAAA! WHAT IS THAT?!
...
HO HO HO! SO YOU CAN SEE IT?
ALLOW ME TO INTRODUCE YOU.
THIS IS DON SLIME.*
HE'S A FOOD SPIRIT.
FOOD SPIRIT?!
HE INSISTED THAT HE COME TO GREET YOU ALL WITH ME.
ACTUALLY, HE'S ALSO ONE OF...
FWAT
!

*SUBMITTED BY MAKOTO HASEGAWA FROM KAGOSHIMA!

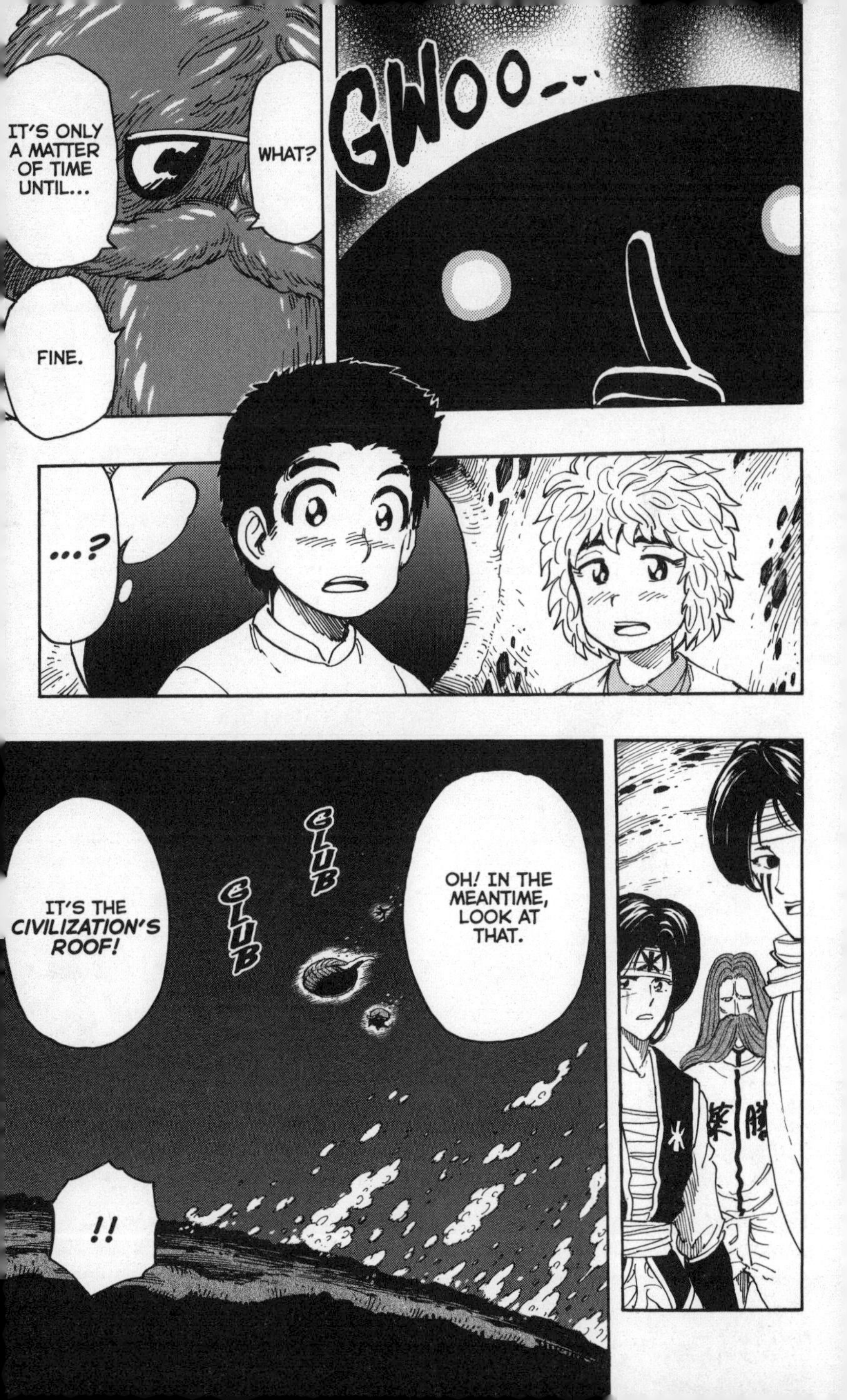
GWOO...
WHAT?
IT'S ONLY A MATTER OF TIME UNTIL...
FINE.
...?
OH! IN THE MEANTIME, LOOK AT THAT.
GLUB
GLUB
IT'S THE CIVILIZATION'S ROOF!
!!

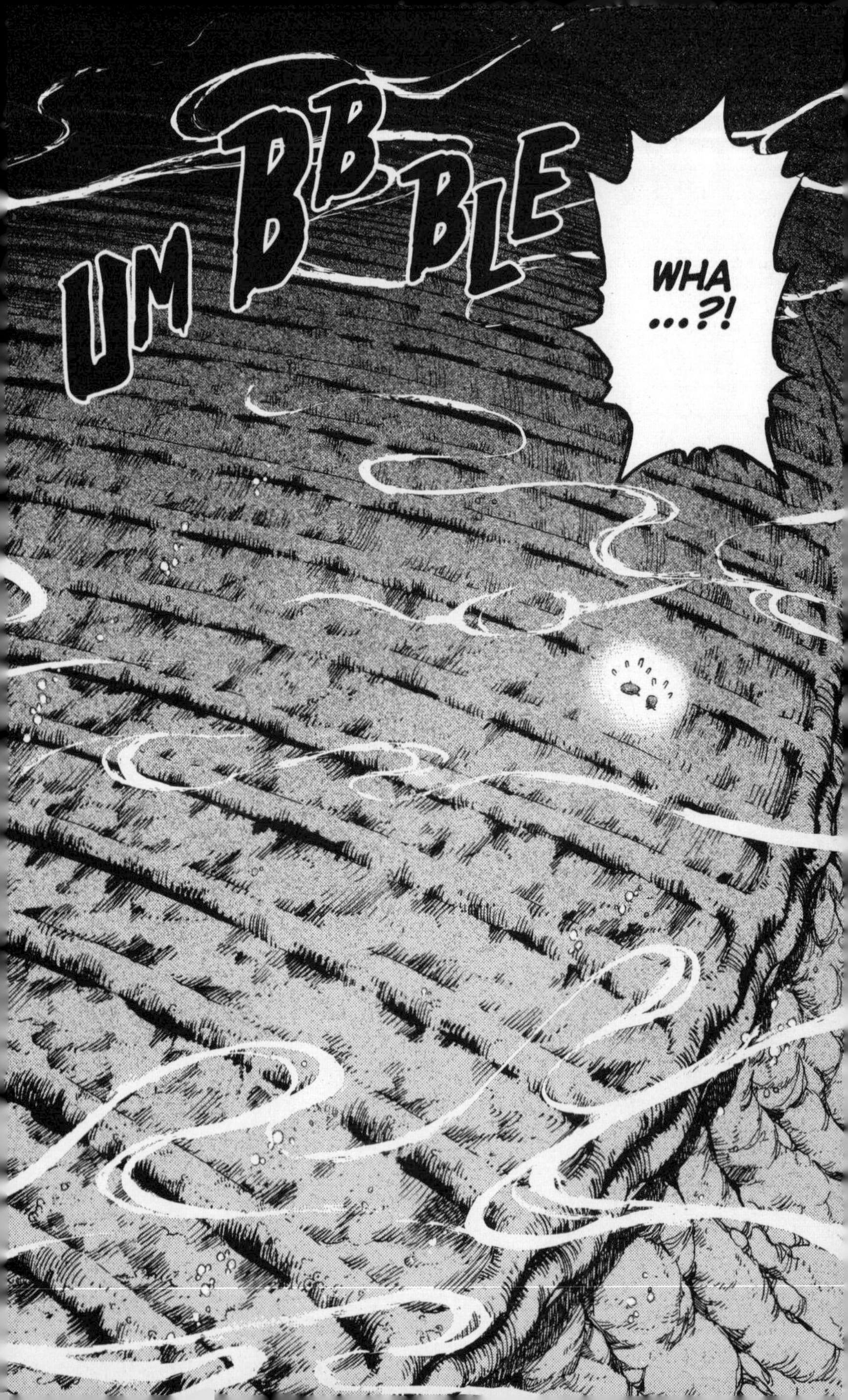
UMBBBBLE
WHA ...?!

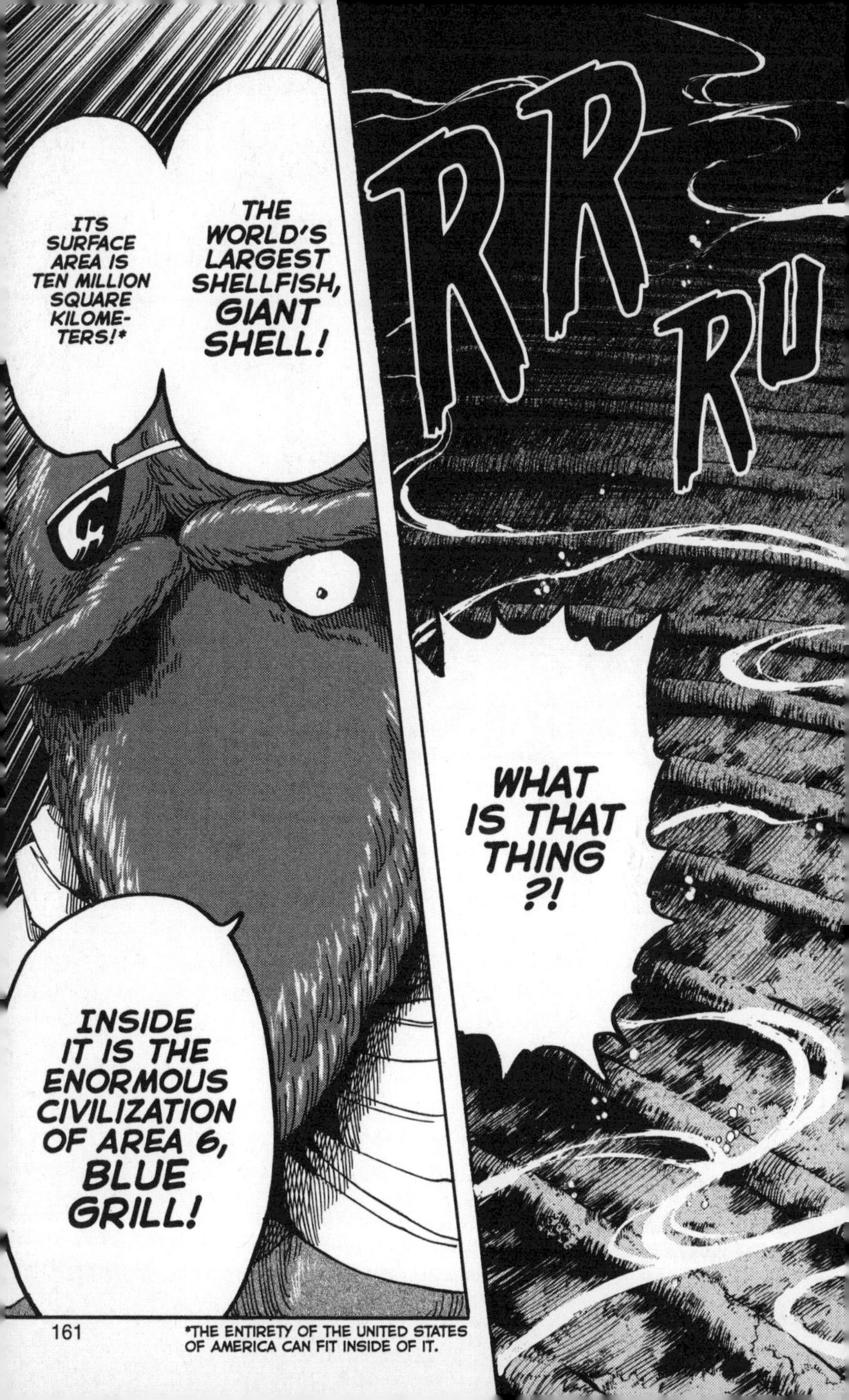
RRRU
WHAT IS THAT THING ?!
THE WORLD'S LARGEST SHELLFISH, GIANT SHELL!
ITS SURFACE AREA IS TEN MILLION SQUARE KILOMETERS!*
INSIDE IT IS THE ENORMOUS CIVILIZATION OF AREA 6, BLUE GRILL!

*THE ENTIRETY OF THE UNITED STATES OF AMERICA CAN FIT INSIDE OF IT.

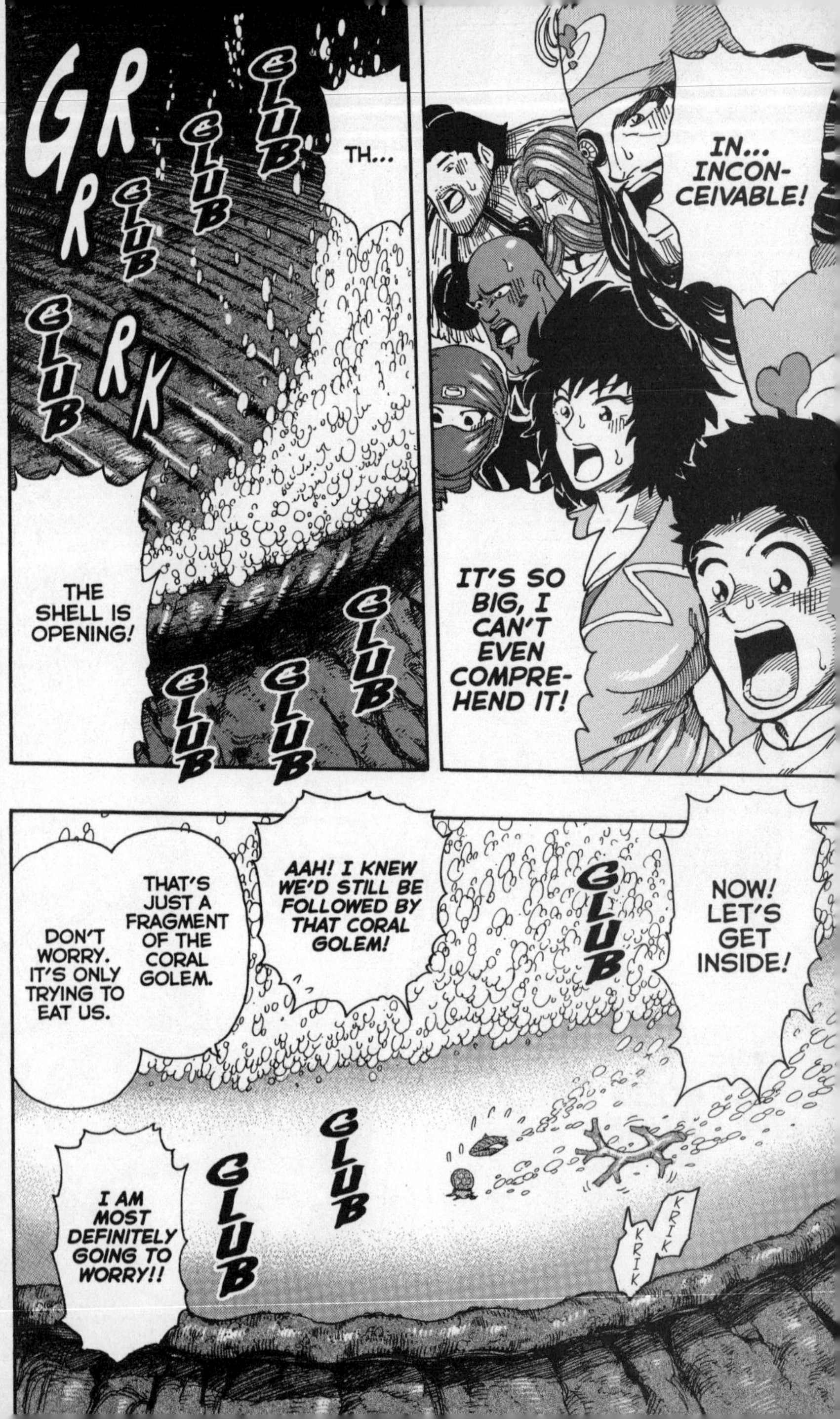
IN... INCONCEIVABLE!
IT'S SO BIG, I CAN'T EVEN COMPREHEND IT!
TH...
GLUB GLUB GLUB GLUB
GRRRK
THE SHELL IS OPENING!
GLUB GLUB GLUB
NOW! LET'S GET INSIDE!
GLUB
AAH! I KNEW WE'D STILL BE FOLLOWED BY THAT CORAL GOLEM!
THAT'S JUST A FRAGMENT OF THE CORAL GOLEM.
DON'T WORRY. IT'S ONLY TRYING TO EAT US.
KRIK KRIK
GLUB GLUB
I AM MOST DEFINITELY GOING TO WORRY!!

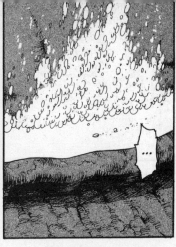

GLUB

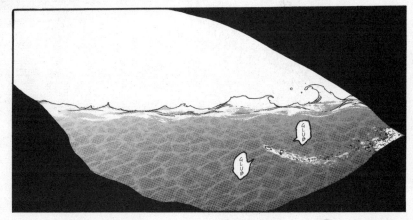

GLUB

GLUB

WE MADE IT!

WE'RE OUT!

SPLOOOOSH

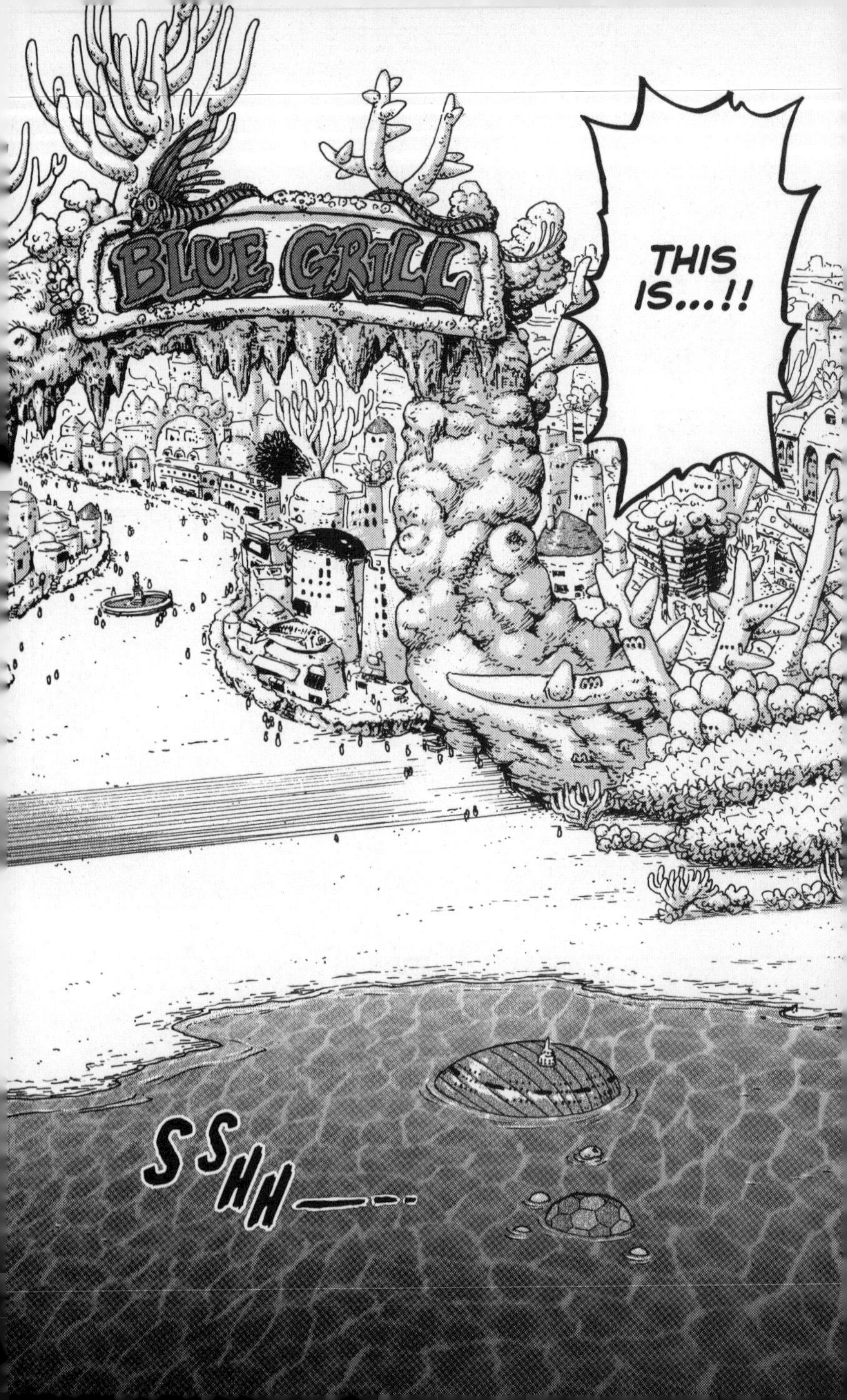
BLUE GRILL
THIS IS...!!
SSHH—

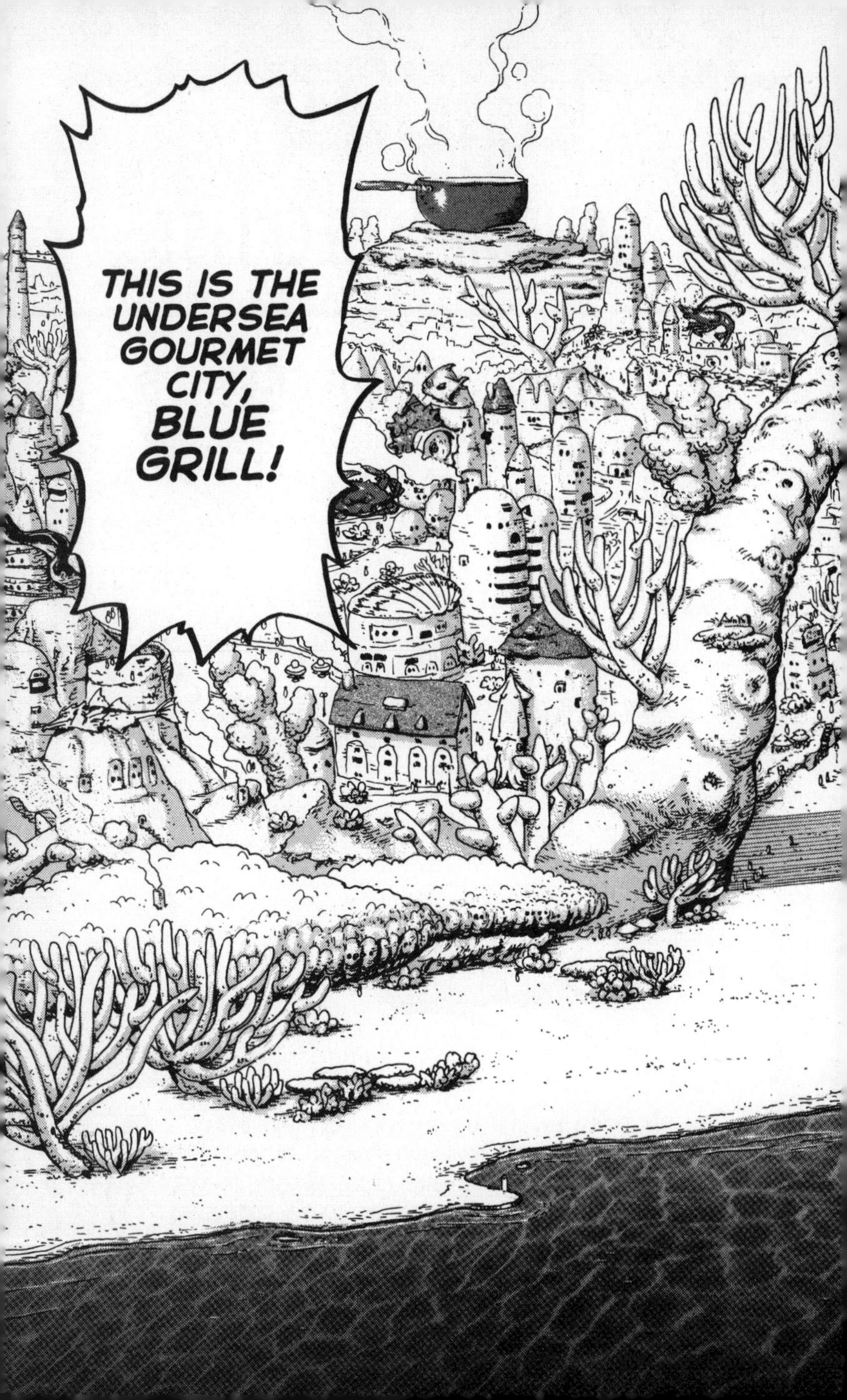
THIS IS THE UNDERSEA GOURMET CITY, BLUE GRILL!

TORIKO

GOURMET CHECKLIST

Vol. 358

TORPEDO SAUSAGE
(BIRD FISH)

NYOOOOM
TORPEDO SAUSAGE*
(BIRD FISH)
CAPTURE LEVEL 195
GN

CAPTURE LEVEL: 195

HABITAT: YUTO ISLAND IN THE GOURMET WORLD

SIZE: 35 M

HEIGHT: ---

WEIGHT: 350 TONS

PRICE: 90,000 YEN PER KILOGRAM

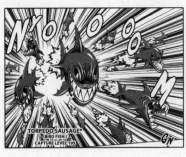

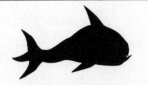

SCALE

THESE BIRD FISH NORMALLY TRAVEL IN PACKS AND THEIR SKIN IS AS HARD AS STEEL. IF THEY HIT YOU, THEY WILL DETONATE UPON IMPACT. THE "TORPEDO" PART OF THEIR NAME IS A TRULY FITTING MONIKER FOR THESE DANGEROUS CREATURES. IN ORDER TO EAT THEM, YOU MUST KEEP THEM FROM EXPLODING BY PERFORMING AN ADVANCED KNOCKING TECHNIQUE. THEIR FLAVOR IS REMINISCENT OF A HIGH-QUALITY SAUSAGE.

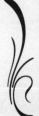

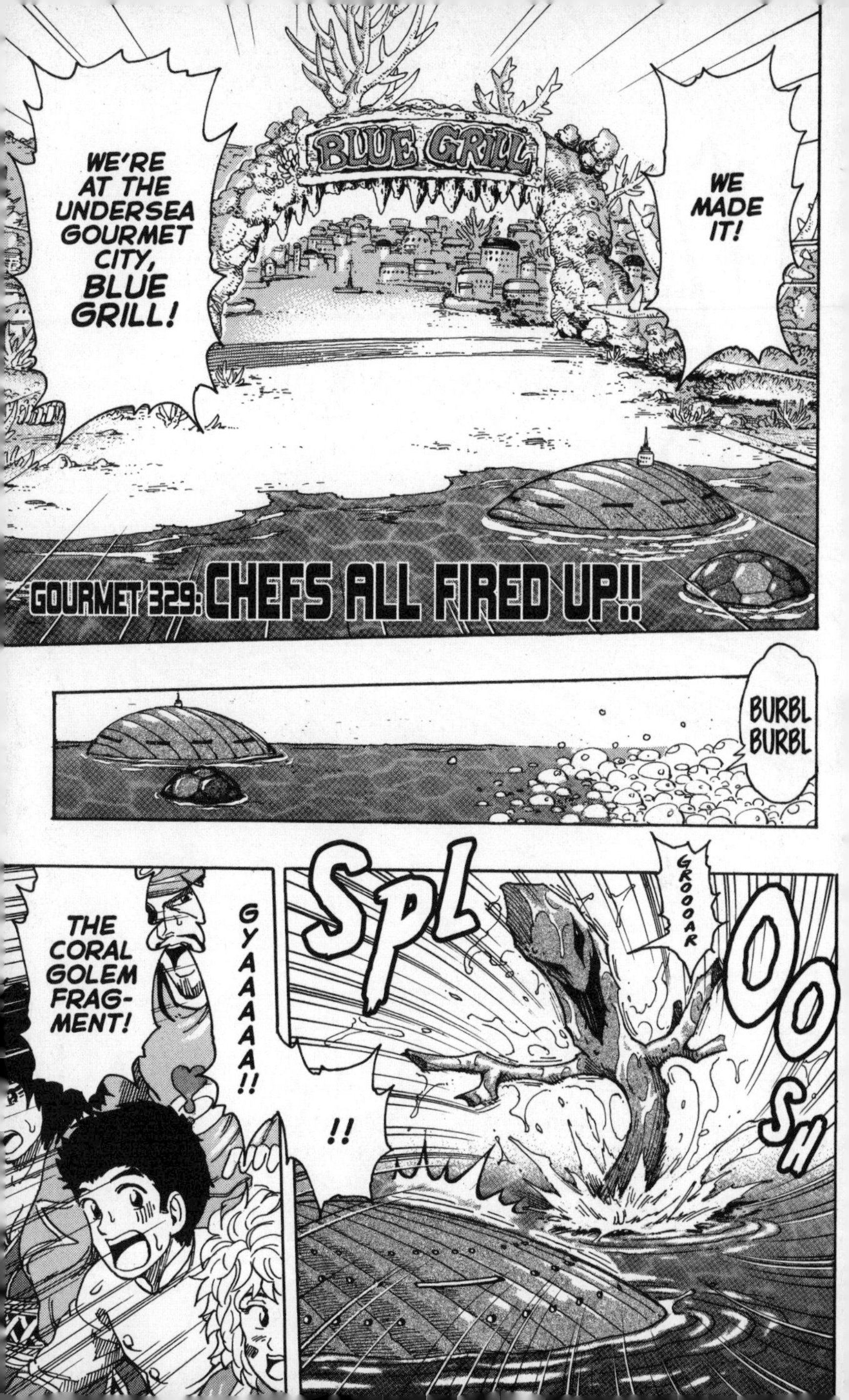
WE MADE IT!
BLUE GRILL
WE'RE AT THE UNDERSEA GOURMET CITY, BLUE GRILL!
GOURMET 329: CHEFS ALL FIRED UP!!
BURBL BURBL
SPL
OOOSH
GROOOAR
!!
GYAAAAAA!!
THE CORAL GOLEM FRAG-MENT!

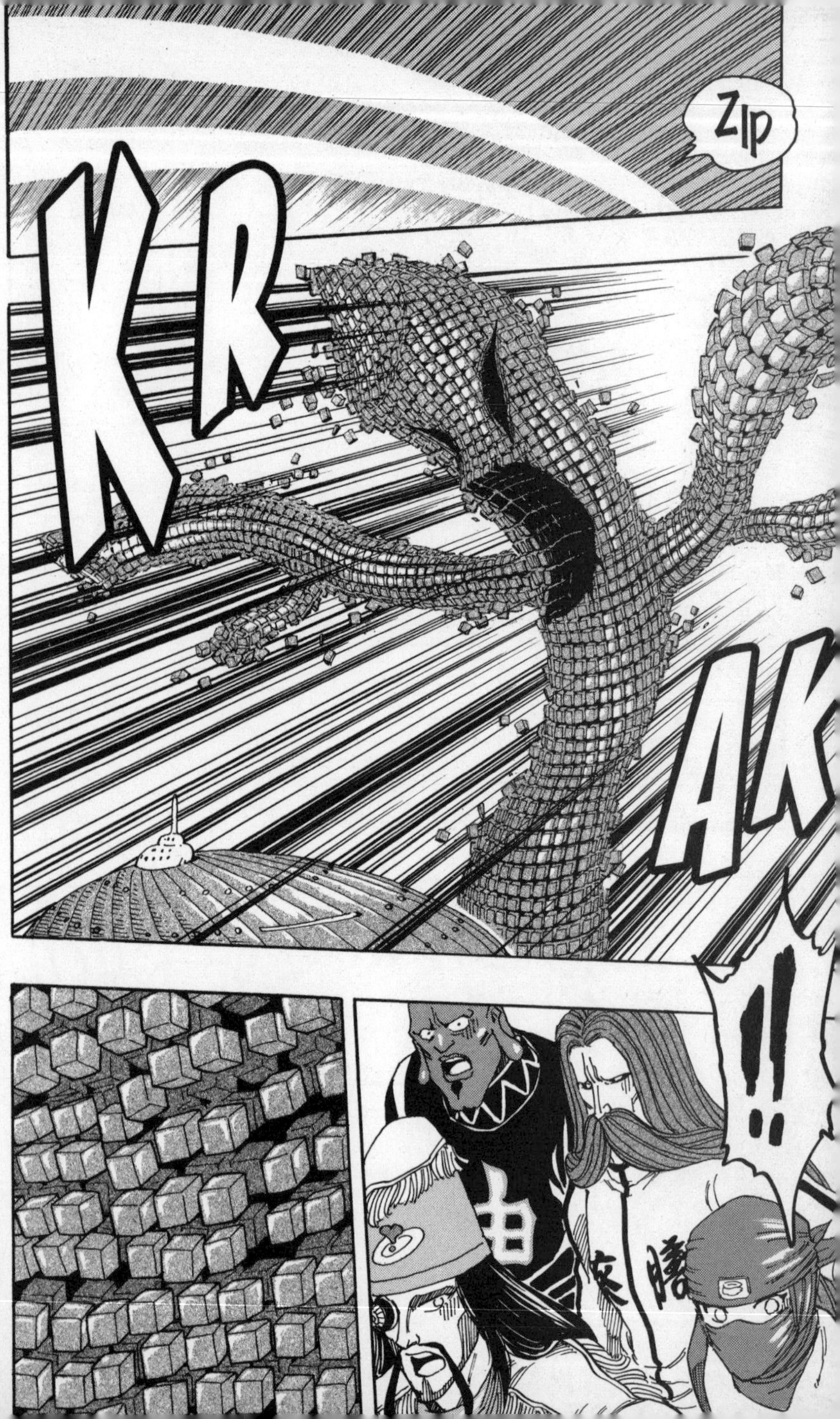
ZIP
KR
AK
!!

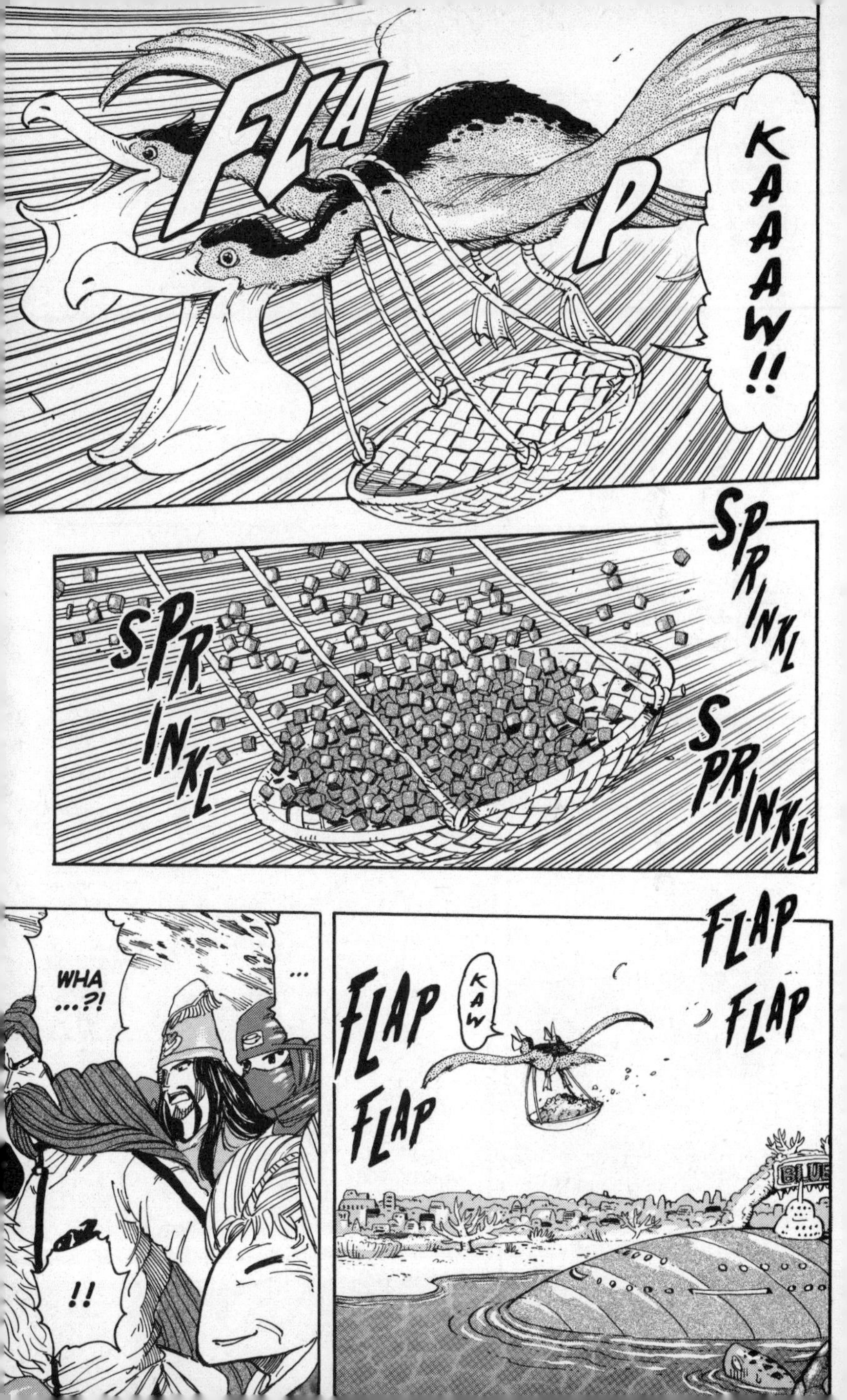
FLAP
KAAAAW!!
SPRINKL
SPRINKL
SPRINKL
FLAP
FLAP
FLAP
FLAP
KAW
...
WHA ...?!
!!

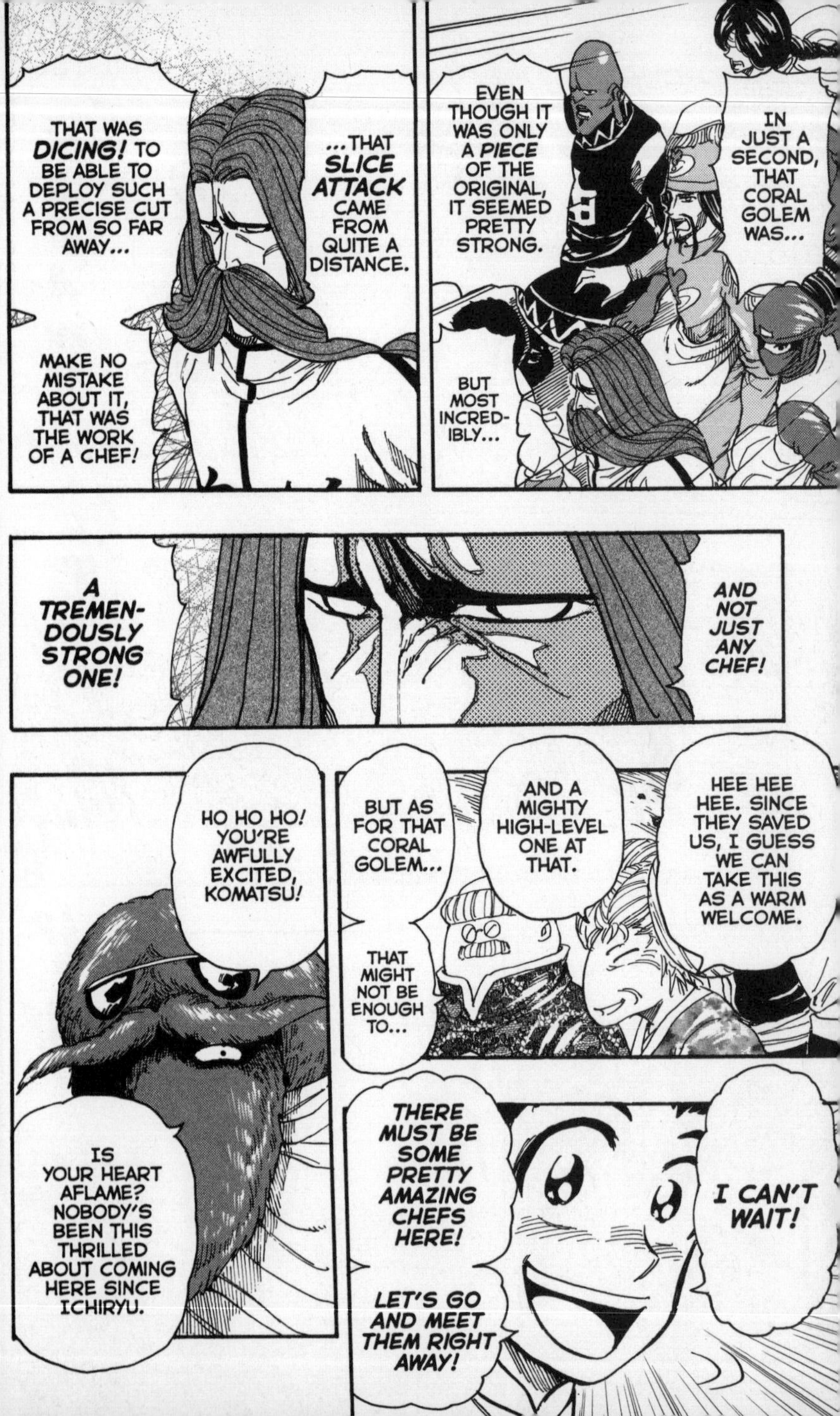
IN JUST A SECOND, THAT CORAL GOLEM WAS...
EVEN THOUGH IT WAS ONLY A *PIECE* OF THE ORIGINAL, IT SEEMED PRETTY STRONG.
BUT MOST INCREDIBLY...
...THAT **SLICE ATTACK** CAME FROM QUITE A DISTANCE.
THAT WAS ***DICING!*** TO BE ABLE TO DEPLOY SUCH A PRECISE CUT FROM SO FAR AWAY...
MAKE NO MISTAKE ABOUT IT, THAT WAS THE WORK OF A CHEF!
AND NOT JUST ANY CHEF!
A TREMENDOUSLY STRONG ONE!
HEE HEE HEE. SINCE THEY SAVED US, I GUESS WE CAN TAKE THIS AS A WARM WELCOME.
AND A MIGHTY HIGH-LEVEL ONE AT THAT.
BUT AS FOR THAT CORAL GOLEM...
THAT MIGHT NOT BE ENOUGH TO...
I CAN'T WAIT!
THERE MUST BE SOME PRETTY AMAZING CHEFS HERE!
LET'S GO AND MEET THEM RIGHT AWAY!
HO HO HO! YOU'RE AWFULLY EXCITED, KOMATSU!
IS YOUR HEART AFLAME? NOBODY'S BEEN THIS THRILLED ABOUT COMING HERE SINCE ICHIRYU.

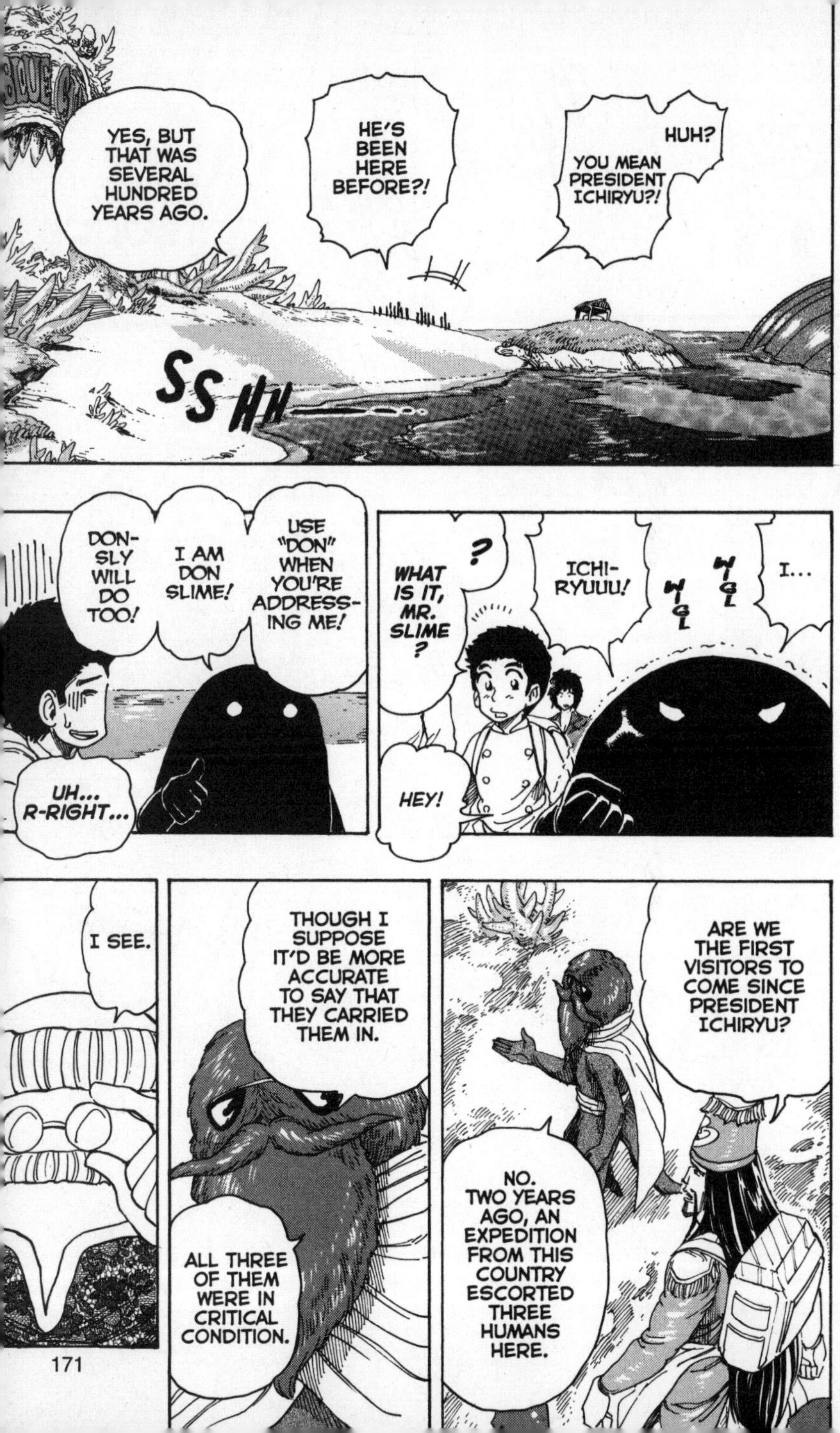
HUH?
YOU MEAN PRESIDENT ICHIRYU?!
HE'S BEEN HERE BEFORE?!
YES, BUT THAT WAS SEVERAL HUNDRED YEARS AGO.
SSHH
I...
WIGL WIGL
ICHI-RYUUU!
?
WHAT IS IT, MR. SLIME?
HEY!
USE "DON" WHEN YOU'RE ADDRESSING ME!
I AM DON SLIME!
DONSLY WILL DO TOO!
UH... R-RIGHT...
ARE WE THE FIRST VISITORS TO COME SINCE PRESIDENT ICHIRYU?
NO. TWO YEARS AGO, AN EXPEDITION FROM THIS COUNTRY ESCORTED THREE HUMANS HERE.
THOUGH I SUPPOSE IT'D BE MORE ACCURATE TO SAY THAT THEY CARRIED THEM IN.
ALL THREE OF THEM WERE IN CRITICAL CONDITION.
I SEE.

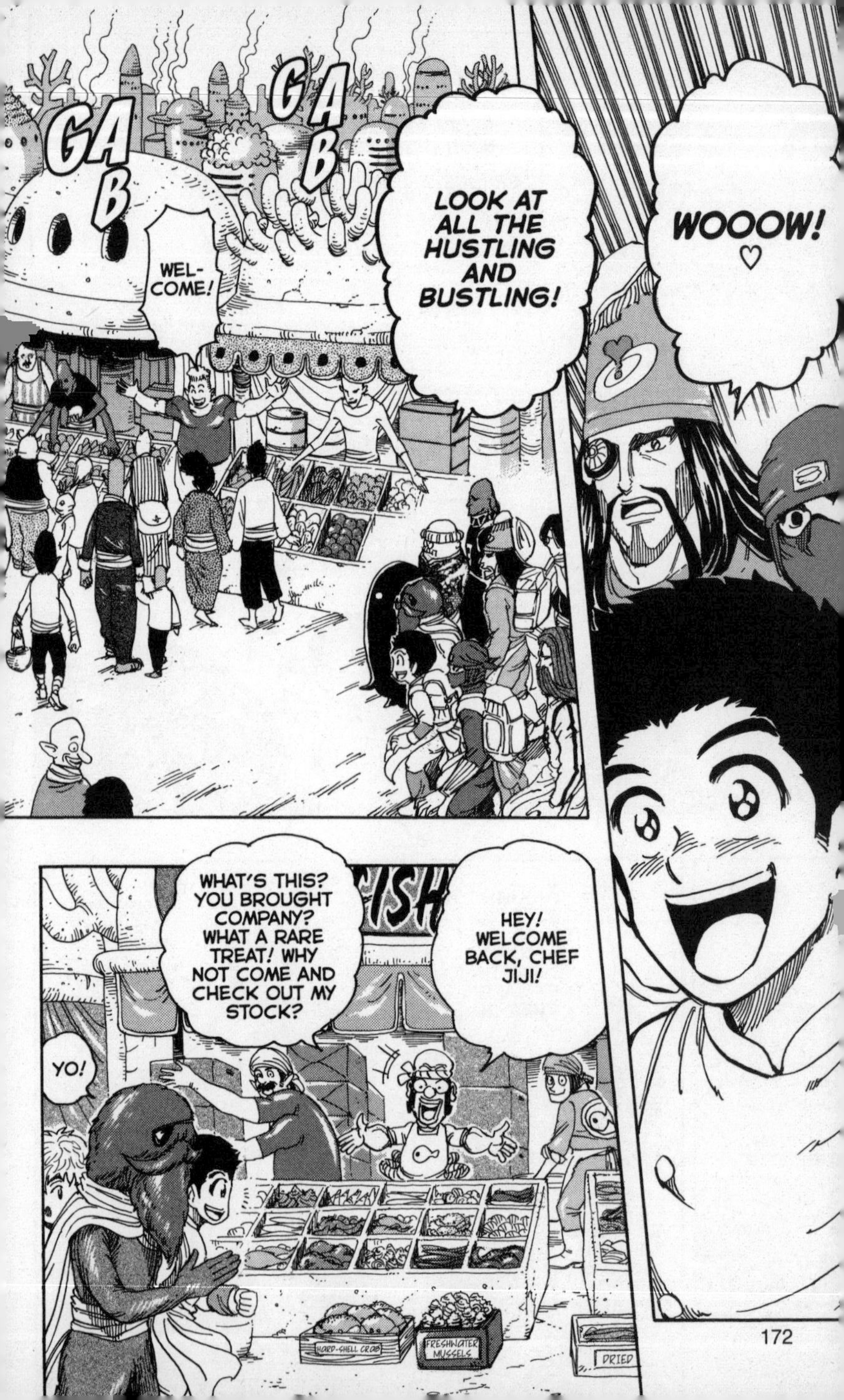
WOOOW! ♡
LOOK AT ALL THE HUSTLING AND BUSTLING!
GAB
WEL-COME!
GAB
HEY! WELCOME BACK, CHEF JIJI!
WHAT'S THIS? YOU BROUGHT COMPANY? WHAT A RARE TREAT! WHY NOT COME AND CHECK OUT MY STOCK?
YO!
DRIED
FRESHWATER MUSSELS
HARD-SHELL CRAB

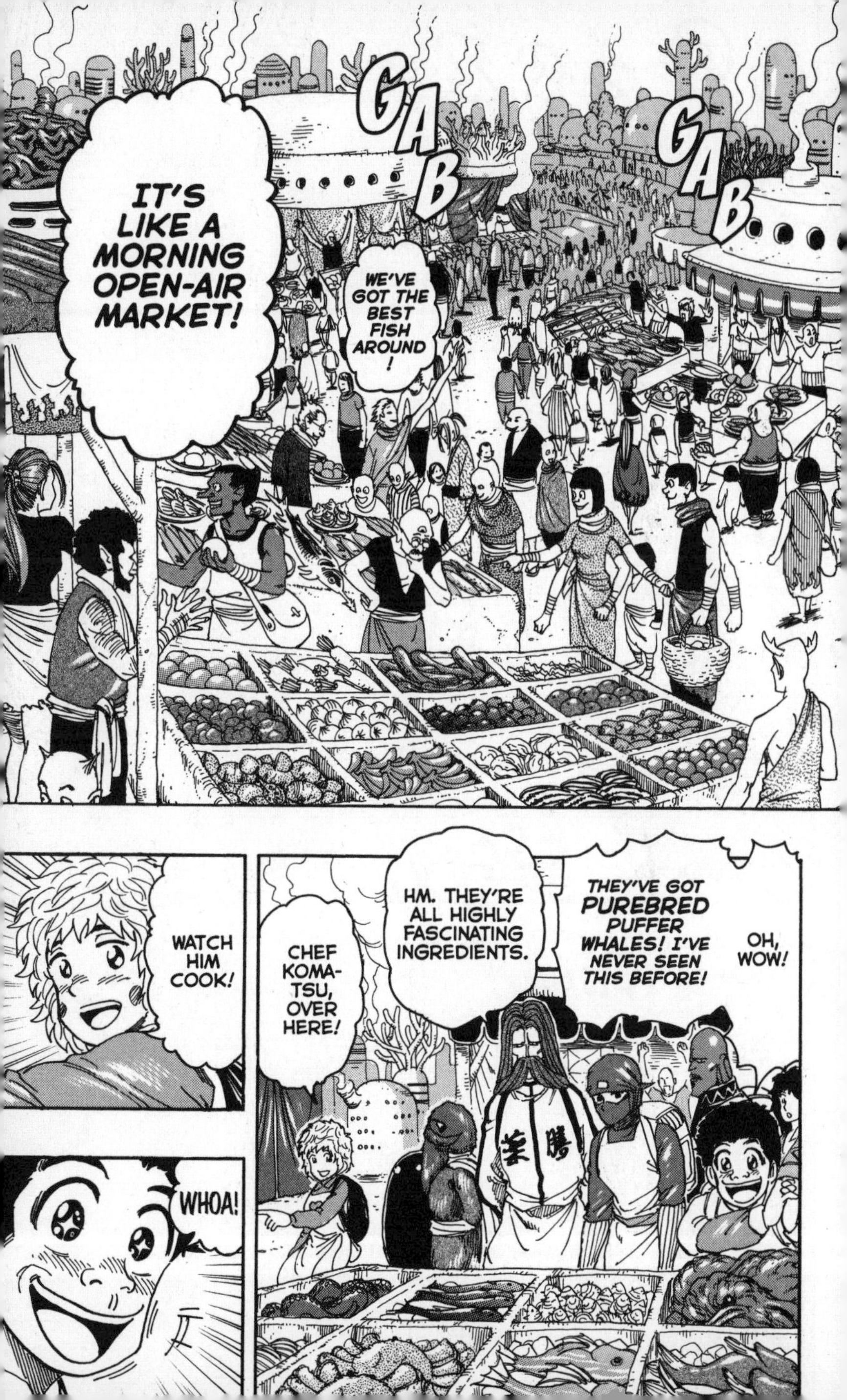
GAB
GAB
IT'S LIKE A MORNING OPEN-AIR MARKET!
WE'VE GOT THE BEST FISH AROUND!
OH, WOW!
THEY'VE GOT PUREBRED PUFFER WHALES! I'VE NEVER SEEN THIS BEFORE!
HM. THEY'RE ALL HIGHLY FASCINATING INGREDIENTS.
CHEF KOMATSU, OVER HERE!
WATCH HIM COOK!
WHOA!

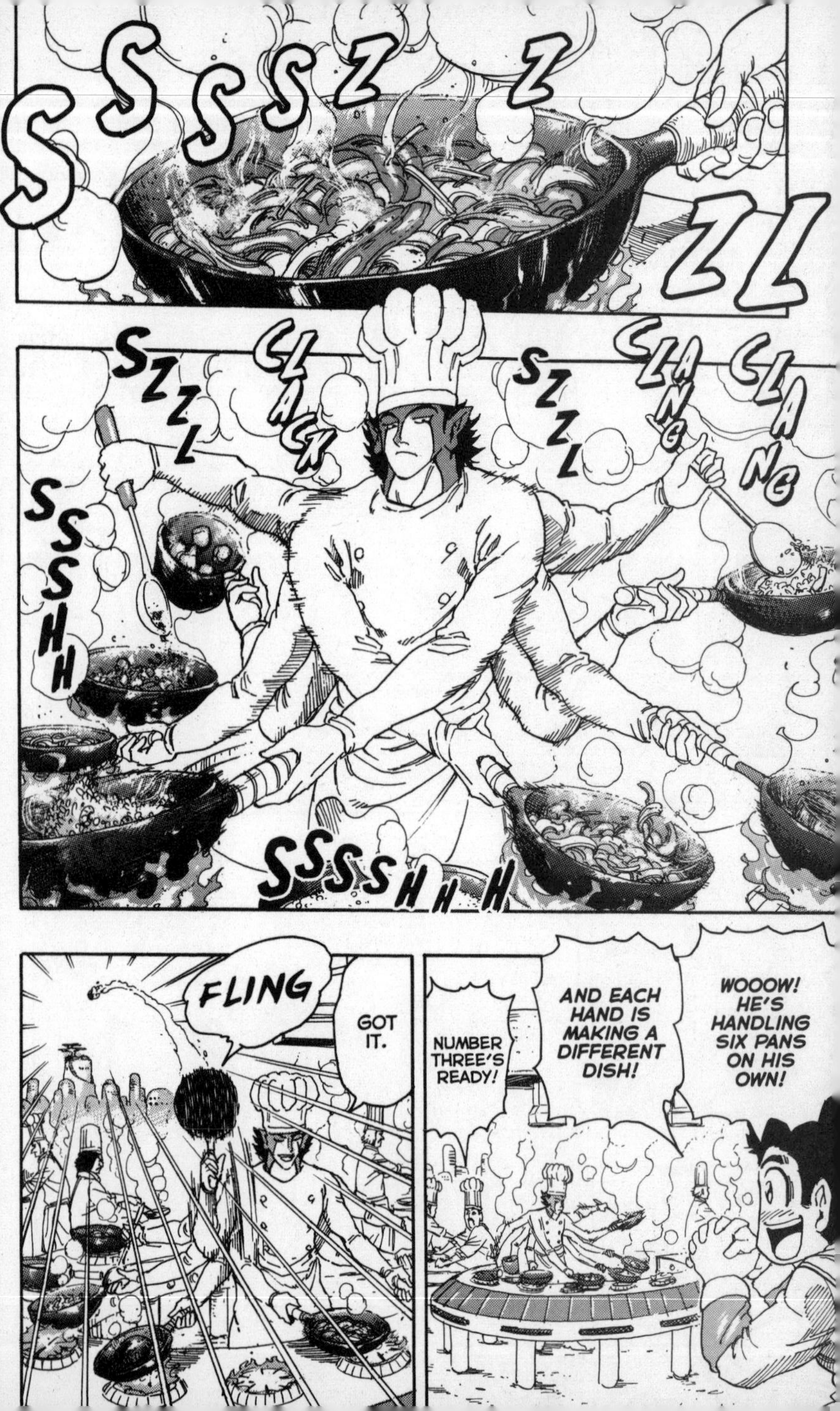
SSSSZZ
ZZ
CLANG
CLANG
SZZZL
CLACK
SZZZL
SSSHH
SSSSHHH
WOOOW! HE'S HANDLING SIX PANS ON HIS OWN!
AND EACH HAND IS MAKING A DIFFERENT DISH!
NUMBER THREE'S READY!
GOT IT.
FLING

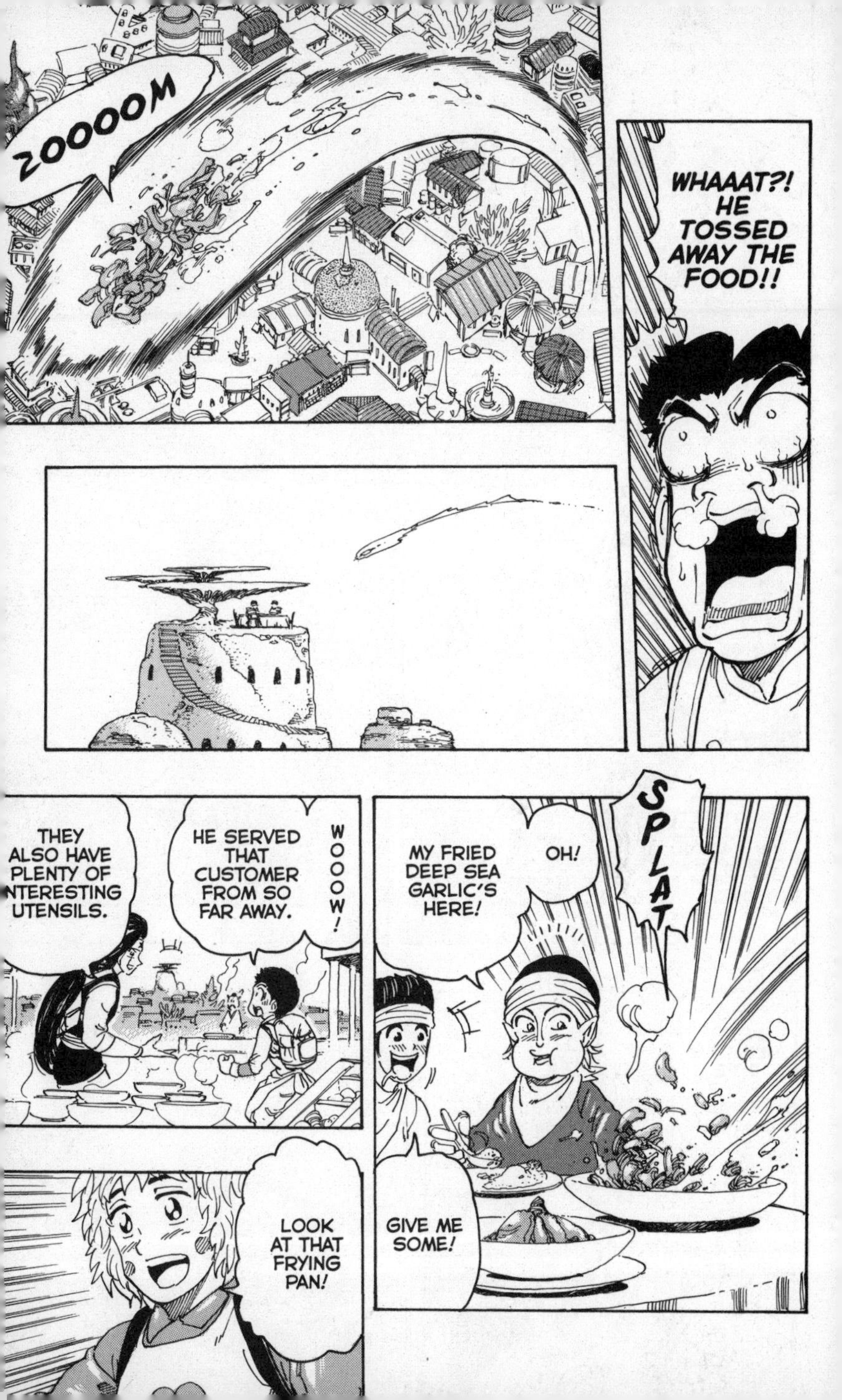
ZOOOOM
WHAAAT?! HE TOSSED AWAY THE FOOD!!
SPLAT
OH!
MY FRIED DEEP SEA GARLIC'S HERE!
GIVE ME SOME!
WOOOOW!
HE SERVED THAT CUSTOMER FROM SO FAR AWAY.
THEY ALSO HAVE PLENTY OF INTERESTING UTENSILS.
LOOK AT THAT FRYING PAN!

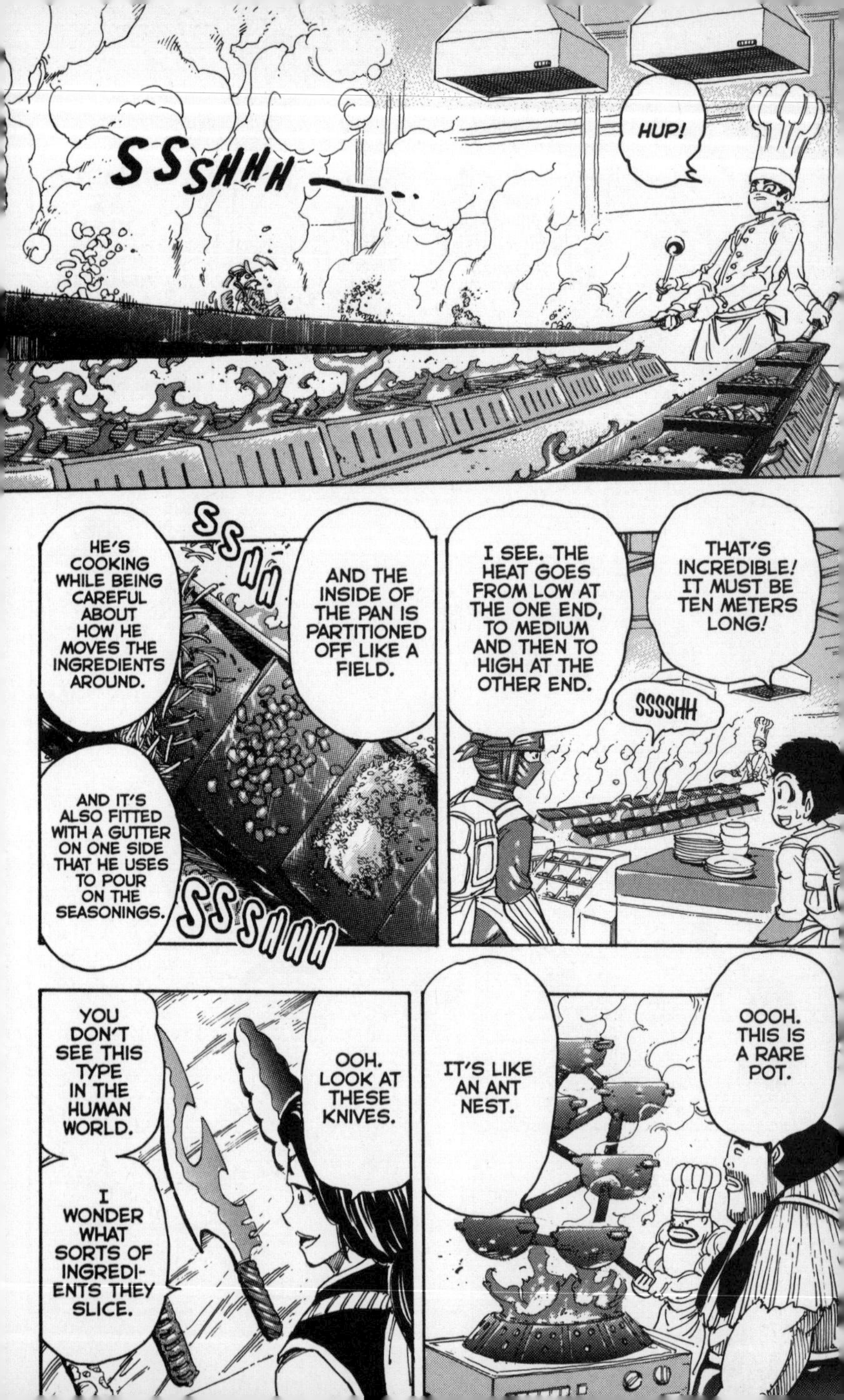
HUP!
SSSHHH—
THAT'S INCREDIBLE! IT MUST BE TEN METERS LONG!
I SEE. THE HEAT GOES FROM LOW AT THE ONE END, TO MEDIUM AND THEN TO HIGH AT THE OTHER END.
SSSSHH
AND THE INSIDE OF THE PAN IS PARTITIONED OFF LIKE A FIELD.
SSHH
HE'S COOKING WHILE BEING CAREFUL ABOUT HOW HE MOVES THE INGREDIENTS AROUND.
AND IT'S ALSO FITTED WITH A GUTTER ON ONE SIDE THAT HE USES TO POUR ON THE SEASONINGS.
SSSHHH
OOOH. THIS IS A RARE POT.
IT'S LIKE AN ANT NEST.
OOH. LOOK AT THESE KNIVES.
YOU DON'T SEE THIS TYPE IN THE HUMAN WORLD.
I WONDER WHAT SORTS OF INGREDI-ENTS THEY SLICE.

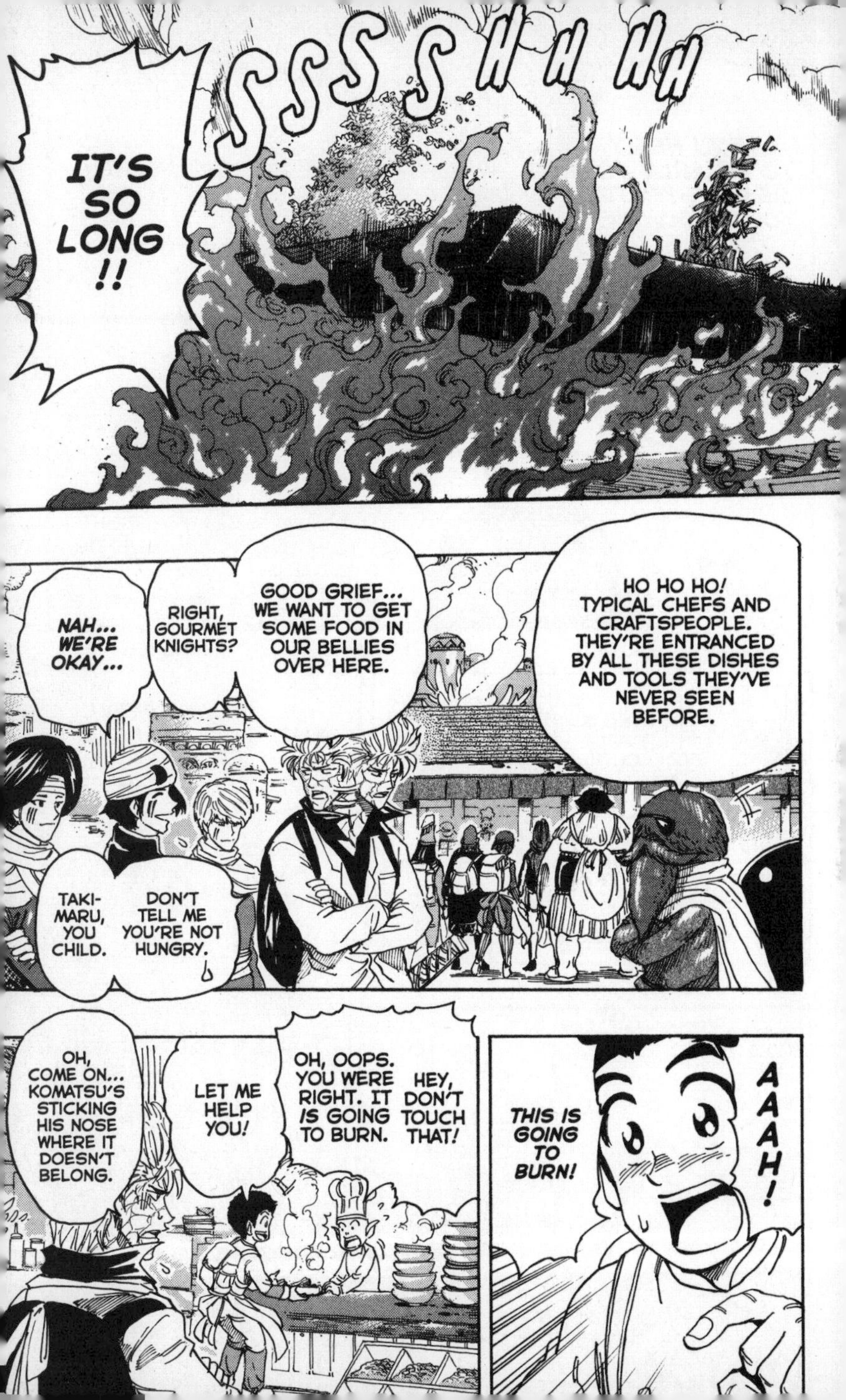
SSSSHHHH
IT'S SO LONG!!
HO HO HO! TYPICAL CHEFS AND CRAFTSPEOPLE. THEY'RE ENTRANCED BY ALL THESE DISHES AND TOOLS THEY'VE NEVER SEEN BEFORE.
GOOD GRIEF... WE WANT TO GET SOME FOOD IN OUR BELLIES OVER HERE.
RIGHT, GOURMET KNIGHTS?
NAH... WE'RE OKAY...
DON'T TELL ME YOU'RE NOT HUNGRY.
TAKI-MARU, YOU CHILD.
AAAAH!
THIS IS GOING TO BURN!
HEY, DON'T TOUCH THAT!
OH, OOPS. YOU WERE RIGHT. IT IS GOING TO BURN.
LET ME HELP YOU!
OH, COME ON... KOMATSU'S STICKING HIS NOSE WHERE IT DOESN'T BELONG.

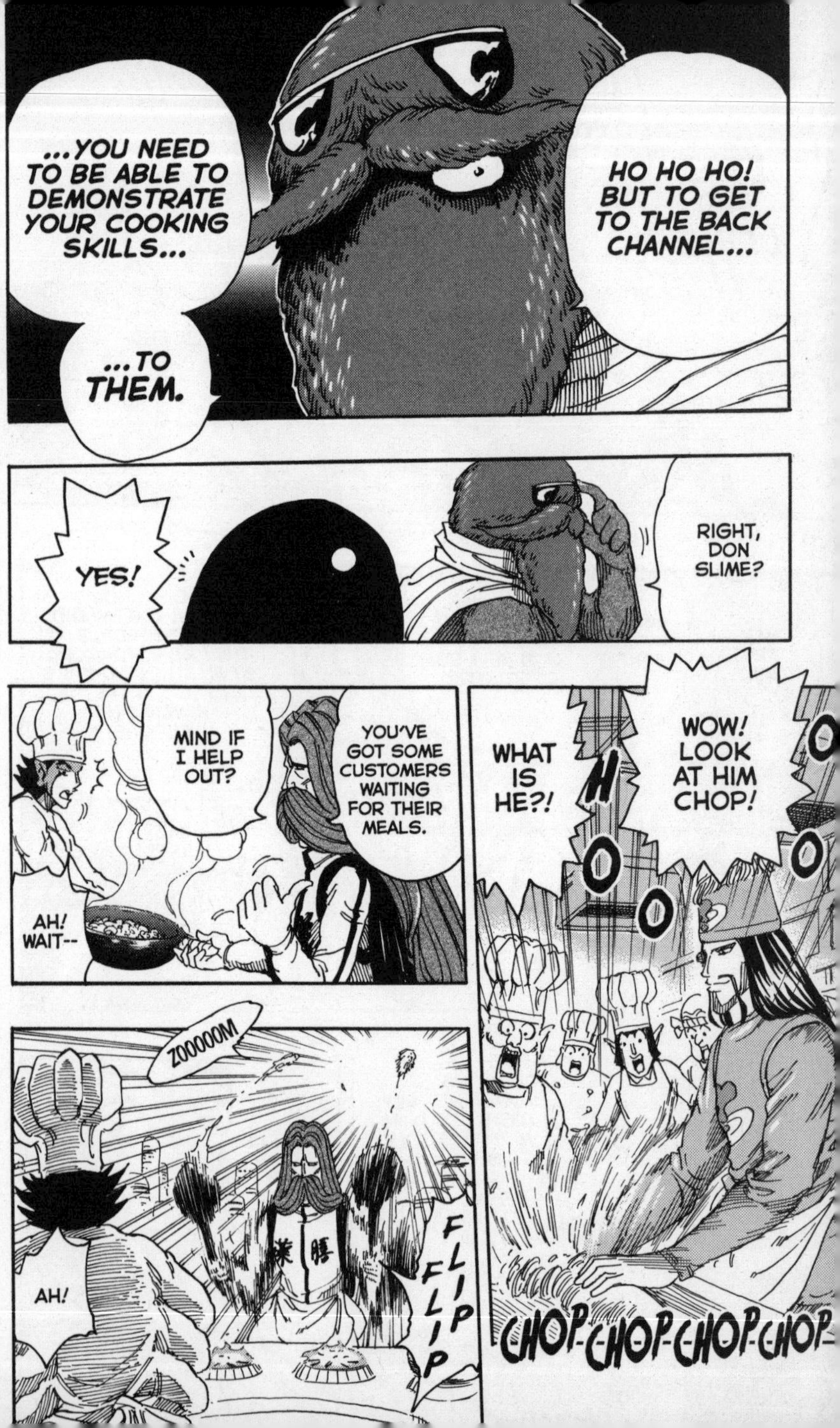
HO HO HO! BUT TO GET TO THE BACK CHANNEL...
...YOU NEED TO BE ABLE TO DEMONSTRATE YOUR COOKING SKILLS...
...TO THEM.
RIGHT, DON SLIME?
YES!
WOW! LOOK AT HIM CHOP!
HOOOOO
WHAT IS HE?!
CHOP-CHOP-CHOP-CHOP-
YOU'VE GOT SOME CUSTOMERS WAITING FOR THEIR MEALS.
MIND IF I HELP OUT?
AH! WAIT--
ZOOOOOM
FLIP FLIP
AH!

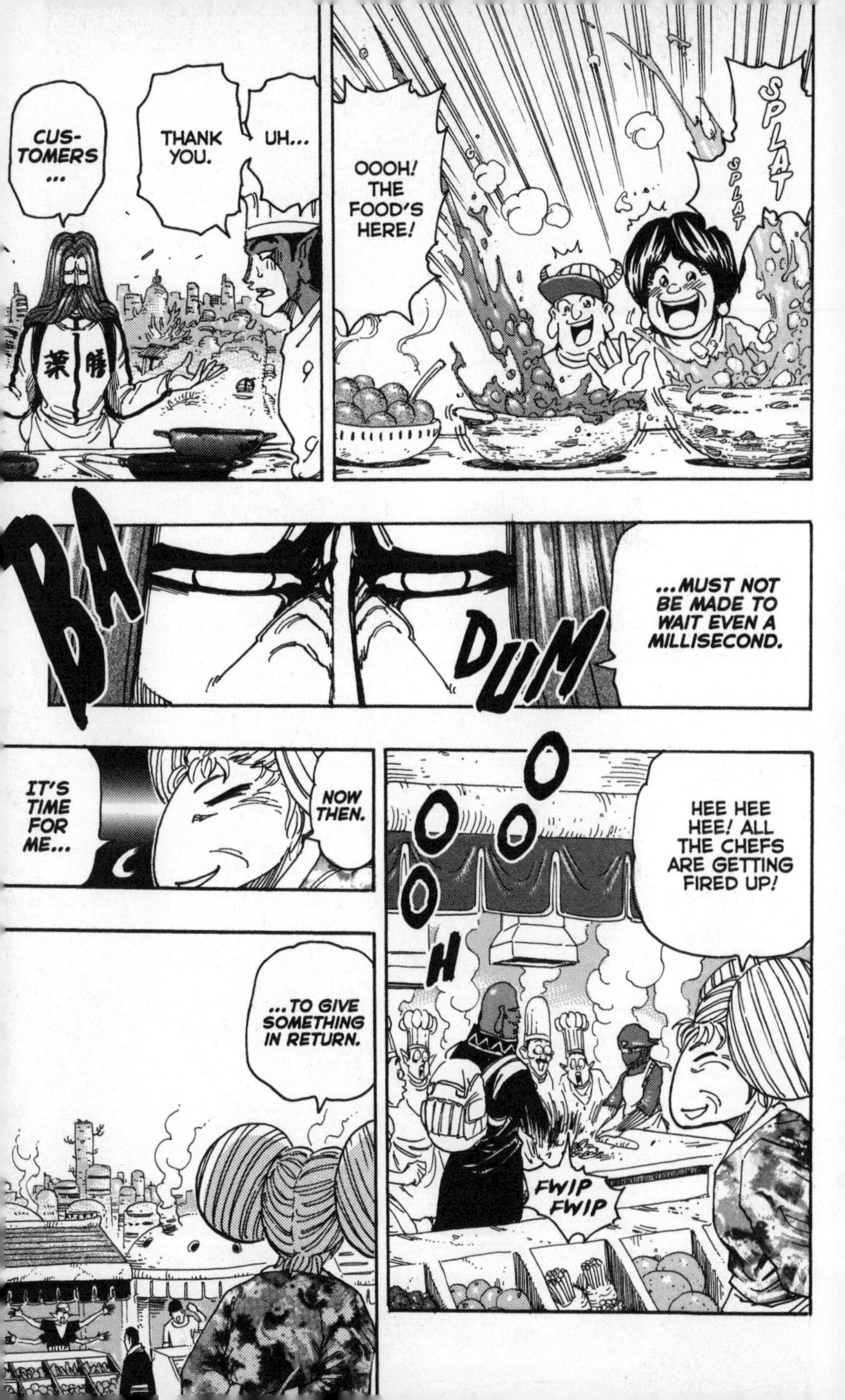
OOOH! THE FOOD'S HERE!
SPLAT
SPLAT
UH...
THANK YOU.
CUS-TOMERS ...
...MUST NOT BE MADE TO WAIT EVEN A MILLISECOND.
BA
DUM
HEE HEE HEE! ALL THE CHEFS ARE GETTING FIRED UP!
OOOOOOH
FWIP FWIP
NOW THEN.
IT'S TIME FOR ME...
...TO GIVE SOMETHING IN RETURN.

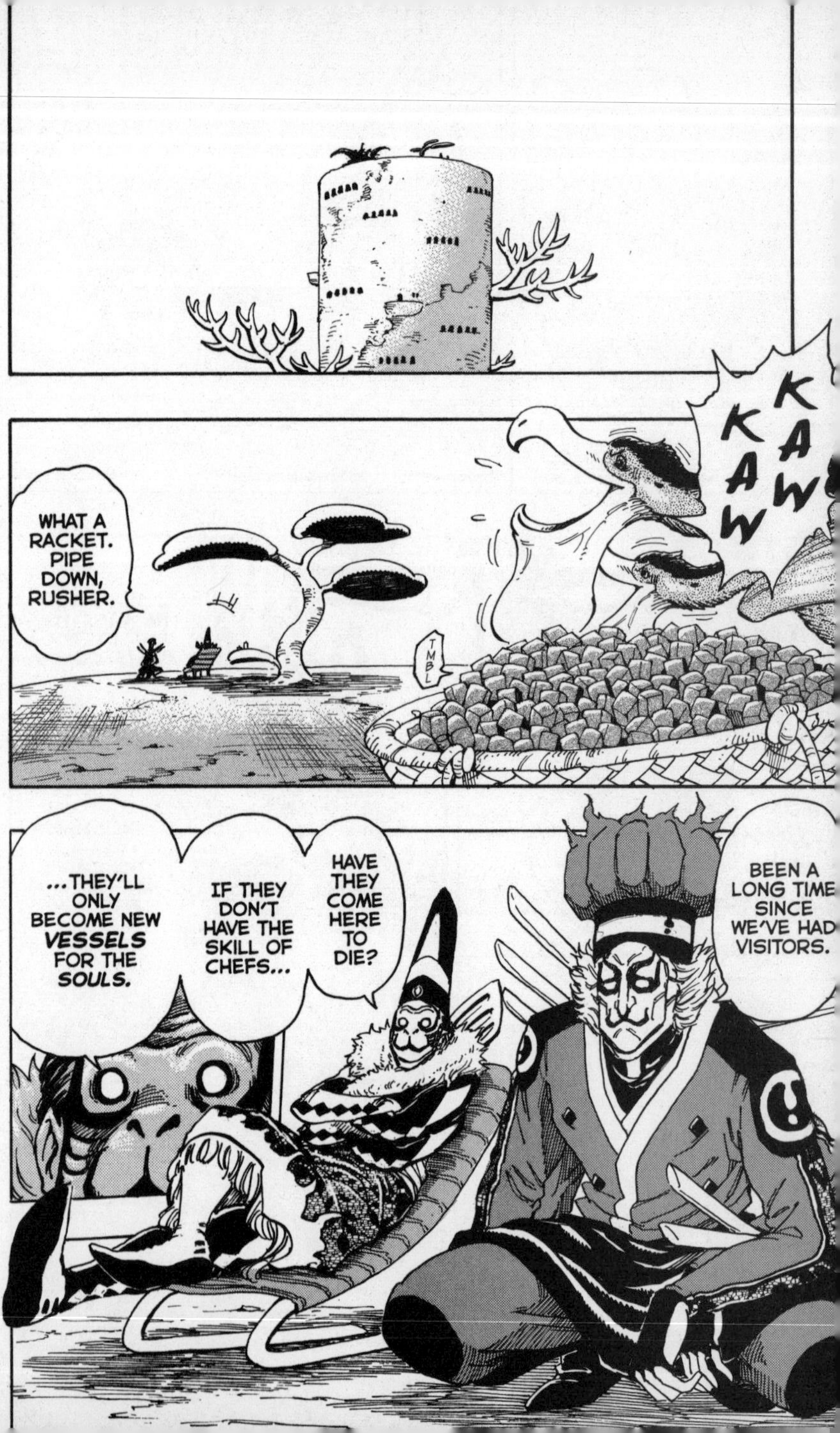
KAW KAW
TMBL
WHAT A RACKET. PIPE DOWN, RUSHER.
BEEN A LONG TIME SINCE WE'VE HAD VISITORS.
HAVE THEY COME HERE TO DIE?
IF THEY DON'T HAVE THE SKILL OF CHEFS...
...THEY'LL ONLY BECOME NEW ***VESSELS*** FOR THE ***SOULS.***

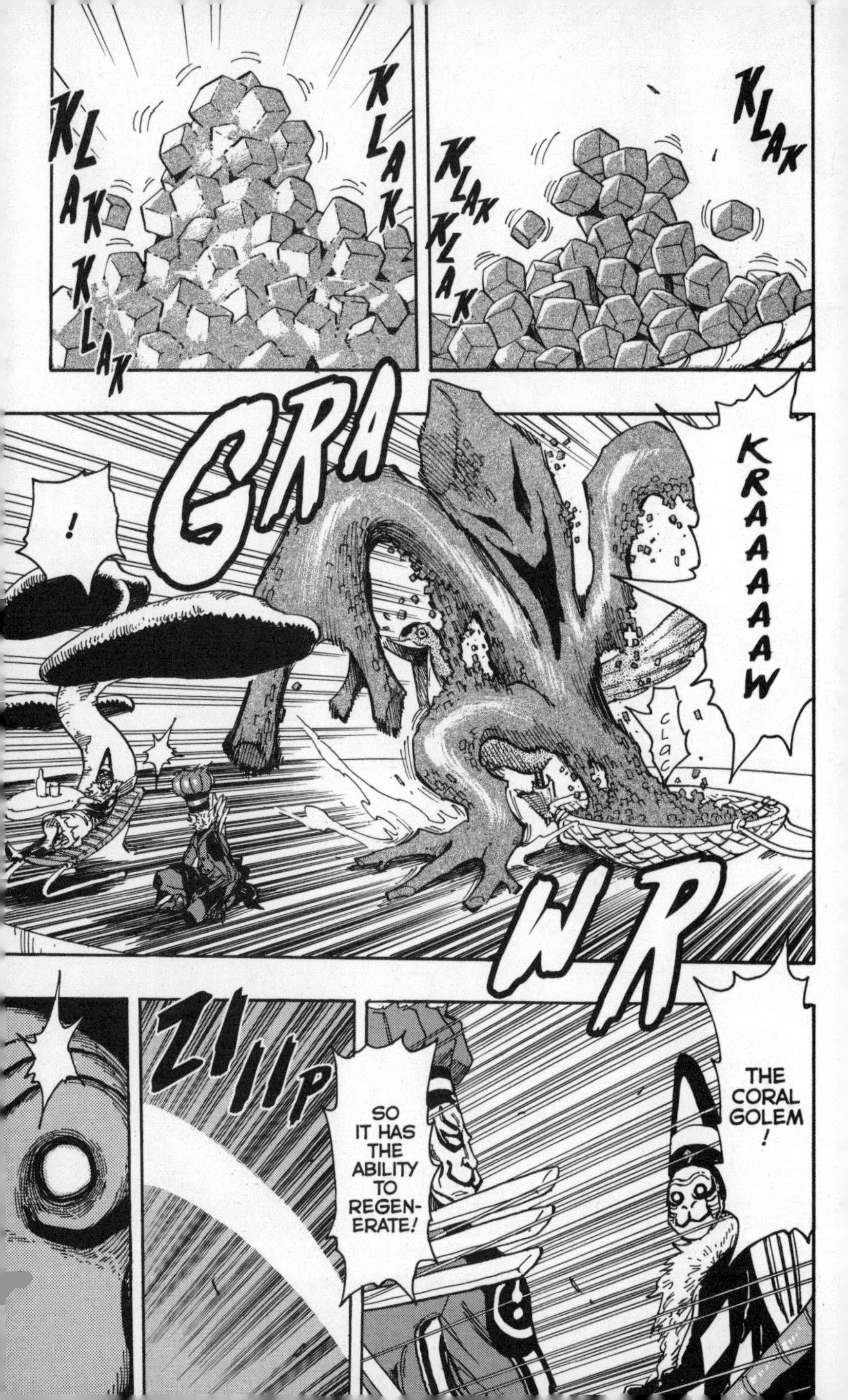
KLAK
KLAKKLAK
KLAK
KLAKKLAK
KRAAAAAAW
CLAC
!
GRAWR
THE CORAL GOLEM!
SO IT HAS THE ABILITY TO REGENERATE!
ZIIIP

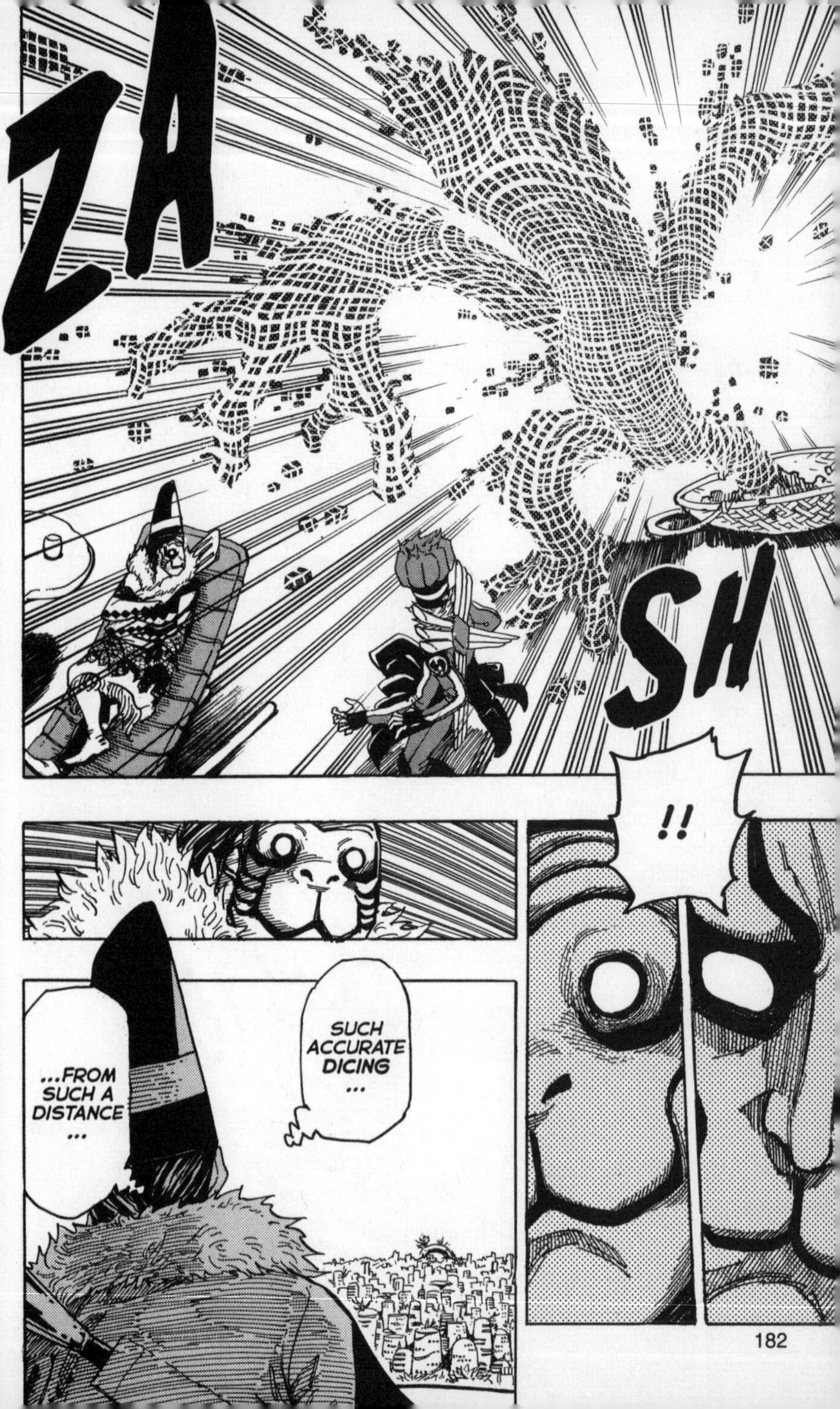
ZA
SH
!!
SUCH ACCURATE DICING ...
...FROM SUCH A DISTANCE ...

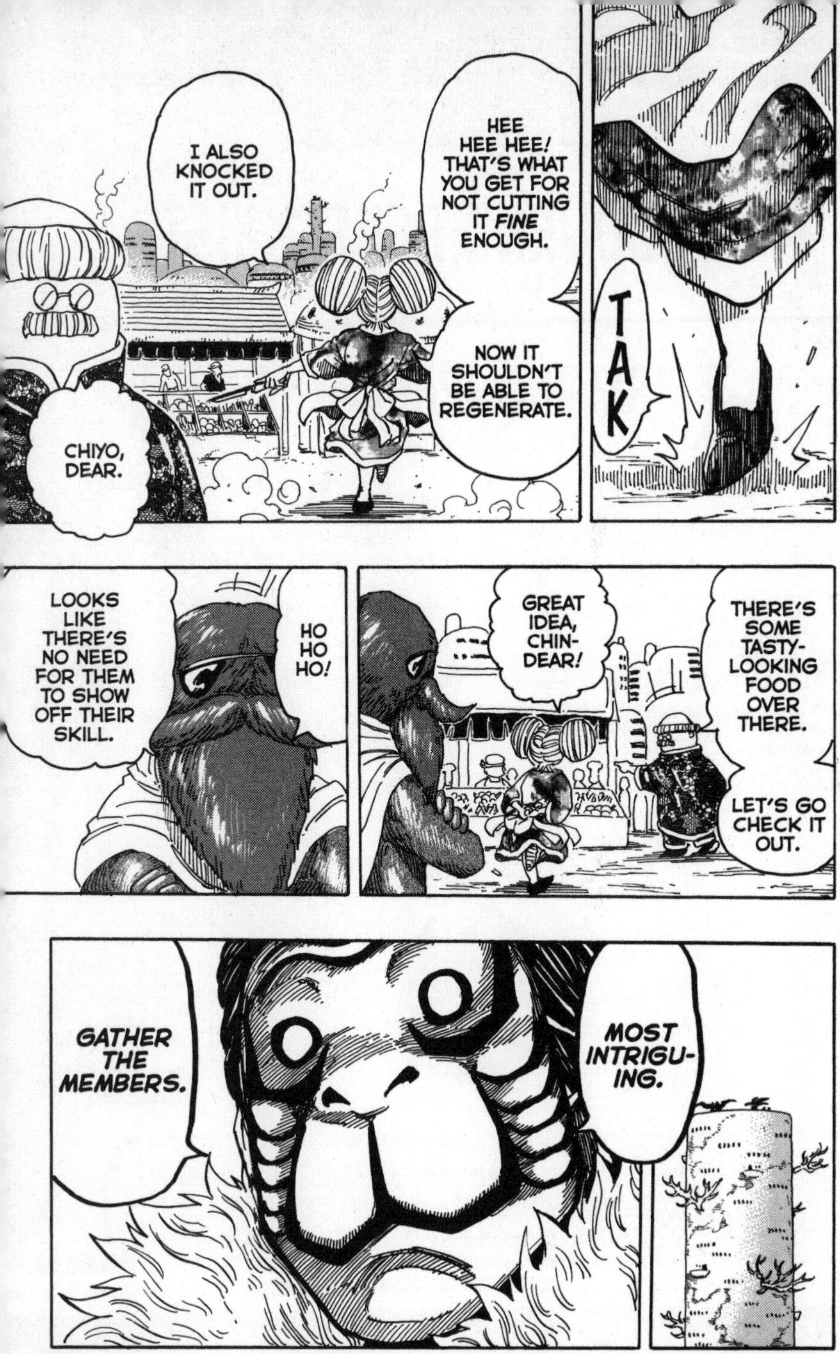
TAK
HEE HEE HEE! THAT'S WHAT YOU GET FOR NOT CUTTING IT *FINE* ENOUGH.
I ALSO KNOCKED IT OUT.
NOW IT SHOULDN'T BE ABLE TO REGENERATE.
CHIYO, DEAR.
THERE'S SOME TASTY-LOOKING FOOD OVER THERE.
LET'S GO CHECK IT OUT.
GREAT IDEA, CHIN-DEAR!
HO HO HO!
LOOKS LIKE THERE'S NO NEED FOR THEM TO SHOW OFF THEIR SKILL.
MOST INTRIGU-ING.
GATHER THE MEMBERS.

GOURMET CHECKLIST

Vol. 359

❧ ARM RHAMPHORHYNCHUS ❧
(PHANTOM BIRD)

CAPTURE LEVEL: 251
HABITAT: YUTO ISLAND IN THE
GOURMET WORLD
SIZE: 60 M
HEIGHT: ---
WEIGHT: 700 TONS
PRICE: 50,000 YEN PER KILOGRAM

SCALE

TRUE TO ITS APPEARANCE, THIS IS A BRUTAL PHANTOM BIRD. THE TALONS ON ITS STRONG ARM CONTAIN A TOXIN AND, ONCE IT GETS A HOLD OF ITS PREY, IT NEVER LETS GO. IT USES CLAIRVOYANCE FOR HUNTING AS THIS LETS IT SEE PREY FROM FAR AWAY. THIS MAKES IT AN AERIAL HUNTER OF THE SKIES ALL AROUND THE GOURMET WORLD'S YUTO ISLAND. DESPITE ITS GROTESQUE APPEARANCE, IT'S ACTUALLY DELICIOUS WHEN DEEP-FRIED.

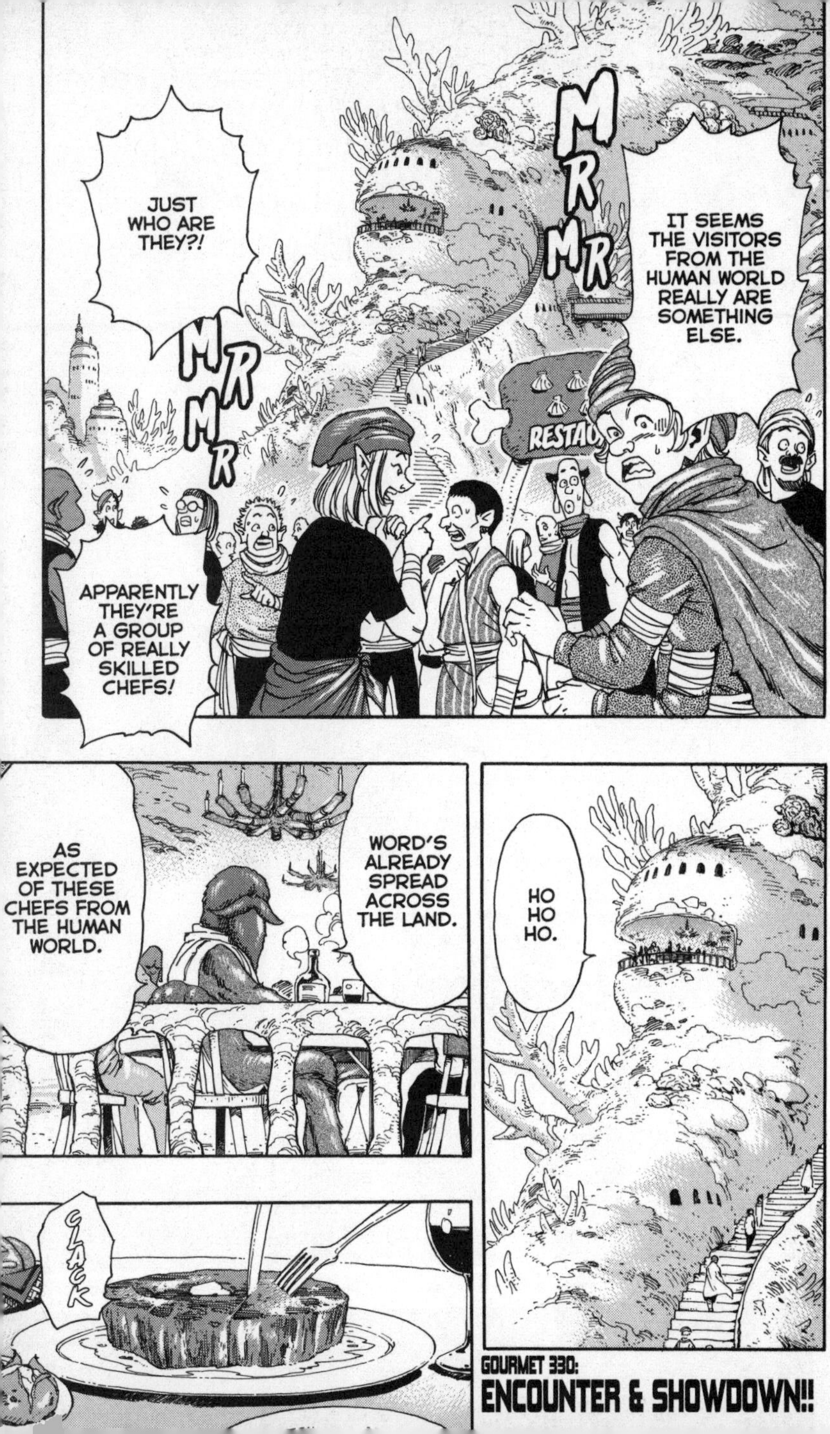
IT SEEMS THE VISITORS FROM THE HUMAN WORLD REALLY ARE SOMETHING ELSE.
MRMR
JUST WHO ARE THEY?!
MRMR
RESTAU
APPARENTLY THEY'RE A GROUP OF REALLY SKILLED CHEFS!
HO HO HO.
GOURMET 330:
ENCOUNTER & SHOWDOWN!!
WORD'S ALREADY SPREAD ACROSS THE LAND.
AS EXPECTED OF THESE CHEFS FROM THE HUMAN WORLD.
CLACK

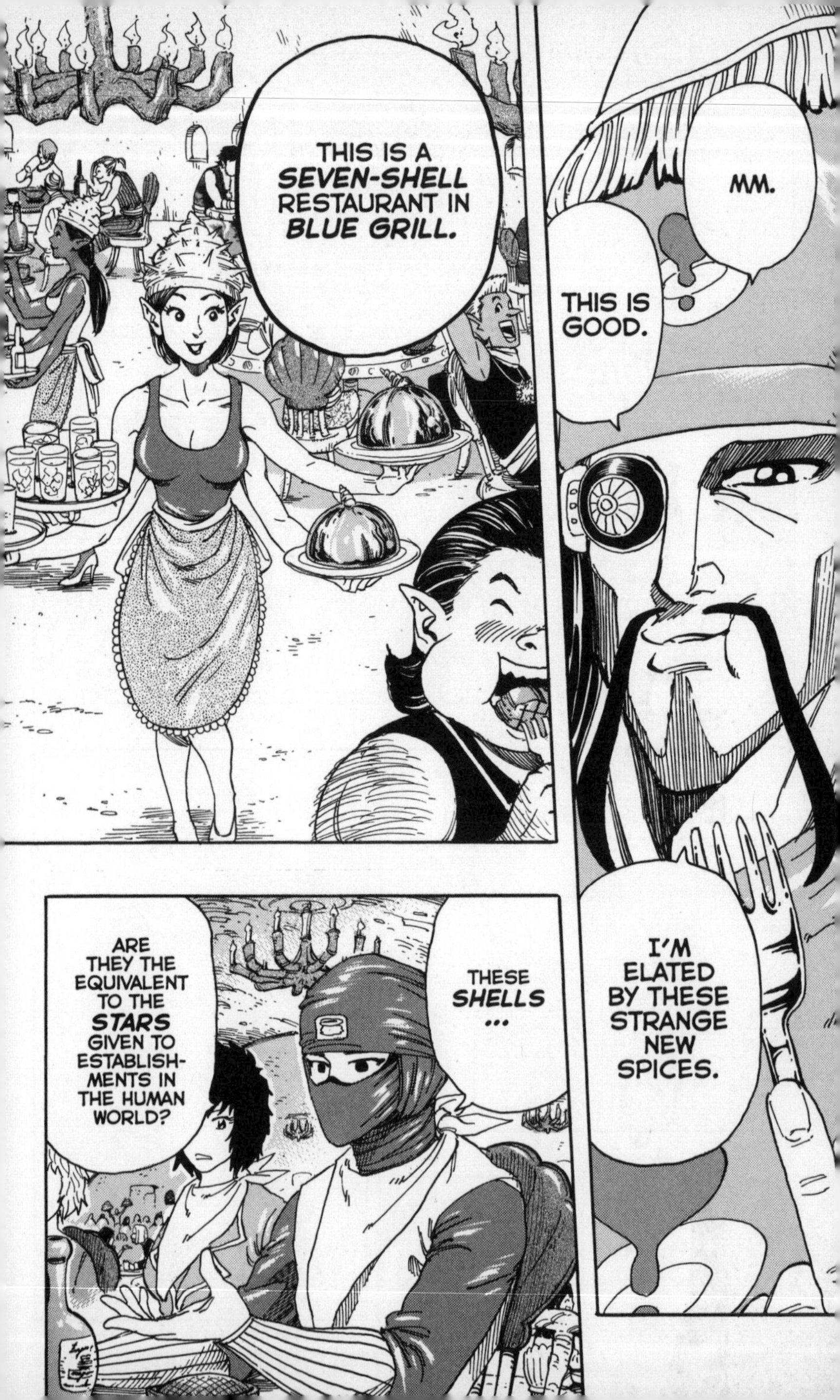
MM.
THIS IS GOOD.
I'M ELATED BY THESE STRANGE NEW SPICES.
THIS IS A SEVEN-SHELL RESTAURANT IN BLUE GRILL.
THESE SHELLS...
ARE THEY THE EQUIVALENT TO THE STARS GIVEN TO ESTABLISHMENTS IN THE HUMAN WORLD?

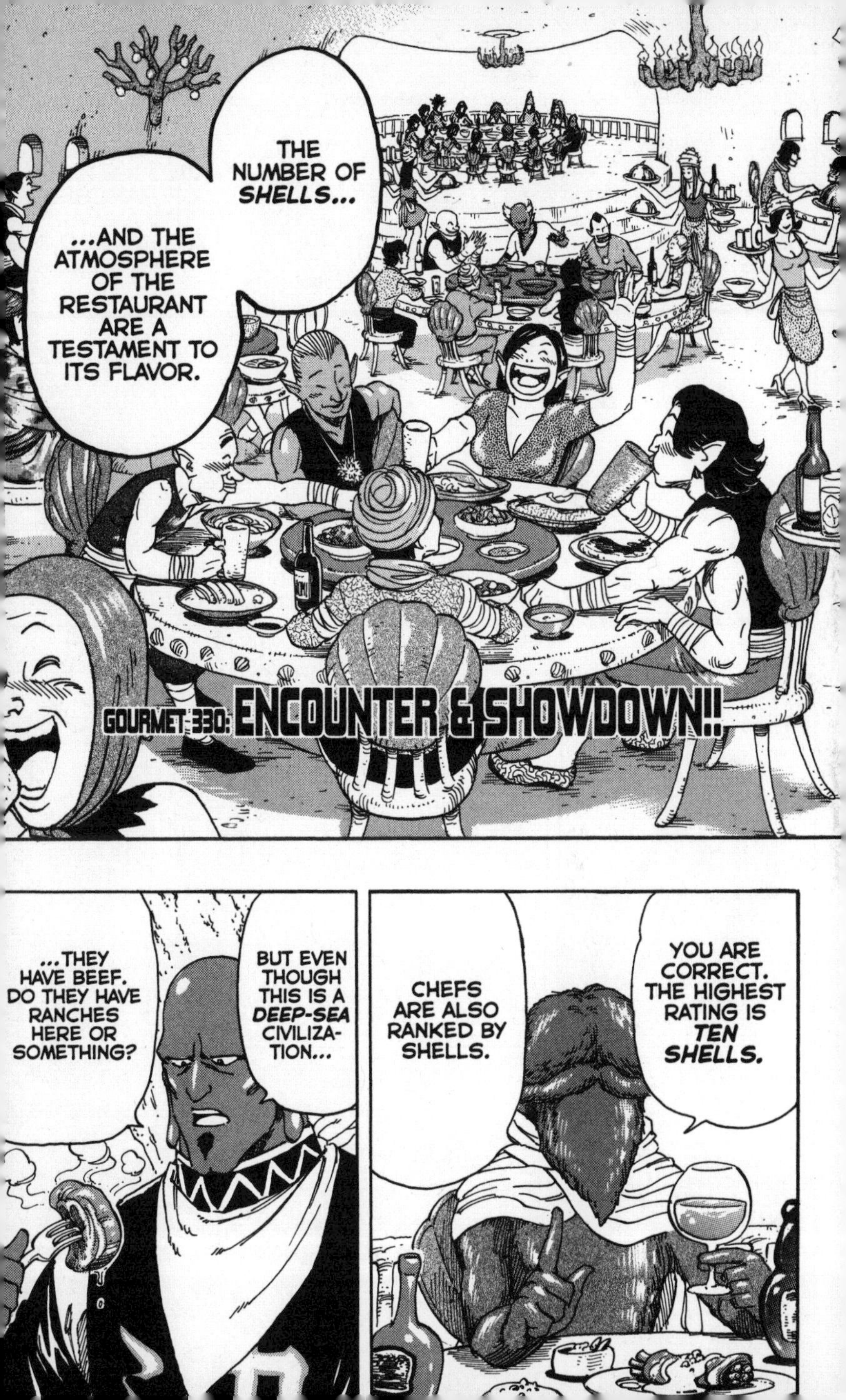
THE NUMBER OF SHELLS...
...AND THE ATMOSPHERE OF THE RESTAURANT ARE A TESTAMENT TO ITS FLAVOR.
GOURMET 330: ENCOUNTER & SHOWDOWN!!
YOU ARE CORRECT. THE HIGHEST RATING IS TEN SHELLS.
CHEFS ARE ALSO RANKED BY SHELLS.
BUT EVEN THOUGH THIS IS A DEEP-SEA CIVILIZATION...
...THEY HAVE BEEF. DO THEY HAVE RANCHES HERE OR SOMETHING?

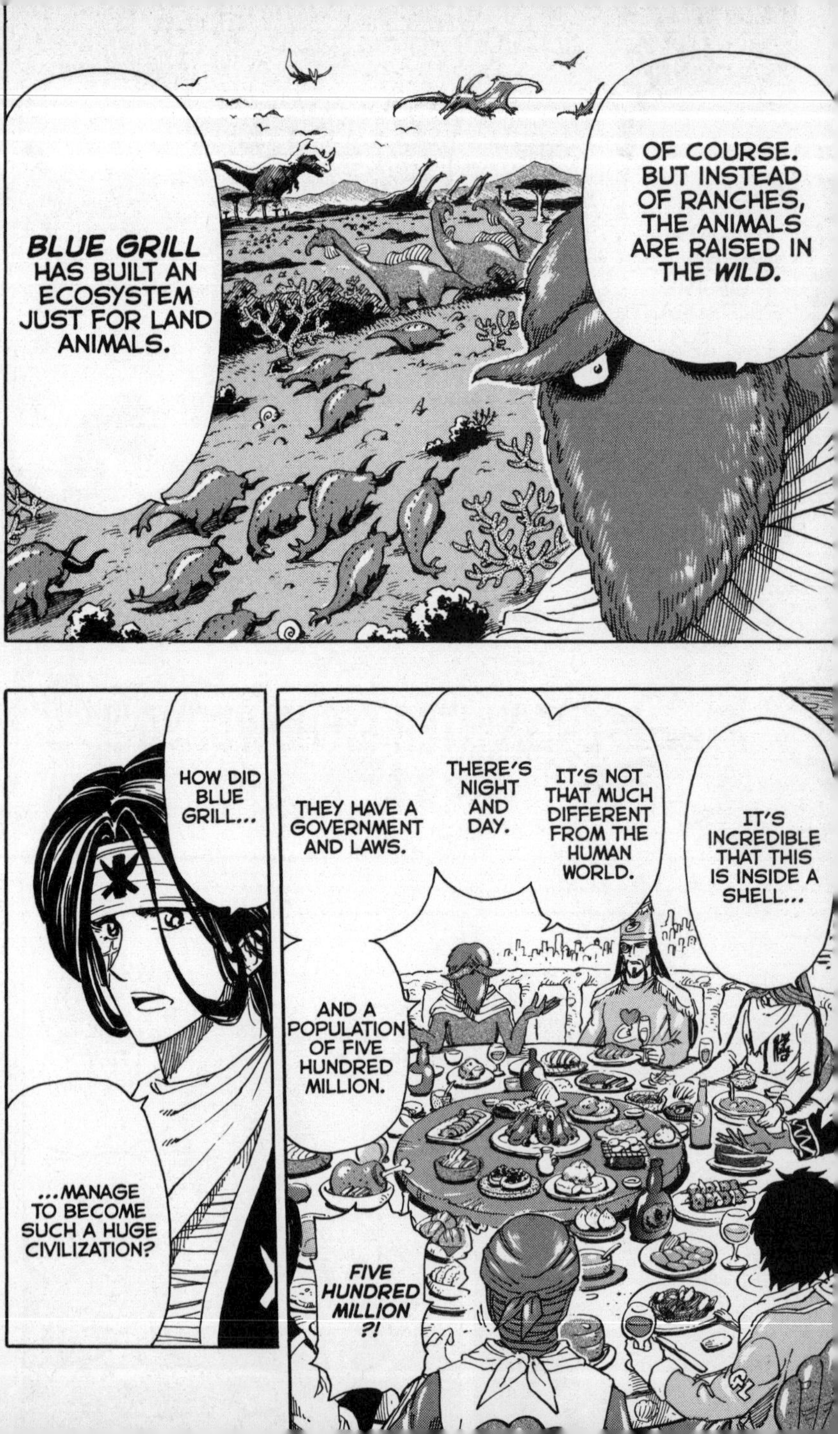
OF COURSE. BUT INSTEAD OF RANCHES, THE ANIMALS ARE RAISED IN THE *WILD.*
BLUE GRILL HAS BUILT AN ECOSYSTEM JUST FOR LAND ANIMALS.
IT'S INCREDIBLE THAT THIS IS INSIDE A SHELL...
IT'S NOT THAT MUCH DIFFERENT FROM THE HUMAN WORLD.
THERE'S NIGHT AND DAY.
THEY HAVE A GOVERNMENT AND LAWS.
AND A POPULATION OF FIVE HUNDRED MILLION.
FIVE HUNDRED MILLION ?!
HOW DID BLUE GRILL...
...MANAGE TO BECOME SUCH A HUGE CIVILIZATION?

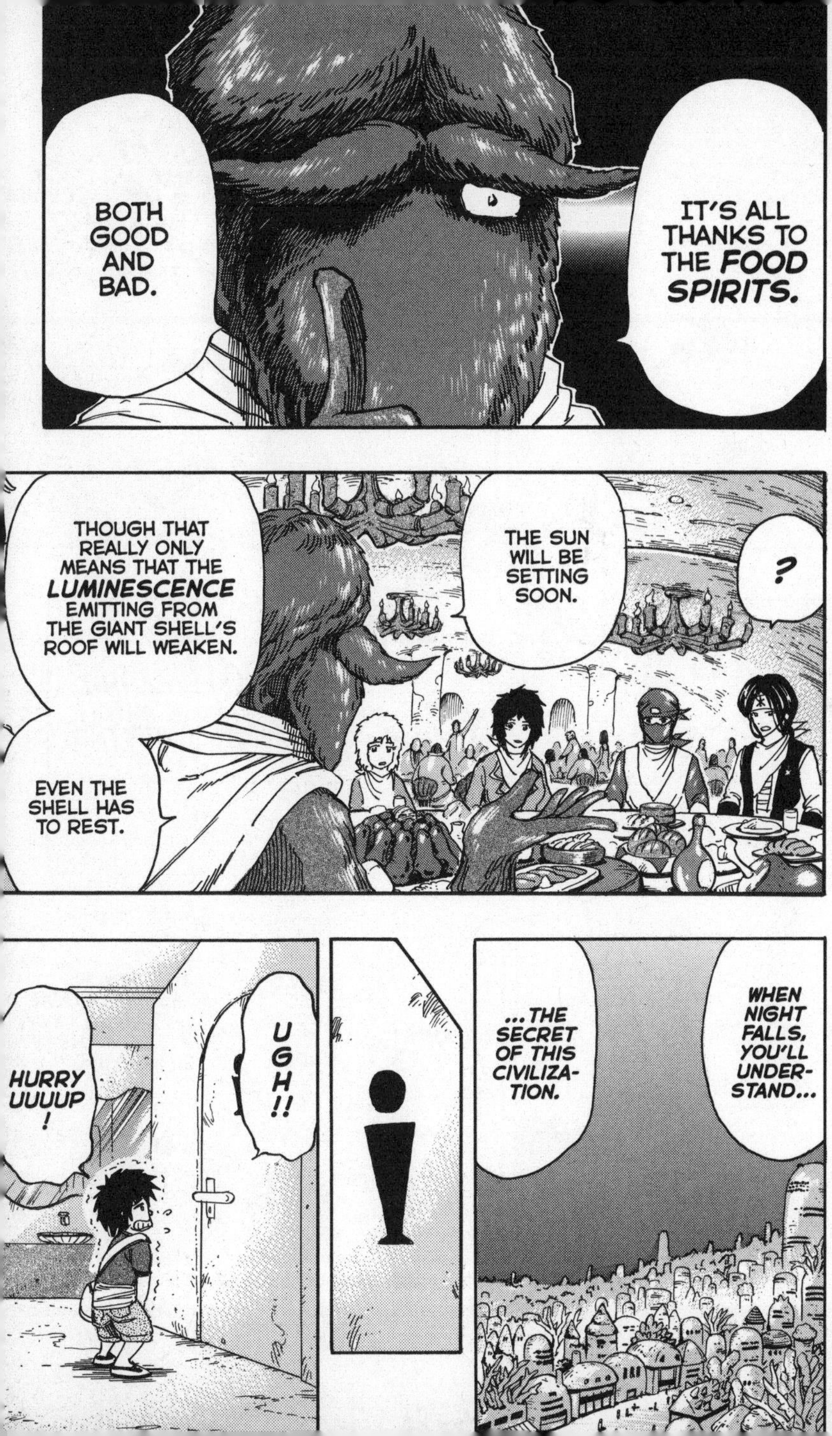
IT'S ALL THANKS TO THE FOOD SPIRITS.
BOTH GOOD AND BAD.
?
THE SUN WILL BE SETTING SOON.
THOUGH THAT REALLY ONLY MEANS THAT THE LUMINESCENCE EMITTING FROM THE GIANT SHELL'S ROOF WILL WEAKEN.
EVEN THE SHELL HAS TO REST.
WHEN NIGHT FALLS, YOU'LL UNDER-STAND...
...THE SECRET OF THIS CIVILIZA-TION.
!
UGH!!
HURRY UUUUP!

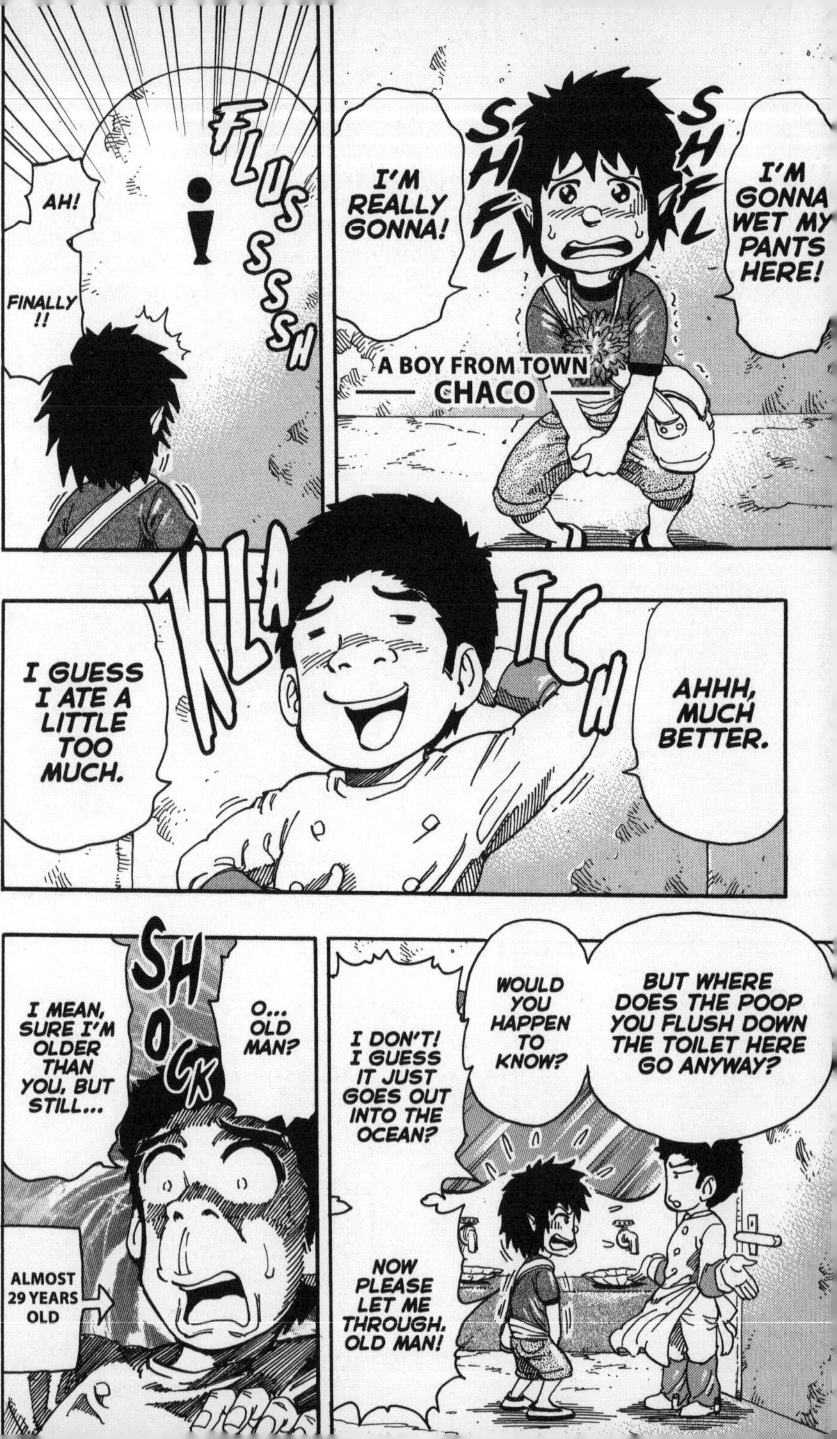
I'M GONNA WET MY PANTS HERE!
SHFL
SHFL
I'M REALLY GONNA!
A BOY FROM TOWN
— CHACO —
FLUSSSSH
AH!
FINALLY!!
KLATCH
AHHH, MUCH BETTER.
I GUESS I ATE A LITTLE TOO MUCH.
BUT WHERE DOES THE POOP YOU FLUSH DOWN THE TOILET HERE GO ANYWAY?
WOULD YOU HAPPEN TO KNOW?
I DON'T! I GUESS IT JUST GOES OUT INTO THE OCEAN?
NOW PLEASE LET ME THROUGH, OLD MAN!
O... OLD MAN?
SHOCK
I MEAN, SURE I'M OLDER THAN YOU, BUT STILL...
ALMOST 29 YEARS OLD

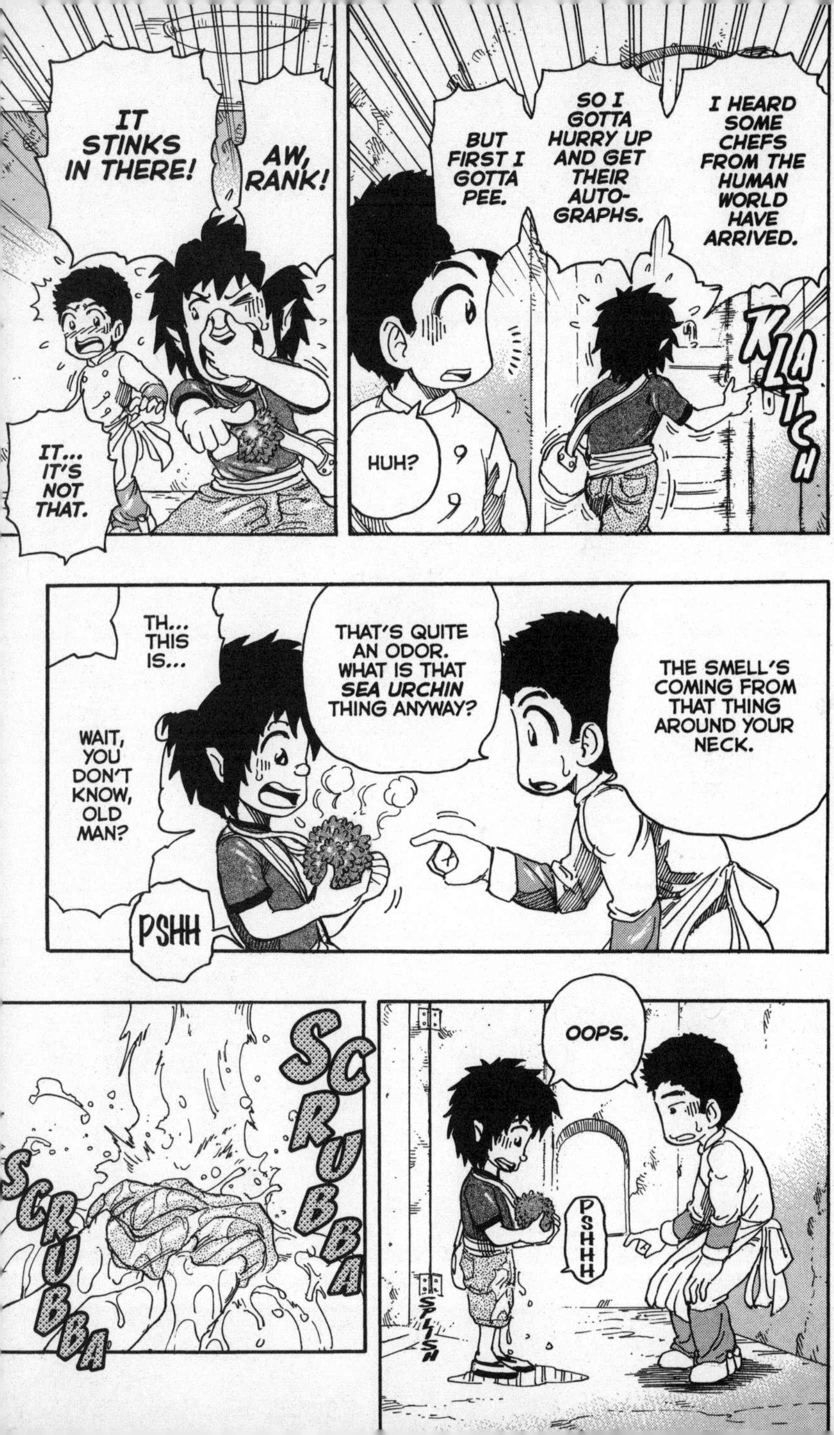
I HEARD SOME CHEFS FROM THE HUMAN WORLD HAVE ARRIVED.
SO I GOTTA HURRY UP AND GET THEIR AUTO-GRAPHS.
BUT FIRST I GOTTA PEE.
KLATCH
HUH?
AW, RANK!
IT STINKS IN THERE!
IT... IT'S NOT THAT.
THE SMELL'S COMING FROM THAT THING AROUND YOUR NECK.
THAT'S QUITE AN ODOR. WHAT IS THAT *SEA URCHIN* THING ANYWAY?
TH... THIS IS...
WAIT, YOU DON'T KNOW, OLD MAN?
PSHH
OOPS.
PSHHH
SPLISH
SCRUBBA
SCRUBBA

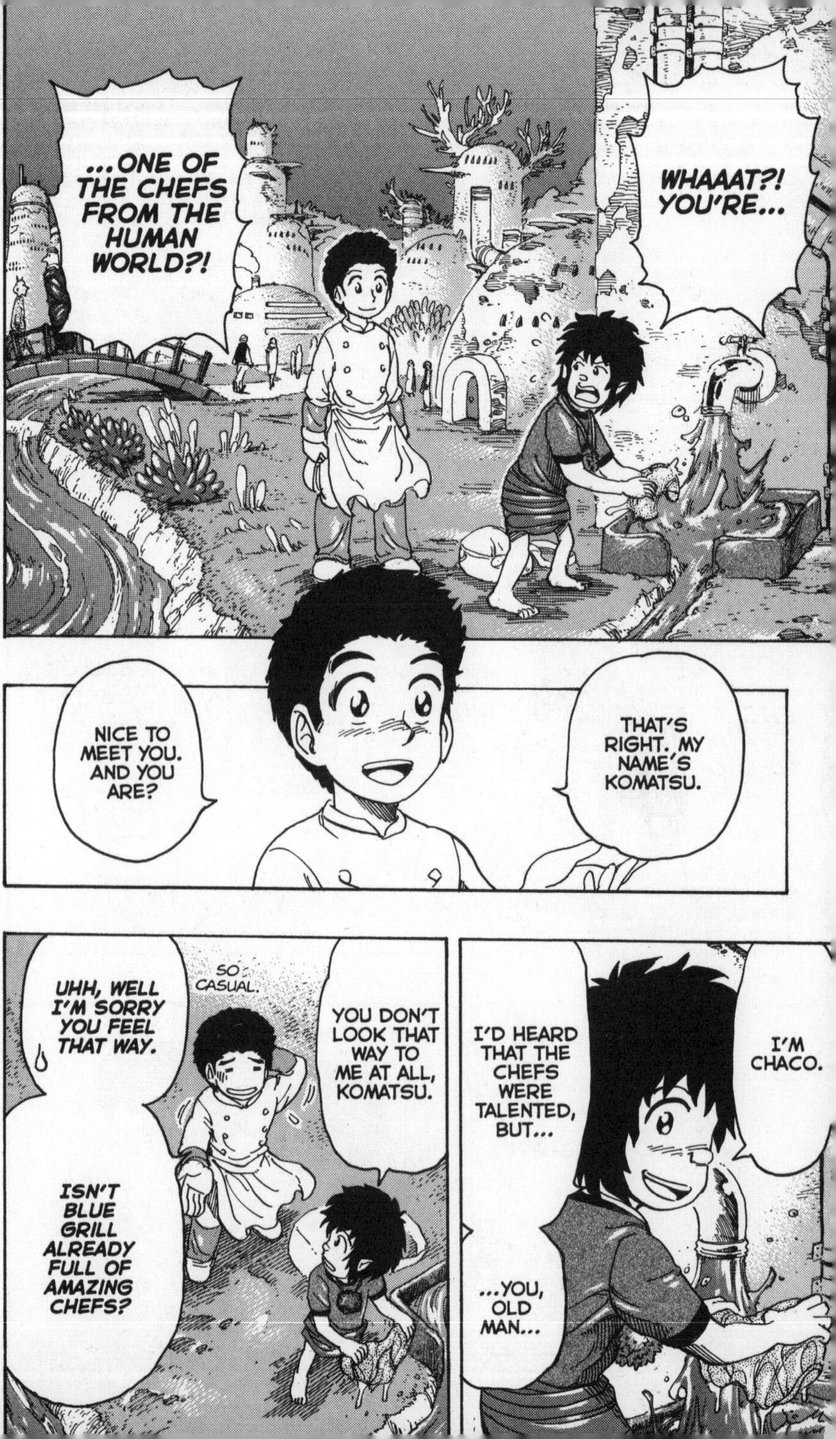
WHAAAT?! YOU'RE...
...ONE OF THE CHEFS FROM THE HUMAN WORLD?!
THAT'S RIGHT. MY NAME'S KOMATSU.
NICE TO MEET YOU. AND YOU ARE?
I'M CHACO.
I'D HEARD THAT THE CHEFS WERE TALENTED, BUT...
...YOU, OLD MAN...
YOU DON'T LOOK THAT WAY TO ME AT ALL, KOMATSU.
SO CASUAL.
UHH, WELL I'M SORRY YOU FEEL THAT WAY.
ISN'T BLUE GRILL ALREADY FULL OF AMAZING CHEFS?

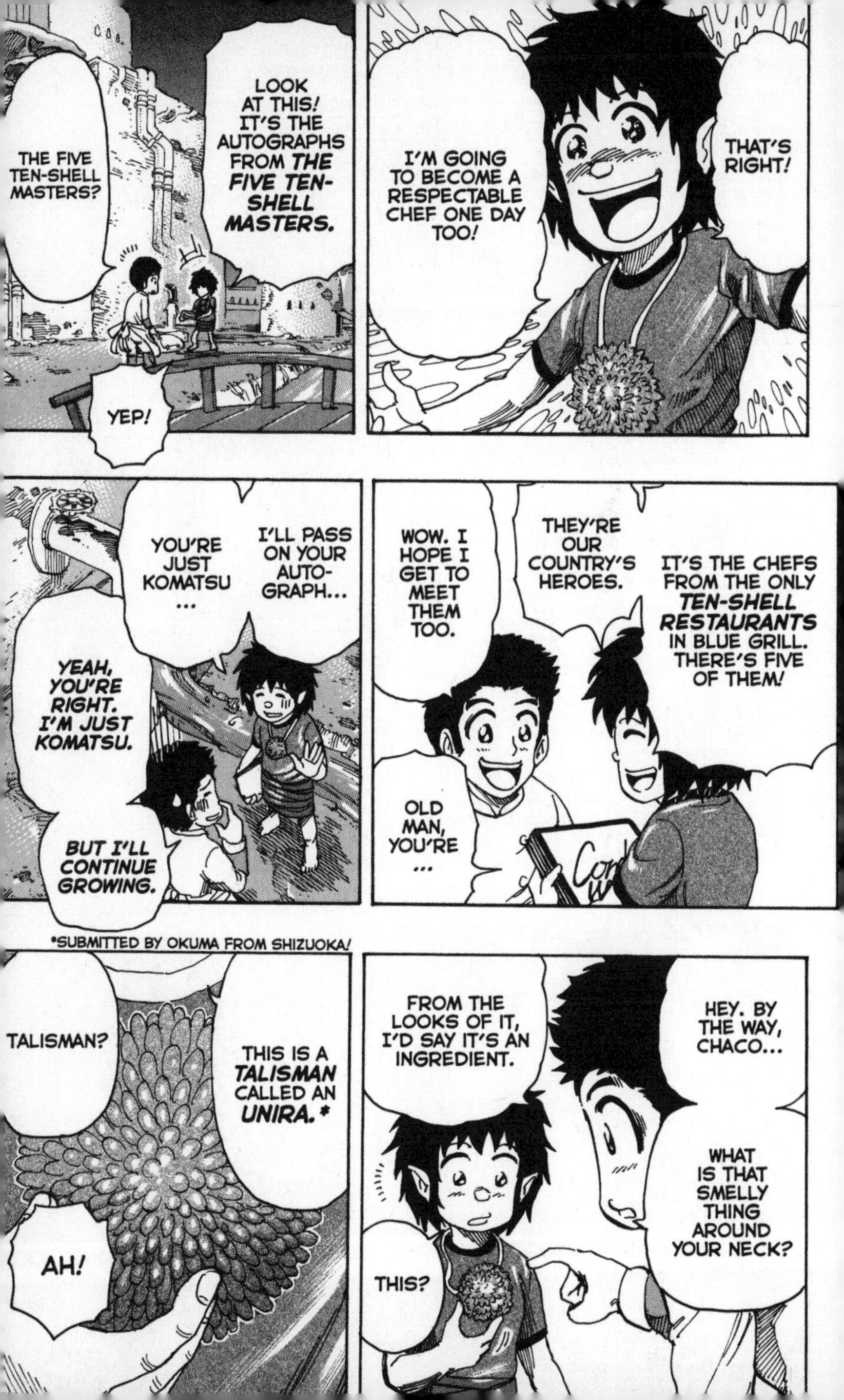
THAT'S RIGHT!
I'M GOING TO BECOME A RESPECTABLE CHEF ONE DAY TOO!
LOOK AT THIS! IT'S THE AUTOGRAPHS FROM ***THE FIVE TEN-SHELL MASTERS.***
THE FIVE TEN-SHELL MASTERS?
YEP!
IT'S THE CHEFS FROM THE ONLY ***TEN-SHELL RESTAURANTS*** IN BLUE GRILL. THERE'S FIVE OF THEM!
THEY'RE OUR COUNTRY'S HEROES.
WOW. I HOPE I GET TO MEET THEM TOO.
OLD MAN, YOU'RE ...
I'LL PASS ON YOUR AUTOGRAPH...
YOU'RE JUST KOMATSU ...
YEAH, YOU'RE RIGHT. I'M JUST KOMATSU.
BUT I'LL CONTINUE GROWING.
*SUBMITTED BY OKUMA FROM SHIZUOKA!
HEY. BY THE WAY, CHACO...
WHAT IS THAT SMELLY THING AROUND YOUR NECK?
FROM THE LOOKS OF IT, I'D SAY IT'S AN INGREDIENT.
THIS?
THIS IS A ***TALISMAN*** CALLED AN ***UNIRA.****
TALISMAN?
AH!

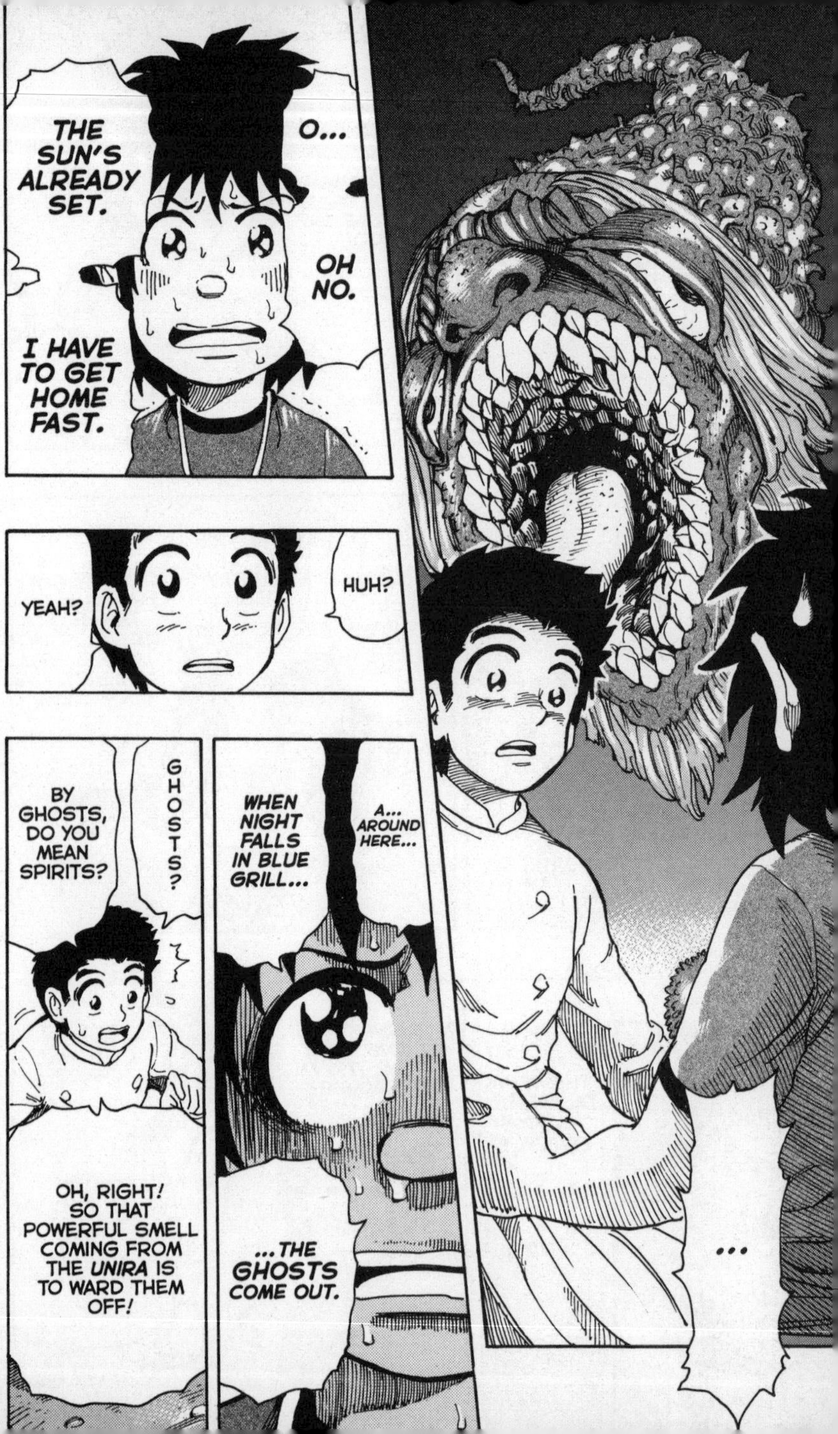
...
O...
OH NO.
THE SUN'S ALREADY SET.
I HAVE TO GET HOME FAST.
HUH?
YEAH?
A... AROUND HERE...
WHEN NIGHT FALLS IN BLUE GRILL...
...THE GHOSTS COME OUT.
GHOSTS?
BY GHOSTS, DO YOU MEAN SPIRITS?
OH, RIGHT! SO THAT POWERFUL SMELL COMING FROM THE *UNIRA* IS TO WARD THEM OFF!

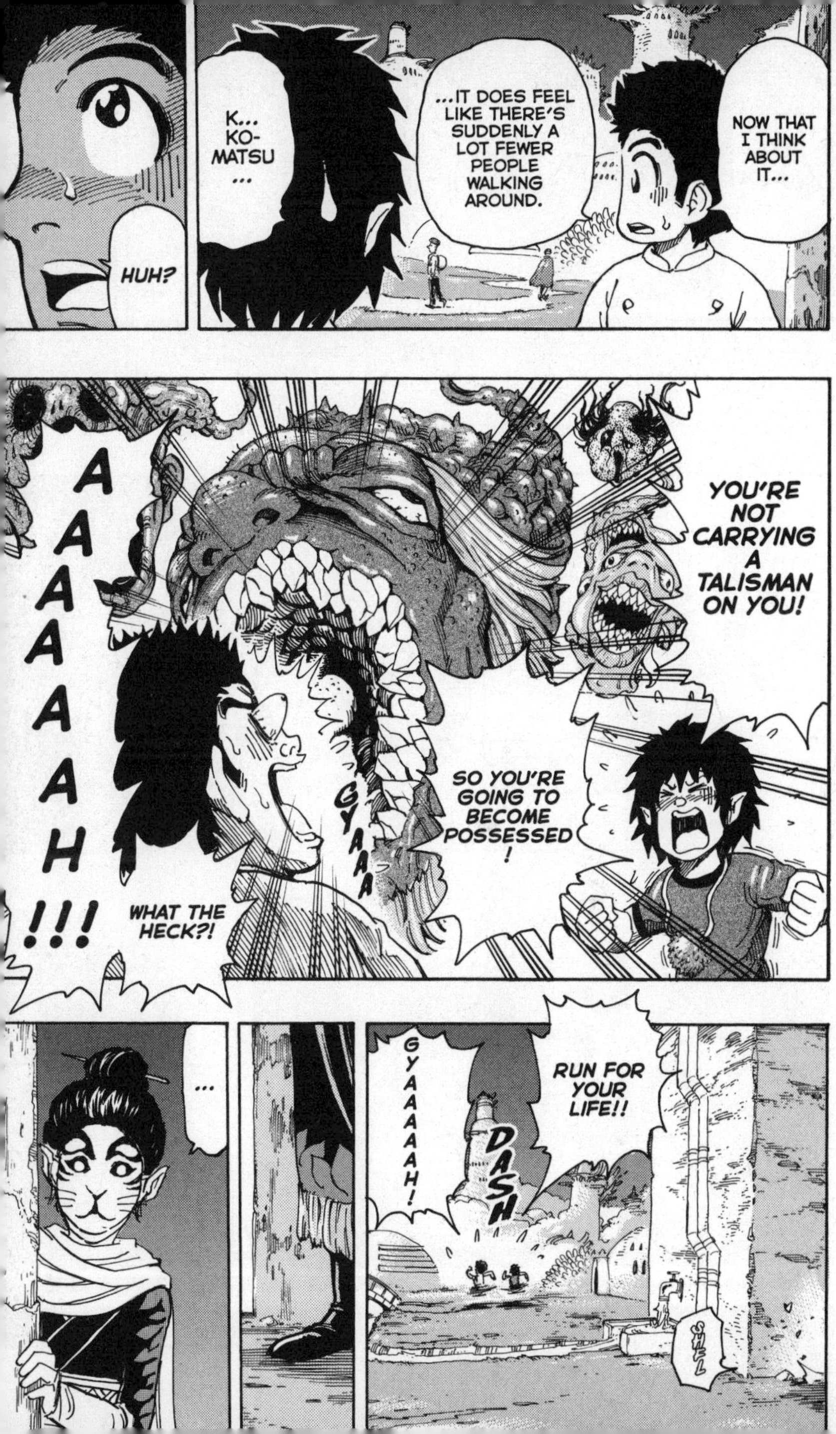
NOW THAT I THINK ABOUT IT...
...IT DOES FEEL LIKE THERE'S SUDDENLY A LOT FEWER PEOPLE WALKING AROUND.
K... KO-MATSU ...
HUH?
YOU'RE NOT CARRYING A TALISMAN ON YOU!
SO YOU'RE GOING TO BECOME POSSESSED!
GYAAA
AAAAAAAH!!!
WHAT THE HECK?!
RUN FOR YOUR LIFE!!
SHFL
DASH
GYAAAAAAH!
...

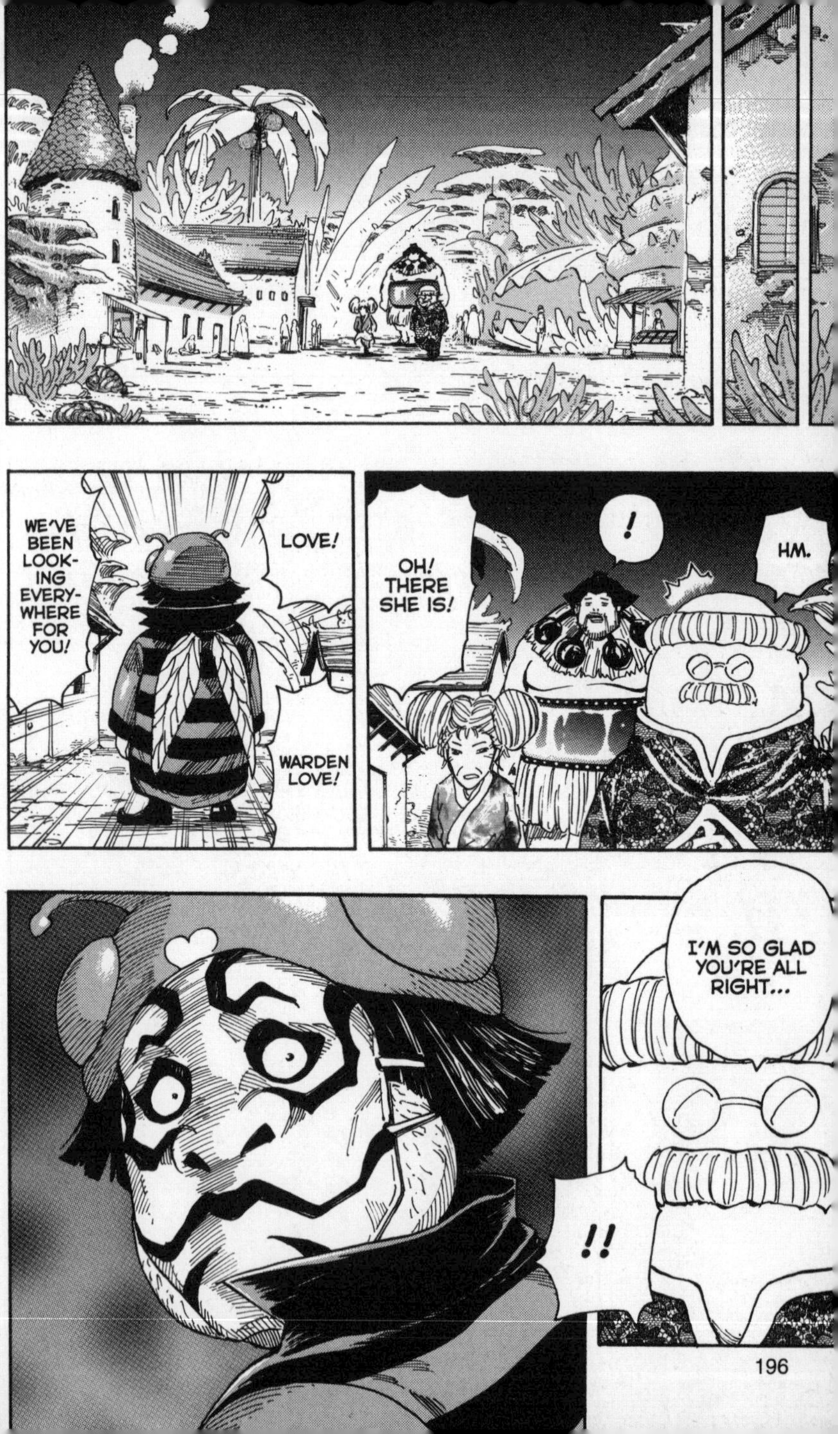
HM.
!
OH! THERE SHE IS!
LOVE!
WE'VE BEEN LOOK-ING EVERY-WHERE FOR YOU!
WARDEN LOVE!
I'M SO GLAD YOU'RE ALL RIGHT...
!!

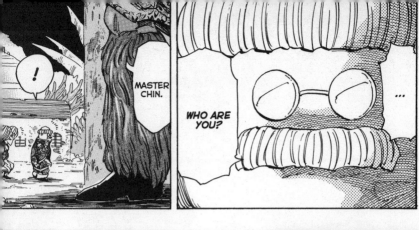

!

MASTER CHIN.

WHO ARE YOU?

...

T A K K !

!!

THIS WAY.

I SEE.

...

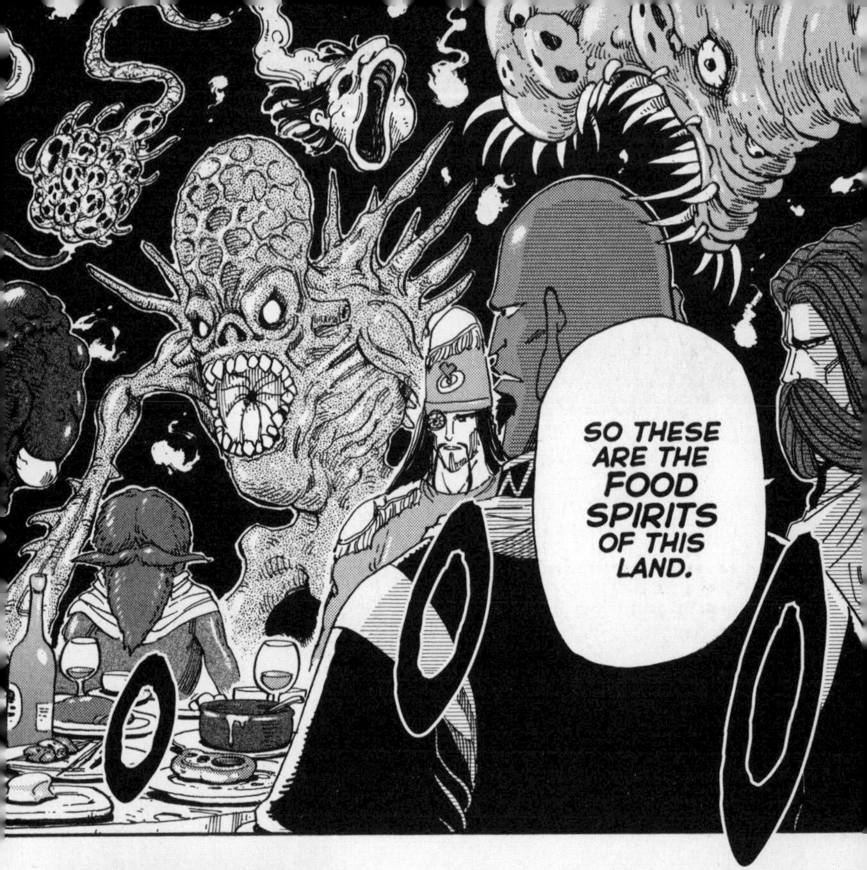
SO THESE ARE THE FOOD SPIRITS OF THIS LAND.

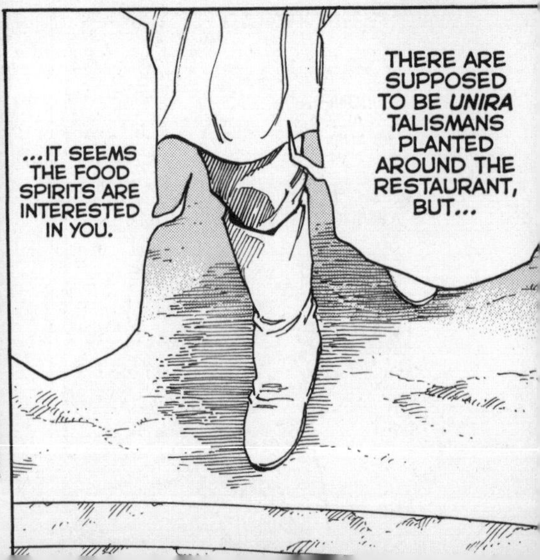
THERE ARE SUPPOSED TO BE *UNIRA* TALISMANS PLANTED AROUND THE RESTAURANT, BUT...
...IT SEEMS THE FOOD SPIRITS ARE INTERESTED IN YOU.

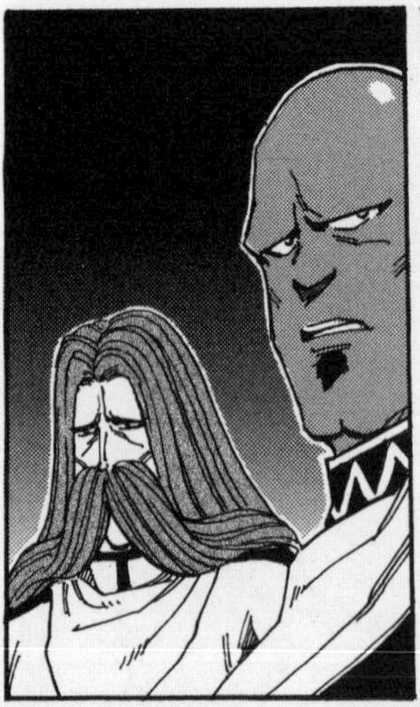

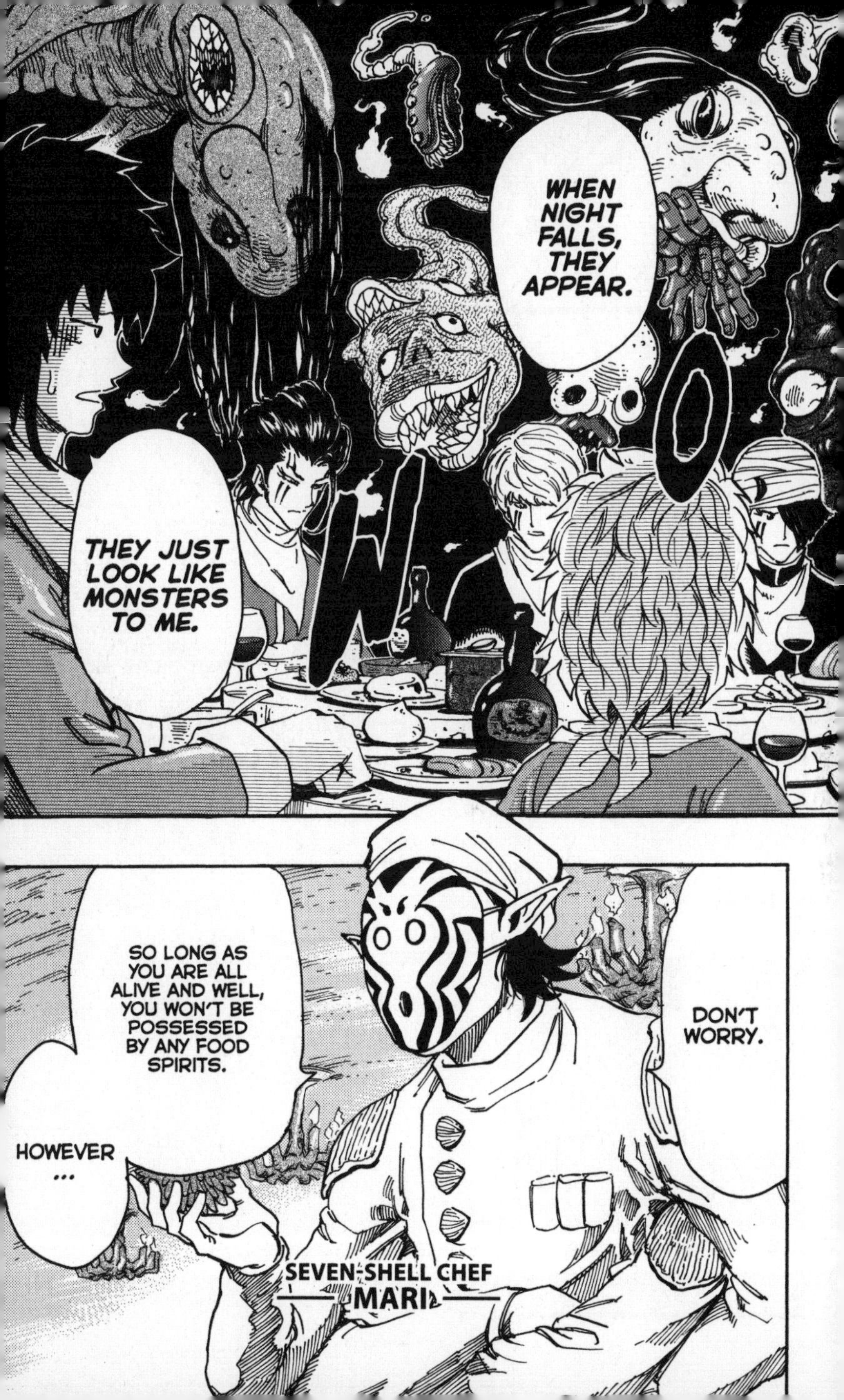
WHEN NIGHT FALLS, THEY APPEAR.
THEY JUST LOOK LIKE MONSTERS TO ME.
DON'T WORRY.
SO LONG AS YOU ARE ALL ALIVE AND WELL, YOU WON'T BE POSSESSED BY ANY FOOD SPIRITS.
HOWEVER ...
SEVEN-SHELL CHEF
MARI

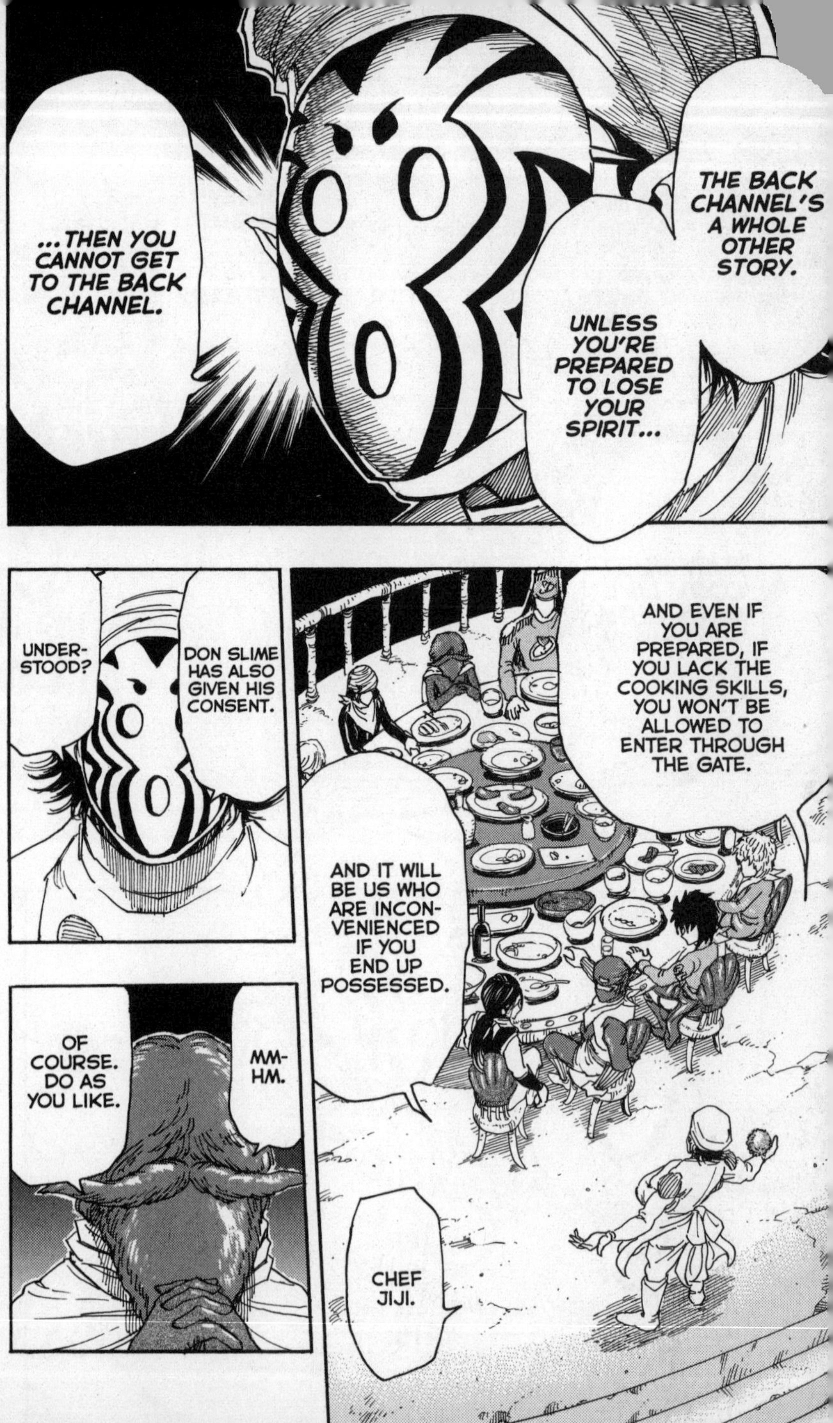
THE BACK CHANNEL'S A WHOLE OTHER STORY.
UNLESS YOU'RE PREPARED TO LOSE YOUR SPIRIT...
...THEN YOU CANNOT GET TO THE BACK CHANNEL.
AND EVEN IF YOU ARE PREPARED, IF YOU LACK THE COOKING SKILLS, YOU WON'T BE ALLOWED TO ENTER THROUGH THE GATE.
AND IT WILL BE US WHO ARE INCON-VENIENCED IF YOU END UP POSSESSED.
CHEF JIJI.
DON SLIME HAS ALSO GIVEN HIS CONSENT.
UNDER-STOOD?
MM-HM.
OF COURSE. DO AS YOU LIKE.

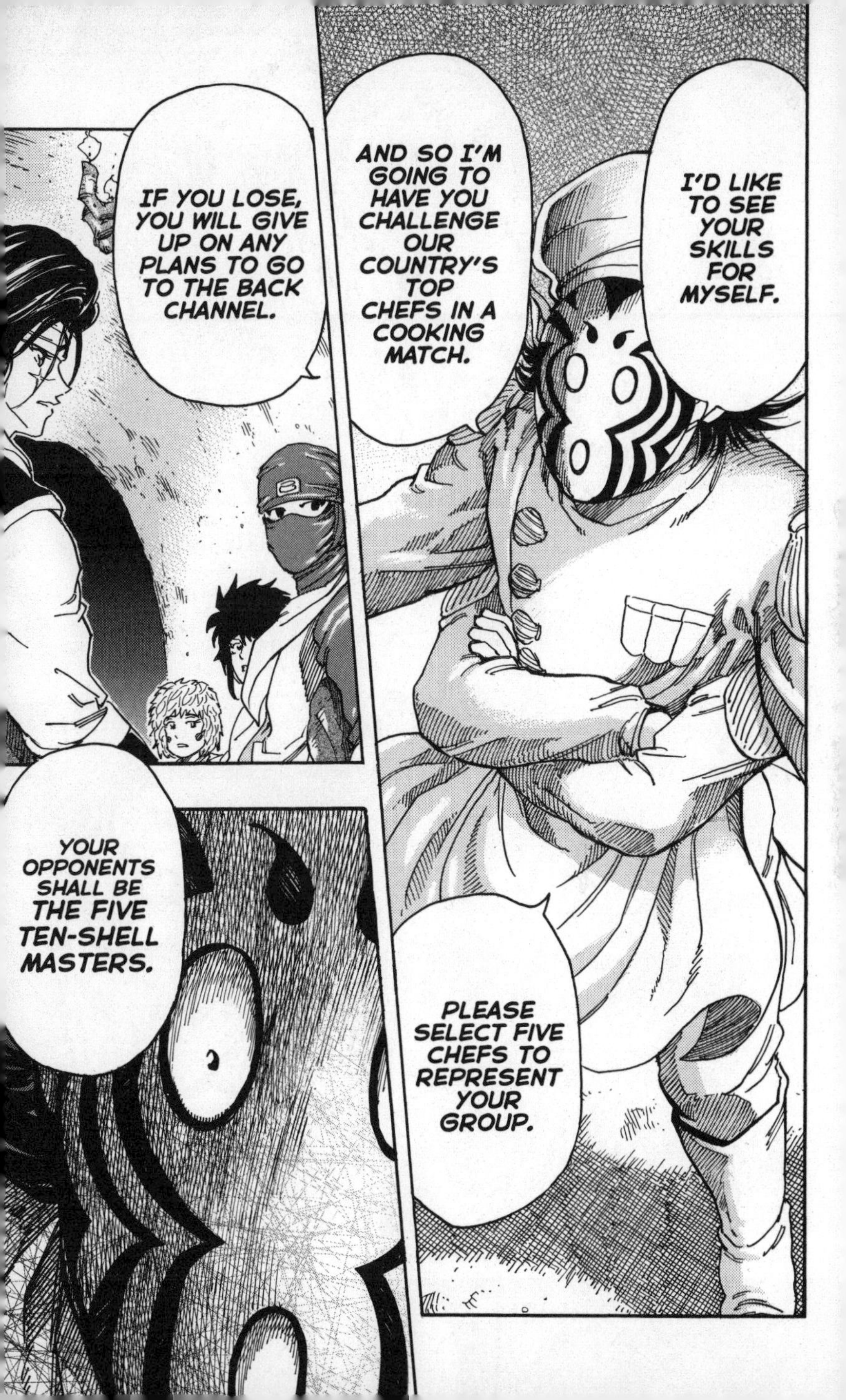
I'D LIKE TO SEE YOUR SKILLS FOR MYSELF.
AND SO I'M GOING TO HAVE YOU CHALLENGE OUR COUNTRY'S TOP CHEFS IN A COOKING MATCH.
PLEASE SELECT FIVE CHEFS TO REPRESENT YOUR GROUP.
IF YOU LOSE, YOU WILL GIVE UP ON ANY PLANS TO GO TO THE BACK CHANNEL.
YOUR OPPONENTS SHALL BE THE FIVE TEN-SHELL MASTERS.

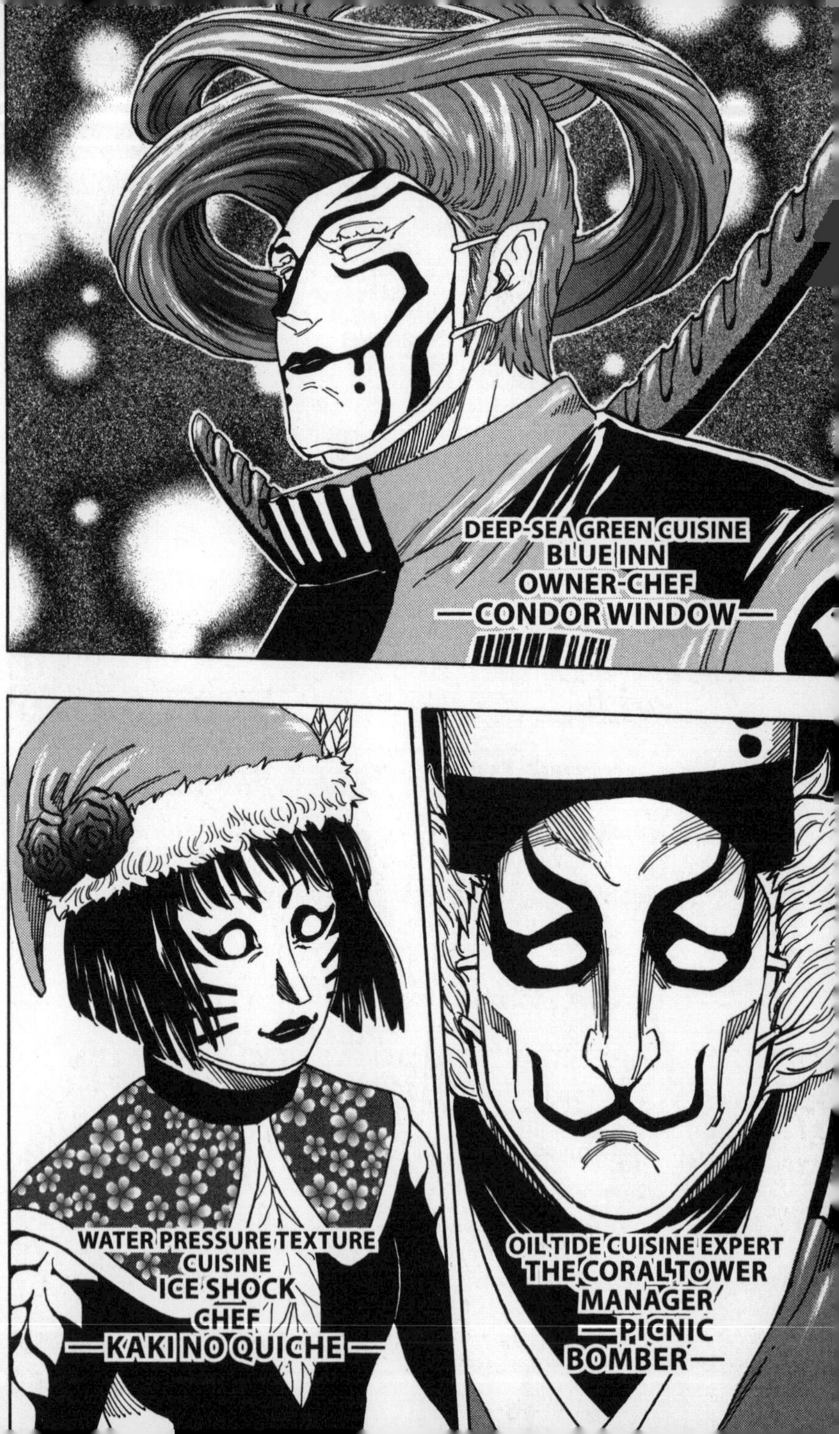
DEEP-SEA GREEN CUISINE
BLUE INN
OWNER-CHEF
—CONDOR WINDOW—
OIL TIDE CUISINE EXPERT
THE CORAL TOWER
MANAGER
—PICNIC
BOMBER—
WATER PRESSURE TEXTURE
CUISINE
ICE SHOCK
CHEF
—KAKI NO QUICHE—

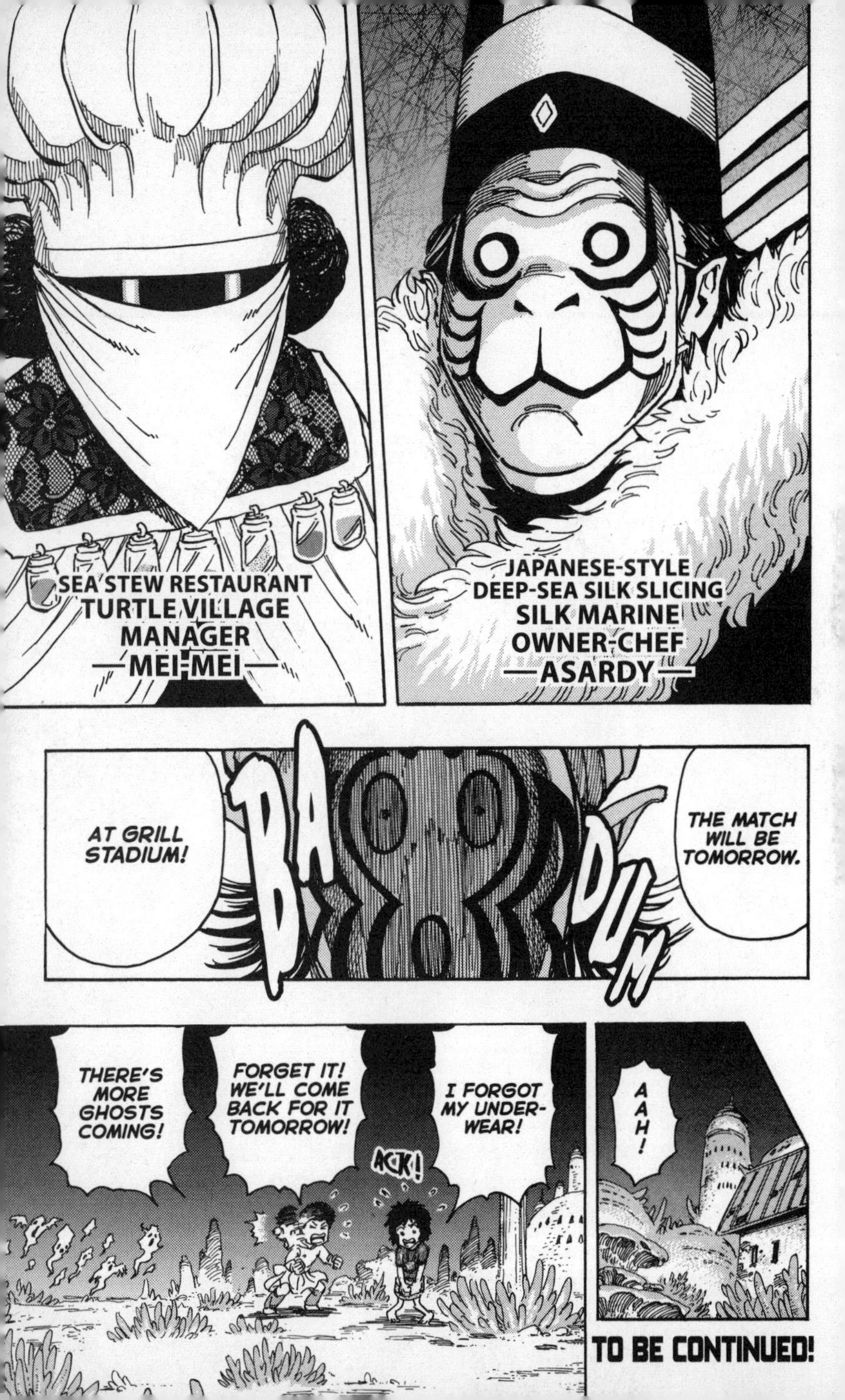
JAPANESE-STYLE DEEP-SEA SILK SLICING
SILK MARINE
OWNER-CHEF
—ASARDY—
SEA STEW RESTAURANT
TURTLE VILLAGE
MANAGER
—MEI-MEI—
THE MATCH WILL BE TOMORROW.
BA DUM
AT GRILL STADIUM!
AAH!
I FORGOT MY UNDER-WEAR!
ACK!
FORGET IT! WE'LL COME BACK FOR IT TOMORROW!
THERE'S MORE GHOSTS COMING!
TO BE CONTINUED!

COMING NEXT VOLUME

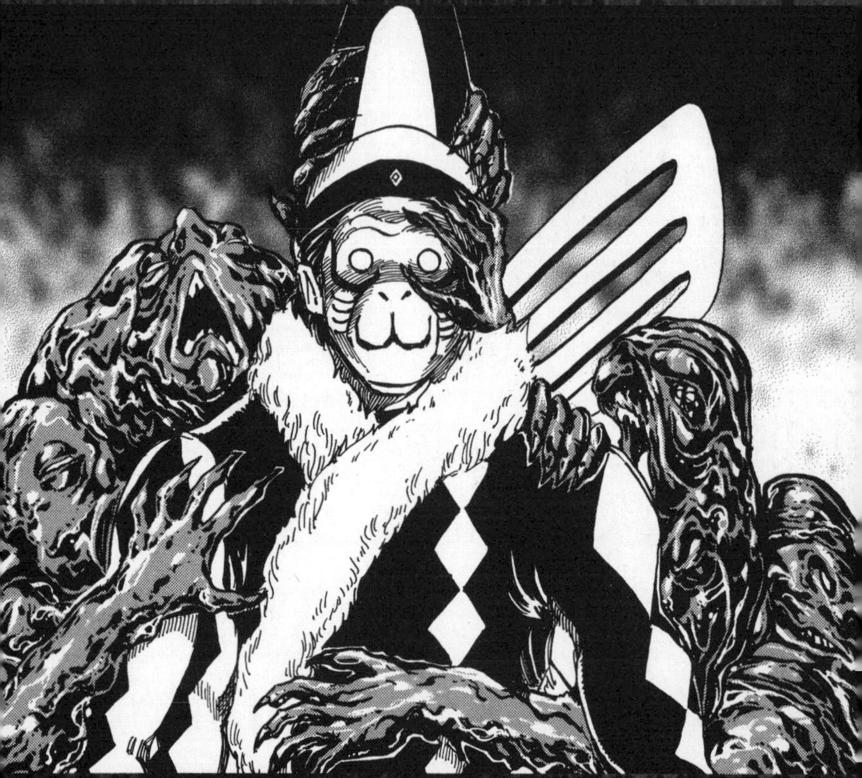

SIGNS OF LIFE!!

Komatsu and the gang dive under the sea and reach Blue Grill, and it's more intense than any of them could have ever imagined! The underwater civilization is full of master chefs with amazing talents and everyone is eager to put their skills to the test! But this Giant Clam is rotten at its core, with a lot of shady business going on behind the scenes. To enter the Back Channel and reach Another, Komatsu and the gang must defeat the masked rulers of Blue Grill, the Five Ten Shell Masters, to prove their worth— or literally die trying.

AVAILABLE FEBRUARY 2017!

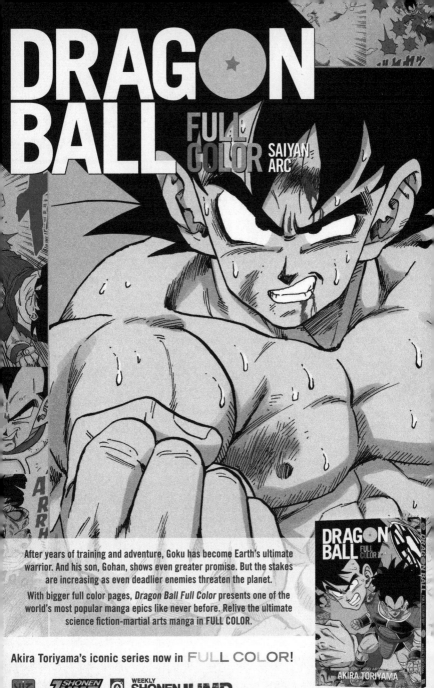

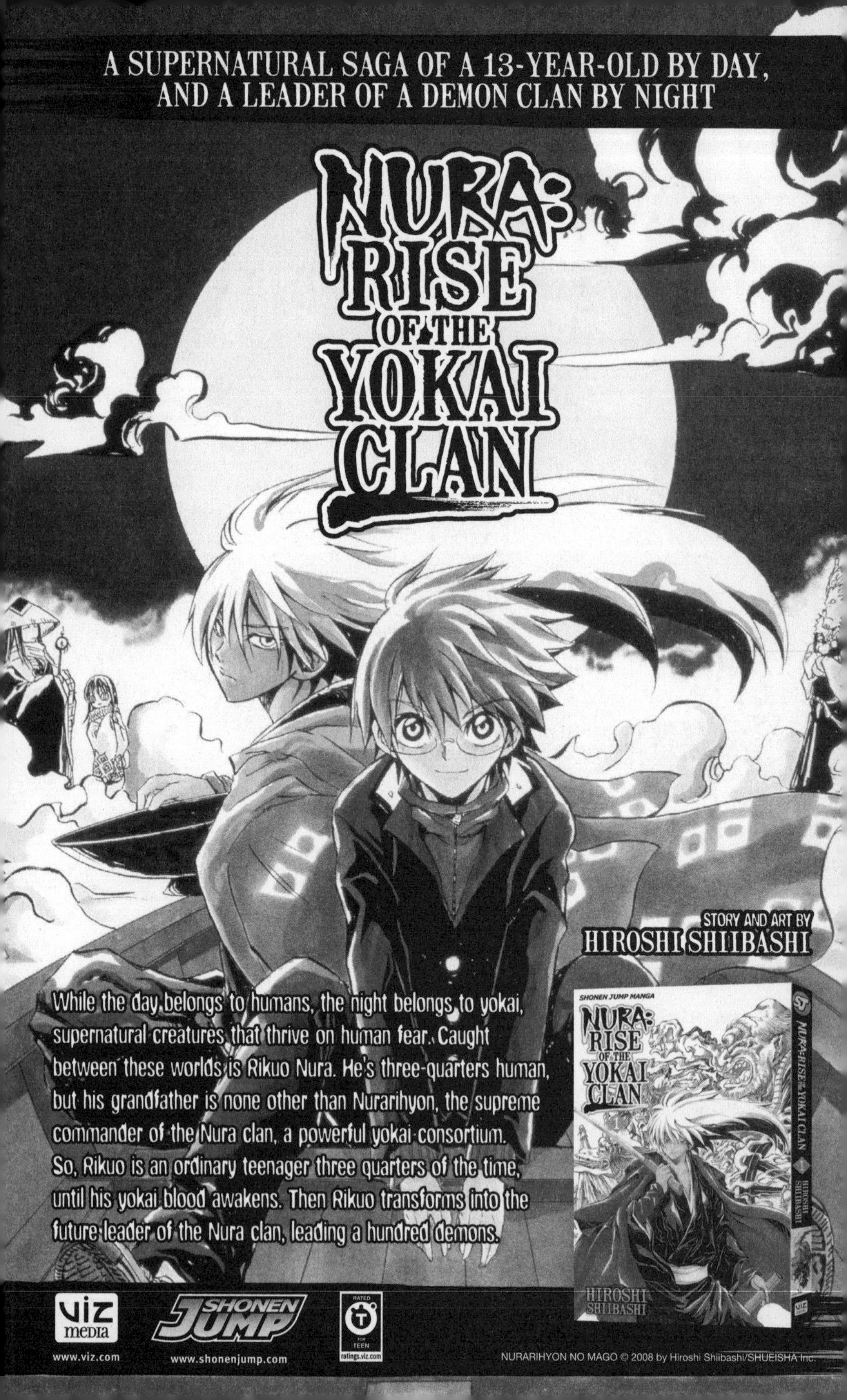
A SUPERNATURAL SAGA OF A 13-YEAR-OLD BY DAY, AND A LEADER OF A DEMON CLAN BY NIGHT
NURA: RISE OF THE YOKAI CLAN
STORY AND ART BY
HIROSHI SHIIBASHI
While the day belongs to humans, the night belongs to yokai, supernatural creatures that thrive on human fear. Caught between these worlds is Rikuo Nura. He's three-quarters human, but his grandfather is none other than Nurarihyon, the supreme commander of the Nura clan, a powerful yokai consortium. So, Rikuo is an ordinary teenager three quarters of the time, until his yokai blood awakens. Then Rikuo transforms into the future leader of the Nura clan, leading a hundred demons.
SHONEN JUMP MANGA
NURA: RISE OF THE YOKAI CLAN
HIROSHI SHIIBASHI
viz media
SHONEN JUMP
RATED T FOR TEEN
www.viz.com
www.shonenjump.com
ratings.viz.com
NURARIHYON NO MAGO © 2008 by Hiroshi Shiibashi/SHUEISHA Inc.

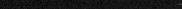

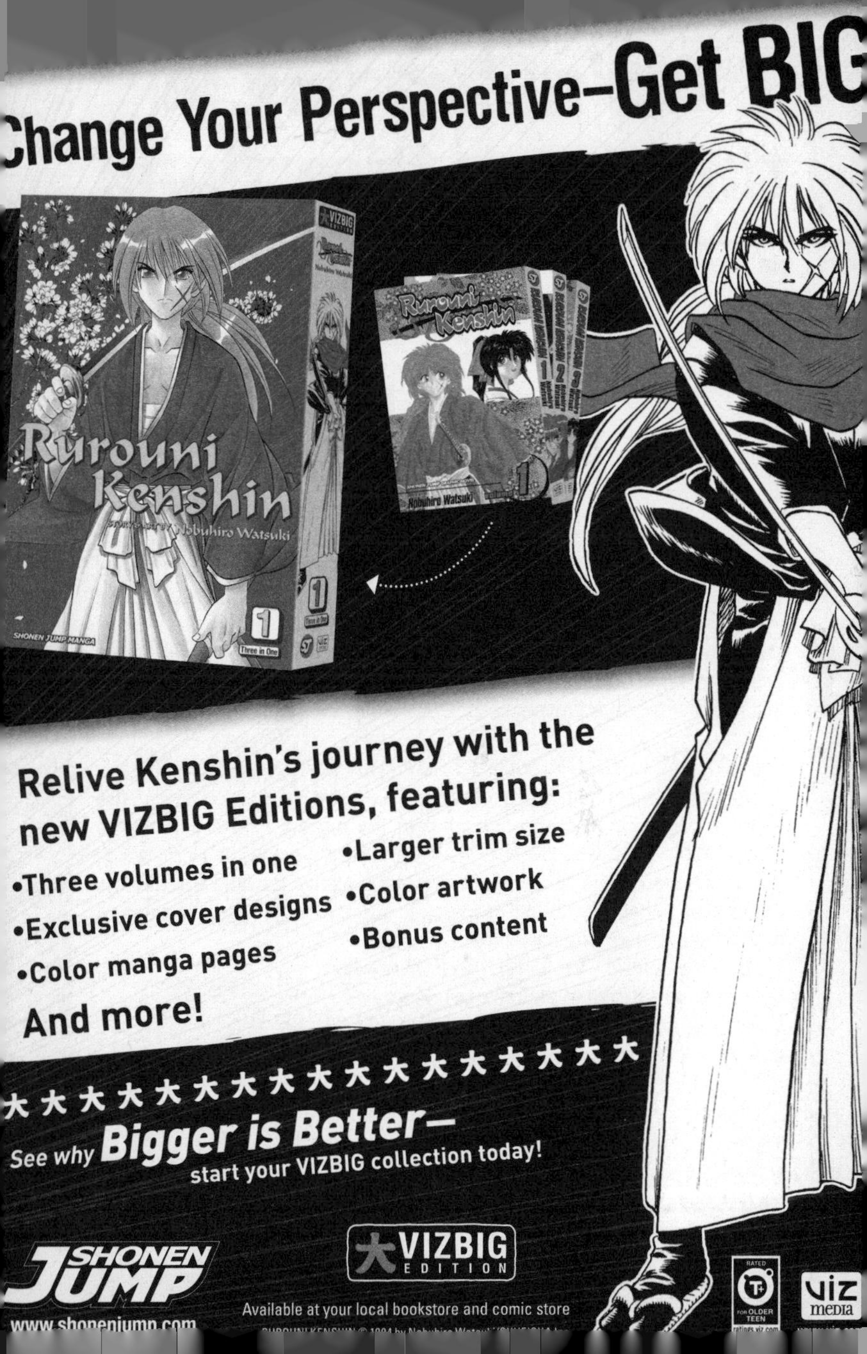
Change Your Perspective–Get BIG
Rurouni Kenshin
Nobuhiro Watsuki
SHONEN JUMP MANGA
1
Three in One
Relive Kenshin's journey with the new VIZBIG Editions, featuring:
•Three volumes in one
•Exclusive cover designs
•Color manga pages
•Larger trim size
•Color artwork
•Bonus content
And more!
See why Bigger is Better–
start your VIZBIG collection today!
SHONEN JUMP
www.shonenjump.com
VIZBIG EDITION
Available at your local bookstore and comic store
RATED T+ FOR OLDER TEEN
VIZ media

You're Reading in the Wrong Direction!!

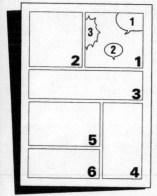

Whoops! Guess what? You're starting at the wrong end of the comic!

...It's true! In keeping with the original Japanese format, **Toriko** is meant to be read from right to left, starting in the upper-right corner.

Unlike English, which is read from left to right, Japanese is read from right to left, meaning that action, sound effects and word-balloon order are completely reversed... something which can make readers unfamiliar with Japanese feel pretty backwards themselves. For this reason, manga or Japanese comics published in the U.S. in English have sometimes been published "flopped"— that is, printed in exact reverse order, as though seen from the other side of a mirror.

By flopping pages, U.S. publishers can avoid confusing readers, but the compromise is not without its downside. For one thing, a character in a flopped manga series who once wore in the original Japanese version a T-shirt emblazoned with "M A Y" (as in "the merry month of") now wears one which reads "Y A M"! Additionally, many manga creators in Japan are themselves unhappy with the process, as some feel the mirror-imaging of their art skews their original intentions.

We are proud to bring you Mitsutoshi Shimabukuro's **Toriko** in the original unflopped format. For now, though, turn to the other side of the book and let the adventure begin...!

—Editor